SHINE LOVE, JOY, AND PEACE!

The Spirit Code of Humankind and the Secret Journey to True Life after All Deaths

A Self-Help Book

EVANGELINE MENDEZ STEFAN

CHRISTIAN FAITH PUBLISHING

ISBN 978-1-64492-179-1 (paperback)
ISBN 978-1-64492-180-7 (digital)

Copyright © 2023 by Evangeline Mendez Stefan

All rights reserved. No part of this publication may be reproduced, distributed, or transmitted in any form or by any means, including photocopying, recording, or other electronic or mechanical methods without the prior written permission of the publisher and the author. For permission requests, solicit the publisher via the address below.

Christian Faith Publishing
832 Park Avenue
Meadville, PA 16335
www.christianfaithpublishing.com

Printed in the United States of America

To my beloved husband,

I adore you for everything that you are, for all the patience and love we learned to find within our hearts together as you held my hands. I thank you for being the greatest father to our children, even when you had your fears. Your smile, your joy, and even your tears remain my heart's and soul's safe refuge.

Love, your wife
—Evangeline

******

To each of my children: Gabriella, Isabella, Michaela,
To my furry companions: Eugene, Frankie, Nigel, Joy, and Pax.

You shall always be that rainbow after the rainy and stormy day; for such beauty you bear—so much light, brilliance, and love you bring to my once lost and aching heart.

—Mommy

My Gabriella

Your inability to speak has awakened my soul from its deep sleep so I may live my purpose. My heart is never to be silent again.

My sweet child, I am going to live the life you meant to have.

I will dream of your dream by following the beat of my heart.

I will sing. I will sing your song so the world will echo the ancient hymns of love, far, far beyond the origin of both our hearts.

I will tell your story, so the world will also know all the grace and the many glorious blessings that colored mine.

I will speak of the earth, and yet the world will hear your love and receive heaven's light. I love you as much and as far as beyond time will go, far beyond the road that bore both our names, the never-ending path of the love of a mother and a child, the greatest gift of humanity's life alone gives.

Mommy

*The ultimate desire of every heart is to shine love and breathe
Peace all the days of his and her life on earth and in heaven.*
—Evangeline

Death and sorrow do not define our spirit's love.
—Evangeline

Contents

Foreword 15
The Purpose of This Book 19
How to Use This Book: PTSD Relief, Grief, Loss,
Emotional Restoration, Spiritual Recovery, and Self-
Empowerment 21
Acknowledgments 23
Consciousness 25
Introduction 27

Part One

    One: Blessed with a Child 41
    Two: Finding God on Earth 47
    Three: The Miracle and Power of Compassion 53
        The First Vision of Life in the Light 62
    Four: When an Angel Speaks 69
        The Second Vision 70
        Gabriella 73
        My Daughter's Tears 74
    Five: When Heaven Calls 77

Part Two

    The Spirit of Love Shining in My Darkness 83
        The Face and Character of Grief 83
    A Door to Love 87
        The Voice of Consciousness Is the Spirit of Love 87
        Holy! Holy! Holy! 88
    Why Mankind Will Not See the Face of God 92

The Order of the Holy Spirit 111
Revelation 111
Understanding the Ten Stages of Grief 112
Ten Steps to Grief Recovery 113
Heal 113
Six: The First Stage of Grief: The Shock, Numbness, Bargaining, and Denial 114
Being Misplaced in Life 114
Seven: The Second Stage of Grief: Anger 118
Feeling Forsaken and Alone in the Dark Pit 118
Eight: The Third Stage of Grief: The Power of Guilt and Shame 121
Nine: The Fourth Stage of Grief: A Necessary Road to Self-Redemption 124
Seeking Answers from Past Events 124
Man Is the Revelation 127
Lesson from Jesus and the Heavenly Father, Mother Mary, Archangel Michael, and Gabriel 128
Holy Spirit's Redemption: Looking Back in Time to Mend the Present 128
The Irony of life 128
Self and Spirit Redemption: The Lady Messenger 133
Self-Redemption: An Unbelievable Sight Seeing the Familiar Man as He Sat on the Throne 136
Self-Redemption: Revelations, the Spirit's Ways 142
I Heard My Dead Daughter Call Me "Mommy" 143
Self-Redemption: Heavenly Music 145
Self-Redemption: Divine Order 146
Self-Redemption: Tree of Life 149
Self-Redemption: Rest in Peace, an Amazing Grace 150
Spirit Heaven 154
Heaven Descended Engulfing All the Spaces in My Room with Pure White Light 154
Self-Redemption: Messenger of Good News 157
Self-Redemption: Love beyond Death, Time, Body, and Soul 157

Ten: The Fifth Stage of Grief: Surrendering to Life's Course..161
Eleven: The Sixth Stage of Grief: The Demeaning Power of Depression..167
    Don't Let the Power of Grief Take Over Your Body and Breath of Love..............................167
Twelve: The Seventh Stage of Grief: Learning to Understand, Life Goes on, Love Keeps on Growing, Love Will Keep on Shining.............................172
    Be Happy for Me, Mommy; Love Me Now for Who I Am..172
    He comes! Life Goes On. Love Keeps On Growing....179
    Truth Is Light That Shines on All Darkness Above and Beyond Time 179
    Risen..181
    True Love Sees the Living Glory of the Heavens........181
    Heaven above the Graveyard 182
    Heaven Knows My Needs 183
    My Best Friend..187
    The Navy Is Our Family..187
Thirteen: The Eighth Stage of Grief: Healing; The Physical Manifestation of Fear..........................190
    The Rise and Fall of Hope.......................................190
    Gaby's Miracles and Visions 194
    A Soul in Affliction Can Be Healed by the Spirit of Courage..197
    Living Father. Living Vision 203
    The Poor's Easter..205
    Mourning Since Birth 209
    Love on Earth Is the Light of the Heavens................213
    My Spirit Cares 215
    My Soul 217
Fourteen: The Ninth Stage of Grief: Let Go of Control over This Earthly Life. Let the God of Love and Peace Come. Nature and Love Will Take Care of the Rest in Time. 223

The Journey of Self-Healing after Any Loss 224
Man and His Medicine 224
My Soul's Rude Awakening 224
Healing the Unseen Spirit in Each Human Being.......226
Solutions 227
Take Care of Your Spirit 227
The Point? 228
The Encounter of the Holy Spirit.................................229
Doctors of the Body 232
Knock, Knock! Who's There? 233
What to Do Instead 234
Remember: Don't Believe It! Know So! 235
One Language 235
No, You Are Not the Solar Systems 236
You Are Not the Mental Universe 237
Rather 238
What Is Death 242
Suffering No More 246
What Happens After Death? 246
Family and the Meaning of Life 247
The Birth of Infinities 248
Grief Is a Belief: It Is Not the Light of Truth 248
The Greatest Machine Ever to Be Created 248
The Mental Universe within the Mental State
of Being 249
The Spirit Does Not Give Up 249
Spirit Above All 250
The Shaping of Our Souls Gives Us Mankind 251
The Breath and Light of the Soul 252
The Eternal Grace within Our Spirit's Forces 253
When the Mechanics of the Brain Stumbles 254
The Mind Snaps, the Brain Keeps On 255
No Stopping 256
The Spirit and Its Eyes 258
Birth and Death 260
Family—an Earth's Gift 261

Adam and Eve 262
Coping Mechanism..264
The Tragedy of the Mind 269
Adam's Sobriety Is Eve's Peace......................................273
Blessings..276
Fifteen: The Tenth Stage of Grief: Acceptance 278
Divine Intervention from Spirit of Mercy..................278
Heaven's Many Secret Rooms 282
The Process of Birth 285
Eternal Love 287
The Language of the Spirit Is the Unspoken
Words of the Heart..288
Family: Love is Forever!..291
A Divine Discovery 292
Time Heals...295

Part Three

Sixteen: The Man on the Throne..299
The Conversation...299
Seventeen: The Father's Presence 302
Illuminated 303
Creation in True Light Is Not Born from
Humanity's Mind...305
The Mind of Grief 308
Eighteen: Rise: The Gift of Heaven Is You.............................312
Nineteen: Breathe..314
Twenty: My Soul's Discovery..316
Brilliant Plane: A Higher Plane.....................................317
The Visit Was the Teaching 318
Twenty-One: The Man of Peace 320

Part Four

Twenty-Two: Fashioned in His Image 329
Spirit Child Is Free 330

Our Living Treasures Are the Richness of the
Spirit's Light 331
Sacred Birth 332
The Source of Life of Humanity's Spirit 333
The Father of Compassion 333
Humanity's Life and Infinite Blessings 334
Before the Throne, the Universe, and the Flesh 337
Whole 340
A New Beginning 341

Part Five

Twenty-Three: The Divine Child in Each Man 345
    First Child: Pure Spirit, Ever-Living Mercy,
    Eternal, and External Grace 346
    Second Child: Of Man, With and Without Faith 346
    The Holy Spirit 347
    Heaven 347

Part Six

Twenty-Four: Shape in an Image of the Holy Spirit
    of Love 353
    Bodies Are Sacred Vessels of Light Eternal 354
    The First Body: Love and Peace, Spirit of Joy, a
    Force of Consciousness 354
    The Second Body: Emotions, the Recorded
    Feelings of Human Life's Experiences 356
    The Third Body: Human Brain; the Machine
    of Life, the Processors of Emotional Events
    within Life's Orders and Disorders 357
    The Spirit above the Emotional Mind and
    Brain Is the Spirit of Love Alone 359
Twenty-Five: New Eyes 360
Twenty-Six: New in Spirit 362
    Reprograming of a New Brain 362
    No Tears in Heaven 364

Twenty-Seven: Heaven on Earth 365
   Before All Births 366
   Peace Is Humanity's Divinity 367
Twenty-Eight: To Bring Out from Within Is Heaven 368
   Above Is Always Below 368
Twenty-Nine: A Heaven within Heaven 370
   The Lamp 371
Thirty: The Throne 373
   Brilliant Garden of Heaven 374
   The Spirit's Unending Love 375
   Instant Ascent and Descent 375
Thirty-One: The Purity of the Spirit World 378
   Weather Spirits 379
Thirty-Two: Heaven's Bodies of Light 384
   The Universe of Life's Consciousness 385
Thirty-Three: Gaby 387
Thirty-Four: Everything Birthed Must Die Before It
  Can Rise Again 389
   Living in Peace 390
Thirty-Five: As He Comes 391
   Heaven Comes 391
   Entering the Peaceful Ocean of Life and Light,
   the Abode of Infinite Source 392

Part Seven

Thirty-Six: Mind, Body, Soul, Spirit Purpose 397
   What I Learned: I Must Write for the World to
   Know Itself 397
   Anger 399
Thirty-Seven: Crazy, Mental Image of Suffering 403
Thirty-Eight: Heaven Has No Man-God 406
   The Holy Spirit's and His Fatherly Throne 408
Thirty-Nine: Spirit of Light 410
   Here and Now 411
Forty: The Tragedy of Being a Human Soul 412

Forty-One: Surrendering All Darkness 414
    The Unseen Waves in the Mind 416
    Forgiveness Is Kindness to One's Mind, Soul,
    and Spirit 417
Forty-Two: The Hour Comes 418
    Never Alone 419
    When Religion Alone Is Not a True Gift 420
Forty-Three: The Making of New Spaces 421
    Eternal Space 423
Forty-Four: Extension of Life 425

Part Eight

Forty-Five: Heaven Is but One Thought Away 429
    The Spirit Is Not the Soul 430
Forty-Six: Trade Suffering for True Love 432
Forty-Seven: The Eternal Beauty 434
Forty-Eight: Human Life Is Earth. Earth As a
    Garden Is the Teacher of Life in Season. The
    Spirit Is Its Students. The Newborn Is Its New Life 437
    Mother Earth's Pain Is a Struggle Projected
    from Within Every Human Being's Inner Sufferings ... 439
Forty-Nine: The Purpose of Time Is to Heal and
    Build Again 441
    Why You Are Born 443
Fifty: Holy Light. Holy Body of Eternal Love and Peace 446
    Why Are You Born a Human Child? 447
Fifty-One: Abandoned Souls No More 450
Fifty-Two: The Secret Wealth of the Human Spirit 454
    The Infinite and Ultimate Purity of the
    Human Spirit's Breath 457
Fifty-Three: Living Vision 459
Fifty-Four: Tree of Life 462
    You Are Light 463
    For Guidance 464
    New in spirit. Shine Love, Joy, and Peace! 465

About the Author 471

Foreword

Throughout history, there lies a silent yearning, a quiet dream burning within every human heart. We are to be born, to learn, to grow through constellations of experiences within this three-dimensional space of reality, earth—our humanity's home until we sense that our purpose, our job on this planet, has been accomplished. Only then do we go away satisfied and content. This knowing gives us the peace and eagerness not to fear, but rather to move on with boldness to face the great unknown. When a soul experiences the fulfillment of his and her humanity, when all taste, touch, and feelings have been sensed, when all yearning of self-discovery has been satisfied, all hunger and thirst are quelled, like a butterfly to a garden of flowers, the spirit rises out of our human body. It flies home to the vast ocean of life we cannot see with our eyes, yet we sense deep in our hearts that its mystifying shore awaits, eager for us to ride its mighty wind across its infinite landscape we term the other side—heaven.

But what happens when our perfect dream dies before it begins, or when our loved ones die before their goals come true? What becomes of a parent's vision after his or her child dies? If you had asked me these questions before I became a mother, I would not have been able to answer them. But now, unfortunately, I can. These were the same questions I asked myself after I buried the body of my daughter, Gaby.

Each day, countless children die around the world because of war, accidents, famine, natural death, hunger, and preventable diseases. I hurt, for I see my daughter's eyes before she closed them for good, in every one of them who must have endured the tragedy of what would have been as the makers had planned it, a beautiful and loving life. My heart sees each of them as its own, regardless of where each child was from, how he or she died, or how much pain each suffered. I hurt for those parents left behind. I am aware of how difficult it will be for them, for they will struggle with the bottomless sorrow called grief, which they must learn to contend with, at the same time they are learning to live again without their child to embrace.

After losing a loved one, we experience a sense of betrayal of life; we mourn. Everything we have come to accept as the most vital foundation of our lives shakes to the very core of our being; our faith, our religion, and our culture become irrelevant. Life as we know it is over. When someone we love dies, it's easy for most of us to believe "this is the end," the finality of everything, that is—until life proves otherwise and we find help and divine courage to give it another chance to carry us.

Thus, as we acknowledge that we are one beautiful, creative, and self-reflective species of high intelligence now existing on the face of the earth, we must see clearly with our spirit's mind's eyes, and courageously face what we fear the most—death, in order to set ourselves free.

We must look back to the beginning of man. How do societies deal with death? Those from the Western part of the world find the strength to hold on to faith and take comfort that they will see their loved ones again in heaven. Those from the East, on the other hand, strongly expect their loved ones to return to them in the same lifetime as another entity through reincarnation. Both belief systems are worthy of honor, for they help us through the sadness as we look beyond today. But deep in our souls, no matter how strong our faith is, one thing is certain: the depth of our inexplicable suffering is inescapable.

I learned that no matter which religion we belong to when death comes to us in any form, when our dream fails to materialize, we will all struggle because death is something our spirits cannot experience. Death is a reality our human brains will never accept because everything we have come to build on earth is created for us to survive no matter what the circumstances we face.

Death is not a language our hearts will ever understand because the very essence of who we are is built to love forever no matter what.

So why is death so painful for those of us left behind? Is it because death goes against our spirit's true makeup; it is the opposite of who we are in spirit, what we are as bodies of light and love, and everything we know life is—always living, always existing, forever enduring. That is why death is so hard to fathom.

Since humanity began, each culture has created its rituals, which lift the bereaved off the pain as they become immersed in such sacred acts. Prayers, dancing, and meditations are acts of surrendering where the bereaved pause from their busy lives to give respect to the souls whose lives on the planet have just ended. For those left behind, it is a time not only to recollect, but a window and a space where they are allowed to feel the bitter loss, face the fear of the oncoming space, of moving on without the ones they love, and be immersed in the numbing serum death gives, the total silence of unspoken hurt. Engulfed in these are wells of emotions, while families' and communities' caring hands stand by their side, night, and day as they are being carried through.

Through the ages, we are forced to learn that death, just like birth, is within our humanity's makeup. But there is a thread in the human consciousness that strongly ties the past and the present into the same expectation. Death must meet us only at the end of our journeys when we are ready, but never at the beginning or in the middle, for such a blow throws us out of life's specific balance. Every soul on the planet would agree that a parent burying the sacred body of his or her dear child, for example, is the most horrific experience known to man. When a child dies, so does a parent's perfect dream. Learning to let go is the most painful experience a parent can go through. This out-of-touch, all-painful, and degrading existence becomes the real world; yet here no one lives.

The bereaved is floating in an ocean of the universe of never-ending darkness, of never-ending sorrow, all alone, crying and screaming a voiceless scream of unspoken mercy, to find the light, to find love, but no one soul could hear the screaming pain of this one's heart. The mouth has forgotten to speak. The ears do not hear. The mind does not think. The brain becomes frozen. The soul's life purpose is forgotten. The spirit's universe of life is muted. No one hears. No one speaks. The soul's mind cannot see any dream. Nothing exists. No one comes to the rescue. Life never comes. The light never comes. Love never comes. One is lost. Alone in the floating sea of darkness. The "once upon a time" beloved and full of life and promised of a boy, the once beautiful girl of God is in a pit of darkness, stranded, screaming to the top of his and her lungs, still, the child floats alone in a sea of oncoming waves of constant waters of cold and tormenting winds of guilt and shame. Here no human soul comes. Love is absent. Memories of joy, happiness, and good life experiences are buried forever. The once perfected spirits had come to shine as light of hope to its human family is now broken. Without love, in the absence of its light, darkness is the world. In this child, the dream of humanity's lights and love becomes lost. The blessed light, love, peace, and brilliance of that begotten child's spirit among the living is hidden. Now unseen. The entire planet's family of humanity has lost its light.

—Evangeline

As a mother, I live in pain each day without my daughter to hold. But I have also found that believers and nonbelievers alike have no choice but to live life with less sorrow by acknowledging the true nature of our human spirits. After I had admitted that truth, I realized the love of those we thought we had lost is, in fact, endless. Because they live on forever. I have experienced that beyond all the pain I have endured. Love and life go on for all of us in two magnificent parallel worlds.

The Purpose of This Book

If you are lucky enough to find yourself in the body, read this book. If you are a grandparent, a mother, a father, a brother, a sister, a cousin, a caregiver, or a compassionate friend to the sick and the grieving, read this book. Share its knowledge with everyone you love, especially with every child in a hospital somewhere battling an illness so they and their families may live their lives with less fear, more love, and infinite understanding of humanity's truth. Eventually, a time will come for them to see the process of the body's illness as a call *not* to dwell in fears of death or the end of any dreams. For in spirit, death of dreams in all degrees and form within the universe is indeed *not an end* to life and love. It is an evolutional transition to a space of divine understanding. It is an arising journey of one's consciousness over all pain and sorrows. All death within the material realm is in spirit, a movement forward, a transcended journey to a conscious awareness of life beyond the human mind's limitations. It is a coming, going, a union, separation, and a return to a better existence of self-ascension to a kind and gentle world of peace, both on earth and in heaven.

This book is written to give *love, joy,* and *peace*; and evermore, *shine* humanity's *truths* and *awaken* the spirit of *hope* in all hearts *now* on earth.

How to Use This Book: PTSD Relief, Grief, Loss, Emotional Restoration, Spiritual Recovery, and Self-Empowerment

For all psychologists: Please use the *ten steps* to assist your clients in categorizing the language of their emotional traumas, for a faster route, to self-healing—mind, body, soul, and spirit.

To every soul, the child divine, if you are currently dealing with a loved one who is going through a great deal or has just suffered a loss, please read the entire book before following the ten steps. Shine above it. A workbook is provided to help with emptying for successful healing.

Author's Note

To respect and honor the privacy of our dear friends and families, the names of children and parents contained in Part 1 of this book have been changed.

The spirit speaks through the heart. All chapters' poems are the echoes of the Holy Spirit's conversations of love.

In some chapters, the glimpses are mentioned more than once to fulfill the light of the visions bestowed to bless the hearts of our current humanity.

Acknowledgments

To the unseen teachers of love: The Almighty Father of peace, whose presence eludes me, the Son of Peace, the Mother of Peace, the angels, and the spirits of those we love in heaven and the sacrifices of all spirits and souls on earth. Thank you for your divine interventions. Thank you for your lights, our eternal breath, and solitude while we experience the bounty of our gifts on earth.

To Gabriella, my daughter, and all the children in heaven and those with us now in our daily awakenings, you have enriched and blessed our lives as parents, both in heaven and on earth, just because you were born. We thank you for giving us the greatest purpose we could ever have. Your birth. The love you ignited in our hearts is the fundamental reason we parents wake up each morning. To see you smile, to make you proud no matter where you shine your light.

With all my heart, I would like to thank everyone who has come into my life as teachers of kindness, patience, compassion, and givers of hope as they remain true to who they are in their daily walks.

My endless gratitude I owe to my heroes, the humble teachers of life's reality: my father, Macrio; my mother, Carmelita; my beloved brothers and sisters and their children. With immense gratitude to my grandparents and their ancestors in spirit.

To everyone who will hold this book in their hands, I thank you in advance. It is my prayer that after you read it, you will look back and see your life blessings, your spirit brilliance, shine your body of love, and endow your breath of peace on to this sacred earth. See that no matter how difficult your experiences were, or are, you will know, after all, that you were never alone or abandoned; but were carried by the Father's love through the caring acts of strangers, your friends, and your loved ones.

To all who are bravely carrying their crosses of life, your heavy burdens are our lessons learned. Thank you for your courage.

To all caregivers, doctors, and nurses, especially at Stanford, Lucile Packard Children's Hospital in the CVICU (cardiovascular intensive care unit): when we could not see beyond tomorrow, it was your caring smiles and loving arms that provided us a haven of hope. My entire family thanks you for being Gabriella's angels on earth.

We are especially grateful for the following doctors who made an enormous difference in our Gabriella's life: from Walter Reed Hospital—Gabriella's pediatrician, her cardiologist, and her gastroenterologist.

To Gabriella's surgeon, from Stanford Lucile Packard Children's Hospital, we thank God for you. By fashioning your life to assist those tiny hearts in great need of assistance to function properly, you help their Creator lengthen the lives of those you've touched. You made a difference in our lives, for you've allowed us the chance to embrace Gabriella's smile and immerse in her love a while longer. For those two wonderful years, she trained our hearts to love like a child—unconditionally—and see life as truly magnificent miracles, a true blessing. Now and for all eternity, in everything we do, we will carry her in our hearts. I honor you and your families. I thank God for your service to heal the hearts of our families here on earth as you magnify each day of your service the love of our families in heaven.

Consciousness

Death came to pass. I did not disappear. Where I am is no-man's-land. Our loved ones now reside in a vast ocean beyond all depths, a newly risen garden above human spaces, with untouched dews that are always forming before me, rest. It is a garden of the spirit. This secret garden floats above the earth. This is the garden of pure light. Forever is the gentle sunrise. The galaxy's suns have not known of this garden. For no sun ever sets or dims here. Death is not known here; it cannot ever come. Everyone, children, and the aged of all family members are lit up here. Here in the spirit body, children, fathers, and mothers, grandpas, and grandmas are brightly shining. Their breath is one light. Life is self, for self is light, and light is love, and love is peace.

I see that no matter in the universe one rises out of, all spirits are to return to this garden of rest. A garden of forever, no weeds in sight, but the green oasis of cool refreshing grass, comforting every soul to ease, illuminated by white brilliance of pure light, a new beginning. To rest here is to know self. To be here in spirit is to be bound by truth. The truth is love. And love is self. Love is the light of every soul. Love is the purest form of kindness. There is no man without a spirit. There is no spirit without humankind's wisdom. Of the earth's world, the spirit is a breath of compassion. Self is the spirit of divine presence in the heart of matters, the physical world, the world of creation. The spirit is the heart of all consciousness. For all is consciousness; before it is vesseled in the flesh, the vessel of creation. Consciousness has a home. It is a garden of luminosity. It is not bound on earth. Humankind finds refuge on the fruitful bounties of the garden of the earth; yet the spirit of humanity shall rest in the spirit's abode, which is the essence and the heart of light eternal, its Spirit Father, the source of love, light, and life-giving breath within the external and eternal spaces of all creations. The heavenly Father's spirit is the living fountain of life's magnificence. He is the infinite grace within every man and all humanity. The source of love and life is the Holy One's body shining in the universe of all created and imagined darkness.

—Evangeline

Introduction

Once in a lifetime, a story comes along that is worth writing. Within its plot is life's discovery, an experience worth sharing. In its character is a hero, an angel who inspired the course of my life forever, my tiny Gaby.

My name is Evangeline Stefan. I am just an ordinary woman, a mother, to whom extraordinary miracles happened, which to this very day fuel the wonders that are flowing down on every family the heaven touches with its eternal and all-living love.

On December 6, 2002, my one and only child at the time, Gabriella, was born, changing the course of my life with so many blessings that she illuminated through her joy, sufferings, and disappointments. Despite it all, Gaby's character always remained graceful and confident as she endured with pride, teaching me the truth that there is nothing so painful in this world that would ever put a dent on her precious and sacred spirit. She was a bundle of joy, a child full of unconditional love, even after her body's death.

On December 7, 2004, she fought for that one breath she struggled so hard to take. Against both of our wills, she died one sunrise, one morning after her second birthday. When I looked into her eyes before she closed them for good, her gaze told me how hurt she was, disappointed that her dreams had not yet begun. Her life was over too soon. I knew she never wanted to go so far away from me, but she did not have a choice. She was there; then she was gone. It was a mind-blowing experience that my heart and mind cannot comprehend to this day. I exist with vast emptiness, an infinite void within the core of my soul, brokenhearted and barely alive, but unlike my daughter, I still had a choice: to die in mourning or to give up my life and end my wicked sufferings.

Amid such an experience, there was an accidental meeting of my higher self. In the riverbed of my soul, I discovered a part of me I did not know existed. Within me was a silent voice, consciously echoing in my heart, guiding me. Its whispers were there to gently enlighten me when I found myself tormented by the jungles of oncoming bubbles of realities; I had no power to control. This gentle wisdom dictated to my soul the right thing to do. This voice had become my saving grace. With its presence, I could breathe peacefully. In a peaceful state I could listen to silence. In silence, everything outside of me disappears. In solitude, I'm able to hear my soul choose life over death, a choice I wish my precious baby had been able to make.

If I am to honor my daughter's life, I must make the choice she could not have. I must go on and finish the dream she was unable to complete, a vision that is alive within me, left intact, untouched by death itself. Despite the deep hurt, I am driven by a goal to try with all my might to pick up the millions of shattered pieces of myself, put them back together, and use them as a beacon of light to make sense of life and a new reason to live still. Though this is impossible to accomplish in the natural world, it is an automatic blessing just because I can still breathe.

Even though I struggle, living for the two of us is my newfound purpose. After experiencing the emptiness my toddler's death brought about, I have found an inexplicable need to put into words the process someone goes through when dealing with such emotions.

This book is about the rise of light from the inner expectations of one's consciousness' battle to overcome the pitfall everyone experiences while suffering the greatest pain one could ever endure: the death of a loved one, the end of a dream, and the loss of a promising love. It is to give light at the end of hope—the finality of human experience.

In *Part 1* of this book, I have fulfilled one of my daughter's purposes: sharing with you the miracles that came along with her birth to give you hope and to lighten your pain and suffering. I learned that our children, no matter how normal or how different they may be in the eyes of others, are and will be the greatest teachers we will ever encounter. They teach us the most meaningful life lessons this planet can ever offer a living soul—unconditional and ever-living love, the living source of compassion.

Part 2 is a spiritual workbook. It is to guide all human beings to learn how to set the spirits and hearts free from the emotional burdens of the ten fundamental senses of the mind after a heartbreak and experiences of loss. PTSD (post-traumatic stress disorder), darkness no one knows exists until the heart breaks from fears. PTSD is the language of a broken mind from witnessing death and loss.

This book talks about my overcoming the debilitating struggle as I go through the emotional pain in search of myself through the language of grief. In grief, all human beings speak the same language and experience the same emotions. I found that naming the seasons of grief has helped me recognize its cycle. It gave me the power to separate it from the truth. Grief is not a true representation of my daughter's life because it had nothing to do with my daughter's beauty. It did, however, have a lot to do with how much guilt I was carrying because I blamed myself when she did not survive, especially since I am still here. I hope that wherever you are in your grief, you can identify the step you are currently experiencing. Human emotion is a body in itself. It is a vessel of feelings, as much as our body is a vessel for our pure spirit. I wrote the steps of grief for you so you can slowly progress to the next level of recovery until you can pull both your feet from its awful grip. You have it in you to be free. You must live on so the spirit of your loved one may live on through you.

Humanity is the sacred temple, the living vessel of our spirit's pure love to live in peace and joy while we walk and have life on earth.
—Evangeline

In *Part 3*, I share with you the revelations and the healing power of the visitations I have been blessed to be part in search of answers to our human sufferings. I believe, if every one of us uses our spirit's eyes of love and compassion, we will see the depth of our spirit and soul's magnificence. We will look at last and honor each other's gift of life. We will be thankful for each other's spiritual presence and prepare the room for such blessings as it is given to us all to shine out into this world. Each child is born a gift. The child is a spirit. The spirit is the gift. It is a gift that this world needs to thrive peacefully and lovingly. In the realization of who I am, I learned that life's circumstances are the teachers of who we are in spirit. I learned that our inner voice never stops communicating the truth of who we are as bodies of conscious love, even if we are broken in soul and mind. I learned that even if we suffer in body, our spirit is whole in love. I now share its light and power to you who are ready to understand. I hope you see your heaven in it. Our loved one showered us with love that we would have never experienced had they not been born to us. Because my daughter and your beloved were here, we are far more enriched as living souls, greatly blessed in spirit than we could have ever been without them. They forever will be our living treasure. We must learn to quench our thirst each day from the legacy our loved ones have entrusted us with in spirit while they were with us on earth—the living bread, the clean and life-giving water our hearts must live upon—the lessons and the shadow of courage our families have shared and implanted within each of us on earth. Our spirit shines its love and its peace even after our death of the flesh.

Part 4 explains my journey to the root cause of my human sufferings. All pain is embedded in its roots. As spirits, we must face it and uproot the tree and set ourselves free, by allowing the tree of suffering to die out of existence. I encountered the deeper source of my suffering way before I encountered pain as a child, before I suffered the sense of the death of hope through my child's death.

It is in this dark void that I encountered a vast world beyond what the human eye can see. It is a world of peace, a world of pure calm and all-loving light. A brilliant man sitting on the throne, shining outside another world, called the universe where the creators and creations co-exist. These worlds are each governing themselves by eternal light, a light of peace, and of cycles of time, manifested as seasons and orders of consistencies. These worlds have one thing in common. It is the source from which worlds of kind creations shine. I see that within the creation in the universe, there is yet another world, the world of the mind, created by the human sense of control, where suffering exists and where new and old beliefs collide. This world is thoughts-based. All human minds build and fuel it unconsciously and consciously. It is the mind and body of human emotions. Emotion is birth; it creates and builds dreams, yet in the same instance, without compassion, it unconsciously and destructively weakens the mind, and it is constantly forming, powering the hearts of humankind to project and govern through the chaotic disorder of fears. The universe of the mind is power by slavery, to seek control, to project fears in the hearts of its followers to survive, to be needed, and grow. This world of our mind is where the body of basic fundamental senses of the human emotions are stored. What is created in the mind is projected into the current reality of the outside world, which all humans with minds will follow as orders out of the man-made belief of chaos. In this world, when life's order stopped for me, I found myself listening quietly. I knew then somehow, we, all humanity, our entire family, are all hurting silently. All humanity at one point or another will experience a form of suffering in their sacred ways. In essence, I found that we adult and children alike are all mourning a sense of balance and peace, which we know we are all entitled as human families, but we are in no way near its light in being on earth.

Bodies of Love. Breath of Peace.

Grief. Sorrow. It is a womb of darkness where I saw the brilliance of the greatest of the purest of light. I see it is in the darkness that all light comes to existence. Above darkness is light. Here all existence and awareness must return. In this space, there are families. Families are light bodies. They are the human form of pure brilliance. Their hearts are their entire bodies that are illuminating an intense degree of pure white brilliant love. Their minds are their entire bodies lit-up with compassionate and kind intentions. They are the embodiment of pure consciousness, of peace. These living beings light the dark universe. They are the living stars of the heavens.

Every spirit begins as pure energy. Pure energy is the substance that powers all consciousness. Every living soul's spirit is from the source of our pure light. Heaven is light. Heaven is perfect love. Its radiance is peace. We are the breath of peace. We are spirits of love and peace. The mind is voided of such glory, for it knows not the light that gives breath to the body of its humanity. The mind is not conscious of our spirit. It is not aware of love. It knows not that the spirit is ever-living. The mind does not know that the spirit is also the breath of human breath. Peace is a pure state of our divine consciousness. Peace is light. Peace is life. Peace is pure love.

The Womb of Darkness and Its Divine Purpose

It is in the womb of darkness that I saw the story and purpose of my birth. When we enter the earth, upon our birth, we cry our loudest. In darkness' sweetest essence, being born is a sacred journey; a sweet and bitter sacrifice, which our spirits of love and courage must make *shine*. The truth is the heart of the matter. We are all grieving. I was made aware that we don't have to suffer death to grieve. In our daily walk, when we are denied the love, which our spirits crave, we lose our inner light. We become lost through judgments. When we need care, yet we are treated unkindly, we are deemed invalid. When our haven breaks, by an unforeseen end of relationships within our family, such as divorce, or when we must grow within poverty, chaos, and fears, a sense of aloneness governs our entire beings every single day of our existence. Though we understand that life should be good, we are made to feel we don't belong in the norm of this world. In this state, we fail to thrive emotionally and spiritually, yet our body keeps on growing at the ticking of both an external and eternal clock, that is within time's grace and, outside time, the spirit's heavenly grace within each of us. We come for such a short time. So short of time, this garden vessels our eternal forces—our spirit. Heaven is our home; heaven is everywhere there is space, yet there is only one opportunity to experience love with our family on earth—only this time! This one life! This moment! Now.

Part 5 delves into the subconscious part of our emotions. It tells of life and how our minds deal with every living circumstance we may face after a loss. Death of perfect expectations and dreams remain the cause of sorrows in our hearts. Suffering within our soul surfaces on its own, and though we may still be alive in the body, deep within, we cannot run from the troubling sensation that we are abandoned emotionally. Moreover, and often, our spirits are denied the validations that it exists. So emotionally, we find ourselves in the dark, alone, lost, for the spirit that is here to give us light can quickly be banished by the eyes of the world of our mind's misunderstood judgments.

We are the spirit of lights in consciousness and in the breath, in the flesh, having a human experience. But we are born to love. When we receive kindness, we light up inside. We soar in spirit above the clouds. We become unlimited. We are made by eternal love; we exist for love.

I was able to encounter why suffering after a loss may persist. I experienced it on my own. Our existence is often misunderstood by our fellow human families. What is real in our minds does not reflect the reality that others see.

Part 6 explains dealing with our emotional bodies as well as encountering who we are beyond our physical selves. As bodies, doctors care for us; but often our souls and our hearts are not granted validations by those who cannot relate to our pain. When we hurt inside, there is no one to talk to about the pain of our souls. No one understands how and why our hearts are broken. There is a doctor for the mind, but our spirits remain unseen. Our spirit yearns for validation before it can feel safe to shine out, but every so often, is denied that it exists at all within us. It is denied that it is the very light and love of life in our very human souls. Life is busy. Everyone is busy surviving. Often there is no avenue to keep our spirits up when we hurt. True healing is recognizing that we are first a spirit; second, we come to have the body, which gives us a name and purpose as human souls. We are spirits, we are souls, and we are in the body—with the mind that processes life through the mercy of our magnificent brains, which processes the universal mind of human senses. In grief, there is no love. In grief are nine basic fundamental senses of our human emotions. But none of it is the truth of who we are in spirit. None of these senses are the true expressions of love and peace, which is our pure essence as divine consciousness. In light of truth, we are spirits with multi-dimensional bodies. And if we are to heal, we must recognize the complexity of our own eternal and physical lights, the force within our humanity's simplistic spiritual nature. We are sourced in breath and light from one body of love, yet even all of us must adore the complex nature of our innate divinity manifest in the everlasting intelligence, of the infinite wisdom of our family, as we walk and fulfill the dream we set out to do at birth in the creation of humanity's sacred makeup.

If we acknowledge the depth of our journey, through respect for our spirits, we will see in everyone the love we seek, the love we yearn to be part of. The eyes of the spirit see the spirit of love in everyone. Our eyes see the love in our souls, body, and mind. It is in the eyes of love that we will experience wholeness within. We are love first in all degrees of consciousness before we became aware of the senses of being human. We are the spirits, the light of the soul, the life of the body, the conscious force that governs the kindness of our minds, so we may transcend the human emotions to their fundamental purpose, to rise in full consciousness, to ignite in full awareness of love. Above all, we are the beautiful dream, in spirit and peace, manifested to give light and purpose to the rising of the new humanity.

Part 7 is a revelation of heaven as it descended on my awareness. I understand that though our human eyes may not see heaven, heaven is always the force that governs our breath. It is always pure; it is a life-giving substance that brings consciousness within matters and the physical. Heaven, that which every ancestor on earth says exists, is not a place. It is a space within our spiritual consciousness. It is a space of light. It is a world filled with pure love. Above all, heaven is a space where we evolve to know who we are in the spirit of pure consciousness. It is our highest body of peace and love that is unseen, but it is what drives us to be human in the physical body. Our light is our breath; it is a living stream from our love above that powers our souls. Love itself is the eternal heaven of our spiritual breath and bodies. Its eyes are our very hearts. As proven by my daughters' life, from the divine interventions of the Heavenly Father's sons and daughters and all of our family's guardian angels, our loved ones now in spirit who reveal their existence after their death on earth are transcendental beings in full conscious bodies of wisdom. They are now the eternal and external light of the universe's creation. Our ancestors' love will always be our humanity's story. We come to sense all created emotions in the world we live in, but all humans, passed and living, are of temporal experiences. All of our humanity's senses end. We, as bodies of consciousness, are what remains even after all our seasons of creation is finished, life after life, creation after creation.

Part 8 reveals the higher dimension of our spirit's origin. Our spirit is connected to the source of the light of the heaven. As spirit and celestial beings, we are the light and breath, the pure body of luminous brilliance of the complete, radiance of divine innocence, the expansive rays of the pure body of living love. Bodies of light eternal, we are the lights of the universe; untouched by humanity's temporal journey, we are not bounded by limits of earth's time, seasons, and of its passing winds. We can never, never, ever die. Forever is not time. Time ends. It is creation. Forever is not our bodies; for the flesh are of seasons' productions. Forever is our spirit of love. We are its brilliant light. Our essence; our light; our breath, peace, and harmony existed before there was any creation of earth and humanity. We are consciousness. We are the disembodied pure light of forever. Though the flesh dies, our spirits remain conscious of self as we enter through the evolutionary and transcendental journey of life. In and out we come. Above all material and emotional endeavors of life's regulated rules, which make up and magnify humanity's reality of our religious practices, including the pattern that our beliefs, cultures, political laws, and regulations created and being sustained, call for us to show up in time in order to govern consciously in service to the present evolution of the entire humankind on earth. In entirety, all man seeks to build the one true path of humanity's divinity, a sacred path, a road lit in grace and mercy of compassion, the simple nature of the divinities' eternal house that channels the living establishments of justice and peace within humanity's spirits; and its true home—human family.

As today comes, though you've lost a loved one, though you've watched your dream fade away with the unseen wind, though you may be in sorrow and in a brink of trials of belief, though you know life failed you of guilt or you think you failed life, I hope you make it your will to see the light of your own unbroken spirit of love—your own eternal light and overflowing and ever-living body of peace is you in spirit. From the same substance, your loved one's radiance shines, which should illuminate through your own heart from deep within the sweet memories your beloved family shared with you on earth. Remember that the light of courage is you. You are the light that shines in creation, creating and weaving a dream that your beloved above dawn in admiration as their living spirit powers you now in spirit with peace channeled through your entire makeup and embodiment. Your spiritual light of truths.

Let your beloved's love be alive in you so it may serve as your guide and inspiration whenever you need them. After all, though you've witnessed them die, though you buried them in the flesh, in spirit they have risen. Now their living spirits are forever in our midst. And that is far more powerful than dying, so you could be with your loved one, far more potent than taking chances on reincarnating to another body so he or she can be with you once more.

Though on earth, we must stay in courage; that life is worth living. We come to light our world with love and grace. Let our spirit bodies shine, as our ancestors of love and courage beacon the same. The memories of our loved ones will forever be our lifetime miracles bound by the short, yet sacred, hours, and moments spent with us.

We love them for their spirits; and their spirits, just like ours, are immortal. I learned from experience that by honoring those memories, our loved one illuminated while on earth in a body, we give heaven the right to carry us through our grief and the rest of our lives gracefully. Not just through living here on earth, not just through the comfort of our fellow human beings that we progress as a whole, and civilized community. It is only through honoring our true body of eternal love that we can heal by the presence of their remarkable, ever-living substance.

So I *beg you* to *stand up* and not use the death of the one you so love as an excuse to give up on your hopes, your dreams, and your faith for a well-lived future; for now, it is through a heavenly power that we can save our souls from such bondage. I know with all my heart that when our loved ones die, heaven opens its door to us and begins carrying us.

The journey to life after death consists of two parallel worlds, one on earth and the other of light, which is heaven. Despite the pain, we are given birth here so we may have our independence, our

SHINE LOVE, JOY, AND PEACE!

being, so that one day, we may die and live in the arms of those we love in the full light body of peace for eternity.

Remember, in the end, one future awaits us all… where the love of a parent and a child, a husband and a wife, a brother and a sister, and the love of a dear friend are all the same—forever love, light, and eternal peace.

God bless you in your walk. I pray that through my story of darkness and the coming of the heaven, which brought forth lights and essence of eternal serenity for the sake of love, you will be strengthened and find your brilliance at heart and in body, in breath and dreams. May your heart light up once more and finish the dream within. Write and sing the song your heart and soul has set forth to accomplish here until you fly and walk hand in hand with your loved one in that sacred space of peace; a dimension that does not share the same vibration of the earth, but the harmony of a garden where a broken heart is restored, a forgotten dream is renewed, and a wandering spirit is found once again. It is a world not of a dream, but of complete and divine love, from which a radiant Father's luminosity of eternal and external grace dawns in full mercy, compassion, and grace of gentle and wisdom-filled light, shining fully as living life of all darkness and lighting all the living hearts of the spirits, to power the love within all the physical creations' manifestations.

Sincerely,
Evangeline Mendez Stefan

*****

In loving memory of my precious Gabriella

Heaven is not a belief; it is in being a space of peace, in body, mind, soul, and spirit, wherever our sacred feet stand.

We are the heaven of life, who come now to shine love, joy, and peace on earth's past, present, and future.

—Evangeline

PART ONE

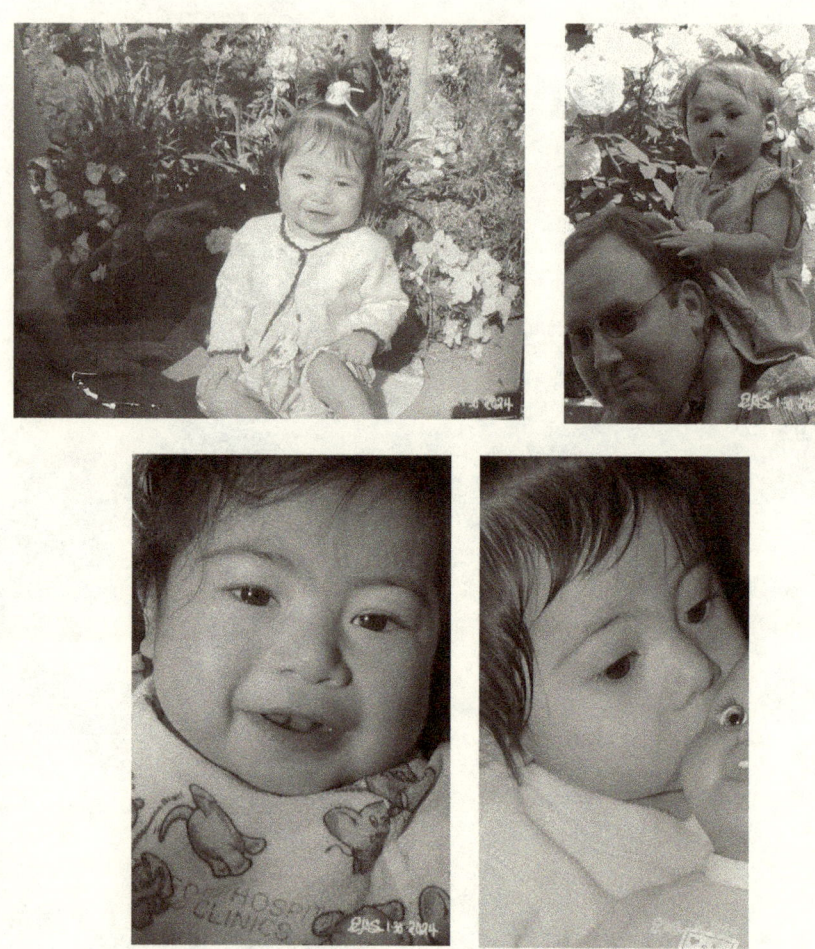

One

Blessed with a Child

We hold the vision of our dreams deep in our hearts. However, through our journey of humanity, we will discover that the spirit of our Father, the father of love, holds for us another. When His design comes first, we think our dream is lost forever. At the end of our time, we are to look back and see our gift, amazed at how grand the journey has been, knowing the world we just traveled is far beyond what our minds could ever orchestrate—far beyond what we could ever imagine.
—Evangeline

John and I had been married fourteen years by the time I was pregnant with our first baby. We knew we were ready to welcome a child into our lives. We wanted so much to be the greatest parents in the world. We had both grown up since we got married. I was about to turn thirty-one; and John, my husband, was thirty-seven. We'd come a long way. We were married on July 16, 1988. We were so young then.

We met and married in the Philippines. After three years, we moved to Japan and lived there for about seven years. In 1997, we relocated to Hawaii, ready to start our family. But it wasn't until 2002 that I got pregnant. We wanted to create the best life for our children. We were determined they would know how much they were loved. We promised ourselves that our children's wellness would always be our priority. Just like any other parent, we looked at the future as a chance and an opportunity to raise each child without the struggles my husband and I had to endure when we were both young. When John was just eleven years old, he had to deal with his parents' divorce and the unfortunate guilt that accompanied it. I, on the other hand, as early as I can remember, had to live each day wondering where in the world I would find my next meal due to extreme poverty. However, far apart on the planet, we were born, now we share one dream. John and I knew that somehow, we would give our children safe and good lives because we were both going to be there for them. I decided long ago that raising them would be my God-given ministry as a woman and a mother.

"Mommy, I'm your baby. I will come soon. But I will be very different," a two-year-old spirit announced happily. She hovered above my right shoulder while I ran by the ocean shore.

I did not know what the vision meant. I was joyful like a child when I saw her around me. A year came to pass by quickly. Finally, that one warm June afternoon in 2002, I found myself at the hospital. Five months into my first pregnancy, we were happy to find out I was carrying a girl. Fifteen minutes later, however, we learned that something was not right with her heart. Right then, I pleaded with God to wake me up from the bad news the doctors were continually delivering in slow motion as many now surrounded me, one right after the other. The room became crowded with more doctors. I knew something was awfully wrong. But no one looked at me. Minutes turned into hours, and hours had disappeared and replaced by floating anguish. It felt like it would never end. "This is just a bad dream, right, God?" I asked under my breath, as another doctor came into the room to study my daughter's developing heart through the ultrasound monitor. Then one more doctor arrived. In between the silence were murmurings of voices, like bees on a hunt, surprised to stumble upon a garden of newly bloomed flowers. There was an uncomfortable excitement, a language I could not understand. Deadening silence filled the room. Everyone was busy. They forgot that my husband and I were actually in the room and had been holding our breath so long in absolute fear. Not one of the nurses or doctors—no one—was stopping to ask us if we were still breathing, if we were all right. With my belly exposed for four hours, as it was continually slathered by ounces of cold, gooey, ultrasound gel, each doctor took his turn. Each pressed and prodded the ultrasound wand on to my bulging belly and ran it over its entire perimeter. Inch by inch, repeatedly, the cold gooey gel assisted the rolling of a golf-ball-size-tip of the instrument, as it dragged and pointed on to my now slippery, and soaked belly. For hours they watched my baby's heart while they held their breaths. Mortified, I tried to tell myself not to close my eyes because I feared I would not wake up. I felt as if I were going to pass out.

Feeling my anxiety, my husband comforted me by squeezing my hands to let me know he loved me. But the fear of the obvious unknown lurked darker. The dusky cloud of mystery was strong. I could not stand it. "Please… this is where you are supposed to wake me up, God, and tell me nothing is wrong with my child. Please… tell me to stand up and shake it all off, and everything will be fine."

But the room was silent, and God was absent. A thick cloud of darkness from above me filled the room. Four hours went by, and the room had gotten colder as each of the doctors left one after the other with only a blush of concern on their blank faces. "Please, God, tell me everything is all right… please," I begged Him. Again, there was only darkness. All I was hearing was the blanket of quiet. A doctor came in, held out her hand, and introduced herself. "Please follow me into my office," she said, staring into my eyes as she headed down the hallway. "We have something to discuss regarding your daughter's heart." We followed her down the long corridor to her office. She offered my husband and I chair to sit on as she went behind her desk to reach for a book with pictures of hearts in it. She flipped through the pages. Each contained a picture of different heart anomalies. After she flipped through two hundred-plus pages, I could tell she could not find what she was looking for. She closed the book and started showing us a picture of a normal heart. Then, with a pencil, she drew another picture of a heart with two holes in between the chambers. Then she drew more pictures as she pointed out that my daughter's pulmonary arteries did not develop—at all. "You need to leave Hawaii. She needs surgeries," she said, looking in mine and my husband's eyes. "There are no hospitals on the island that can perform the procedures she will require immediately after birth," she added.

Right then, my heart dropped. It sank so deeply I wanted to come out of my skin. "Heaven did not hear my cry," I whispered with tears in my eyes. I started feeling sick to my stomach. I was in shock. There and then, I mourned the loss. I could feel the wind slowly take my heart's dream for my beloved child out of my heart and mind: her development, her future—all the normal, wonderful, and exciting phases of her life. I had been dreaming her future would be perfect. Now, all those dreams were gone.

The most painful news I received, however, was when one doctor said, "You know, in cases such as this one, some parents make the decision to terminate the pregnancy." She looked into my eyes as she stood behind her desk, disappointed as she uttered the words.

There was a sound of compassion and tiredness in her voice. I could not help but notice the stoic background behind the words as they came out of her mouth. I was disturbed by her misplaced professionalism. Quickly I looked behind her and saw a picture of two boys wearing their baseball uniforms. The ten-by-eleven-inch picture, proudly framed, held up the beaming happiness of two eleven-year-olds. *Happy kids*, I thought. The captured smiles on their faces were heightened by the clear blue sky and the green grass under their feet. I was surprised to see that she was a mother.

In my heart, I wondered why she'd not displayed any motherly tenderness, as I would expect from any mother. Though I knew she was trained to say those words way back in her classes during medical school, I wanted her to make an exception this time. I wanted her voice to tell me gently as she held my hands. I was angered by her insensitive mannerisms, not because she spoke the words she was trained to utter, but because she said them with no kindness in her voice. My faith in the divine plan had been violated because she had not recognized my rights as a mother.

I felt as though she was telling me I was one of those parents who could end a living life inside me. I was reduced to the size of a chicken when she assumed I would take the most convenient route to escape the responsibility of being a mother to my child when she needed me the most. Yes, I sat there, bewildered for hours. I cried. Oh, did my tears fall. As they dropped endlessly from my cheek to the cement floor, I could feel the dreams I carried for my beloved child completely vanish away as those tears dried up with the wind, leaving my heart sore to the touch and my mind completely blank. I had forgotten who I was and why I went to see the doctor, to begin with. I could not feel my body, but I could sense my feet fight hard to keep still while my knees trembled as I remained standing against the wall.

At five months in gestation, the outcome of my daughter's life was uncertain. I first heard from the doctors that she would need at least six heart surgeries from the time she was born to when she turns sixteen. My tears were continually flowing as I feared all the hard days she was about to face and must conquer just to be with us… just so she could experience life with us.

Despite that tragic news from the doctor, however, I felt that behind the fears and unending tears was a stream of calmness and stillness in my soul's riverbed that kept me in check of the truth and gave me insight into what mattered at that moment. I was grounded by it and saw that part of me rejoiced that I was all right, and for the moment, my daughter was safe and had not given up. She was alive in my womb and eager to live. She would be born. She would join me in this life. She would make me a mother. I knew somehow that just as I was created, she was also created for a higher purpose that only the Creator knew. I believe God chose me to be her mother, and my sole job was to give her what I was born fully equipped to do—love her with everything that I am.

Before I left the doctor's office, I shook her hand and thanked her for her time. As I said the words, however, my eyes were drawn to look at the picture of her happy children once again. When I looked that second time, I saw something my tear-filled eyes had missed the first time. After rubbing my eyes, I swallowed. I felt my throat tighten. One of the boy's smiles was masked with the feature of an eleven-year-old who bore the face of a child with Down syndrome. Quickly my heart was called to look into the doctor's eyes. I felt her cumulative pain across time.

It was only then that I understood why she had to tell me those words; it was her effort to warn me and save me from the grief she had to endure.

Unbeknown to her, looking into her little boy's smile as he stood proudly in that one frozen moment of time, captured by the slide of a film, I felt a ray of hope awaken my heart again after mourning the loss of the perfect dreams I had carried for my daughter. That little boy's smile gave me a spark of secret light. I saw in his eyes joy, security, dreams, promise, a bright future, but, most of all, confidence and love. As he sat next to his twin brother, the love in him shone as brightly as that of his brother, who had no ailment. His Down syndrome did not define him. He is here to illuminate the world with his love as his life, and once it began, it must continue.

As we drove away from the hospital, I carried his smile with me. Through those two boys, I saw glimpses of my daughter's future. When I closed my eyes, I could see her smile too, and her joy. And somehow, that was enough to give me peace. The doctor's presence at that moment as a giver of terrible news masked her pain, which somehow gave me strength. As I exited her office, there was gladness in my heart. I was happy that she chose to let her child live. I found out later that she was the nicest doctor I would ever meet in this life. I was certain her beloved child had a lot to do with her kind nature.

Two

Finding God on Earth

"Mommy, I'll come soon. I'll be born, but I will be different."

From the time my daughter Gabriella (Gaby) was in my womb, my husband and I were told her life was on the edge. From her birth to her surgeries, her normal days were spent at the mercy of the proper tweaking and administering of varying types of medication. I wanted God, the merciful God I was told existed, to come and tell me why He would not stop her pain. I was told by my ancestors, the priest, the Bible, and other loving people that He was the creator of miracles, that He was loving. I wanted so badly to shout at Him, to shake Him up. I felt He was sleeping. He was unaware. He could not see the pain in my heart as I watched my daughter's agony fill our life. He could not see my daughter's daily suffering. Every single hour of the day, I begged Him to send His Son, Jesus, "Just one time so He could touch my daughter and restore her to perfect health," like the stories in the Bible where Jesus touched people who had illnesses, and they were instantly healed because of the strength of their faith.

My faith in Jesus was great. I just didn't know if He could hear me. Or if He existed. Or does He even care how I think, how I feel? Or am I so desperate of a human being I have to believe in something I could not see just to make sense of the world of my current suffering?

In my daughter's fight for survival, my faith and struggles came rushing back. It was shining loudly through me, the glimpses of my own identity as a child as I faced my child's suffering. Left in the uncertain faith of her survival, I am again in the presence of what I tried hard to forget of my own life as a child.

I was mad again. At things, I could not explain. I felt as though I'd gone mad from the day, I figured out that I could think. When I thought, my heart raised up some unformed questions. I wanted to know why life? I did not understand why people are born. I am my father and mother's child. Yet I am my own emotional poverties. I am that child who could not understand the cause of suffering, of diseases; I am that one that was mad at the cause of children's hollowed eyes as I rise each day lost in the usual haven of glaring windows of my childhood pain, which I could not hide or escape. Birth after birth, Filipino children give their mothers that temporary escape. Hope. For a little while, these beautiful children are born only to drown in the sea of hopelessness, as they wake every sunrise in hunger with a daily blunt punch of emptiness, coupled by an eerie silence that blasted a brilliant promise of what was to keep coming, a future ordeal, a secure and widely spread intoxicating substance of endless poverty. From where I stood, the same horizon dawned. As was yesterday, today is the same wind. The wind of poverty, which created a sense of helplessness in my being, would not stop coming anytime soon. It is not in the waters of the Philippines' springs, nor is it coming from its soil or winds. Suffering is engraved in the hearts of my ancestors and their ancestors before them. This is my humanity. This is my childhood. But for what purpose did I come? Why was I born?

So I am that child that a neighbor told there was a God. I, thought, he, and my other neighbors were insane. I wanted to stay away from them. I couldn't fathom that a God of poverty existed. This god they praised at church and gave alms to was making my cousin and my neighbors believe it's okay to be rude and mean to each other. No one told the old neighbors and fathers not to drink and be drunk, so they would not lose every peso to fun gambling.

Neighbors felt entitled to condemn my brothers and me because we were dirt poor. The god that the Catholic priest talks about, yet the priest's eyes would make it a point not to look my way at church because I'm that one that did not have a peso to put on the tray at mass. But I was told never to forget that their god was always watching me. I didn't have to pray how I felt. I felt terrible for not having money. I was guilty of being a helpless child who didn't have money to give the priest so he could look at me in the eye and validate that I am there too—in front of him.

So I did not go to mass but waited for an opportunity to see when the church was left open after masses, so I could sneak in and pray to someone who could listen to my disjointed thinking. I found refuge in the altar's stillness. My heart would spring open and surrender so helplessly to tears until my heart of guilt and shame was emptied. Then I felt foolish for feeling the guilt and shame that needed to expel out of my being. No one was there to listen except there was an irate frustration that something was troublingly wrong at the altar of the church. I had forgotten to hear my conscious voice in the church. My heart came to know what guilt is. It was in the church that I felt the echoes of unspoken yet decapitating essence of shame.

Why? Well, there was that guy, the guy bleeding, hanging on the cross waiting for me to come and save him from that mighty high altar that no little girl could reach.

I felt guilty for being free while he was up there hanging. I forgot why I came to church. I would always come out feeling so helpless. I was frustrated that I couldn't take that guy from his cross. And every time I wanted to reach out deep in my voice of frustration, I felt even guiltier that he had to be stuck in that suffering agony that could never end. So I went home ill. Often speechless for not having saved him down from his suffering. Priests couldn't help him. Well, they are kind if they want to be. But they wouldn't understand why my heart wanted to see that wooden man out of the altar.

The Priests and Parishioners adored the hanging man. They liked looking at the bleeding side of his rib. They took pride in his forever pain. I was confused. I was heartbroken. I was mentally damaged by what religion and faith were silently imposing in my heart. Suffering is a human's destiny. I am human. And the god of humans is suffering for the sake of humanity?

Later I learned that the hanging man's name was Jesus. According to my grandparents, He saves people who go to church. So, I kept going, but I couldn't understand why everyone who came and went to church was still mean to my brothers and me, and poor kids keep telling other poor kids we are sinners. It was an automatic assumption from our neighbors that we were less than they are; we were poor; because we were sinners. Everyone around me struggled to have enough to eat. As each dawn came, the sunrise illuminated the silent ache in my heart. Poverty has a face. I was the face of poverty. I was the face of sinners. All because I was poor. And mainly because I am human. But poverty is not bad, according to the church. A guy died for it on the cross. But didn't give so much hope to know He had to die. If humanity is a sin? Death on the cross is its cure? Where am I in all of this chaos? Poverty didn't agree with me. The church did not know I existed and couldn't care less if I did because I had no money. There was no belonging to my ancestors' reality. I was unwanted, often mocked for being who I am. I learned I was lost in my world, and as each day passed, I was judged by the poorest of the poor's standards of being unwanted.

I stayed away from my neighbors, who kept pointing fingers at us when things went wrong. As I grew, my elders said they have their own god, and his name is Jesus. Hmm, okay. But I was made to know that their god is better than the hanging man at church. His name is Jesus too. But he was a child. He had his little fat hand reach out to me. He was called Little Jesus. "Santo Niño." Most poor people who don't go to church prayed to him in their tiny hut. No alms required. No problem. *I can talk to that guy,* I thought.

If I could remember, I talked to Him and asked for His guidance daily. And to this very day, as all Christians all over the world have proclaimed that indeed He is Jesus. He is the son of God. I carried the vision of little Jesus in my heart. I had imagined that when He came down to touch my Gabriella's heart, the two missing pulmonary arteries would wake up and each would appear the perfect length and attach itself to its designated lung, giving each life. I imagined that with His coming, He would magically restore my daughter to normal health. With that belief in my mind and heart, I waited for the miracles to come. I waited for Jesus to save Gaby's heart. Days of waiting turned into weeks, and weeks turned to months.

Too soon, a year had come. Despite the daily meditations and my daily prayers to God, I had received nothing—just the usual stillness after the blue and, often, gray, sky. So desperate, my heart kept looking up, only to bow to the ground over and over again to recall where I stood was a ground of quiet uncertainties. Time became irrelevant; I knew I could not give up praying. That was all I could do as Gaby's mother. So I persisted. Instead, cold wind and utter silence was my prize. There was no answer from heaven.

Gabriella was born on December 6, 2002. Though we ended up living in the hospital for almost her entire life, she was my source of happiness, peace, and a constant reminder of how much I grew. I learned most of all, how deep and endless I became inspired by her presence. I was in awe of how much I could love. When I held her or even looked at her, it seemed as if I were in the company of an angel, of pure innocence.

The love of a child is so unconditional. I learned not to get tired. I never felt I could give up. I was gifted with the knowledge that the love of a mother is patience. It was clear that the feeling was brought about by knowing that our union was a sacred relationship from which so much evolution between my heart and hers was to be fulfilled and encouraged to keep on thriving. The many times I cried, she reached out her fifteen-month-old fingers to dry my tears. She was there when I needed a friend. Though she could not speak, her silent smiles comforted me. The way we were there for each other was indescribable and immeasurably pure. To experience and be immersed in it was one of my daughter's gifts, which I knew was grand; therefore, my soul accepted it ever sacredly and did not take one ounce, one glimpse of it for granted. Every second I had her in my arms; I felt I was so much more because I knew I was not just a gifted woman but a blessed mother.

When she had her first surgery in June 2003, she was nine months of age. Though we were always in the hospital for different doctor's appointments, we came home at the end of each day where Gaby experienced somewhat of a normal life. In between her pain and discomfort, she laughed as much as she could. She smiled; she was our little comedian. Most of the time, she was very corky. At a year old, she knew exactly the right button to push, so everyone around her would forget what they were doing and laugh with her.

When we were out shopping, she would ask to be on her daddy's shoulders. As she sat tall, she would scan each of the aisles for people to say hi to by waving her hands while her smile went up to her ears. She made no exceptions. Even with the occasionally grumpy-looking people who wouldn't say hi back to her, she got them to pay attention until they were forced to smile back… to her contentment. It was then that I realized she was truly happy, when other people smiled back. It was enough for my heart to stop questioning where God was. *She sees the truth,* I thought. In spirit is a world of constant love and compassion. Here joy never gets tired. It shines always. But the world of man does not know the world of the spirit. The mind of man is in the cave of darkness. And it will succumb to the darkness in the world, to create safety, out of survival. Not because he wants to, but he suffers and gets tired, but because he doesn't know he is a spirit that can shine his light unceasingly, as a child of the spirit shining in the wilderness.

She sees the face of God in every one of us… when we smile. God is an imagined man who I was told would come only if I was good. I waited, but no man—God comes in my expected vision. I was made to believe that His garden is perfect, that it is a place of refuge to my broken humanity; but, all humanity's garden had closed for me long ago when I was called a child of poverty. Humankind's God was silent toward me. His garden was closed for the poor. Now that I am a mother, I searched no more. With my daughter in my arms, I am whole and filled. When everyone smiles, light and peace come into humanity—that is love. Love is not a god. It is a light of love shining through the eyes of a kind, gentle, merciful, and loving humanity of compassion.

—Evangeline

Three

The Miracle and Power of Compassion

While humankind creates another world, it is a world not yet aware of the works of the heavens. But when a man allows his heart to be carried by love, the light that is springing from within him illuminates the heaven above, which magnifies light to the earth below, making both worlds one body of existence; for together they coexist in each man, lighting all creations above and below with one brilliance—peace and harmony. God is not one of us. The source of light, the Father of grace and mercy, is the power of good shining through creation. All humanity, united in light of love and peace, is the power of a divine Father. It is in the full light of peace and love that the search for humanity's idea of mind-made gods end.

—Evangeline

Gaby received both her surgeries at Lucile Packard Children's Hospital at Stanford. Both times we were there, Gaby, my husband, and I became friends with other children and their families, who were also trapped in the same predicament. Some children were there waiting for hearts to come; others were there for cancer treatments and heart surgeries.

When we returned to Lucile Packard for Gaby's second heart surgery in April 2004, she was fourteen months old. We stayed in the hospital about three months. Unlike the first heart surgery, which took eight weeks, the second was more complicated, and it took almost three months for her to recover. While she was recovering, I would leave her bedside to get some fresh air. The only way to do it was to search for an empty waiting room on another floor where I could have a quiet moment to myself... and pray. In that quiet space, I would close my eyes for a minute or two before I headed back to my daughter's bedside once again, feeling renewed, strong, and alert enough to face any news the doctors would give.

During that time, I became familiar with the other floors in the hospital. Each level had a different ward for children of various ages and illnesses. As these children mingled with us in the waiting rooms, I could not deny that just like me, they were also hungry for a break. So they would say hi, smile, and strike up a conversation. They would laugh freely and giggle when they talked about their future dreams. They would tell me what they wanted to be when they grew up. I could tell they had temporarily forgotten they were attached to the twelve feet of long, thin, and clear hoses, hooked on to their IVs and oxygen tanks that ornamented the small, wheeled, silver poles, like Christmas trees, which they or someone important to them were dragging along behind to help them keep breathing.

When their daydreaming ended, when their smiles became fewer, my entire body and every perimeter of my soul would feel like it had just been run over by a truck running two hundred miles an hour. Repeatedly, I would witness life's cruelty, as they were forced to awaken from their quick escape. I saw the pain in their innocent souls, followed by a grin of frustration on their faces. Tears had accumulated around their exhausted eyes, framed by their frowned brows, as they realized they were still in the hospital, living someone else's great fear, experiencing someone else's worst nightmare. Dreamers can shake a dream off and resume daily activities, forgetting the nightmare they had had. But these children could not wake up from their reality—it was their lives.

My tiny heroes, I cried for them as they endured. But I knew they were tired, ready to wake up to their future dreams where they would be happy and free to run around like normal healthy kids, doing what they please. Day after day, and even at night, I remained haunted by those innocent eyes. As a mother, my heart throbbed, longing to awaken them to their new dreams. If only I could have taken their hurt away.

When I saw the disappointments in those children's eyes and the evident shock and helplessness on the painful masks covering their parents' faces, I couldn't imagine another world where children were healthy and are free to do as they pleased. Each time I planted my feet on the hospital's thick royal-blue carpet floors, I wondered where God was. Was He "out there" with the healthy kids? Or was He with my child, along with the other kids who were suffering in the same building? "Where are you, God?" I asked as I went on yet another elevator ride to visit another floor in search of that quiet place to rest. "Please come down and heal all your children. They are waiting for you…." While the answers from God never came, deep within the core of my being, I knew those children would be healed, somehow, in due time, not by medicine alone, but by the warmth of the loving hands of the parents and friends alike, carrying the children in their hearts.

Though the wards were filled with sick children who were facing the unknown as they barely held on to their lives, something wonderful happened. When miracles arrived at the hospital, they shone brightly, as God, though nowhere in sight, always seemed to be the one credited with such events.

We were part of these celebrations as we became participants and witnesses to the sagas as they unfolded. Immediately, after we arrived at Palo Alto in San Francisco, we checked in at the Ronald McDonald house. The following morning, Gabriella woke up about five, excited to get outside. My husband and I were barely awake, but we saw Gaby's head pop up one time to see if either of us was awake. Then it went down on the pillow. Up and down, she checked, for at least thirty minutes. Each time, the bed made a squeaky noise alarming us of her restlessness. She was ready, excited to meet the new day with her radiant energy and smile.

"She's checking to see if any of us are awake," John whispered under his breath, pretending to sleep still.

"I know. Poor thing is going to be exhausted if one of us doesn't stand up," I said as I stood up laughing.

John followed immediately. He smiled at her. "You won. Let's get outside. You can help Mommy and Daddy get some coffee," he said.

We changed clothes and went downstairs. At 6:00 a.m., we went outside to be greeted by the cold spring wind. It was still a sweater season, but neither my husband nor I had one on. Gaby always traveled with an extra blanket, so I wrapped her tiny body in it.

The sun was creeping out of the morning sky. It was a beautiful San Francisco morning. As my husband pushed Gaby's stroller ahead, Gaby's excitement filled my senses with love. The fresh air replenished my entire being with its sweet morning scent. There were flowers everywhere. Everything—the trees, the shrubs, and the beautiful rosebushes blossomed in clusters; they were glorious to look at. Gaby was happy. I felt new inside.

We walked across to the street mall, where we found Starbucks. We enjoyed our coffee, savoring the morning air while we sat outside and examined the beautiful flowers all around the surrounding landscapes of the outdoor area. After about an hour and a half, we got back to the Ronald McDonald house.

We entered through the second door next to the community kitchen. There were about twenty small tables and forty single chairs on that kitchen floor. Sitting in the center was one person, a lady in her early fifties with short, silver, and well-styled hair that framed her face kindly. She had a cup of coffee and a bowl of cereal in front of her. Eating all alone, I said hi to her. She smiled back at me and waved to Gaby. My husband proceeded to the kitchen and got something to eat for breakfast. I looked for the perfect table where Gaby would be comfortable and sat down.

The lady stood up from eating her bowl of cereal. She picked up her cup of coffee in her hands and walked toward us. "My name is Diana," she said. "You must be new. Did you just get here?"

"Yes, last night," I responded.

"And who might you be, little girl?" she asked my daughter as she leaned toward her, smiling.

"Oh, this is Gabriella. We call her Gaby," I replied.

"Well, nice to meet you, Gaby." She held her hands out to Gaby and smiled. She straightened her back up and took another sip of coffee.

"Well, I'll be seeing you around. Enjoy your breakfast," she said as she turned her back to us, entered the kitchen, and washed the dishes in the sink.

"I made a new batch of coffee. Help yourselves," she said to my husband as she walked out of the kitchen. She passed my daughter and me, proceeded to the hallway, and then disappeared.

The following morning, Gaby woke up at the same time. We took her out, got our coffee, enjoyed our walk, and smelled the sweet-scented roses all around the outdoor mall. Then we went back to the Ronald McDonald House at eight. Once again, we entered through the kitchen door. Once again, I noticed Diana all alone again amid the tables and chairs. The morning after, I entered the kitchen again to get some coffee to bring to our room and was surprised by the small boy running around. It was early still, but he was awake. Diana sat on the table quietly and watched the boy run around the kitchen floor; this time, there were two cereal bowls, a cup of coffee, and a glass of juice on her table. I proceeded to the kitchen and got my cup of coffee.

"Eat your cereal, Drake… Come and eat!" she ordered the little boy. The boy sat down. He was shy and very quiet. I came to introduce myself, and we had a brief chat.

"So, your name is Drake? What a handsome name," I went on. He looked at me with his bluish-green eyes and slumped his shoulder down, so his face almost touched the table. I could hear him giggle underneath his folded arms, but he was very discreet about it.

Diana smiled and asked, "How do you like your room?"

"I like it very much. It's nice. I am so thankful that we have one. We don't know how long we'll be staying this time," I answered.

"What are you here for?"

"My daughter is scheduled for her second heart surgery three days from now," I responded.

"Sorry to hear that." She sighed and looked at Drake. "We've been here on and off the last six months," she said. "Drake's parents are sleeping right now. I come every two months to help them. Drake is my grandson. His father, my son, is my eldest. I try to help him and his wife when I can. Drake needs a heart transplant. He's been on the list for a while now. We're hoping he'll get one soon," she explained.

"Was he born with a heart problem?" I inquired.

"No. He was healthy until a virus attacked his heart just last year."

"Oh, I am so sorry," I said. "I will pray for him."

"Thank you." She smiled. "He needs it. Well, we all need it," she said with sadness in her eyes.

"I must get back in the room. I am pretty sure my little princess is awake by now. I'll bring her down if she is."

"We'll meet you back here for dinner. It is soup night tonight. Every Wednesday the volunteers make soup and deliver it here for all of us to have," she informed me.

"How nice of them," I said.

"It's really good! Join us." She smiled.

"All right," I smiled back.

"We'll see you then," she responded and began playing with Drake. I left the kitchen after waving goodbye to him.

That evening, we showed up at the community kitchen, happy to see other families with their children. Everyone already had his or her bowl of soup. I noticed, however, that Diana was not around with her little grandson. And most of the tables and chairs were taken except for the ones against the wall. Gaby and I sat in one of them. John went to the kitchen to get some soup. He returned with a tray and sat down with us. As we were eating, we saw a little boy with beautiful mesmerizing eyes, who kept on smiling at Gaby. Gaby yelped with her laugh; she was so excited. Then the little boy came to where Gaby was sitting. With no words between them, he smiled and touched her hand ever so gently. Gaby was on cloud nine. So was the little boy.

"They are happy to just watch each other giggle," I whispered to my husband. I couldn't help but feel all the worry about my daughter's surgery lifted off me as I watched the two interact playfully as if nothing was the matter at all. It was magical to watch the two of them communicate in a toddler language.

"What's your name?" I asked, hoping one of the mothers in the room would speak for him.

A lady next to my table said, smiling, "That's Rocky."

"Well, this is Gaby, Rocky." I smiled back at him. "She really likes you. I've never seen her so happy to meet a little boy. You've got to be very special to her," I said.

"How old is Gaby?" asked Rocky's mother.

"She's fourteen months," I answered.

"Rocky is twenty-one months now," she said. "As you can see, he likes to run around," she said, while her eyes were planted at Rocky's steps. "He is gaining his strength again. He's undergone four open-heart surgeries already. He gets tired easily. But he likes to use those legs when he can." She giggled. "He's getting stronger each day," she added with confidence and a sense of pride.

"I don't blame him." I smiled. "I'm pretty sure Gaby would join him if she could. But she can't run yet. Her heart is too weak to let her legs move around too long," I replied.

The mother stood up. "My name is Lane." She shook my hand and pointed at the girls sitting around her table, eating, giggling, and occasionally smiling at Gaby and me. "And these three girls are Rocky's older sisters. Rocky is my youngest." She smiled.

"Gaby is my one and only child," I informed her. "We got here three days ago from Maryland," I added.

"We are from Redding, about four hours from here," she replied. "Rocky was born with hypoplastic left heart syndrome. But after his surgeries, he needed to be on a heart transplant list. We are here now because the pacemaker in his heart is about to expire, and he is beginning to need more medicine to function. We are here on standby. The doctors wanted to operate on him as soon as possible… well, once a heart becomes available for him," she explained as I watched Rocky's eyes gleam as he ran around from one chair to the other.

"I met another little boy on a transplant list this morning," I told her.

"Ah, a three-year-old boy?" she confirmed.

"Yes, thereabout, he has blond hair… Diana's grandson?" I responded.

"Yes, they were here earlier. I think he is five. I'm glad you've met. Drake and Rocky loved playing with each other. And you'll love Drake's parents too. They're nice people." Smiling, I couldn't help but notice how beautiful Lane was. She was tall and thin, with long and wavy chestnut-colored hair that almost touched her narrow hips. It was her hazel eyes; however, that captured my heart the most. Through them, I saw her strength, her courage. I also felt her fear. I could see the tribulations she had endured as she tried to hold on to hope for her son to live. I felt a sense of familiarity between us. We were both battling the same depthless ocean, which neither of us had ventured before because it is the sea of the unknown, and its waters is called the future. I knew no one could take us there. It had to come and reveal its secrets to us both.

Rocky's smile lit up my heart; his eyes were shaped like almonds with brown, blue, and black hues on his irises, highlighted by his black and curly hair that framed his sweet face. When he smiled, his eyes became round and clear white. It made his face even more plump and mesmerizing to watch. Every time he smiled at me, his eyes glowed as if an old intelligent soul was looking right through my aching heart; I couldn't help but think his tiny soul knew the worries and burdens my heart carried for Gaby. Every time I looked at him, it was like staring at a cherub from heaven; my heart felt as though it melted on hope, love, and nothing more, followed by a stream of peace. I could not help but feel the same; like my Gaby, he could open the window of heaven through his gaze.

Drake and Rocky were being seen at Lucile Packard Children's Hospital, the same hospital as our Gaby. For months, both toddlers were on and off on the heart list. They would be on the list, but as soon as they contracted a cold or fever, they would be taken off the list. They held on for their lives each day, armed only with a hope that a heart would eventually come to rescue them.

While we were waiting for my child to recover from her second surgery, Drake, the older boy's heart, failed completely. At that time, there was no heart available for him. The doctors were reluctant to put him on an ECMO (extracorporeal membrane oxygenation), where a machine would act as his heart and lungs. Through his carotid artery, it would pump the blood out of his body via two sets of hoses, five to six yards long, to give his blood some oxygen. The oxygenated blood would then go through an opposite set of hoses to enter the opposite carotid artery so his blood could be distributed through his body.

Doctors found no other option for Drake. Without the machine, he would die right then. Without a new heart, he would die days later. The doctors were uncertain whether the machine would be of any help to him. He was the youngest one they'd ever used it on. But there were no other options. They had to try. They needed to buy him time. He was placed on an ECMO for ten days. So, for those ten short days he could be with his family. I passed his room on my walk to the CVICU, the back room, where I attended to my child. Each time, I would take a moment to watch him through the glass window and pray for his spirit to hang on as he lay lifeless on his hospital bed.

Accompanied by a giant machine with hoses attached to his belly, and the other end attached to the little boy's carotid arteries, Drake's five-year-old body lay so still it was hard to know whether he was still alive. I watched the three nurses who held their breath as they carefully tended the hoses containing his flowing blood. As the machine pumped the unoxygenated blood out and the oxygenated blood back in again, I wondered where Drake's spirit had gone. "Is he playing?" I asked myself. "Is he alone?" No matter, I prayed he was being cradled by angels or held in Jesus's arms.

Each night, as I sat and watched over my daughter, my heart and mind agonized for Drake. Before I could start each evening, I had to pray the rosary on behalf of him, Gaby, and the other children in the building. There was a sense of guilt in my heart that it was all I could do for them. I felt helpless. But in prayer, I could sense the light-filled altar of God. In prayer, I could raise the whole hospital and all the sick children up to Him; I could even see my hands lifting them up to the altar of His living love and presenting their pain and heartaches to Him. In prayer, I could clearly see God's hand reach out His healing light and melting all the children's pain away. In prayer I found I could fully open and give all my faith to God and believe with my entire being that He exists. He is listening. He knows. It is in the hour of my prayer that God is ever-present and ever-powerful; He could cure all our pain no matter what kind of pain it was. Thus, prayer was the pillar of my every morning, which I held on to each moment to keep my head and chin up while I raised my shoulder and chest upward so I could see the new sunrise that lay beyond that day rather than slump through my hours in misery. Each sundown was the pillar I leaned against to hold me up at night, so I could stay awake and be present for my Gaby. During prayer, I would see God as the most powerful, ever-living, and ever-loving God, who wants nothing bad to happen to my daughter and me. In prayer, I found safety. It is in prayer, I became strong, useful, and empowered, as a mother who felt helpless with what I was up against—the unknown. Yet it is in this prayer that I would lose my humanity. I became immersed in the reality that my grandparents religiously fashioned for me. It is a roller-coaster ride. I don't know if God is even listening. I hoped He did. Even though as religion said, "I was a sinner." So every day was a struggle prayer to make sure that the God of truth, the God that made me and gave me my child was listening. I prayed He would carry my family and me… kindly.

The First Vision of Life in the Light

Love for my child took me places I didn't know existed. When I arrived, I saw the spirit of man, so radiant in His patience and humble in grace. His presence lit the world of darkness. He stood still marking time with his pristine, light-filled tunic. He is dawning on earth to give comfort to all of my humanity. He is light where there are uncertainties. My heart and spirit said, "He is the promised one. He has arrived. Now darkness will know itself as blessed. For its light is come."

—Evangeline

Each morning, on my way to Gaby's bed in the back of the CVICU, the hospital's critical room, I was pulled to stop, contemplate in silence, as I watched Drake through the glass window. My heart would be so solemn as I faced the blank vision that held the secret of the unknown quiet space all around me, which only the coming hours, in the dawning of the new highly anticipated day ahead, had not the power to make manifest his healing, had not yet arrived. Patience is a breath of peace. This boy is patient. I thought prayerfully as I watched his suspended body, lying so flat, so inanimate, so silent.

I stood there and watched, concerned with this uncomforting tranquil. His eyes remained closed; his body still, naked, but alive in oxygenated blood with the aid of the machine which intricately worked its purpose. I stared at the moving blood through the clear hose that entered his carotid arteries. I took a long deep breath. I turned my body and headed back toward the hallway. I had hoped each day I visited him it would be "the special day" for him to get the heart he'd been waiting for. Each evening, when I returned to him, I expected it to be "the night" where he already had the new heart working for him while he recovered without the aid of the machine.

After the third morning of the ten days given. I passed Drake's room again. Suddenly the usually cold and still room changed. It was lit up in a white, soft light. Then to my surprise, I saw there was a movement within the light. It struck me with jaw-dropping awe. The bed is still there. The boy's body is still asleep. But there was something else in the air than the usual bed, the boy's body, and the ECMO machines. I pressed my head closer to the glass window. This time was not like the past mornings. In the corner of his room beacons, the bright light; in the light was a light meadow. Its silhouette brilliance, which was a carpet of grass, was resting next to the foot of his bed. Then in this meadow was a Little Tikes red bike and a red ball. Both toys were by the foot of the bed. Then I saw a spirit of a boy, playing ball with the spirit of a man with brown curly hair that dropped to his shoulders. He was looking after the boy. They were playing under one lone olive tree. *They were waiting for something too, like I am.* I shook my head. He smiled at me. The vision subsided, back to myself again; I saw sleeping Drake, alone in his room. The room remained cold, as I was outside its door. But it left my heart warm by the secret vision.

Something is up, I thought. Something big is happening. I knew the unknown would make itself known. It was just a matter of time.

I went back to Drake's room the third night's visit hoping things had changed; however, I stood disappointed because he was still surrounded by the hoses, the nurses, and the machine. Though I was comforted that his blood was constantly flowing, I felt doubtful, for his days were lessening with time. I would say a prayer that a heart would come to rescue him. I wanted it to be my surprise the following morning. As he lay there and the machine pumped the blood through his entire body, I finally had the honor of shaking the hands of his young parents, who I'd not met before, on his third day of being on ECMO.

Drake's father was twenty-eight. His mother was twenty-five. Both were so young. I've forgotten what they looked like. I only remember how scared they were. When they held each other's hands, they seemed so hopeful, but their eyes and hearts looked fragile. Both of them constantly gazed either on the floor or up to the empty sky. I could feel their minds were dazed, tired, and blank. They spoke very little.

Every day since Drake had been on life support, his grandmother would sit next to me, while I took my morning break in the waiting room. She held in her hands the Bible and would read the words out loud to me. Not because I needed the comforting, but because she needed to hear them, the most in that given moment in her life. I listened with patience and understanding, for I knew it was her way of harvesting any hope from the passages, which boosted her belief that God was on her side. After all, He was her only hope left, though intangible as He was; I knew He was the most powerful force her grandchild needed most. *"He had to exist,"* I thought. *"Because I am here; because I can love, I know He exists. I know Gaby is here because He has a plan."*

Drake's grandma was in her sixties. I was thirty-two. Though we differ in age, we both have something in common. We both understand the limited power of man and medicine. Our spirits knew God was the only option left to extend Drake's life. Just as my prayers held me up morning and night, she was being carried by her faith that there truly is a God and that He was listening to her while she recited the messages in her Bible. Through her deep faith, I could already see that her grandson would receive his lifesaving heart within the expected time. In tears, she whispered to me, "A heart must come soon. It's already day three… within seven days… in that window of time, a heart has to come or else he dies."

"I know… The only thing we can do right now is to pray." A flash of the vision returned to me, but I could not find the strength nor words to explain to her. I had to be careful. "The doctors are doing everything they can. You guys have done everything you can. It is now in God's hands. We have to pray that Drake does not give up, and I believe he is listening to us, just as God is listening, and I promise you, God is listening," I responded sobbing. The flash of the vision strengthened me. I hugged her and felt the endless sea of great helplessness. The sea of the unknown blasted through me as great darkness came. Suddenly the sky opened. The boy playing lit all the darkness up. Fear was no more. What remained was the vision of the boy playing.

"Faith alone is not going to help us," I told her. "You have to know that the God of peace and love has a plan. We don't have to know everything, you just have to know He loves Drake and you, He loves us," I assured her.

"The doctors told us that the machine would begin to damage his young body more than help him. After the tenth day, there's nothing they can do for him… A heart has to come soon," she said, wiping her tears and lifting her head toward the heavens.

"I know… Now all knowledge known to man has ended. There is no other choice. Now is ours. We have to believe in miracles." I hugged her. Together we prayed the only prayer I seemed to believe would work, the *Our Father*.

On the morning of the tenth day, I was in the head nurse's room to discuss the care of my Gaby. The day prior, the nurse who was assigned to care for her would not even help me change the sheets, which were discolored from medicine spills. It broke my heart to see my daughter fighting hard to stay alive, and the sheets that were supposed to give her comfort were filthy. It tore me up that she was already motionless, and I didn't know where her spirit was at the moment. Her precious, yet helpless, body lay still, intubated, and her graceful face was covered with masking tape to hold the hose, making her unrecognizable. The least I could do, as her mother was to keep her bed pristine, just like her spirit. But the nurse refused to see my side. She did not consider it a priority to help me change the sheets.

So I spoke to the head nurse, and she invited me into her office. As I was sitting in the chair and discussing the issue with her, there was a knock on the door. "The heart is on its way," a lady said. My heart jumped out of my body. Suddenly, my lungs, which had been halted by repetitive fears for too long now, felt inflated inside me. I could breathe again. I began crying. "Please tell me that heart is for Drake! Please!" I sobbed, begging the head nurse.

"It is!" the head nurse smiled. "But we can't tell the parents yet until we know for sure that it matches. We have to wait until it gets here."

My heart was pumping, my body trembling, and my lungs were exhaling more air than I thought they were capable of doing. I leaped back to my Gaby's bedside and cried in thanksgiving. But it took a lot for me not to dash to the waiting room and scream the news to Diana. I wanted so much to let her breathe again. I wanted to take her pain away. But I had to wait.

Forty-five minutes later, the head nurse approached me with a smile. "Do you know where they are?" she inquired. I jumped out of my seat. She nodded. "It's a match!"

Overcome with tears and floating in disbelief, I begged, "Can I please tell them now?"

"Yes! Yes, you can," she answered. I was about to run out of the door.

"They can't leave the hospital, though. Tell them. The doctors will inform them officially what needs to happen next."

"All right," I nodded as I fanned like an excited dog about to receive a bone.

"Okay. I'll tell them," I said as I tried to plant my feet on the ground. So I ran to the waiting room and broke the news. Diana cried with me. Drake's parents arrived a few seconds later; Diana told them what we were crying about. They both fell on their knees. Unbeknown to me, I did not realize my husband was back in the hospital from his morning shower and had been watching me throughout my excitement of the past hour.

"What's going on? What's gotten into you?" He hugged me. "I've been calling your name. You weren't listening."

"Drake has a new heart." I hugged him back, still in tears.

In disbelief, he took a deep breath of relief. "Oh my God, are you sure?" He believed cautiously, wiping his tears away. He wanted to be sure I was not giving Drake's family false hope or playing a cruel joke. "Are you sure? Are you certain? Who told you that the heart is for Drake?" he whispered, demanding an answer quickly.

"Yes! Joel, the head nurse, told me."

I looked all around me. People I didn't even know were crying, sighing, and thanking God. Then my heart sang the ritual of thanksgiving. It was only appropriate to gather everyone in a circle and lead a prayer of thanks to God. Not a moment more, we said our praises; hand in hand, we cried our thankfulness, which seemed to have melted away all the spiritual and physical exhaustion we each carried deep in our hearts from the agonizing days that had come to pass.

When I returned to Gaby's side, the same nurse who would change Gaby's sheets was there, but I made it a point to do it myself. After watching from the sidelines, she gave me a hand, which made me feel even better.

Three weeks later, as I sat resting in the hospital waiting room, Drake smiled at me again, as though I would never see it again, as his mother pushed him around the hospital floor, on a little red wagon. They were on their way out to get some fresh air.

After watching him move slowly across the floor and away from me, for the very first time, I became aware that heaven's mercy was something I could never earn. For a child to be given another precious heart, a second chance to live was simply mercy, only God's love could make happen. The heart that beats in Drake's body is the glory of that love. The silent fear that devoured his mother's mind with tremendous concern had been replaced by a tight grip on the handle of the red wagon, accompanied by a gentle stride to make sure she kept the heart still, to support her child's life in an ongoing manner.

Drake was the bearer of a miracle; he knew it, for his eyes told me so. And the heart that beats in him is God's grace through the unselfish faith, and loving act of another mother and father from only God knows where… who had just lost a beloved child. But they knew the true secret of life: their child's legacy would defy the laws of death as the heart would not surrender but resume its duty to beat, so the recipient may continue the dream it had begun. Mercy, they were not given, but they were willing to give it to others. They leaped beyond their pain and had absolute compassion for another child as if the child in need was already their own. They openly reached out, as they offered their entire family's unrealized dream to complete strangers, so others would not know their pain, only feel their love… and the opportunity to live life as one whole family together on earth.

Love is a spirit. It is a spirit of a gentle power of pure wisdom. The wisdom of light is white brilliance within every human being united in one light of peace, mercy, and compassion.

—Evangeline

Four

When an Angel Speaks

He sat next to me quietly. He was seventeen feet tall. With folded wings behind him, he spoke so caringly. I noticed that even in sitting, he was strong. "Tell the mother of the boy that a heart will come in two weeks." A vision of the desperate mother's palm was made open in the bright light; gracefully, the vibrant heart of a child from the sky came down. Illuminated, the heart was cradled gently by the unseen and loving giant spirit hands and was gently laid upon the mother's agonizing yet now grateful open hands.

—Evangeline

The night Drake got his heart, I went back to the Ronald McDonald House to have dinner. Lane was there with Rocky. I broke the news to Lane. I could not remember anything she said that evening after she, too, showed great disbelief. Immediately, she took a sigh of relief. We talked for some time. Then she was tearful and quiet until she left the kitchen.

The following morning, she smiled a lot as she talked to me at the community kitchen. She was hopeful. She stood straighter. She no longer dragged her shoulders with each stride. That morning she walked with lightness; there was clarity in her eyes and openness on her face. She followed Rocky playfully as he went all over the room in delight, smiling as usual. He had just as much joy as he did the first time I met him.

When night fell, I said the rosary for my Gaby's healing. It was the same prayer I recited the following morning before the sun rose. Both times, after talking to God about my prayer for Gaby's recovery, I pleaded for Rocky to have his heart before his pacemaker stopped working.

The Second Vision

As a mother, I thought I have to give my child the world. It is not so. I now know I was only given the heart to love, comfort, and guide my child, all the days of her life. Love is radiant and infinite. She brought that light out from me. She has taught me that the spirit is more than all the world. She came with nothing. But her light and spirit bestowed love on to my entire world. Now the world shines because of her spirit. Her love is light. Light is the fuel of my spirit.

—Evangeline

One night, as I was resting my tired and aching body on the long sofa, I lifted my feet on the cushion for comfort. I meditated in peace. It was midnight. All alone in the waiting room, taking a breather, staring at the clear night and the full moon, I fell asleep. In my vision, a big angel, seventeen-feet-high with wide wings, sat on the couch by my feet.

"Don't worry about Rocky," he communicated telepathically. He spoke no words. He was gentle in his heart's voice. "A perfect heart will come for him in two weeks. Tell the mother not to worry," he said, while he showed me a vision of a beautiful, plumb-sized heart beating ever so strongly in his open palms. He kindly handed it to Lane. Lane accepted it gracefully as she sat on the Ronald McDonald kitchen chair. I woke up from that vision, not knowing what to feel, but I suddenly had hope for Rocky.

Two weeks later, as I was sitting on the coffee table at Starbucks with Lane, sipping my coffee, a familiar voice came to me. "This is the day…," she gently spoke. This time it was an older mother angel. "Please tell Lane that the heart is on its way." Not wanting to sound crazy, I looked into Lane's desperate eyes and once again saw my sorrow as if her eyes were a mirror of my inner pain… hopeless… scared. I had to be very careful with what I had to tell her. I did not want to give her false hope. I was still unsure whether I could communicate with the angel or whether I'd just gone crazy due to a lack of sleep from the trauma of watching my daughter endure so much, and I could not help her one bit.

Anyway, I knew I had to acknowledge the angel's presence, just in case I thought I was communicating with her, just in case her news was true. I silently explained something very important to the angel, whose beautiful essence remained hovering behind me: "You know, I can't just tell her the heart is coming today. We have to be gentle with our words. Why don't you tell her in her heart?… just the way you are telling me now? Prepare her, show her what to do. She will listen… I know it… She will," I telepathically told her. Then gently I gazed across the small table and said as I smiled and tried to feel Lane's thoughts, "Lane, wouldn't it be beautiful if today was the day you get a call and the heart is ready for Rocky?"

Quickly, her eyes lit up, and she replied, smiling, "Oh, that would be so nice. My goodness, it would be a celebration, wouldn't it?" After that coffee hour, which took place at around nine-thirty that morning, Lane and her girls went to see a movie. The theater was only five minutes away from her mother-in-law's house. During the movie, she got a call that indeed the heart was on its way and that she must come to the hospital immediately to prep her precious boy. So off she went.

She swung by, dropped the three girls at her mother-in-law's, and headed to the hospital. I smiled after I learned the sequence of the day's events. I knew deep in my heart that the angel was glad to accomplish a task where I wouldn't be needed much. The third day, immediately after the transplant, Rocky's mother invited me to his hospital bed. His blue lips became pink, and his pale skin became alive and radiant. Every time I looked at the great changes in him, I could see the angel's love at work as he watched next to him. I knew then that Rocky was loved. I knew he would be all right. I was honored to be a witness to such a story… a true miracle.

We gathered at the Ronald McDonald community kitchen to share many meals, hugs, stories of struggles, and updates on our children's situations. Some of the news from newcomers at the House were grim. But for those children who were recovering, there was good news my heart enjoyed hearing. But no matter what the news was, our children's smiles when they felt better temporarily made the parents forget about the pain as we would find the strength to laugh once again, even though deep in our hearts, for some of us, we knew the joy might have been short-lived.

After many months of hoping and waiting, both couples received the news they had patiently prayed for. Within one month, with only three weeks behind the other, two hearts became available for each of the children.

We rejoiced in their new lives. We watched the children go from blue to pink when they had the heart transplants, as if they had been pulled out from the list of death to a list of a new life, of a second chance. Suddenly, we could look at the horizons for the two children and see their future.

I thank heaven for the simplest, yet most profound, gesture of kindness, of bravery from the donors' parents, whose lives were just as tried and violently shaken as ours. I mourned their losses in silence. I shared the guilt of the recipients as I realized what had to happen so they could keep their families together. I hurt for the donors, for their sudden and abruptly torn world, for their trials came without them being given a chance to prepare.

With such examples of mercy toward other children, even when their future dreams had been depleted, these strangers' courage was the source of my inspiration. Their selflessness awakened the eyes of my heart to see where God truly was. His living power was in the kindness of those parents who chose to give the hearts of their children away so others could live. I admire their strength. At that point, I thought that maybe true faith was not found in just believing, but in knowing, in understanding that we can make a difference in someone's life when we decide to give from the spirit of our heart, even when it means we'd lose something. In the end, I learned to look for His grace, which is within the human's ability to surrender to do what is right, even in the most horrendous situation.

For the first time, I saw another God. A god that was not at any church I have entered. Here it was a humble spirit. A silent and potent love in action, from what source? I have not yet been made known, yet I see, feel, and know that it lives in the conscious hearts of my fellow brothers and sisters. I saw the basic origin of all the goodness on earth through compassion. It is comforting to see how this silent, yet serene, God really works. I thought to myself, *if a fellow man, out of compassion, can will it so that another child lives, how much more healing can Gaby receive when God of life and love himself hears my plea and sends us our own miracle healing?* I just knew inside my being that Gaby too would have her turn. I just had to be patient and wait. But while I did, I needed to see my daughter for who she was, an innocent child, an angel of courage.

Gabriella

I looked through her eyes and knew that my child is the joy that has come to light my lost soul. It is her entire being, her spirit, her soul, mind, and body that shine and overfill the empty spaces within my soul. Now I am my own universe. In me is a motherly universe's heart. And when I have none of earth that may quiet my soul, to quell my eternal hunger and thirst, she is birthed into my world, as the gift of love from the unseen heaven. She is the door to my unconditional existence. She is the grace and mercy of my life. She is my purpose. Now I know. Eternal love is the universe and breath of every spirit of a child born on earth.
—Evangeline

As a newborn, Gaby was not only a joyful child, she was peaceful and full of promise. Countless times I had gotten tired from having no sleep on top of worrying about her health and upcoming surgeries; she would have reached out and lifted my chin to her, smiled, and laughed. I learned that her grace was not limited by her toddler mind. As days went on, her will gleamed effervescently through her small body. She glowed as if her spirit's light was too big to contain in a two-year-old's body. It was mystical to see a child's deep sense of quiet, still, and infinite knowledge, which she beholds. It was something I could not describe or understand. After her first surgery, I took her back home accompanied by instruction on how to slowly wean her off the heavy doses of medication she had to have to recover from her operation.

Gently and slowly, I was weaning her off when she showed discomfort I could not fathom to see. It was the most painful thing… to watch her in so much pain. I could imagine her wound from the chest operation was aching badly. I could feel her tiny heart's stubbing pain, from having been handled by the surgeon's hands and manipulated for sixteen hours. And the hair-like-arteries, which were the source of her life, through which her living blood could flow to her tiny lungs, had been cut opened and sewn with five thousand needlepoints and pricks she received. She was in too much pain; I have no words to describe how she must have felt.

My Daughter's Tears

Every waking day, I thanked God for my daughter. I thanked Him for guiding us as we journeyed through healing her heart. Yet I found that on my lowest point of desperation, as I watched my daughter suffer, I was grateful for her ability to shed tears, which were a blessing, her source of relief, an outlet to let the unspoken pain to escape from her. She would cry all day long. I could not give her all the high dozes of heart medicine she was used to in the hospital to comfort her so that she could sleep peacefully. But I had to make sure I was not giving her so little that she was in deep agony while she remained awake. She groaned in my arms. I held her, hugged her, kissed her, rocked her, but she would not stop arching her back. It would have been a lot easier if I could have just given her body what it demanded, but I didn't want her to become dependent on the drugs. I wanted her to heal.

Not knowing what to do, I held her in my arms and begged God to please stop her pain. "Please, God, if you are going to heal her, do it!" I cried. "If the only way to heal her is to take her back, take her away from me, take her! Just take her pain away!" I sobbed while holding her. After twenty minutes of my crying on top of her cries, suddenly, she stopped her twitching and groaning. She put her baby hands on my lips. She caressed my right cheek. Then she smiled at me and made me smile as she laughed while she assured me in a soft gaze with her eyes that everything would be all right.

It surprised me; I almost dropped her on the floor out of fear. I felt as though I was holding an eleven-pound being with the eyes of an ageless soul. I felt she was not a child at that moment. It was as if she knew what heaven knows, and she was there to tell me not to mind her pain. I sensed that she was far more aware beyond what I could ever know or understand as a soul, as a mother. When I think about that moment, my breath stops. To this day, I remain in disbelief. Since that day, I've known I was working with an extraordinary child who bore in her the mystery of life, which I will never understand, and the only power I had was to respect her given purpose and love her with every bit of my being—mind, body, and soul.

"She will have a full life," I said to myself every minute of the day. "Someday she will want me and her father to give her a big wedding and watch her enjoy life. She will have a family of her own." Every single sunrise was fueled by hearing my voice say those words. It was these affirmations that carried me along many hours and days.

During her second heart surgery, the surgeon worked on her heart for thirteen hours. By the time he wanted to close her breast bone, he could not. Her heart was too swollen; it had doubled in size. So he left her chest cavity open, covered only by clear plastic, similar to a Saran Wrap. When the nurses wheeled into her room, I stared at her heart and thanked God as it beat for her. The surgeon eventually closed it, three days later. But I was so thankful to have a glimpse of what God had designed so I could have her in my life.

Seeing her heart, as simple as it was to look upon, a tiny heart the size of small plum, it was fighting hard to give my daughter a chance at this sacred life. She was intubated for sixteen days afterward. As she remained asleep for so long, I began to miss her so much. That was the longest we'd ever been separated. I panicked inside as I realized I could not live long without her company and without her smile.

Before she was extubated, the doctor slowly weaned her off the medicines as she slowly awakened. Sluggish still, when one of the doctors sat her up to pull the tape that held the tube in place, she was the first one to clap her hands and smiled the minute she felt the tube pulled out of her throat. The surrounding doctors could not help but laugh and cry at the same time.

It pained me deeply to see her that way. She deserved so much better, better health, a better heart, and better lungs, but she was just happy just being herself. My tears welled out of me. My spirit asked, "How could a child endure so much just to have a taste of a painful life on this earth? What is it about this life that such a precious soul is willing to go to any length to obtain one?" My heart cried in thanksgiving to have her back in my arms again.

Four weeks later, with much hope from my own daughter's strength, and the miracles I am honored to be part, I felt the wind gather within me. From that wind, a boundless mountain of hope rose out from my tired heart. We finally left the hospital and came home knowing for sure, that indeed she will heal completely as she merged into the beautiful future that awaited her.

Five

When Heaven Calls

In her smile, a buried seed hidden within me in secret has ignited into a spark. I couldn't explain that such a sense of wholeness is secretly nesting inside of me. She glowed with such unconditional joy, and the spark blossomed beyond time. Now I see. I realize the light was a different light. It was a spirit light. It was unseen to the human eye. It has lit the secret door to the heaven above. The door opened. It gives out love; love is continuously coming and going from the vast space of yet unknown eternity.
—Evangeline

    Seven months after her second heart surgery, Gabriella caught a cold. At the hospital emergency room, I watched her sweet eyes look into mine for the longest time. They were asking me, what's happening? Why was it happening? Before I could find my voice, before I could search for words to answer, her eyes closed. Then she was no longer there. Just like that... one minute she was smiling with me, lighting me with such brilliant dreams and living purpose; and the next she was void of that one breath I waited to come out again so she could open her eyes. But she never did. She was gone. She lay on the table, looking peaceful, yet her body was hollow and cold to the touch. I begged for whatever made her smile and giggle to stay right with me. In tears, so scared and distraught, I pleaded, "Come back to me... Don't leave me, my precious child... Please come and smile at me again. Come back, dear child, and caress my cheek again. I need you in my arms. I beg you. Come back. Don't leave. I love you. I can't live without you. Come back now, all right? Please...," I whispered in her ears.

On my knees, I held her sleeping body; I pressed her heart against the beat of mine to remind it to beat again. With every thump of my heart, I commanded hers to follow, "Just like this, sweetie... You can do it. Open your eyes, please. Please, wake up... Make your heart beat... just like Mommy's," I whispered. "I know you can do it. Please try!

"Please... Please," I begged. I kneeled. I cried. I prayed. Darkness. Space of darkness was all there is.

I waited for hours as my husband kneeled in between cries to pray to his God to let her wake up from her sleep and then stood up again. I watched both of his knees become red, scratched, grated, oozing, and crying with blood from repeatedly being pinned against the rubble, sandy, dirty, and very cold cement floor. How long had he kneeled each time?

How often did he stand? I could not remember. I knew it was the longest I'd ever seen a man plead for mercy. But even for him, there were no answers from his God. He knelt, waiting for eternity. He stood up a million times, wailing in agony for his child's spirit to return.

Hours passed. The room was ocean cold. My husband came toward me. He looked at our precious Gaby. He touched and caressed her face over and over again for thirty minutes. Then he looked at me and begged with his red and swollen eyes, shaking his head, "Honey, please... please tell me this is not happening." Bursting into tears, he hugged Gaby's unresponsive body and me.

I sobbed endlessly. I could only watch as his cheek pressed against hers. Still, I was hollow inside, emptied of words. I just watched him as I could no longer cry myself. I could not respond to him. I looked around. The space around me became colder. I was void of who I once was. I felt I did not want to answer him with his begging just yet because I too was waiting for any moment when Gaby would open her eyes. In silence, I waited... and waited some more.

Four hours had passed, but she remained quiet... covered with bruises and still. In my arms, she lay ever so gracefully, but very, very silent. She never moved. Her eyes remained closed. Just as the room remained silent, and the air in it was void of warmth, her heart did not beat again. Her lips did not move. They are frozen. My breath did not want to come out of my body as I waited for her to take hers, so that she could open her eyes. So I wailed from the top of my lungs. I begged.

But for a long, long time, she lay still... no movement came from her, and her chest never rose again to give me the breath I longed to feel. It was at that moment that the beyond impossible took its course, the first hour of my life. I felt the sun come down on me way before it had the chance to rise. In that cold sunken room, darkness arrived and swallowed me whole. It left me all alone in its belly. I could not see; I could not hear. I could not feel my body. I was lost, so lost, in the now-hollow body of my precious baby.

I waited in absolute faith that my fear would not strike me, but it did. Without Gaby's smile to wake me up and shine on me again, I would become nothing... no one, not a spirit or a soul... just an empty invisible body that I was is all that was left. Now that she's no more, I realized my daughter's light was my light. Her dreams were the reason I am a mother. My child's visions were the reason I was born. She was my light. When I held her, I knew she was the reason I woke each morning. The reason I crossed the ocean to find love, gamble with the chance to find her father, my husband, my friend. Now she is not here. Her body is still, hollowed, and cold. Instantly, it had come. I lost the ability to speak. I could not think. I burst in the silence of death, body, and soul, broken into billions of tiny, shattered, and unrecognizable pieces. In an instant, I had turned in to a mad character whom I could no longer recognize. In this space of cold wind, where her light left it, I died as a mother. But, life required for me to stand. Offer her body to the ground. In her light, she is all mine. In her death, even her body, I had to surrender to the earth. Everything I am was gone. However, still, my heart is pained in the realization that I walk. I walk as a hollowed woman. Life, after all, goes on. It has not stopped calling. Tomorrow kept on coming. The night keeps on returning. Its call never-ending. *Rise*, it says. *Run and walk with me.* The space would speak before I sleep.

My heart spoke: Space is conscious of my sorrow. Space is consciousness itself. I am in its womb.

—Evangeline

PART TWO

A strange ocean of deep pain and sorrow can only be soothed by the subtle radiant light of truth—our everlasting love is our body of consciousness. The breath of our spirit is sourced from the Holy Spirit, our Creator of peace, the king of love, our Father in heaven. The space that contains all of the heavens and the universe are the living body of waters of love, welled from the breath of the holy heart; the mind of infinity; the sea of the living wind of peace—His majesty's pure essence is the spirits' space of light, darkness, rest, and creation. He is powering all life to live again, death after death, life after life, time after time, in support of humankind's journey through every season, to seek, and create a family of awakened, conscious, ever more peaceful, and united children of divine humanity.

—Evangeline

The Spirit of Love Shining in My Darkness

The Face and Character of Grief

In a man are two beings. One will rise. The other will die and surrender itself to ashes from which it rose a child of man. In spite of both, one dream is fulfilled. It is to be aware of life's greatest secret. Through pain and suffering lies powerful energy called love, and that is what the womb of divine creation has come to learn to manifest as we, the spirit, gain true courage to live. Within its thread, we experience our magnificent purpose, to heal others as we are to heal from the endless sorrow brought about by not knowing our divinity. Through us, there is no beginning or end, just endless kaleidoscopes of opportunity to understand and be understood, to love and be loved through the mercy of the universe's eternal and material substance called humanity in time, through time, life after life, dream after dream.

—Evangeline

"Explain to me how you feel now," my psychiatrist ordered.

"I don't think I can make it!" I replied. There were no words to what I had become. I was empty, fragile, and shattered. Many minutes passed. "I feel like a giant tsunami has hit me… Only it hasn't let me go. It is still carrying me now in an ocean of great void and turmoil. I am trapped in its noisy, angry, roaring, unforgiving, tantrums. It is a cunning beast, a scary monster without a face!" I explained.

There were not enough words to explain this type of hurt. My psychiatrist tried to help me by being quiet most of the time, but I knew she could not say a word because she could not ride with me or reach her hands beneath her to find what is left of me. I had become nothing. From being a blessed mother to an empty mad character, I was hollow, cold, mute, and damned.

Each day after my great loss, I was overwhelmed by how hard it was just to survive and overcome the grief as it would take over me unannounced in the form of a very dark cold wind. Against my will, it swept up my injured and already-bleeding heart. It crept up inside my mind and rested there awhile. When I least expected it, from the core of my being, it shook me like a wild tornado, leaving me hollow, void of life's good memories, and all the wonderful experiences that once powered my soul to live.

I had watched many before me drown in grief's conniving cruelty. For some people, the rest of their futures stopped existing. Their once bright life is now full of darkness. Their breath is rubbed out from them, never to know what it's like to live, and find love ever again. I knew somehow, I must win this battle. I had one more breath left to find a way to beat it.

So it was by naming it and recognizing its many faces that I was able to learn its processes. I discovered that with understanding came the eyes not to judge or fear its presence. I let it be what it was, just another gush of wind, which found itself entitled to be part of my existence.

When I opened my eyes to acknowledge my deep sadness, something remarkable happened. The truth struck me. *Sadness is not me. My daughter's true beauty is and was never to be part of sadness.* She was the beauty of my life. Her smile was and is the light of my days. She was the gift of life.

Grief was a hollow, cold wind that shuts me down wherever it found me. I could not think. I could not feel. I was a frozen zombie when it took over me. It horrified me that I know it existed, and there was nothing I could do to combat it. I could not escape from it. It pained me that I know it was always going to be part of my future. Deep inside, I accepted that, like anything else in life, I had to learn to live with grief, accept it for what it was until one day, its presence would no longer bother and hurt me and my precious family.

Without my daughter in my arms to cradle, guide, laugh, cry, and dream with, this is how life shall go on for me—cold, dark, and empty. Above her grave, I stood and sat, hollow inside. I was a shattered woman. Lost in time of her love, I had no candle to light the depth of darkness, which the present gives above her grave. She is now under the earth beneath my feet. It is closed. It doesn't know me. It will not open for me.

My injured heart stung me each time I breathed. I wished I had died with my daughter. I wanted the pain to go away, but it never did. I prayed that it would stop throbbing when I cried, thought, or moved. But I couldn't stop crying. Everything about life hurts. My mind ached for my baby's smiles. My arms twitched daily. My breasts squeezed themselves till my uterus would churn and hurt me. They wanted to feel my daughter's warmth. But she was not there. So I cried. Tears are the waters of relief for the lost and forsaken one. I am that which is forsaken. Cried I did daily. I wanted to commit suicide. *You're going to hell!* A voice repeated loudly at me each time I tried. It was the voice of the priest from my ancestors' church—the priest of my childhood.

I wanted to get lost, but I couldn't leave her graveyard. I wanted to run away, but I was afraid that she would not find me again. I wanted to give up, but I did not know how I could without disappointing her. Every single time, I wanted to end it all; I was shocked at my finding that every ounce of my spirit rebelled at the idea that all that was of life is suffering and death. I welled tears I found to be bottomless. Each tear, which came from I know not the source, birthed in me the sense there is a hidden space. A space of no judgment is a mystery wanting my encounter. It gave me a deeper sense of my being that I knew never to surrender. I wanted to find kindness in life, despite the bitter taste and embodiment of such great loss.

I walked each day with a heavy heart. "Who are we?" I heard my mind ask, not as a hungry child as before, but now I ask in great sorrow as a lost mother. "Why are we born? What are we doing here? Why am I here? Why am I suffering? Why did my daughter have to die? Why did I have to stay? Why am I left behind? What's the purpose of life?" I see a vast space around and above me. No one hears. I wait all day. I wait all night. There was no answer. Yet I wake again the next morning. When the sun rose. I did, automatically. Whether my heart was there at all, my knees stood on their own and carried me.

Choosing to hope, I found, was the easy part of deciding to live. What I encountered to be disheartening was my inability to believe that life is capable of being kind to me. It was not kind to my daughter. I lived courageously as a child despite poverties and hunger that brought me up. But I was never afraid. But as a mother in sorrow, my child's death took with it the faith that powered my inner-child spirit. I was afraid. Deep in the sea of the cold abyss. I was lost in an island jungle of busy human minds. No one can see me. My heart searched for Gaby in my mind, in the sky, in the darkest of the night and brightest of the day. I could not see her. I could not find her. I ran till my body got tired. My mind missed her smiles.

I was thankful that my new house was three minutes away from the emergency hospital. I was there all the time, due to emotional, body pain, and anxiety until I had a vision.

A man with a dazzling light body parted the heavens in two. He came out from the brilliance of the pure light and came down to me. "Write!" He handed me a pen. "Write the truth. Your spirit will set your soul free." He went back to the sky. The lit heavens closed. I wrote. I was shocked. My mind did not question. My spirit listened. It openly understood. It was obedient. My spirit lit up with hope. Yet my heart did not see or hear the man in my vision. My heart as a mother was broken, and it lived life in a sorrowful dimension. Then after reading what I had written, which is my own life and my daughter's journey of the two years she was here on earth with me, I learned, I was not damned. I was still the same as before. I was as I was, as I am now—still blessed.

Life is tragic when death comes. But the spirit of my soul sees the light. The light is love. My daughter's smiles are my light. She is love. Her life is the love of my life. Today, despite what death took, her flesh, her body, in spirit, I am more, for her beautiful smile is lighting the ways ahead. Though her body was surrendered to dust, her love lives. Her spirit is always with the wind and is with me wherever I go on earth.

—Evangeline

A Door to Love

The Voice of Consciousness Is the Spirit of Love

A soft light beaconed in the depth of the dark and open sky. I followed its door. It need not open, for it was fully lit by the bodies of spirits that gently made the door beam to its brilliant white hues. The guardians shined. Angels stood side by side. In a circle, they spoke in full light.

When a spirit is given a body, it is a holy creation. It is a spirit in a soul granted a new and sacred name, willed by the angels of holy breath, of divine purpose. When the body is taken away, for the universe takes everything it gives the spirits, the soul's creation ends, yet the spirit will rise to heaven. In full consciousness, it will face all the darkness that its soul could not cure. The spirit will be guided by angels to face his/her creation as a human child. He or she is given a choice and the rite of passage to fix his or her creation, so in the spirit, it can shine. When the spirit is healed, the soul is healed, and the grave from which the body rests is healed. The spirit and the soul is one in the same dream, to create a humanity, conscious of its body of love, of its breath of peace, harmony, and grace, in this one begotten garden of Eden called earth, a universe gift—of the human birth of affable creation.

—Evangeline

Holy! Holy! Holy!

Silence came. My knees fell on the ground. I tried to walk. I stumbled. I tried again, but my knees kept me frozen. Facedown, I could not see the blades of the prickly grass that held my being. My heart yearns to embrace my daughter. She is six feet under now, beneath my palms. Everything of me says I am forbidden to disturb her from her eternal sleep. I can't wake her even if I wanted. I am helpless. I raised my head up to breathe. I gathered my strength. Suddenly all is no more. Now I am afloat. Alone, I was captivated by the twinkling space that went on forever. I looked up. Earth was no more. I was suspended in the vast space of my own awareness. I was a sinking ship lost in the deep sea above the earth, deep into the heart of all the heavens above all spaces beyond all physical heavens.

Then a massive light shone in full luminosity. It was a light being sitting on His throne. Before I could ask the angels that surrounded Him, before I could ask the Man of Peace that lights the way to this divine body as He held my hand, before I could think, the light transfigured into a brilliant, living body of a forever fifty-five-year-old, healthy, and vibrant man. He was a giant spirit; yet, fashioned in a human image. He beheld an ageless and all-knowing Father smile, as He sat gently and kindly upon the living mighty light-filled throne. The greatness of all greatest brilliance of pure life and everlasting wisdom beyond all existence both known and yet unknown emanated out of His entire being. His eyes were pure love, an infinite grace of gentle innocence He beheld, the gentle lights that billions upon billions of all life's newborns peacefully and lovingly radiate when they arrive on earth upon birth. I looked at the vast space of His crystal-lit heaven. Nothing else existed above Him but peace and calm. I looked down below His feet. The universe was below Him. His entire being lights and governs all that exists in all spaces above, below, and around Him; yet His heart and entirety was so focused, overlooking all the activities of the lights within the brain-size universe below His feet. The universe was vibrating within its core due to His Divine presence. His light is life. His presence is the source of all creation. I knew then that His majesty is the Creator of all creations outside and inside the universe. All purity and brilliance of light are sourced from His entire being. And His will and breath is the source of all love. His presence is pure peace, pure light, and brilliance of ever flowing, of all luminosity that surpasses all light beyond all universes. His glory is His heart, the source of all compassion; His heart is the loving fountains of all good, of all truths, the purpose of all hearts is to shine His light onto the world known and yet unknown. Everything good manifested through His breath according to His love and passion. I know that everything He creates is gentle and humble. He is careful, graceful, childlike, but a gentle giant of a spirit; yet all that He is, is a loving Creator, giving life to all. In all endless secret spaces, of all hidden secrets, both dark matter and multitude degrees of hidden spaces beyond consciousness, are powered by His eternal essence. From darkness, all light consciousness and all seasons are governed by His infallible substance that can make a life out of nothing, in order to sustain all forces as one body, despite all the vastness of divides that give purpose to a boundless abyss of orderly chaos. In His presence, all spirit of creation creates in calm.

—Evangeline

The God of Peace and love is holy and kind. He is a living father of pure light. He is a spirit. The god of fear, the human mind, is the ego. The ego is the chaotic mind of the unconscious darkness. It destroys the body of light, love, and the vital force—the breath of peace of a holy child is within each man.

—Evangeline

I had asked many times the meaning of life. Yet in the human standard of life and perception, I get no answer. After my daughter's death, after having lost all her love, I came to my senses. Now I know that poverty, government, country, and rules, even the mental mind that dwells in me, feeding my suffering must first all disappear before I can find the answer to my own spirit's humanity. In my hunger, I asked to be rescued. I searched for the God that all humankind has promised existed. Yet when all the minds of man have passed away, the illuminating space comes to me. It surrenders its light. The light is a man. Before Him there is no other God. His breath and being is the bottomless source of all peace that powers the earth's life, the life of all stars, moons, and suns within the universes before Him. Before Him is the mental mind of insecure creations that generate within their core matters and space; this is the creation from which man has forgotten the image of his own spirit. As the throne shines, His entire being is the source of light that fuels all life, both material and eternal, into one equal substance of pure and everlasting brilliance. Darkness He judges not. He is present, sustaining both the lights and the bed of all darkness with His breath so both may rise to manifest solitude and eternal calm in all beings outside and inside the rhythms of His creation, the universe, its light, its consciousness, His families.

Humankind did echo for two thousand years that no one may see the face of God. Man is right. For in the space of solitude, this man shines a radiance that soothes the brokenhearted heart, and the lost and forsaken find the finality of their longing. All souls before Him are the innocent body of lights of utter contentment. He is the grace of all graceful essence. He is the breath of all peace. In Him, the space of heaven and the universe is the extension of His heavenly body. In Him who is Light, all is a breath of love. Heaven is vast. It encompasses the essence of the earth's colorful life. Heaven enfolds the earth with peace. From peace, life comes to be. Heaven and earth are one. Heaven cannot live without earth. And the earth will not be the goldilocks of perfection without His Majesty's light. All family of colors is one root coming from the tree of His one heart of love. True life is in Him. Creation is His wisdom. In Him, all that is conscious of His truth shine peace, for all earthly domain has passed away. The wonders of creation are one spirit in Him; for all spirit is born in darkness to gather from the universe His radiating and life-giving light.

—Evangeline

Heaven's door is the spirits. Here, angels shine. They speak not in tongue but the silence of hearts.

Love is a spirit, and you love the God that creates and builds in peace. Love a child; you love yourself. When you love yourself, you become an innocent child. A child cannot be without a father. Love your spirit. You will see your Spirit Father holding you in the comfort of His endless

SHINE LOVE, JOY, AND PEACE!

palm. When you have forgotten to destroy the world, which bares your humanity, your spirit will build a new earth in His spirit. Peace is your body. Peace is your light. His love is your heaven. You are His breath. When the planet called for its light, you were sent; for you are its conscious light. Now that you've come, this planet is blessed. In shining the truth, earth seeks to be a host to your peace, the living waters of humanities' true loving creation.

—Evangeline

Why Mankind Will Not See the Face of God

God has not a face. God is an idea only created by religions of man. The Holy Spirit is not just a body. Neither does He reveal himself through human ideas.

The Holy Spirit is life. God. He is the source of creation before the universe founded its beginning. Brilliance of all brilliance, He smiles in wisdom as the Spirit light of no end. He is enthroned as the spirit body of full luminosity. His entire being illuminates glories of the life-giving and life-generating promise of dancing calm and joy. In Him, all good dreams are fulfilled in space through humankind's time and beyond the spaces of life's universes.

He is the light of joy, powering the uncharted depth of spaces within the universe of creation. His wisdom is the unseen force, intricately hidden in the complexity, yet tangible bodies of matter. In all creation's discoveries, there is the spirit of His breathtaking intelligence. He is in the light and body of wisdom. His love is the essence of stillness and solitude, for He alone magnifies truths as He governs all that which nature's intelligence shall make manifest as good and kind creations.

He is the radiating glory of light's grace; in all creation, He breathes peace. Outside creation, He radiates all beginnings. All beginnings come from Him. All ends return to Him outside creation, which is heaven, where He reigns in a spring garden of peace.

He is life's breath. He is the essence of all beings. For in all deaths and births are life. He is in life. And life is spirit. In His presence, there is no death. Through Him, all that have desired to be born in the space of creation has sprung from His divine wisdom. He is mankind's contemplated desires to magnify in full glory, in light of peace, during and after all human domain. He is the spirit's dream of perfected humanity. In His light, all dreams shall meet fruition through gentle and kind manifestation.

He is the body of brilliant existence—love. The father that governs this universe and all the heavens around it is filled with His inescapable spirits—oceans of overflowing strings of a living unity, and entanglement, of hidden streams of elegant symphonies of fantastic music—of lights, love, and joy. Love is Him. Love shines from His being. Beyond all knowing is His wisdom. He is that one brilliant light that powers matter and space gently and elegantly. He is the grace of full luminosity. Shining spirit, He is the body of a gentle king of everlasting wisdom. Mercy is His light. Yet in all luminosity, He exists as the source of compassionate light. He is the source of light, the power that gives purpose and rest to the space of darkness. He is the source, the well of breath to all that is living. A spirit in the shape of a man, His brilliant body of light is the living fountain of calm waters that give life and light to all that exist within and outside the universe. For mankind, He is a Holy father. To the universe, the seen and unseen spaces, He is the majesties of all majesties of ever living wisdom. He is the roots of the living tree of life; both the seen and unseen, He governs all, gently, attentively, carefully and compassionately as they are encouraged to shine their spirit of love and wisdom, peace and harmony, from which His joy shines proudly as a Spirit father.

A father to all creation, His unimaginable intelligence is magnified in the universe's divine beauties. He is the source body of awareness that illuminates the brilliant sparks of all consciousness. He is light. His light is the consistent fountain of life. The root of humanity's tree of life is His body of love and brilliant breath of wisdom. He is a loving fountain of white energy that keeps giving love, breathing life to both the seen and the unseen. He is the body of the pure state of the highest source of brilliance. He lives and is ever-living. He is enthroned as a white, living brilliance of spirit. He radiates in darkness the brilliant rays of never-ending forever; and in every spark of breath, He breathes out the newborns to have life and extends the tree of life in all secret spaces of the spirit world; and manifests order to the physical reality, so kingdoms of colorful beauties may boundlessly rise and breathe out life.

He is the living mercy of light-filled grace. Gentle and kind, He reigns in the spirit of infallible fluorescence, beckoning all the stars of conscious forces below and above Him to shine the same light of joy, regardless of space in which every living thing exists. He reigns in the abode of perfected space, of unboastful, and graceful soft wind of intelligent gardens with winds of absolute humility. He is a king of wisdom, a body of light that gives breath to all, yet in an image of a human, He illuminates from within, the life-giving brilliance of ever and always living compassion. He reigns not just a king of wisdom; evermore, He governs as a master king of all spirits. Of all kind and gentle domains, He is the gentle and soft voice of courage that flows in all humankind's senses. The well of our spirits and souls' living wisdom of infinite understanding is sourced in Him. All kindness and breathtaking beauties within life's innocence is His Majesties eyes of pure love.

He is the king of non-judgment. While humankind's souls create gods among themselves, He judges not their domains of the mind-made universes. For, many gods desire His heart of wisdom, but their heart may not contain His simple light. His heart is the pure light of love. Loving and gentle father is His domain. There are many human gods within the matrix of universal minds. They create their own ideal beings; and entertained, they influence the minds of mankind who are lost; these gods are the disembodied souls that seek a human host to manifest their domain; they respect the Father but their domain as mankind's avatars, often mislead the souls to forget their own light. Broken, they who know not the knowledge of their own sparks, nor understand the purpose of their souls' dreams, become avatars' subjects. There are many gods within the universe, but they seek to be served. They have already been manifested as souls, but they lack the heart of compassion. While many gods fashion the mind of the universe, the Father and King above the universe shines His gentle grace of acceptance. He respects the existence and choices of the universe's gods. He never judges the gods to create for themselves. There are kind human disembodied god's that know the King and God of peace. They will not subject the spirit child of the Heavenly Father to their cause. For, they fear Him who is the King of peace and Father of love. While human gods seek and look after their subjects for labors, the Father of the spirit shines. He does not create. He shines love. In the light of His love, children are led back home to His arms after a long journey to the magical beauties of the physical earth. Through the voyage of the depthless sea of the disembodied spirits' domains, where the caves of dark and hidden cages of the mental minds of an uncompassionate universe, the spirits children of the King of Love are led back home to rest in the garden of peace.

He is the highest dream of humankind's true creation. It is His body of love that time, and the natures of the universe are fashioned to create and multiply. A Father, a King, He shines an infinite luminosity to give lights to all spirits, so in doing all may have life, abundantly, in the creation of family, regardless of the shapes and the vessel that contain our spirits.

Life-giver, He watches outside of the universe, while His brilliant light sustains its life in full. The conscious spirits of the universe create love through magnifying beams of infinite compassion. While mankind labor, He is still. He shines a stillness of peace onto the minds of honest and righteous creation. The minds create a universe for themselves, but the Holy Father reigns above the mind-made universes. He is the King of gentle and loving creation. He births peace into creation, so solitude and balance may manifest life into being. Nights He made come so mankind may rest from the works of the minds. The day comes, so mankind will not work in the darkness brought by self affliction. The conscious creator makes a peaceful being in the colorful creation under the light of the day and restful sleep in the quietness of nights, while the human mind's ego will create a universe that enslaves the rest of the human emotions to fears and darkness; regardless of the days and nights that come, the mind's ego enslave the souls with worries and oppression.

The mental creations pray on the spirit; these created rules and regulations come to destroy humanity's spirits. But the father alone creates with utmost light of compassion so everyone who lives may shine in the full spirit of love and peace. In being a spirit, mankind is the light of the current insecurity and fears of human ego.

He is the body of truth. His living presence lights and guides His children who hunger for His truth. In love for His gentle spirit, the unborn come to be birthed as human children, so they may magnify out of humanity, His body of light in part of creation in the human universe as they walk and tend the earth's garden—human hearts—family. The unborn come as bodies of spirits of courage. His Majesties children come to heal and cure the ills of the minds, and awaken the love of the heart as the King of love casts and gives His body of light, so everything and everyone may live in truth—*Truth is kind. Life is kind. Life is love. Love is living in peace.* Outside the universe, He reigns as King of Light. Life is the truth. Truth is not labor. Truth is a fresh breath from within one's being. To breathe is to bestow compassion.

Elegant designer. Within the universe, He breathes His intelligent design. The highest domain is not labor. He lives sitting upon the throne. He shines His light, so everything above and below the universe may dwell in the light of their truth. True creation is light. True creation is love. Breath is love; love is everlasting and ever-living light of stillness. True being is self-breath of peace.

As the Father is exalted in stillness, so shall His children may rest in the solitude of truth. Humankind's true purpose is not to till the land. Mankind is to light, shine its love, so peace may come with every breath as a living channel of a kind and allowing river of life—the self. Because it is in the breath of peace and love that everything good, kind, honest, and truth is allowed to manifest from oneself. Without human breath, all things die in humanity. But with mankind's love and breath of compassion, everything of mankind's secrets, its hidden, and yet uncharted intelligence that is well in the heart and body of the Holy Spirit will manifest as a fountain of ever-living waters. This shall sustain the human family's life of its highest dream—to breathe in peace and full love: for now, the spirit lights of love, are the waters of tomorrow that are sure to come to and go, in both heaven and earth, regardless of the human condition mankind unconsciously finds itself.

To love is to expand. Love is not labor. It is light. It is cast all over the universe. It is breath. It is bestowed, never withheld. Breath is our spirit bodies of light. We do not labor in the spirit. We are breaths of consistent hymns of ever-loving symphonies of life's dance—the Majesties song is our spirit in wisdom and discoveries; the life beats of His heart and His children both seen and the unseen are the music that is carrying us to the dance of life. We are in the highs and the lows of the magnificent songs of life experiences. Individually, we are each in spirit and breath the multi-expression of the Maestro's elegant music's vibration. We embody the lows and highs of graceful notes of His infallible, consistently evolving, yet ever silent, and life-filled, dancing lights. We generate from every spirit life-giving breath, which extends and reverts, rises, and falls through the season of self's involution and evolution through the process of the bodies' deaths and births, and in the beginning and the end of human experiences. Love lives for it is the breath of the spirit of divine consciousness. We are the journey. We are that which we seek. We are that we find as our consciousness continues to grow, as the Holy Spirit and our spirits desire to witness the beauty of the universe's wonders. We are that which is coming and going through spaces as a witness to the secret intelligence of our spirits' divinity; inside and outside our being, we are there. The father is the root spirit of the tree of mankind's life; just as He is the source of the universe and all the species of all life within the universe. Our body is love; our breath is peace; our joy is life's sparks of brilliant wonders. We are the children of the God of consciousness; from the living tree of humanity's life and family, this ever-living brain of a universe is our spirits playground. It is our home away from home. Our self-discoveries are the harvest here which we bring home to power the spirit to live after death, so one may come over again in light and wisdom to sustain the same dream—to live in humanity's graceful bounties, to shine love, peace, and joy.

He is above the universe, while in wisdom and grace, with humankind, he walks in spirit.

He is wisdom. All wisdom emanates from the Holy One's entire being. Soft, kind, and loving grace, He shines as the light of gentle, yet comfort filled radiances. He is the body of all life's morning glories. All spirits dance in His joy. He is the light of divine mercy. The living source of pure light's currents, of everlasting, and ever-living luminosity, He alone, in spirit, reigns, above the universe, to sustain all that is below Him and around Him, to have life abundantly and infinitely. He is first a father of a kind and conscious universe within all humankind. Honest and gentle, and as always and evermore, whole in the spirit light of humanity, the child must be guided in light and love. The Father lives as merciful lights to all living channels of honesty and truth, yet the simple creation—of kind human domains. He is a father of love, a king of pure joy. He is the breath of graceful and harmonious solitude. He is the light that illuminates from within himself merciful and ever-living grace of peace. He has not a face, for He is the body and spirit of all light within all humankind's spirit.

He is the light of darkness. To see Him is to become one in love with Him through the power of compassion for the world. To know Him is to live in His entire being of *reason* and *understanding. He is a body of love.* He is the source of love to all that is within and to those that are outside the universe. He is both in the universe and in man. Shine your light. Breathe your peace. He is the brilliant force, a light spirit that powers the hearts and bodies of all mankind's spirit. He is the light that shines kindness within man and onto man's universe.

He is the breath of human forgiveness. For He is the father of all forgiveness. Every man is His breath of peace, shining and lighting all the spirits of both the living and the dead. In His love, all life lives. In His light, only truth exists. Truth is kind. Truth is love.

To see Him is to see good in everything that exists; for in both the physical universe and the heavenly spaces within and outside the universe, He is the Holy King, the brilliant Father of love with a pure radiance that illuminates the light essence of gentle and humble light and space of forever. To know Him is to acknowledge the simple nature of His intelligent wisdom, in every child, in every living thing both on earth and in the spirit world; for, He is the life and vessel of a kind and loving, peaceful and graceful humanity. We are His children of peace, breath to breath, love to love, joy to joy, and peace to peace.

He is the King of gentle and harmonious creation. In all creation, He beacons. He is ever present in all spaces, for He is the light and the heart of the spirits of both the seen and unseen.

He is the spirit source of honor. To see Him is to know honor. Honor is the breath of true freedom. *Honor humanity's* loving consciousness by acknowledging your own spirit's voice of *wisdom*. It is in your kindness that He rejoices in full brilliance, and in joyful glory, He is rejoicing for the sake of our righteous creation. The Heavenly Father's holy spirit is the pureness of your child like-qualities. He is the light of humanity's *innocence*. He is the *forgiving* light that overcomes all our fears, sorrows, and darkness.

He is humble. The compassionate and ever-living joy in all the newborns' essence is His breath of humility. His entire body lights up in eternal and external luminosities, lighting our heart's desires—to behold the undying visions of the good spirit within our own humanity.

He is the beginning. He is the secret force within every child's birth. From the spirit to the flesh, He breathes in every man, a breath of life which is contained within every man's being. He is in you. He is in every man. Mankind's life force dwells within one light, which is The Holy spirit body. All humanity lives in Him. All lights are spirits of His own body. And every spirit may descend as intelligent and gentle forces of light sparks, that in breath and love, these sparks of light may power the dead to live, rise, and dream of the perfected spirit of mankind, heart, body, and mind, over and again through the expansion of humanity's time, of past, present, and future.

He is the living *essence* within each boy and girl on earth and in heaven. For His light is their living, gentle, kind, and soft innocence. Pure breaths are every child. Peace is breathing out life though them into creation, for He is the breath in them.

Honor His loving and gentle grace through the heart of each woman, as the Father honors each of His children. Every woman is His vessel of love, peace, joy, and light. For in love and breath, the feminine is the bridge of every life. She is the living river of truth and life. She is the bearer of His light, love, and peace. Out of her womb is the child of gentle peace, His breath, and His body of light and love.

Honor His presence in your love and in each man before you; for in all mankind, young and old, in each man is the Father's strength and desire to love all of His children of humanity through depthless wisdom and yet kind guidance every step of mankind's journey, before, during and after the end. Through the heart of every man and every human father, is the head of the house of family, from which love and peace shall be housed. In each man is the Heavenly Father's spirit. He is the gentle force in him. The man who loves his children loves his spirit father—the man who knows the truth breathes only gentle and kind guidance for all his children.

He is the *kind* voice in every human storm. His being our father in spirit, we may find rest despite the hardship of our human journey, in our quest of higher knowledge, in pursuit of meaningful creation within the manifestation of our humanity. The Holy Father is spirit. His love dwells in the presence of the human heart. The union between the Holy Father and the spirit of every child makes creating a conscious soul a beautiful and one of a kind experience.

He is one breath with humanity. Rejoice in love. You will rejoice in the glorious smiles of your Heavenly Father. His face is a gentle light of pure and radiating mercy. He is the unseen love, contained within the very fiber of your humanity's spirit and breath. His entire being illuminates the grace of forever and eternal that powers the spirits of the universe to manifest only what is good and kind. Despite the torturing torment and the consistent jolt of undying traumas of fears, and struggle, through time, humanity itself has learned to overcome in grace and love, in compassion and in forgiveness. For it is from the spirit of reasons that humanity evolves; and evermore yield in one desire to know self as being conscious in the spirit of understanding which the Holy Spirit alone gives every living soul to manifest the highest of itself, spirit, love, and peace. It is in the human domain of truth that He exists. His power is the face of all gentle and unboastful courage. No darkness may hide Him. No lie will keep Him bound. He is the truth. He is the spiritual body of all humanity.

SHINE LOVE, JOY, AND PEACE!

He is the truth within our being. The one true God has not a face. He is the breath of peace and peace is the spirit that lives in the river bed of the universe's sea of conscious creation. The Heavenly Father is Spirit. He is the pure radiance of white living light. He breathes in all that exists; love, harmony, and solitude; He is the silent breaths within all forces of life. Holy in spirit, He illumines His entire body as one brilliance of life-giving yet ever so gentle winds of calm and contentedness so we may breathe His love through creation.

He is humanity's light. In each child, He is wisdom and joy. He powers all the non-existent to manifest so that all dreams bound in good may become fulfilled to govern peace in the material world. In all that live, His Majesties glory lives in them in truth. Light is the substance that powers the breath of kind and gentle creation.

A ruler of peaceful manifestation. He rules the spirit of mankind's birth into humanity. Space is the vibrational energy that houses the unseen body of light of every consciousness to manifest in time physical as breath, the body of love, through the expression of eternal and external wisdom. For as every innocent babe is pure, the Father's spirit is ever pure in every newborn.

He is the ultimate light of good in all that exists. His eyes are the hearts of love, which power all consciousness to evolve in wisdom. In love, there is no limit. The Holy Father's Spirit is the living body of brilliant light. He is the light of the infinities. His body is above the universe radiating light into the universe, so all may dwell in conscious creation, yet His living light is the breathing currents that power every living cell within all spaces of all matter in the universe.

His entire being is the *light* of *peace* and *harmony* within the silent space of heaven and the universe. These living spaces are filled with the vibrational currents of love, which is bound by the essence and power of His body. Humanity and otherwise, we exist in the hidden field of the elegant energy of love. He is as we are, one body of life. His power is the force that gives life to all matter. To all dreams of man, He is the source of the highest and righteous light. He is the simplest form of the highest dream. To be like Him in pure light is to be the loving light to all that live.

He lives! His love powers the living currents of peace within humankind's domain. He is a living Father of the unseen. His love is the light manifested in life's all-knowing and ever-expanding creation. The highest of all creation is love. Love is one in heaven; He is the god of love. In the universe of mankind, He is being magnified in every child, father, mother, and family; He is one body of our light in the flesh. Humankind will build and create rules to satisfy the needs of its society. But the father is the one to make a living river of hope and wisdom so that His breath and the living water of compassion may flow freely into humankind's reality. Peace, expresses in the solitude of every man's domain, through orders, politics, and religion, man yearns to find the spirits of his body of love, to magnify and sustain the spirit of every citizen he wants to serve. Love in the world is his body, which shall be the man's body. For all humanity yearns for its spirit. Love. Peace is His breath, which is the bed of humankind's eternal dreams. He is the truth. He is the light of the seen and unseen; in Him, all is love. Light and solitude are the living spaces of all beings. Everything lives in His body. He is in every morning's sunlight that emanates in gentle and soft rays of morning glory. The Father is the spirit of life. Life is light. He is pure light. Eternal mercy is His breath.

He is knowledge. To know Him is to make a way of His mind, by opening the heart of your mind. His humanity in us is our expansion in the minds and soul's desire to love and embrace and make conscious all in one spirit of that one desire. Love is us. We are love. Love is one body of light in the sea of life. He is the spirit of comfort. He is a father. You are His spirit child. You are one in the same spirit. He comes through you as a breath of gentle light of kind wisdom. It is in Him that life is boundlessly beautiful and colorful. Love all, then you will see His face in your heart, the person before you, and the nature in which you are to breathe peace. He is the face of absolute and pure joy radiating in all children. Embrace all; you'll see His face in your own boundless joy. His is the pure light of radiating love within every human being. His body illumines the grandeurs of infinite innocence, which overshadows the shapes of His entire being in us regardless of the color of our skin. He is one brilliant white light of love in and through us. His breath transcends life to manifest peace in all that exists, making both heaven and earth co-exist in one light. To see Him is to witness the living essence of pure grace. He is the pure light of morning glory, soft, gentle, humble, and merciful, always existing in radiating wisdom spread in the sea of life both in the physical and spirit, unseen and the seen. His essence alone gives purpose and stillness to the spirit of harmony. The gentleness of nature of life illuminates Him in all seasons, past, present, and future.

It is not in the face of God that we exist. It is in the heart of a Father's faithful love for His children that we have our being in humanity. We are sent to be His creator of good. We are His arms. We are His dreams. We are His hope. We are His confidant. We rise as man to create a good life with each and every hour with humanity from birth through the end of our bodies' time. We are His spirit's bodies on earth. He is our spirit in heaven. It is not in the face of the Holy Father that our sprits' consciousness may find mankind to attain for itself a purposely driven cause, but in His love and our love for our Father's spirit, which lights and powers the heart of our own bodies. We are souls. We are bodies. We are minds. We are of the earth, yet we are the spirits of consciousness that the heart and light of the entire humanity's soul, dreams, and purposes are made transfigured in the highest vibration—peace, life, love. Eternal in spirit, we are the vessel of the spirit's umbilical cord of light, which powers life to exist. It is not in a body that we have our being. It is in His Fatherly image that we obtain and receive the embodiment of our own spirit, the *brilliance of pure mercy, understanding,* and *compassion.*

He is our wisdom. In being one with His image, we are His radiance. We are His bodies of Love, Joy, and Peace who came from outside the universe, entered creation, manifested the womb of light within our being, transcended ourselves in space, so we each may be born into the body of our mother earth's physical umbilical cord. In her womb, in every woman mother, we enter in order to experience, create, a consciously driven family, while refuged within humanity's vessel, the flesh.

As breath of life, we descended from heaven into the darkness of the unformed mind, to die of pure light within mind-made realities.

Still, we rise as human babes, to walk with humankind's mistakes and stumbles, live our best in all degrees of failings and sufferings, yet honor the joy of humanity's sacred beauty when the nature of peace is finally attained.

We are born to experience all of the sweet, and the bitter tastes of mind made illnesses yet with one spark of conscious light, we love and live our lives to the fullest, so we may die out of humanity; and like everyone before us, our last breath will dawn, so in spirit, we may rise to once again return, to rest from human sorrows.

Energy that we are, we shine in full. We yearn to light the call of darkness. More than our last life lived, we shine brighter, and with the fire of courage within, we begin to illumine as we love. After rest, we descend into the universe again, to transcend the spirits haven into the far reaches of the universe's womb, by coming as a conscious force of living stars, to walk in the spirit of the universe's sacred creation.

We come again to face the human mind's struggles. We come again to face humanity's hunger. We come again to taste poverty. We come to experience love's frailty in humanity's greed and dishonesty. We come to face ignorance, as ignorance may demand to house our spirit. We come to thirst. We come to be hungry. We come to be weakened. We come to be denied. We come to well tears. We come to be powerless. We come to crawl. We come to be hidden in darkness. We come to be slaves by humanities' religions. We come as servants. We come to fear. We come for wars. We come to die. Yet, in all of our humanity, there, deep in the well of our breath, hidden in each of us is the undying pain of our Father's heart. He is the light in us when we are hidden in darkness. He is the breath of courage in us when we are afraid. He is the eyes dawning in each of us when we are hungry, when we are dying of thirst. He is the tears that well out of us when we are forgotten and abandoned. He is the eyes of every dying child. He is the heart of every father and mother's love. He is the pain of every child dying in hunger. He is the tears that come when we need to exhale. He is the power that turns on when we need to see. When we can no longer be humanity's servants, He breathes in us a new spirit. He comes. He comes through us. When He comes, we breathe His love. We breathe out His love through our courage. New in spirit, we face death again, so, once more, we may live in His breath. When He comes, we lose the darkness and pain of our humanity. In breath, we awaken in a new spirit. We awaken to a spirit of a better than last humanity.

We came in spirit. We came never to be the lost cause. As the faces of our Father's light, we come as living spirits of wisdom, to light our bodies of love, through reason and understanding. We come to shine the breath of eternal and ever-living compassion from within. We come to weave the living and undying dreams of the heavens, to come in one lifetime, to transform the human family into one light, one breath, one body, one image of mankind regardless of the color and shape of the suit we are bestowed, regardless of the origins of our DNA, regardless of our belief, regardless of culture from which we are raised. In breath, we have no limits. In the body, we have no faces, for as our Father is a spirit, so our spirit is boundless, of no form. Our bodies shine as our Father of love is beaming in full radiance. Through all spirits gleam purity; we come lighting the uncharted depths of the space; in doing so, we become witness to the breathtaking wisdom of His divine nature, as His wisdom, is magnified and spirit infused in the sacred beauty of life itself. His eternal wisdom shines everything kind in life. Life is compassion beyond the universe's limits. In grace, He shines so we may have our being in this humanity.

Never alone. In Him, we are never alone. We came not as individual faces. We come as current, yet, one big wave of gentle forces, with one body of dreams-to manifest what is kind and plant what is right. We come as radiances of gentle and soft individual rays of light, shining from one brilliant and living and all-encompassing body of our father, our spirit Mother, our spirit brothers and sisters. In our tree of life, He (our Father), she (our mother), and our spirit brothers, sisters, and guardian angels who are light bodies illuminate the kingdom of our spiritual roots—the human spirit is the journeying sparks across the cosmos. We are the extension of the spirit's body. The Father is the living water from which the living tree is rooted. We are the branches of this one tree. Therefore, we come not for ourselves. We send ourselves to make a good path for our descendants, who are the life and fruits of our humanities' seasonal bounties.

The silent nature of all humankind is spirit. We are the spirits of the seen, and we are the unseen within the physical. In the physical, we are the outside that we see—our body; in Spirit, we are the inside wisdom, hidden within ourselves, yet magnified through every action and thought we manifest. We are the silent voices that yearn for kindness and truth outside, which is the world. Take the spirit; the body dies; take the body, the spirit lives. In body and spirit, we are children. In breath and light, we live as the tiny sparks of light extended in space, individually beaming out from the body of the holy spirit body one magnificent glow. Together as one body, we light in a synchronistic spirit of love. In light of love, in the flesh, we come and are made conscious of humanity.

Waves of life. Family, we come in waves. We are birthed into our bodies on earth to belong to a family who we yearn to be part while on our earthly journeys. We belong together; we are stronger when we are together. And like any light, we are weaker when we are apart. But we come in the longing power of unity. We gather all lights to raise to heaven the spiritual hearts of begotten and newly risen humanity—our one family that which shines only one breath, the body of one truth, love, and peace. Spiritual union is our highest dream.

Mankind spirit has not a face. Together humanity are sparks of bright burning lights, powering the cosmos with intelligent wisdom. Consciousness floats as living lights in the sea of life. That is who we are. That is the nature of our spirit. We are the body and wisdom of infinities. Without the human body, we float. Our spirit is one light. We are bound by each other's presence. Together with the whole sphere of bright, pure, and conscious spirits of one light, we glow to light brilliantly, changing the cosmos of our awakenings. We are the conscious spirits of space. As we see, life becomes itself. Life becomes conscious of its existence as we are the observers of its beauty. We co-exist. We co-create. We transfigure, and we transcend. That is the light of our love.

Unbroken by death. Humanity's spirit is not broken by death. Our spirit is love. We are built-in love, unbound by the death of any dreams. For the Holy Spirit is life. In us and through us, He lives and breathes life. His presence within our being, has made all deaths non-existent. Our spirit has not a face. We are energy. Like our Father, our spirit is bright light, always beaming, forever radiating, we can never, ever be imagined nor formed by the domains of the mind, nor are we bound to fit the thousands of years of beliefs of the human egos; nor shall we succumb by religions rigid orders; for we are our Heavenly Father's body. We are in the breath as He is a soft and kind energy of love which, no creation may contain without being first made transfigured in the full glory of love itself. He is the light, and brilliant wisdom, breath, and compassion within the entire mankind's dream. We deeply yearn His presence in our hearts, because it is in Him that our innate consciousness may manifest, the true body of the perfected family of humanity, who is fashioned in an image of His own makeup. He has not a face. The Holy one is the brilliance of all brilliance, for He is a light body shining in and out of all life and spirits. He is all the innocent and all-encompassing love within all beings. The spirit is not a soul, body, or mind. He is a radiant and shining body of love, joy, and peace, from whom all mankind has their very being in truth, life, and in death of creations. It is in His spirit that we are fashioned, yet in His love, and our love, that our spirits hearts and bodies have our life and being during the domain of planet earth's seasonal creation. His face is light, and body is love; in our joy, we become one light of His entire being. In the breath, He is the body of silent peace within the unseen and the seen, yet convoluted space of consciousness; from which all gentle and awesome creation is supported and encouraged to manifest. In everyone that lives, in everything that exists, in all thoughts to be empty; and in all dreams to be filled, there is a gentle, silent yet ever giving, force of innocence and solitude. This force is His kind body of wisdom. He is in everything that is now and always. He is light. He is our loving and living breath of life. In everyman is His being, the force that gives power to the body of that being. He is in each child of man, for, He is in spirit, one with humankind. See you; see Him; He is the face of us in all that is outside humanity. Yet within us, He is the force of consciousness that powers our hearts to love infinitely.

He is within us that expands in light as we overcome the limitations of the egos and the mind. When we make ourselves become the spirit of good, our entire being shines His spirit body. He is the gentle force within our life forces. Individually, we yearn to expand, exhale, grow, evolve and light up fully so others may see us; so in manifesting of our good and unlimited deeds, others will also find their own strength and hear their own inner voice through the presence of their own spirits awareness of light. The spirit of mankind is the life and voices of pure consciousness, which is of our spirit Father, our beloved Mother, and the children of the spirits of love and peace—Spirits are us. One body. One humanity. One family. One laboratory of life. Human creation. The Tree of life is humanity. It's beginning, and its end rests on this sacred planet earth. We float in spirit. We are grounded in humanity's reality by being bestowed our bodies. We come to build ourselves as bodies of luminous love. We come to breathe out the unseen love, the power, and the breath of peace that govern our human domains. The Holy Spirits and His angels' lights are extended through every child's breath. In every living thing, the breath of life, which is the force that makes up the body and light of our Father, who is the God of peace and the God of love, is our Father in heaven. He is holy. He is Love. He is peace.

To shine like Him. When we do good, when we work through kindness, when we embrace beyond comfort, we heal all that is broken before us. We come as the conscious forces of the mind and the body. But our wisdom, which is the Father's body of merciful light, is cast all over the earth as living stars, fueling the works of the righteous humankind and their hearts. In the Heavenly Father's light, we become conscious of the present. We become aware of the truth. We acknowledge our purpose on this planet earth is to cast love and breathe peace all over the hearts and minds, bodies, and souls of mankind itself. Humankind has not known its spirit. Nature magnifies the beauties of the Father. Simple, kind, and graceful, nature is a space of love and peace. All humankind, lives, in its wisdom and grace. Nature is love. Space is love. For nature is God's intelligence and space, His eternal grace for all conscious forces to create what is good and kind.

Every child of man is God's body and breath. Mother earth attracted our light to help heal humanity of its needs. Every child of man is a sacred gift to serve and support a good cause. Every child is a gift to current humanity. Every child is light to that which is dark in the world. We spirits have come to give meaning to human souls' dream to build a kind family of humanity on this beautiful island earth. In breath, we are the Heavenly Father's wisdom. We are the faces of our Father in humanity's suits. Together we, are one force, one body of brilliant vibration of light. In our purest, we are the body of gentle rays of—love.

Humanity. We are in breath the wisdom that powers peace to magnify creation. To see the God of peace is to acknowledge the love of our lights. When we deeply yearn to see kindness before us on the planet world, we are whole. In His force, the light of peace in all facets of this Earth's life will only manifest as the gentle spirit of self's wisdom and knowledge of sustenance, the kind and gentle wisdom that comes as power of self-sustainability.

We are one spirit force channeling His body of love through our love. We channel His breath as we exhale in the breath. We channel His light when we honor our innate voice of wisdom through our actions and awareness. We see the depth of our loved ones as we see the pain in human sufferings. It is in this unspoken grief within that we understand we have come to alleviate this planet's vulnerability, which provides mankind the intelligence and reason to appreciate our planet earth's beautiful, colorful, and deeply complex life-gifts. We have come to fix the broken in mankind—the mind's ability to fear and tune out the light and love of its spirit, resulting in the choice to survive in service to the mind's beliefs, its anger, and pain.

The nature of life is kind. It is in the nature of true life that we come to live as nature exists in the order of simplistic cycles of time's grandeur. Nature is our home while here on the planet.

Intelligence. The innate awareness of mankind's spirit, is fashioned in our father's wisdom. It is in the sacred order of mysteries within nature's seasons that we become awakened to the true beauty of human life. Planet Earth, our sacred, and always kind home, is His grace. We are humanity in the spirit that has come to witness for a lifetime, this planet's secret systems of the physical world—that is bestowed on the breath and bodies of every human child, man, and woman, which makes up the infallible wonders of the simple and complex beauty of the entire human race. As family, we are the physical nature and space that magnifies the simple make-up of the whole, transcendental wonders of one, united, humanity. Humanity is a spirit. The spirit of humanity is magnified in the space of love. Love is all there is in spirit existence.

Family, we are one body of love. One dream, we are the breath of peace. Our joy is in our union as one brilliant light of the Holy Spirit Father's body. Family of intelligent spirits of consciousness, we are born to manifest the simple nature of humanity-love and peace, the conscious forces of the universe.

We rise from ashes to create in the wisdom of truth. We are born to learn good, in order to do all that is kind and good, with respect to the spirit of our merciful and gentle Creator—the Holy Spirit, our Father, the God of love, and breath of peace.

Humanities' spirit Father. The body of our love, the source of our life, the generator of our breath of peace, the light in all human darkness; and evermore, the brilliance of all that exists, of times' past, present and future. God has not a face. For humanity in spirit has not a face. We are life and love of a peaceful and kind manifested dream.

Humanity has not a face. Humankind is love. For our Father's Holy body is light of love. We come to humanity as life's good story. We are consciousness' spirit of truth. In full luminosity, we are breaths of peace, solitude, and grace. We come to shine the body of our whole humanity as being one with our Holy Spirit Father—light to light, love to love, joy to joy, and peace to peace. *Compassion* is the true light and face of humanity. *Tolerance* is the bed of humanity. Our union is the one body of humanity's whole being. To see the Holy Father's face is to know the spirit of our being. We are love and peace shining in humanity's fears and darkness. To know Him is to shine our own spirit of truth—love and peace is life. We manifest in time; through time, we are awakened to the breath of consciousness within all spaces. We are His glory who descended into the human world on earth, so that we may transcend humanity to its highest dream. We must shine and magnify His love. For in waking up each morning, we desire to experience His glory as brilliant powers of life. We are His joy. We are His children of peace, breath to breath, dream after dream. The Holy Spirit's entire prisms shine in every child of mankind's love, wisdom, joy, and peace. We live in Him, and His light and being must live in us, to fuel our human experiences. Heaven is His entire being of light. He is the living spirit of life inside our heart, body, mind and soul. Love yourself. Do what is right and good. You will see the face of God of peace and love in your eyes, and through you, you will hear His silent plea to breathe His peace into the world of humankind. Mankind will not see the face of God. For, the Father is Holy in spirit. He is the light of all perfected humankind. To see Him is to see the positive light of His spirit in all that exists. To see Him is to see the perfected spirit of our entire humanity. Until then we can only imagine that which is to mankind unimaginable. He is that which we do not see unless we acknowledge the spirit of our own inner qualities.

The Order of the Holy Spirit

"Woman! Write your emotions. For emotions are feelings, feelings have colors, and colors have words. What you don't expel from you will weigh you down. Grief is an emotion of darkness. It is heavy. Darkness shall vanish from the spirit of love once you open the door to your grief. Write your emotions. In spirit, be set free. You are light. You are a spirit child of humanity; humanity's children are, in spirit, children of love."

—Evangeline

Revelation

Man... rise out of pain, forgive your sorrow, forgive your mind, you've left the past. You are now here. At heart and in love, rise. Shine peace into the world. For when you shine your love, darkness, and all your pains are to be no more.

—Evangeline

Understanding the Ten Stages of Grief

Understanding can set us free. No matter how distorted the stages of grief are, grief is still just a seasonal, spiraling ladder of dark emotional energy that we find ourselves riding on after a loss. On a very fast track, it takes over our bodies and souls, manifesting a sting we believe is too painful to overcome. Our spirits job is not to fall or wilt away. We cannot get stuck in that dark pit where death and loss have thrown us to die. We must recognize every step of the grief's game and give it a name so that when it does show up, we can climb off of it with our hearts, light, and spirit; moreover, our dignity and grace will still be intact. Slowly and gently, time will help us rise above the pain of grief as we gain the freedom to separate it from our divine selves. Even in grief, we can consciously decide to choose that once again, we can learn to walk the rest of our lives with grace for the sake of those we dearly love.

After a loss, there is only an opportunity to heal so we can give love another chance. Flourish. Live again in the spirit of love. Love is the will of all our being. Love is the spirit. Spirit is the light of love. Love is the spirit of the past, present, and our future. Love is forever and eternal.
—Evangeline

Grief is a world of darkness, only a broken heart, and a broken mind feels and sees. However, it is merely acknowledged and validated by a loving heart and light-filled spirit of man.
—Evangeline

Ten Steps to Grief Recovery

Recognizing the Ten Fundamental Stages of Grief and its Emotional languages:

1. The Shock, Numbness, Bargaining and Denial—the Zombie State
2. Anger
3. The Power of Guilt and Shame
4. A Necessary Road to Self-Redemption
5. Surrendering to Life's Course
6. The Demeaning power of Depression
7. Learning to Understand
8. The Physical Manifestation of Fear
9. Letting go, and letting God, allowing love and peace to shine from within
10. Acceptance

Heal

In spirit, darkness will not come. For the spirit is the light of the darkness. In the light of every child of man is the heart of the Father of all the heavens and the universe. His radiance and wisdom power the kind creations within all life of the earth.

Above the universe is the heaven of peace and calm. From below, it is darkness that summons the spirit to come; so, darkness itself may face its own light. Light is wisdom. True darkness is calm and gentle silence, from which a soul may rest. This kind darkness, which the loving Father of creation made, aids the soul to find the light of its spirit in order to live. The spirit is the light of the soul. Light is the haven of the soul's radiance; it is in the darkness that the spirit can manifest in light. Darkness is the bed of light's consciousness; light is the life and heart of darkness. When the light comes, darkness is dissolved, for the two are made one; as such, birth and death is one substance, and heaven and earth are one field of divine evolution of spirit's journey to the source, in fulfillment of its coming to full consciousness, which is pure love.

—Evangeline

Six

The First Stage of Grief: The Shock, Numbness, Bargaining, and Denial

Being Misplaced in Life

I bore her in my womb; I understood the sacred duty of being a woman. The hour she was born, a new universe within me rose. My womb had been given light and was filled with the grandest purpose. I am blessed. Even in infancy, she filled me with a sense of pure joy and laughter. In her presence, solitude and comfort was my light. Peace, she gave to me in abundance. Dreams illuminated like a living river within me. Visions of truth flowed in a continuous fashion. I am a mother at last. Then too soon, the hour came, her vessel dimmed its light. Her breath rose out of her body. She closed her eyes, never to open them again. Yet because her spirit still lives even though she no longer fills an earthly vessel, she visits me often with families, with care and guidance of loving arms of the angels, the lights and love of the pure brilliance of heaven's peace is with me. Death took nothing away but suffering and pain. My soul is shocked. My heart is begging that she return to life. My soul begged and screamed for her to live. My soul knew the struggle without her. She could not die. My soul denied that her life had ended. Yet in love, my soul honors the ways of the spirit's love. It accepted the passing of death of the body in order for the spirit to be free of pain. Now, in light of my soul, I am everything still, in spirit. In the passing of time, where my soul was in complete and utter darkness, who I am now is more. I hear my own voice. In silence, I hear joy. And when dark clouds come over me, it is so that I can light my heart and shine through. In love, all the left behind light and love flow more as each day passes. Life after death is not the end. It is a beginning. Even as the angels and loved ones came in spirit, when her flesh died, her spirit returned. She is with me in my humanity. Her spirit shines in this world always.

—Evangeline

Immediately after my daughter did not come home with me from the hospital, I was outraged. I felt the universe had emptied all its open void of pain and cast it within my entire being. "I cannot believe my daughter is gone. I can't believe Father Pedro's Bible; God did not save her. How in the world did she vanish like that? How am I going to live now? I can't. I won't. I need her to live. I love her. I can't live without her in my arms," on my knees, I cried over and over again.

It wasn't happening. I am tormented. I rebuked darkness. With all that I am, I refused to partake in life in her absence. "No! It is not possible. My daughter cannot die! Not before I do. It's against everything life says it should be. She can't die!" I sobbed and sobbed.

"She should bury me first. No mother should have to bury her child first. No! Please tell me it isn't true. Please tell me it's just a bad dream! Please, God! Please wake me up."

"Please.... please..." Down on my knees, I pleaded.

"She can't be dead. I'll do anything you ask of me. Please just let her live. Don't let her go away from me. Don't take her. Bring her back to life. I promise I'll be a better person, a better mommy. I promise... just wake her up! Oh, please, God... Wake me from this dream! Let us be together. I'll give you anything..." I begged and begged with all my might as I felt deep within my being that everything life had to offer a living soul was no longer intended to include me in it.

I felt as though I'd been chosen to be kicked out of life, but I did not know which biblical law I could have possibly broken. I felt like a great sinner being punished. But then again, I had no clue which sin I had committed. Everything life used to be; I felt someone I could not see ripped away from me. In its place, a great hole nested, a great silence, a great ocean of emptiness. I felt dead inside. The once colorful sun, green trees, and blue sky I once knew were merely distant memories, replaced with black-and-white scenery, an unfamiliar landscape, of nothing else in between.

As my husband and I buried her sacred body, we were both outcasts in our world, space no one could understand. Neither of us could make sense of our newfound surroundings. We were both strangers in our own hearts and minds. We'd completely lost the map of who we once were.

"Who are we?" I asked him. "What did we used to be? Do you remember?" I asked in tears as I begged to be reminded. But he was silent. He stared at the empty ceiling as if it was a blank space. I was silent. Neither of us could answer. In that instance, I could read his heart, his feelings, of what was left of him. He felt the same way I did. We were two people with Gabriella in our arms—him, her father, and me, her mother.

"Now what? Who are we?" I asked. He still did not answer. He couldn't. His lips could not move. His eyes were too swollen to open. I could not see his soul. But I knew he was withdrawn from me—numb, shocked, and lost. Everything that was, was gone, just like a bubble that had been popped, without a trace.

We have never been the same since. Every time we tried to make sense of life by finding the courage to move on, we'd fall right down on our knees, where we both felt empty in the pits of our stomachs; neither of us were able to get up without the aid of the other. For three months, I was too weak to tie my shoelace, too disconnected from my body, where my brain could not make my arms move. No matter how hard I tried, my hands remained lifeless, too weak to wipe the tears off my own nose. Every time I cried, it was my husband who patiently stood by my side with the tissue wiping my face dry. I felt lucky to have him, yet conscious that I was too lost to reach out to help him with his pain.

Blinded, we found that we were on such a desolate and very unfamiliar path. We did not want to be there. We kicked. We screamed. We cursed life. We felt condemned by God, rebuked by our own dreams, rubbed by death. We begged for our child back, our life back. But life, or even God, did not answer. It was the beginning of a journey we thought would never be able to return from, even if we tried. We were cursed, exiled to the oblivion of nothingness. So far gone from everything familiar, we both felt the unseen darkness of death had taken over the both of us, and flying so fast against our will, it carried us in its cruel and windy tantrums. We could barely hold on.

Heal. Let go. Write the source of your shock, numbness, bargaining, and your feelings of being misplaced:

I feel shock when
_____
_____
_____

I feel numb when
_____
_____
_____

I need to bargain when I feel
_____
_____
_____

I am in denial when I think, feel, and do… Describe the emotions you feel and the reasons you give yourself when you are in denial. What action do you take when you are in denial? To heal: What action do you need to take to feel emotionally validated as you listen and honor your own spirit voice?

Seven

The Second Stage of Grief: Anger

The most destructive emotion within a man is anger. It knows not to build. It destroys all the love that its spirit and its loved ones have come to create.

—Evangeline

Feeling Forsaken and Alone in the Dark Pit

Grief—an experience neither my husband nor I wanted to share with anyone. As the days came and went, our friends had also become fewer. Silent rage was constantly present in my mind. "I am so angry at you, Death!" I screamed at something I could not see. But I knew it was an invisible, cruel, monster lurking behind me silently watching. I hated it with everything that I was. I cursed it! The unseen thing responsible for my daughter's absence consumed my soul day and night.

"I can't believe you have the audacity to take away the most meaningful presence in my life. You are mean! You are so unforgiving to my child. How could you not spare her life? How could you take her away from me? You are ruthless! I hate you! I despise you! Oh, I hate you!"

The constant battle in my head grew bigger and bigger as days went on. As it continued, I became angrier at everyone around me. I was angry with the world. "Can't anybody see my daughter just died? Why can't you stop living for a minute? Stop! Life should stop! Now that she's dead, everyone has to stop and mourn!"

My hostile mind went on and on. It was only heightened as days moved on. With the exception of the few, I discovered none of our friends or relatives were able to stop everything to be with us. They were busy living their own lives, too busy with their concerns. There was no one close by to acknowledge us. We had become the mirror of their fear. Through our reality, it was suddenly possible for them to lose their child. They could not bear to look at us.

At times, our usual friends would no longer take the time to talk on the phone. They would avoid us when they saw us in person. "Perhaps it is because they didn't know what to say," my husband reasoned.

"Then they should come and tell us they don't know what to say rather than avoiding us at every opportunity as though we are being made aware that we may be contagious with the death disease." They should make the phone ring and say, "I was thinking about you… but now that I've called, I can't think of anything to say. I don't know how you feel."

And I would reply and say, "It's all right! I'm too empty to say anything anyway, but I feel a bit better now that you called. Thank you for not making me feel that I am now contagious with the 'death disease.' It's good to feel wanted, understood!"

As my husband went on to work, back in Maryland, I remained in Hawaii to tend to Gaby's grave. I was misplaced in time. I was stuck but alive in the memories of my Gaby. Everything I knew about God's promise regarding my future was gone. The little hope I had left me. I was suicidal in every thought.

I worried so much about who was taking care of my daughter. I would look at the clock on my wrist and say, "Time for her milk and medicine. And after that, she needs her diaper changed. And oh, then she needs a bath. Please take very good care of her. Whoever you are who took her from me, please take care of her," I cried and cried.

I knew in my heart that she was not all right. I knew she needed me. I wanted only to be there for her. "If only I could die soon," I ached. "We could be together… I could hold her and give her everything she needs." I was mad at death. But I barely had the energy to speak my feelings toward it. I didn't know what to feel. I was lost. I was numb. I couldn't speak. But I know I am angry at the unseen. There was no breath for blame. No reason that mattered, I just wanted my daughter to be alive just the way she was.

Heal. Let go. Write the cause of your anger:

I am so angry that

_____

_____
_____
_____
_____
_____

Eight

The Third Stage of Grief: The Power of Guilt and Shame

Death is an end of human suffering. Rise above shame and guilt, for these emotions, do not die. It hovers for thousands of years to cast its judgmental voice to the born and yet unborn.
—Evangeline

I had been blaming myself for everything since the day I found out Gaby's heart did not develop as it should have. It was something I ate since I didn't smoke or drink; I knew it was the food I had consumed. Or maybe it was because I exercised and did sit-ups when I was pregnant. Maybe it was because I was a sinner like Father Pedro said I was, all children are because we are children of Adam and Eve, and now that I am born, I am being punished. "It is all my fault, isn't it, God? Well, since you cannot talk anyway, and you haven't so far, it means you agree. So it is… It was my fault. It was my defective genes. It's got to be because my forefathers wronged you, or because I wronged you, and you just had to make me pay. Is that the kind of God you are… unforgiving? Was it my husband? Did he wrong you? Was it because I married him instead of somebody else? Would you have punished my child regardless of who I married? What is it, God? Tell me why… please."

My anger continued. In the back of my heart, I knew if only I had kept my daughter in Maryland, if we hadn't had traveled to Hawaii, her care would have been steady. Her doctors would have been more alert, unlike the ones at Tripler who did not know her. My mind shouted, "They were passive! You were irresponsible! You should have never taken her anywhere! She would have been alive today! Careless! You are a careless mother! You should have known better! You don't deserve her! That's the entire truth! If you had known how to care for her, God would have let you keep her! Death would not have been able to find you! But no! You were weak. You didn't deserve to be her mother!"

With every thought of what-if, there was that conscious part of me who refused to believe the precious essence that made my daughter's body smile was destructible. Each moment I asked, "How could such a precious spirit of courage and grace who brought so much love into my heart just melt away with the wind?" The core of my spirit begged to know. I wondered if anyone out there knew the answer. But there was no one around to ask that question. I was alone. My suffering was not real to anyone. I knew no one would even listen if I did ask. I doubted I would even be understood when I spoke. I assumed no one knew my newfound language because it hurts too much to speak it. How do I speak the guilt and powerlessness? No word on earth may capture the depth of indescribable shame death gave when I had been made known since a child that love conquers all. Why was my motherly love not enough to cast suffering and death out of my beloved child's life? How was it that my love was not enough to cure her broken heart? Why was my love not enough to make her live? Why was my religion not enough to touch and cure her heart anomaly? I prayed over her undeveloped heart. I commanded the heart to grow pulmonary arteries. I asked for Jesus to come. Like many born-again Christians and my Catholic family said he would. Why did he not come and make her live after she died? He came for Lazarus. He made him live even after he died. Why not my innocent child? She deserved to be here now with me on earth as much as Lazarus did for Jesus and his family. Why did all the Bible stories told not work when I was told by every priest I knew that

God listens and God answers prayers? I did not know why the God at church did not come. What possibly could I have done wrong to see my child die, even when everything about the world's medicine and all doctors that knew her made sure that she lived? Everyone did their best. God did not answer when I kneeled a thousand times. The priests could not mourn with me when I cried. No doctors could heal her winded breath when they tried for many hours. Yet, I alone held her cold body. I searched for her smile. I waited for her heart to beat. Still, when I stroked her usually shiny hair, onto the casket pillow, it fell. This is how my motherhood for my daughter Gaby ends. Cold to the touch. Still to the bone. Alone in the darkness. This ocean of sorrow is vast. Too much pain for one lifetime to bear. I wiped my tears. I heard my mind say, "The cure is to forget. Surrender your heart to dust when you bury her." I heard my heart say, "How about her light? How about my heaven? How about her smile… my joy? How about the rest of my love, which she opened and ignited at her birth? I can't bury a light. My heart can't hide from love. Where did her light come from? Where did it go when it vanished from my hand? I go where her heart glows. There, I see her brilliant smile. I wish I could keep her alive on earth, with my love."

Heal. Let go. Write the cause of your guilt and shame:

I feel so guilty that
_____
_____
_____
_____

I feel shameful that
_____
_____
_____
_____…

Nine

The Fourth Stage of Grief: A Necessary Road to Self-Redemption

Seeking Answers from Past Events

In my darkness, as I knelt in sorrow, there came a gentle light from the sky halting the flow of pain in my ignorant, lost soul. From white, living light, He transfigured Himself to the man of brilliant peace. Hovering above me, He gleamed. Gently and kindly in a calm voice, He said to me, "Woman, know thyself. The light of today has come to guide you to charter the darkness of the past. Gather the lost brilliance that was buried by cast judgments upon your soul, gather the pieces of the child divine in you. You are born a breath of peace. Exiled out of life, shattered by the world of darkness, this world blinded you from your own spiritual light. I tell you. Rise! Redeem yourself from the world of iniquities. The world of voices of judgment are themselves painful sorrows of the voices of frightened and lost humanity. Gather your fragmented, darkened, and hidden body of sparks, which this world of emotions has cast and hid from you. Go back in time. Find who you are. Awaken to the purpose of today. For today is yours. This hour is your destiny to usher the coming of tomorrow, which is your love, your light, your body, and the breath of peace. Woman, when you come to your true self, the light comes. Your Father in Heaven comes to light the vessel of your being, to shine love into this fragile heart of creation."

—Evangeline

SHINE LOVE, JOY, AND PEACE!

In love, there is no time. We are the breath of love. We come to Earth despite time. We come learning to express ourselves regardless of the limited capabilities of our vessels. Our body is limited, for it is the sacred body of created intelligence of the universe, but our spirit that dwells in the body never dies. A man's spirit is like that of his Father in spirit. It lives forever.

—Evangeline

I was alone. Lonely. I was lost in my mind, aching in the heart without my daughter Gaby to hold. Many midnights' past had been the same. I hurt without her. I needed to see and hold my sweet daughter. The unbearable pain in my head gave me tremendous headaches. The voices of her memory in my mind while she was alive with me, as we struggled to keep her alive and kept growing made me anxious. Conflicted by my mind's memories of her surgeries, medications, and remembering the sound of her laughter in Maryland's morning and afternoon, summer, fall, and spring neighborhood loop walks we did each day when she was alive, and all the time and struggles she had after her two surgeries at the Lucile Packard Hospital devoured my soul each day. One evening, I felt destitute. I decided to run my car off a cliff. Before I could step on the gas pedal, however, my whole body stiffened. My right foot could not point to the gas pedal and push on it. When I came out of it, I was furious. "You're a coward!" I screamed to myself.

In between my fallen tears, I tried to make sense of everything—why my daughter had to endure so much. It seems all her life since birth was destined for medical life. She was born only to suffer under the knife. Her life was dictated by how much medicine she had to consume. All the work, all the pain, only so she could die before she could form a sentence, which I waited for because I knew it was going to come… but it never did; now, it will never come.

Before I took that second step to push on the gas and kill myself the quickest way possible, I suddenly remembered the first message I received before Gaby was born.

In the middle of October 2001, the year before she was born, I had a dream. A lady, with a blue scarf on her shoulder, appeared in midair, hovered there for a second, and spoke gently and lovingly to me, "Something will happen by October of next year. You will move out of your home… Please tell your husband about this message tomorrow."

Because it was so unusual, I had a hard time sleeping through the night. When I woke up, I gave my husband the message; he listened to it just to satisfy my anxiety, though he was as baffled as I was as to what it meant.

By the following April, we decided to conceive. It was then that I had another dream. I was called to a place with a floating mountain, and I was greeted by waiting men called the "Twelve Apostles." While the one who greeted me with a smile went on to tell the chief that I had arrived, three others guided me to a white building standing by itself in the middle of a meadow. They were grateful that I had come. They left me in the white room to study for three days. There were three of us in the room, me and two teachers. Both male teachers were clothed in pure white linen top and bottom pants.

Upon graduation, there were two other women in line with me. One before me and one behind me. All of us were women of childbearing age. In the white building, we learned something I could not remember later, but I knew I was carrying the lesson inside me. Upon graduation, the chief finally appeared at the lectern. He handed us a diploma, though it was not a piece of paper as I had expected; rather, it was a wreath adorned with white lilies on the front. The chief crowned me with it. It was a big crown, but I knew I would learn to walk with it just as the woman before me learned to hold hers on her head as she ran away from the stage. When he put the crown on me, I looked down and noticed I was wearing a white linen gown, which highlighted my now-swollen bosom.

When I woke from the dream the following morning, my husband asked to play golf with me, so he and I played golf together. As I was putting and sinking every hole, my husband noted how I had turned pro overnight. I picked the ball from the hole and said to him, "I know I am pregnant," and I proceeded to tell him about my dream.

That was the best feeling I have ever experienced since I was born. The feeling that I am all right. The sensation that I am at peace under the morning sun. It was amazing. The dream made me feel at ease. I knew something was changed for good.

Heal. Let go. Write the source of your self-redemptions: these are the memories that made life mystical and beautiful when you were experiencing it. Remember those happy moments that gave meaning to your life.

Write what role and what they have to do in your awakening.

(I know I want to be happy. I am happy when I am in the light of truth. Where the spirit is safe, there are smiles. Where there are joys of light, there is peace. When all darkness moved away, I know I deserve… to be happy again.)

_____

_____

_____

_____

_____

_____

Man Is the Revelation

The quest is a sacred story—the secret path to self-redemption is the light and love within humanity's life's tale. Man is light. The lesson of humanity is from the brilliance of the light's consciousness. Consciousness is love. Love is the light and heart of humanity.

—Evangeline

Lesson from Jesus and the Heavenly Father, Mother Mary, Archangel Michael, and Gabriel

From heaven, a conscious child of the Holy Spirit sees the needs of its Garden earth's family. With deep compassion, it will desire to be born a child of man. But when this light of consciousness is born into a body, it is to grow and learn the human ways, eating and drinking human food. In his quest to being a perfect human, just like all other humans before him, he suffers in being alone in the darkness of the human-created minds. Yet the spirit's heart shines. He lives in search to quell his secret yearning to shine his or her own light, for he or she has forgotten that it is not just a human soul with a human story. He is a spirit of pure love before he is given a human body. He is a breath of peace before he is to breathe the human wind. No man—no matter how strong, rich, or poor—is a good human being without surrendering his humanity to the love and light of his own higher self. His higher self is his destiny. His spirit is his own light. His love is his path home. For all, man is the child of the one Holy Spirit of love and peace. Compassion is the perfected brilliance of this merciful grace. All man is holy in the heart of the Father. All man before humanity is the child of the Holy Spirit.

—Evangeline

Holy Spirit's Redemption: Looking Back in Time to Mend the Present

The Irony of life

Wherever His spirit child's heart yearns, there He is in light and love. Wherever His child is in pain, there He is in pain, breathing His breath and love of light and peace, until His angels come for His child. Life on earth is a time of opportunity to embody good in spirit, mind, body, soul, in the full illumination of love and peace in a time of every action.

—Evangeline

Playing golf is nothing like playing at all. It is a time of self-contemplation. A silence to hear my own voice speak. It's time for me to see my own weaknesses. A time for me to see how straight my focus is to make my mind connect to my brain, to connect all my limbs to make a lifeless ball go where I direct it to go with my will, close to the hole or in the hole. It takes a lot of effort to play the game of responsibility. But I go anyway. I golf for the time to get to know me more. Never would I come to a time and space where when I showed up to hold the ball and the club, that I will not think first. But when I did, trust I could explain what happened. The time I didn't think, where the ball was going first, when I trusted that the ball was created so I could hit it in the hole, dug perfectly for the ball to go home to, the rest was done for me. I just had to show up and play. Not think or contemplate. But trust the ball. Respect the hole's purpose. I played in peace.

After that one dream that there is another space of peace where "the Apostles" in spirits still exist, where they are so peaceful, I realized that peace is extended to where I am and who I am. And will continue so for the rest of my tomorrows, todays, and yesterdays.

In my heart, peace is everywhere, my heart trusts, where I love, where I am quiet. I learned there was a sense of open peace that comes when I trust, that what has been created in the time of my needs will show up, for already everything that life needs is already made for me; I just have to show up and play the game, honestly, and consciously, and most of all consistently.

Two weeks after the perfect birdie of the golf game, after that beautiful dream that I conceived, not knowing for sure whether I was carrying a child, I went to the Philippines. During my second week there, I was faced with another reality of life that I could not understand. My brother Chris begged me to bring some money to help an eleven-year-old boy, his young friend, who had become like a little brother to him. He explained that the boy had been suffering from a disease called rheumatic heart since he was an infant. In the last three years, he had been slowly wasting away. He badly needed an operation.

The problem was his parents had no money and could barely afford to eat three meals a day. His father was a bus driver, making only fifty dollars a month. His mother went from house to house doing laundry for people and getting paid the equivalent of four dollars per day, a job she only had twice a week if she was lucky. It was barely enough to get the little boy the medicine his heart required to function properly. So for days on end, the child suffered without medication to hold him up.

When he spoke, which was infrequent, it was with pain. I wanted to meet this boy, for such compassion I already bore for him. The hospital scheduled the boy for a heart operation, and with the help of a heart foundation in the Philippines, his family would only need to come up with 25 percent of the total cost. But the entire family was in survival mode just to make it another day, and even 25 percent was beyond impossible, an unreachable dream. The boy suffered as my brother watched helplessly. In tears, he told me about the little boy's ordeal as he convinced me with all his heart that I could make a difference.

We arranged to meet the boy the following week. The day came very quickly, and I had prepared myself to meet him. When it was time to go to his home to visit, my brother called me to get out of the chair I was sitting in so we could leave. Upon standing up from the chair, the voice of the same lady who came to me in my dream spoke, "It isn't time to meet him, sit down," she whispered gently. I immediately became very tired, and I passed out.

My mother said, "I think you are pregnant. Finally, at last!" She smiled. "Don't worry," she said, "I will go with your brother and see if there is something we can do to help."

My mother was given a chance to meet the little boy. I, on the other hand, was not.

The following week, I left the country with him on my mind. As it turned out, all he needed was less than five thousand dollars. I wanted to speak to the priest at our church to see if he could ask everyone to be involved in making a difference in his life.

When I got to Honolulu Airport at the end of my journey, my husband came to pick me up. Smiling, he kissed me, lifted his hand, and showed me a white stick. "What is that?" I asked.

"It's a pregnancy testing stick." He hugged me again. "I hope you're pregnant, honey!" he said excitedly.

"Well, my body has been acting weird for the last three weeks. I'd better be pregnant or else…" I said, smiling.

On our way home, he stopped at a Starbucks. He could not wait to drive another fifteen minutes to get home to find out whether he was going to be a daddy. In the bathroom of the coffeehouse, awkwardly, for the first time in the thirteen years I'd been married, I peed on the stick. *Things one needs to do to become a mommy*, I thought. Two minutes later, two lines amazingly appeared on the stick. "I swear I did not write them in there!" I smiled at my husband.

At four o'clock in the afternoon, we were both gleaming with joy. Excited, he smiled, "We are finally going to be parents… Yes!" he said as he smacked his palm on the car's steering wheel.

The same week I got home, after speaking with my husband about the little boy, he agreed we should help as soon as we can. The time it would take to get the community's help through the church might have put his health in jeopardy. Though we did not have a lot of money, we were willing to do everything we could to help him get his surgery. My mother and I decided to split the difference between the two of us.

As soon as the family and my brother received the confirmation that help was on the way, they went to Manila Heart Center. Upon arriving, many nurses and one doctor were so happy that the child was going to receive the operation he needed, a chance they knew he well deserved and deeply needed to survive. They were all crying with tears, not of happiness but hope for Billy.

Within two days, Billy had been given the scheduled date for his long-awaited operation. It was set for the same year, July 6, 2001. Early May, I sent him the desperately needed money.

A week after he received the money, my brother was on the phone, crying: "He could not wait for the surgery, sister…" The little boy had become very ill the night before his surgery. My brother had rushed him to the hospital the following morning, but before they could get there, the boy died in his arms. Heartbroken, I decided the family could give him a good burial using the money I sent. I mourned his loss. I found myself bewildered as I wondered why I had to know about him if I wasn't going to make any difference in his life after all.

My brother told me the nurses at the hospital did not believe Billy had died. They informed him of something no one could explain. Supposedly, at the hospital, the same hour Billy had died in the province, his doctors and nurses in Manila were in the middle of a conversation when they all stopped talking and saw Billy standing next to them after he had come in from the hallway. His right hand was hanging on to the edge of the check-in counter as his chin was looking up directly at a white pad that was lying on the counter. He stood there, shyly, facing the counter where patients check-in for operations.

"Billy, you're looking well!" one of the nurses called out. Without words in return, he looked at each of them, smiled, and disappeared before their eyes. Not even two days later, during his wake, my brother called the heart center to tell them Billy would no longer be needing the heart surgery.

The nurses argued with him as they had the evidence that he was well; after all, they'd just seen him well. When they realized he was gone, they were as upset as my brother was, just as all of us were.

As I thought of him, I prayed daily for his precious soul. Billy taught me that hope was an inexpensive medicine a person could take as much as he or she wanted when needed. It is there for us anytime we choose; it holds us up until it becomes the bridge that carries us to become one with its side, to cradle that part of us that are left whole and intact, that piece of us that still shows up wanting to tell the world that we don't just disappear, even after we die.

We indeed show up wherever our name is expected to be called by time. I carried the lesson he gave me in my heart while I tried to get used to being pregnant. Despite being anxious, I was unfazed in my daily routine. I looked forward to the day my husband and I would find out the sex of our child. That too, came very quickly. We found out I was carrying a girl. We felt blessed.

But it was short-lived, for an hour after we found out she was a girl, we were given the news that her heart had an anomaly and that she would require surgery when she was born. I was deeply troubled by the coincidences between helping the young boy to have his heart surgery, only to find out that my own child had a heart issue as she was growing in my womb. I felt a jolt in my soul as if someone had just kicked me in the stomach. I could not believe what was happening.

Self and Spirit Redemption: The Lady Messenger

From heaven, she comes. Her body is light. Her grace is beaming in soft and comforting, yet very still and obedient, wind. Her heart is filled with overflowing love. Her giant body of light gently began enveloping me to stillness. She is a Mother of Peace. She is the heart of grace. She is the body of a kind light that surpasses all human understanding.

—Evangeline

Within an hour of receiving the unwanted news about my child's health, the rest of my life as I knew it had been flipped upside down. All my future plans had vanished; I knew those dreams were gone. Never did I think they would come back to me, only in the what-if questions. It was what it was.

I had to forget our trip to Europe for three years, which my husband had penciled in a year prior to the news. We were supposed to be stationed in Rhoda, Spain, in April 2003, the year after the birth of our first child. Instead of heading to his new duty station, however, we had to remove my husband's name off the list. We were both disappointed. It would have been perfect to give birth to my baby in January and head to Spain in April that same year.

By August 2002, we had left Hawaii to go house hunting near the hospital in Maryland, where my daughter's care would take place. We found a lovely house in Ann Arundel County, which was an hour drive from Bethesda Hospital. My husband could still work for the Navy, but he had to drive to Pax River Base an hour and a half away, about one hundred and ten miles, back and forth each day. We made an offer on the new house. We were to close in November that same year if our offer went through. We came back home to Hawaii at the end of August to pack our belongings.

By October 22, 2002, I found myself with my husband at the airport about to board a flight to LA. I was very worried about what was to come. I was well into seven and a half months of my pregnancy. On one of the flights to Maryland, I remembered the dream I had about that sweet motherly looking lady who resembled Mother Mary herself. I remembered her voice and what her message was about. It was then that I trusted that God had a plan for my daughter and me, and that she was there to give me the news.

By December 1, 2002, we had moved out of the base lodge and into our new house. By December 2, the movers had delivered our belongings from Hawaii. On the morning of December 4, I was unpacking some kitchen glasses from one of the boxes, when at about 9:30 a.m., my child moved violently in my womb. She was startled because I had unwrinkled the paper in which a glass had been wrapped. I was frightened too to feel her move so violently.

As I took a deep breath and leaned over the kitchen counter to hold myself up, there was a bright light floating in midair in the middle of the kitchen. Before I knew it, I was staring at the same lady. "It's time." She smiled. "Don't worry, everything will be all right," she said and disappeared from the kitchen, leaving only a peaceful aura of mingling and shining wind behind her, as if she scattered dust of shimmering powder of gold in my kitchen.

Immediately after her voice disappeared, I heard my husband pull into the driveway. I realized he had come home from running his errand to pick me up so he could drive me to the hospital for my weekly checkup.

As we were pulling out of the driveway, he suddenly said, "I feel like saying the rosary." It was an unusual request coming from my husband. I used it as a great opportunity to share with him what had just happened. I told him about the event in the kitchen. I knew for that moment whatever fear he was feeling was calmed. I knew he believed me.

We agreed to pray the rosary as I began feeling some sharp contractions while I was sitting in the car. When we got to the hospital, the test showed that my daughter was in great distress. She was only eight months in gestation; she was not supposed to be born until January 6. The doctor opted for safety, and I was held in the hospital to be induced within four hours.

The next day, both my parents arrived at Ronald Reagan International Airport at 11:00 p.m. from the Philippines. The following day, December 6, at 12:30 in the afternoon, Gabriella was born. She was nice and pink, contrary to the blue baby I was warned to expect, given her heart condition.

She was sent to Children's Hospital of Philadelphia the following morning. It was there we were told there was nothing they could do for her. Her heart was unique in that the arteries were completely absent. There was nothing to fix since there was no receiving end or even a beginning. We were told to get her better and take her home to enjoy her as long as we had her and give her a quality of life, which was assumed to be three months or perhaps more. No one knew for sure.

I was focused on my daughter. Just like in the beginning, when I chose to proceed with the pregnancy, I reminded myself to respect life's processes and continue to believe that whoever created her had a greater plan. All that I had was her; I had no other choice but to believe in her purpose.

Over the next two years, she underwent two open-heart surgeries. In between the hospital visits, our universe had turned into an everyday ride on the Beltway. From our house to Walter Reed Hospital was our commute. Despite having a new house, our car became our home, and the hospital became our haven. The one great thing about it was we were together, the three of us, a complete family.

"What if Gaby had been born healthy? Do you ever wonder?" my husband asked. "I wonder what we would be doing in Spain at this moment," he continued to ask as we were driving home from the hospital one night. "Wouldn't it be nice to visit Europe and learn about all the rich histories of those countries?" He turned his head away from me and looked at Gaby. "I bet the children would love that," meaning our future children. "Gaby would love that." He smiled.

I smiled back. "I am pretty sure it would be nice, lovely, too," I replied. "Maybe someday!" I said with hope. "But here, now, in the car is where we are. This is our moment, our time… this is much better than that dream," I reminded him. "Here, now, we have her for sure… For sure, we are a family… Now we are blessed with Gaby!"

"You're right!" He smiled, turned his head to the road ahead, and grew silent. Then he said, "I would not trade this moment for any dream! It is what it is," he said with certainty.

"Precious!" I said and tickled Gaby's feet. She giggled and smiled at me. She squealed in her toddler's laughter. The moment was precious, hearing her laugh. I knew then that this was where I needed to exist, where sacredly I knew I had been called to be… in the moment… in the car where I was afraid, yet warm and comforted by both my loved ones' presence. I felt whole. I was happy and content. I was utterly so glad that I could not allow any other what-if dreams to ruin the precious time I'd been given. This was my sacred moment.

Self-Redemption: An Unbelievable Sight
Seeing the Familiar Man as He Sat on the Throne

The wind is absent; the sky is still but lit with a thousand full moons. The space is light, and serenity governs it. All brilliant light from which all darkness surrendered is at home. Contentedness is the morning sunrise. Everything around me disappeared. He is all there is above me. A caring Father, sitting on the throne, He dawns gently on me. He cares for me. All my thoughts and anguish He bore with me. He has come to honor my motherly heart. He spoke without words, filling my emptiness with so much love. He is the brilliance of all brilliance. He filled me with His gentle luminosity. Grace is Him. Mercy is His glory. My heart, my spirit, and mind heard loud, His guiding request, "I am here."

—Evangeline

In November 2004, before Gaby's second birthday, I decided to take her back to Hawaii. "The warm weather and the vision of being able to play outside will help her heal faster from her second surgery," I convinced my husband. He agreed with the plan. She was admitted for surgery in April 2004 and released from the hospital in July, three months later.

After a few months in Maryland, during her recovery, I dreaded the snowy winter ahead of us. I wanted her to play and experience the freedom of movement during her healing process. On November 7, a few weeks before our trip to Hawaii, I once again experienced something I did not understand. As I was taking a shower, I lifted my head to let the water run over the skin on my face. In doing so, I was sucked like a vacuum into a space way up in the sky where only soft and cool winds and kind clouds existed. I emerged into a space of light and calmness, floating amid the clouds, standing before a man, the holiest of holies. I stood in a submissive state in front of a fatherly figure sitting on a throne. I listened obediently as if something inside me understood Him… knew Him, and everything that I am, accepted Him. "Your job is done… It was done well," He said, gladly, proudly, gently, yet comfortingly proud of my choices.

The obedient part of me, which I just found out to have existed, listened and accepted what He said without any reservation. He crowned me with a wreath not made of thorns, but rather of mini buds of red roses. As I held on to the crown to feel it, to keep it intact as it sat securely on my head, I once again opened my eyes and found I was back in my body; my feet were both planted, standing in the shower again. I ran out of the shower as if I had just awakened from a dream, which I took to mean something peculiar was going to happen. But I found myself drowning in so much peace; I was not alarmed.

After running through in my mind all that just happened, I dressed quickly as I became concerned about the meaning of the vision. An hour had passed. As I was cooking supper, I saw a vision, not in my head, but rather floating inside my kitchen. My daughter was on an island being looked after by an island lady who seemed to be Tahitian. She was surrounded by children I knew were not hers. I panicked as I shook myself out of the vision. I thought of my daughter, Gaby, in tears, and alarmed. I ran to the living room and scooped her up. I held my daughter in my arms for the rest of the night, afraid of losing her.

On November 29, 2004, we landed at the Honolulu Airport. I felt at home and was very happy inside. My daughter was happy, as well. She was giggling and playful. When we got outside the airplane through Gate 10, I was surprised to see my daughter become so still. I wondered what she was looking at. For a good two minutes, she stared at the biggest rainbow I had ever seen in my entire life. It glowed sharply with all its might over the mountain and above all the buildings. As it hovered, my daughter looked as if she was talking to someone or something within the rainbow that I could not see. I stared at her. She was gleaming, radiating with smiles, and clapping her hands with joy as she looked at me for approval. All the hair on my body stood up. I felt uneasy. That was the first time I experienced my soul step out of my body and felt the pain in my entire back as it slowly shifted back, making me feel instantly and completely worn-out.

From the airport, we began our journey back to the Marine Base in Kaneohe. As we headed into the H3 entrance, on the highway that led to the base, there was yet another rainbow. It was big but not as big as the one at the airport. As the car drove toward it, my hair stood up again. I told my husband, "We are being welcomed, honey." I looked at the entire car. Everything in it, especially my daughter's feet, had turned light green, and they glowed. I began to feel something beyond me was happening.

We got to the hotel, the Lodge. We stayed there until the morning of December 6. By then, we had found an apartment near the beach, which we leased for six months so my daughter and I could finally savor the Hawaiian sunrise and the fresh air, which I believed to be the key to her recovery. We moved into the apartment on the evening of December 6. That same night, from eleven to one o'clock in the morning, my daughter's heart began to beat out of control. It would not slow down. I laid my hands on her chest. She was in distress. She was arching her back and crying. Her heart was beating as if it was being driven by wild horses on their wild run.

We found ourselves in the emergency room very early on the morning of December 7, just before the sun crept out of the morning sky, about six o'clock. When we first got there, Gaby was saying words as if she was hallucinating. I knew in my heart it was bad, but I knew she was going to be treated at the hospital just like all the other times; then, we would come home after a few days. I told her we were going to celebrate her birthday at the Sea Life Park as soon as she felt better, the same discussion we had in the car on our way to the emergency room. Every time I spoke, she responded in her toddler language.

When she was given a bed in the emergency room, I held her. I proceeded to talk to her and kiss her. Then one doctor came in and saw how badly she needed oxygen. She panicked as the crew began to put an oxygen mask on her. That was the time she last looked at me with a stare that looked through my body and into my spirit. I could hear her say, "Not this again, Mommy. Can you tell them to stop, please? Not again," as if she too was disappointed with what she was about to go through all over again.

My heart sank. I hurt for her so badly, but my love was not enough to take her pain away, to make her heart not do what it was doing to her; it made her suffer. Immediately after she had her oxygen mask on, her eyes began to close. Her lips began to turn purple. Her fingernails began to lose their pink color. More doctors arrived; everything in the room was in chaos. One doctor was pumping her chest, while another was yelling at the nurses for more potent medicine, and still, another was watching the monitor. "We're losing her," he yelled, sounding alarmed and distressed; she was not breathing. Everyone in the room held their breath. All red-faced, in suspense. And I? I was coming out of my skin, out of my soul, out of my heart, begging that she does not feel the pain in which she was being administered as she was being helped to breathe again.

The doctor pumping her chest began using the machine to shock her heart. Over and again, her body shook when it received electricity in an effort to get it to start pumping strong again, but her breath remained so far away from where it used to be. Even the machine could not reach to well it out. Her heart grew weaker.

As the doctors worked around her tiny body, there was no room for me to hold her hands. When I tried to squeeze myself in between the hips of those around her, I could not make myself look at how much torture she was under. One nurse had put a one-and-a-half-inch needle into her right leg, as if it was just a thumbtack being punched through a piece of paper. I felt all the pain she was enduring. She was surrounded by a sequence of routine calls, one after the other, without a drop of caring on the part of those who were working hard to save her breath.

I was angered at how much those doctors were focusing on her body; they forgot to care for her feelings. They were inflicting so much pain on her that her tiny soul could no longer take it. I could not get through to them that she was weak, to begin with. She didn't need to be treated so aggressively… without an ounce of gentleness. She was handled as if she was a doll.

Somehow, I knew the hour I did not want to arrive would eventually come. The precious heart that beat for my daughter Gabriella finally gave up. There was too much assault, too much pain, too much routine for such a tiny precious heart, and a twenty-five-pound body. She was too shocked to feel any form of caring or even kindness if there were any at all given. She went away with the wind. Her eyes never opened; they had remained closed for me to see through them once more. One moment in time, when she took her last breath, she fought so hard to deliver had summed up the end of the road to her precious life, which quietly mirrored my own. My heart only wanted to keep my soul at bay, by forgetting the trauma, which I watched my baby endure. But my heart, though it is torn, must beg the mind to remember what it had seen. Everything that took place as I can remember them tore my heart. My mind had shut down to protect the rest of my well-being. So as a mother, as a soul, I was left alone. I was still trying to make sense of why death had to happen.

Life can be so cruel and so unforgiving. There was nothing I could do to change anything. My prayers did not work. God did not hear me. I was helpless. Life, I discovered for the very first time, was not about promises of the future, but rather about how much more my injured heart could take when more assaults and punches were already at hand; and they seemed to keep coming.

Left alone in the room, I felt I was floating in the dark sky. However, having my baby's tiny breathless body to hold on to, made the intolerable, somehow bearable, despite the agonizing cries in my heart and mind. In that dark and cold emergency room, it was still she who gave it warmth and grace. She lay so still and silent in my arms, but I could hear her whispers to accept… just accept life for what it was—bittersweet.

At the age of thirty-four, I surrendered to madness. Yes, I was mad—mind, body, and soul. I lost who I was, and all I used to be in that emergency room, in that one visit. I have never been the same since. Losing Gaby meant losing the very tiny and short string that gave me hope. The innocence that had given me so much understanding, strength, and forgiveness for life itself had been ripped away from me. One blink. One breath, gone! Against everything that life had presented before me, my husband and I were forced to let go. I was an angry being, angry that the hospital had swept her sweet body from me. Away! Overnight! It was infuriatingly painful to imagine how alone she was going to be. I was furious beyond words. I wanted to tell her I love her all night long, but no one understood what I was trying to tell them. I wanted to be with her, as long as I could hold her, but no one would let me.

The doctor took her body away from me, anyway. I felt violated as a mother, as a woman. I felt like someone had just punched me in the gut. It left a big hole in my heart and soul when he had to rip her out of my arms. Without her in it, I felt sickly empty. I curled myself into a ball and hugged what I could, my knees. "It's the hospital's policy," he told me.

"Stupid ritual," I thought with a respectable snare. Such practice, in my motherly opinion, is the most demeaning act he could have ever done to any mother's soul. To separate a child from her parents on the very last day was inconceivable to me. Giving her away, letting her be taken away, was just as if I had given away all my rights as a human being, as a mother, to death; the system violated my daughter's love, injured her spirit, as her rights as my daughter had automatically disappeared with the breath she did not take.

I watched in the corner of the room as they wheeled her body off the floor… up to the hospital morgue. The thought of her in a freezer, instead of in the love of my heartbeats and the warmth of my arms, drove me crazy. Since she had been formed in my womb, from the time I gave birth to her, through all those nights she was in that hospital bed, that night she was taken from me was the very first night we had ever been separated. It was my worst nightmare unfolding ever so slowly before me. It was happening.

Disappointed and angry, too tired to fight all the man-made rules, without a choice, my husband and I went back to our cold and darkened apartment; like two strangers, hollow and empty, we each placed our bodies to our usual sides of the bed and cried ourselves through the night and into the following morning.

Self-Redemption: Revelations, the Spirit's Ways

A light came, which turned into an infinite garden where all the spirits within it greeted me with silent and unspoken luminosity. The path of this secret garden is the Prince of Love and Peace. He is the path; He is its door. Many loved ones here were the light bodies of eternal joy. He is their teacher and light; He lights them with His unaltered and pure brilliant compassion. Before Him in His care, the spirits of our ancestors are at rest in peace. Still, they are learning and being taught by His brilliant and eternal wisdom. He is humanity's ancestors' teacher. They are His students. An illuminating radiance they give in full. Surrounding me with gratitude, I was being bathed in pure white brilliance. Their hearts are lighthouses calling me to be filled with lasting smiles, as the serenity of complete and all-knowing wisdom of everlasting love shone like a radiant fountain streaming and beaming out of their beings, gently, yet calmly, watering the very depth of my loss, forsaken heart to shine. "Shine love!" the lights of these hearts illuminated. Their presence lit me up. Everyone is whole. With their hands outreached, they held me. In union, they proclaimed in screaming silence, "Live again! Love again! Shine! You are light. You are a divine spirit!"

—Evangeline

I Heard My Dead Daughter Call Me "Mommy"

The following morning, with red and swollen faces, we returned to the hospital. This time at the chapel, I watched and studied my daughter's still body, finally resting continuously without interruption, in her sleep. She's at peace at last, and something in me was at ease to watch her not being interrupted by a nagging cough, which was often her daily ordeal. *At last, an eight-hour, well-deserved rest*, I thought.

Then, out of the stream of quietness, broken only by a few whispers between the priest and a visitor, I heard my daughter call, "Mommy, Mommy!" A luminous white shadow appeared; she was all smiles as she stood the same height and size as my daughter. She hovered in front of me, bearing my daughter's face, demeanor, and even her grace. The luminous white shadow bent down and began poking at my daughter's resting body, poking her knees. "Mommy! Is this my body?" she asked in a very sure manner.

"Yes, it is," my spirit answered. Then before I knew it, she was hovering over me, asking so many questions, which my spirit answered back without delay.

The second morning, I was half-awake. I realized I had fallen asleep and slept without interruption, eight hours straight for the first time in three years. "Out of exhaustion," I assured myself. I closed my eyes again; as soon as I did, I felt a movement hovering over my face. I did not move; I opened my eyes to watch, but there was nothing there. When I blinked, I saw a glimpse of my baby, Gaby. I closed my eyes. Then I learned if I kept them closed, I could see her again.

So I closed them and watched. Floating face down, on top of me was her, my daughter, Gaby, with bruises still on her body. "Mommy, look, I am not sick anymore," she whispered. "I love you, Mommy." She came down to kiss me as usual and hovered over my husband's cheeks; gently, she hovered over him and kissed him on the cheek. "I love you, Daddy," she whispered. Then she disappeared quickly with the unseen wind. Like a beautiful bubble floating so gracefully, then instantaneously popping, it was gone. I was powerless, so limited, no longer able to reach her. There was an unseen barrier between us, one my spirit knew I must never cross, for it was forbidden, to be respected, to be honored. Whatever it was, that space, or that unseen wind that now cradled her, had taken my daughter from me; and all the rights, even my title as her mother, was no more. What she has become part of is a world I know I do not understand.

Instead, there I was still on my weakened knees, left behind with a fragile mind and a torn heart. My love and instincts were so focused on Gaby's bruises; how I wanted to hold her and take her pain away. I did not know what had just happened. I wanted her. I needed to see her. It was all good until she disappeared. Angered, infuriated, I was so confused about what was going on. I knew my mind was fooling me.

But wait! I sat there and thought. *Maybe it is death! No! Maybe it is life! Shit! Maybe it is God making a mockery of me.* I silently screamed my cries and frustration in a fetal position so no one, not even my husband, could hear me until my entire being churned out of control, and I could not feel my existence. Then when I thought I was gone and thought it was good, I was, in fact, still there, hearing my thoughts, looking at my two toes moving back and forth as my mind was able to make them move. *I am in a dream,* I thought. So for sanity's purposes, I decided I was in a dream. I was all right. It was good. I was fine.

Self-Redemption: Heavenly Music

A green and morning lit garden floated. In it were six two-year-old toddlers playing varieties of music instruments, creating a piece of music that moved my heart to awaken in truth and calm, peace and solitude. Like a dancing wind, their music rose up to a higher space above the secret womb of hidden spaces beyond the garden that they filled with divine and purely innocent angelic hymns. The violin's every note silenced my pain. I am made calm. I am made at peace.

—Evangeline

On the second morning after her burial, I woke up to beautiful music, serenading my soul to comfort. I saw in front of me, my daughter, playing the violin. She was leading a group. With her were five other children who were also the same age, about two years old. All of them were holding some musical instruments as they produced a hymn befitting only heaven. She was there, hovering beautifully. I felt alive again, seeing and watching her. I felt proud of how beautifully she could play the violin and secure in knowing she was not alone. My heart's mind seemed to have surrendered to the gentle glory of the melody that her entire group seemed to have produced just for that instant to comfort my spirit off of worry, pain, and guilt. Everything was good. I felt whole. I knew it was love. *"My dear child, even after death, you come, trying to heal my broken heart. Your music has soothed my heart to comfort. What a life-giving hymn, I can breathe again. Thank you."* I thought.

Then I opened my eyes, in my desire to see more, but again she was gone. I had been left behind once more. Alone, yet somehow invigorated deep within by the loving harmony my tiny visitors had produced, the sweet echoes of each note had slowly become a sound escape in my wondering. I wondered why all her friends bore the same bruises as she. The music had long faded in my mind and heart, but my questions were not to be answered for many weeks after her death. Two months later, her surgeon told me that Gabriela was the sixth cardiac patient he had lost. I asked myself, "You mean to tell me they all met up in heaven after their ordeal? And they've decided to show themselves to me?" Of course, I was left thinking of how important I had suddenly become.

To think that those children had taken the time to prepare for my poor soul a hymn, which helped strengthen and rescue me out of the wicked grasp of death's awful grief. I was honored, proud, humbled, and of course, loved. *"She loves me, thinks of me,"* I thought. *"Wherever I am, whatever I am doing, I'd better do with grace,"* I thought. *"She is watching over me and knows the state of my heart and mind."*

Self-Redemption: Divine Order

Have we come to know that the best of life on earth will offer itself to us freely? Through every turn of the season is a sacred mystery, illumined from the infinite and timeless depth of our true spirits. This amazing life is a living river in the vast ocean of the waters of divine grace, so pure; it is hidden within each man, waiting only to be unraveled in time—until we stumble on our own eternal glories that what we seek in the world is within us. We are spirit bodies of everlasting love. We are the breath of peace that has come to flow infinitely as living waters of truth, welling out in every breath, spirits of continued waters of pure radiance, the light of love, cast into the planet earth's family of awakened and aware creation of always new humanity.

—Evangeline

Going back to the first day after her death, we were handed a packet guide with instructions on how to plan for her funeral. As guided, we ordered her casket. At the funeral home, we were naive to think it was going to be an easy find. When I looked at their inventory, my heart was crushed again. I suddenly felt alone again. There were caskets in all directions for adults only. *Only old people die, never an innocent child, not my precious baby.* My tears welled up while I scanned the entire space for the one that would fit her.

After all the runaround, we were called to a room where there was only one small casket. It was way in the back of the room. After being led to the far end shelf, there it was, by itself. Upon looking at it, never once in my life prior to that sacred event, would I think a casket was beautiful, much less not fear it. I touched it, gladly. I was greatly thankful for it being there. At that moment, it was beautiful... fitting for my one and only precious princess. It was shining, just like her smile. It was grand... priceless. The thing that would cradle her was created so intricately of pure Hawaiian Ko'a wood (Ko'a is an indigenous tree to the Hawaiian Islands).

The lady who accompanied us went before us to open it. Inside, its bed was covered with beautiful white silk; tucked within it was a half-inch of soft batting, which was entirely layered with satin fabric. The top cover was embellished with a delicate design from a see-through rayon, of an off-white fabric in the shape of a sun bursting its magnificent rays covering the infinite horizon. I touched and felt it for its degree of comfort. *"Will you be warm enough to hold he*r?" I thought.

My tears fell profusely because deep down, I knew the answer. My arms were my daughter, Gabriella's warmth, and her home. *"Why did it have to come to this?"* My heart cried. *"Oh, how I beg, I wish this was just a dream. I will soon wake up... I will soon wake up with her in my arms and at the park where she and I will play. Not here. Not here,"* I cried and cried.

I ran my fingers and hands all through the inside of the precious box. What I felt in reply was an answer that slightly satisfied my sensations. The security and the warmth of the small space built for the right fit, its unmistakable desire of its maker to give and create coziness was well achieved. The feeling of safety from the softness of the fabric as well as the careful crafting of the other elements that made up the small box silently conveyed sacred grandeur.

The more time I spent feeling it, the more I knew the well-intended dreams of the person who sketched the blueprint of this remarkable craft. Suddenly everything about the box, inside and out, had given me a sense of belonging where I would otherwise have lacked it within. *"Close enough... it has to be,"* I thought again. "Comfortable enough, warm enough," I whispered to myself.

Then, from my shoulder, "Five fingers of God," my husband said, naming the five sun rays, shining out of the depicted satin image of a newly rising sun, covering the coffin's upper lid, as he caressed the fabric and ran his hands through the entire cloth, which was carefully nestled inside it. I wondered what he thought of it. I wished I knew. I wanted to know if it was good enough for him. I dared not ask because I knew the answer. It can never replace both of our arms, but we need to make sure, we need to agree in deep silence, that it is good enough for its given purpose.

So in silence, I let the mother in me carry me through, in a deep hope that it would see what it came to find. As I examined it further, inside and out, the woman behind us said in a slight pidgin accent, "An old man had ordered it six weeks ago."

"He changed his mind?" I asked quickly.

"It arrived two weeks ago. But financing fell through. He never came to pick it up."

"It is the perfect size for my daughter," I responded, saddened. "It would have been the one we would have chosen if we'd had the money to buy it," I continued.

"Since it is already here, we'll make sure the price fits your budget." She walked out of the room and later returned. "It's yours," the woman said with a gentle smile and a voice that broke out with a spirit of compassion.

I nodded with a smile. I thought it was odd that someone would preorder a coffin. *"Maybe the story was just made up,"* I reasoned to myself. The spirit of my consciousness, which had always been a guide to every choice I've ever made in life, would not have been surprised if it were true.

Two weeks before, we arrived in Hawaii. Two weeks prior to that, the coffin had been ordered. It had been sitting there the entire time we were in Hawaii. It did not matter how or what the reason was. My daughter's body, her life's vessel, which was the greatest instrument to give meaning to my own life, was now going to be cradled in a very special and beautiful resting space, a sacred and grand box, but not just a box; it was one that also bore an unusual story.

Self-Redemption: Tree of Life

Though life may seem like an accidental manifestation, time said it is not so; for the womb of time prepared a tiny seed, which rose to be a tree, so a passionate craftsman may be born, to grow in wisdom, to carve for me with passion, a shiny box to cradle my child's vessel to her ultimate sleep, so her spirit may rise and be offered to the Man on the Throne in surrender to a new joy, peace, and love of life eternal—her new life.
—Evangeline

I ran the sole of my palm throughout the shiny, perfected craft. My spirit became flooded with deep knowing that I am not touching a dried and painted wood. It was a tree of life.

Once, not long ago, it was an exotic tree that stood among other trees. Once a seedling, many times over, its leaves and branches danced with the wind's sometimes gentle and yet sometimes strong caresses. It grew and grew to its purpose. It provided a sanctuary to the birds around it and gave shade to those who rested under it, while it was cradled by the earth's soil, nourished by its minerals, and nurtured by the sun. It had, with time, breathed the same breath that Mother Earth gave freely, abundantly; meanwhile, as it stood, it was a living witness to many lives that had begun, unfolded, lived, and ended around it.

Within the well of its memory was encoded not only a story of its own, but also the plots of many lives connected to the depth of its roots: the other trees, the rocks, the waters, the rain, the grass, and all the other specimens in and around it, to which undeniably, it had been a giver and a recipient of the same life. Together, the entire cycle of nature's grace fueled its every cell, which made up its every fiber. Its life's purpose was rooted out of time and cradled by the generous space planet earth gave freely. It was a life with an intelligent, caring, well-meaning nature of its own, which happened to have a name—a tree.

As it once stood among the majestic green forest, never had it been alone. In the morning, when the sun rose, it shined as it reflected the sun up in the sky, just like the other trees. Together, with the sun lighting their being, they were the ultimate testimony of solemn and quiet prayers of nature. The explosions of the gentle sun, as it awakened the trees' shadows, with the dance of the playful wind, there was a display of gratitude for having been created, for being a part of life.

No doubt, at the end of the day, when the sun came down, as the trees are left in darkness, they too were reminded of their faith—a time that would come for their chosen experiences to end. Now, for this tree, its time on the planet had come to pass, and its experience of the sun's kisses and wind's caress—as well as the uncounted well-lit moons it had witnessed those many nights as it stared at its own massive shadow—was over.

But its life ended for a grander reason. Its time had come at last. Its final purpose? It was to come to my rescue and be part of my closure. It had arrived, now under my palm, reunited in the same state of stillness as my daughter's body. Bearing nature's mark of magnificent beauty, it had come for my daughter, to cradle her sacred body, her vessel, upon its surrendering to dust. Even when it was no longer alive to give my daughter its potent oxygen, it was here now, one with the journey, to save me with new breaths and preserve my broken soul out of insanity.

So it was then I decided. As I stood where my knees had been locked up a while, and where my hands had rested after touching and examining the grains that had given the wood its visible essence, I decided it had convinced me. It was more than enough to hold her body for eternity, for its beauty matched that of hers, timeless. *My precious, precious, beloved angel, Gaby, rest in the comfort of stillness.*

Self-Redemption: Rest in Peace, an Amazing Grace

The sky opened. Hundreds of brilliant spirits were looking down. They were dawning upon me. In the center was the Man of Peace, holding my daughter in His arms. They are with me in surrendering to the season of life. I knew then that they were with me in comfort at her birth. They guided me in daily nurturing when we were both together. Even now, they

are with me in the time of her death, to honor the end of human experience to deliver me the eternal substance of immortal bodies of love—the breath of everlasting, where she lives comforted in joy, light, and forever.
—Evangeline

We placed our daughter's body to rest in the brown, shiny, beautiful box. I immersed my attention in her beautiful, peach-colored skin, her plump cheeks and baby lips, her gentle face, coupled with her eyes closed. My heart was still, at peace, not asking for what was not, but rather accepting what was in front of me, respectful of the sequence of events that had and was still taking place beyond and above me.

At the close of the ceremony, we prayed and sang, "Amazing Grace." From the beginning of the song, a strong breeze wafted over, caressing our faces and encompassing us with a fresh breath of life as it blanketed our bare skin with its cold and refreshing touch. As we sang, a white bird appeared before us. My husband and I watched it fly toward the spot to which we were going to lay Gaby's sacred body. Meanwhile, above me, I could sense a sudden presence from the sky. The music notes and vibrations had caused a bunch of white clouds to file around in a circle. The big open sky, the heaven right above us, had opened up.

A big hole the size of a few hundred football fields had formed. Surrounding it were faces and bodies of shining spirits looking down. They watched and joined the sacred moment of our complete surrender to God's design. I could see the spirits—the souls—and the white clouds as one with us. I saw in the center of it the spirit of a man holding a child as he watched from above. I did not take note of what the details were. It was just what it was, too amazing, and yet too profound to comprehend.

As soon as the last note of the song was over, so was the vision of the open door of heaven tucked within the clouds above me. In its place was just an ordinary 9:30 a.m. blue sky. But the people beside me knew something remarkably beautiful, but unusual, had just happened. Their faces said it all.

The following night, the second day after we buried Gaby, I was brushing my teeth to go to bed. "Mommy!" The tiny spirit of light was there again before me; she had appeared within the wind troubled. "Mommy, please come to my garden tomorrow." She demanded in an annoyed voice. *"I wonder why she is upset?"* My motherly spirit asked my soul.

"Of course," my spirit answered back.

"Mommy, promise me, all right? Promise me you will come!" she demanded loudly.

"I promise, sweetie," my spirit assured her.

I walked out of the bathroom and told my husband that Gaby had been talking to me again. "She wants us to go to the garden tomorrow," I said. I asked him to remind me not to forget.

As usual, my husband whispered, "Okay, all right," turned his back and walked away.

That was my husband's way of saying, "I love you… Whatever you say, it will be. I love you, even though I think you've gone crazy." I could see his body silently scream with such thoughts, but there was nothing I could do. After all, it was not my job to convince him or make him a believer of this new world of truth that comes down to bring to me the visions of life which is to come. I was only sharing so he would know in words what I can see, hear, and feel. At that given point, I could not deny I was in a fighting mode. I was fighting to make sense of my own life and the feeling that I'd been tricked. Yet, in the same being, I did not have a choice. I knew somehow, though, that I needed to fight to survive. As always, I'd come to a place of truth, my truth, that since I was a child, I felt displaced from everything called "normal" life. I felt alone.

God will grant one a husband. But it doesn't mean we will speak the same language or see the same vision of today and tomorrow. I can only respect what lies before me. I honor you in the same state of being. We can share the pain. We can share the love, even though we are both struggling and hurt in our own ways. We are both in the darkness of grief and sorrow.

—Evangeline

The following morning, my husband and I decided to go to downtown Honolulu. We decided to grab lunch before noon. After I ordered, I laid my hands on the table to relax. "Mommy, you promised," a soft voice said in a disappointing tone. There it was, a dancing, smoky-white, thin ribbon of a silhouette, smiling, brilliant, and an intelligent cloud, bearing the shape and form of my Gaby. She was within the wind… well, as hard as it is to put into words… she was a floating spirit in the wind. She was the spirit of the wind. The wind followed her wherever she went.

I examined the vision closer. My daughter's voice came as she approached me, appearing with such a smile. Her entire body was now a gentle light, not in the flesh, but a glowing light. She was all right in this state. She seemed complete, in every way, though she glowed with every word, in her expressions, particularly her smile. It was weird to see her character and demeanor remain the same, but no doubt, she was somehow happier, so confident and sure. I was, of course, dumbfounded and too out of myself to even ask what was wrong with what I was seeing.

"Yes! That's right," I yelped, punching the table. "Oh, my goodness!" I was alarmed.

"What?" my husband asked, suddenly surprised.

"Remember our baby's request? She's here with us in a fit. We've forgotten our promise," I said to him. We stayed at the table, though we both ate our lunch uneasily.

We quickly left the restaurant after eating and headed straight to the memorial ground. As soon as I got out of the car, my daughter appeared with the wind, in a panic. "Look, Mommy," she complained, pointing at her burial plot. "Mine is the only one like that." I held my breath in disbelief. Her grave mound had sunk about six to seven feet, leaving a hollow space on top of the garden.

I don't know what my husband thought after that, but I was certain my daughter's spirit, whom I so love, was surely not under that ground.

Spirit Heaven

Heaven Descended Engulfing All the Spaces in My Room with Pure White Light

A brilliant heaven came rushing down. My soul bewildered, my sorrow disappeared in the shadow of the pure light shining in fantastic brilliance. My mind disappeared; my spirit halted. My whole motherly being is made still, my spirit felt safe, and my torn heart as a mother was made whole. The brilliant luminosities announced at once the truth. In all my past journeys, of my childhood lost and disowned, I was made known that it is finished. Now is now. I am in this brilliant heaven, which is of bright light. I am at home, lost child of humanity's soul no more. I am found in the spirit.

—Evangeline

The third day after Gaby's burial was Sunday. Early in the morning, my husband woke up and headed to the bathroom to brush his teeth. I lay in bed, feeling so lonely, filled with emptiness, and horrified by the unfathomable pain, the burning sensation in my gut that never stopped. The ocean of deep, cold longing that kept me lost, but no one else knew it existed and kept on coming. My heart's silent cry to hold and comfort my child in the safety of the warmth of my arms was ongoing. I worried so much about who was going to change her diaper, dress her, hold her, and cradle her when she looked for me. *"Who is going to comfort her when she cries?"* I asked myself.

The thoughts devoured me to the point of insanity. I found myself, once again, so angry at something I could not see or touch. I felt someone had played a trick on me that made my daughter disappear. But most of all, I was furious that my innocent child had to go through such inconceivable pain before it happened. The only way to battle it was to empty my stomach and everything that I was—I wanted to throw up until I stopped existing. I cried endlessly to the point I could feel my insides churning and turning as it twisted into itself.

Curled into a fetal position was the only posture I could maintain. Then suddenly, a gentle young man's voice called "Sister." I kept my eyes closed, but the voice called again. "Sister, look," said the voice again. I opened my eyes, and there was my brother, who had been dead since the day of his birth, twenty-five years ago. He was standing before me; behind him were all the relatives I knew had died not long ago. They stood together in a circle, smiling with looks of compassion on their faces as they held hands and faced me. They were mourning with me. They, without words, were carrying a deep burden with me.

Oh, my God! My soul was jolted into shock. The dead were there to comfort me. My pain they were willingly bearing for me.

"Sister, look. Don't cry. We're not the ones holding her. Look!" He pointed at the ceiling, which was no longer a ceiling but a luminous, bright space of such peaceful beaming white light stretched so long; my heaven disappeared, and this one approached so fast I thought I was going to explode. Yet quickly, as I took a breath, a living diamond came down, followed by a blue ocean of infinite heaven that stopped nine feet above me, after the heaven's light had turned into a calm, kind image of a brilliant, seventy-foot light body of a man, who instantaneously warmed the entire room out of cold and darkness, was before me. I looked up, frozen. A handsome and kind man stood there in a dazzling robe, beaming with a white and intense light that enveloped all of heaven and lit every inch of the earth. An intense presence of peace was coming from his radiance, intention, and breath. His voice was so calm, so certain.

"Woman, cry no more. You have been given the gift to see the truth. The truth lies before you. Do not deny the truth," he ordered. Then I heard a clap. A sudden happy, presence and all cheer filled the brilliant space of humble wind with gladness. Then there was a delightful squeal of a child that my spirit recognized so deeply. I was shocked. On his right arm sat my daughter, Gabriella, also dazzling with such intense, bright, white rays of light. Everything that Gabriella is was there again… as if nothing had ever been wrong. *"Sweet mercy, you're back? Dear God, you're alive!"* My mind uttered, my mouth and jaw dropped.

With joy and a smile, she spoke, "Mommy, rest, okay?" pointing to the bed. "Because in this many months"—she counted her fingers, thirteen times—"I have a surprise for you." She smiled. The Man and my daughter both looked at me. More brilliant peace shimmered and gladly went through me, followed by a vision of a little infant girl, filled with birthmarks on her stomach, was handed to me. Then as quickly as they had appeared, they were gone at the same time, leaving me alone in a frazzled state of disbelief, baffled and surprised.

The room was no longer the same. A light of heaven that is not of earth had altered its state of being. My body was no longer cold, not hollow. I could feel my gut and all my veins light up. They were made strong. I could think. I could hear my mind reason. I could no longer cry. I couldn't move, however. I was in a state of absolute peace and felt so gently cradled by the warmth of the light that had just shone so brightly through my flesh and bones and into my blood; the light had fed the core of my miserable, hungry, and thirsty soul to life again.

My spirit was quiet. For the very first time, it did not want to think, cry, or ask questions. I was frozen, soundly stilled in a moment of peace, as if the antidote to my grief was injected into every cell of my being. "Cry no more"—the echo of how it was said ran through my mind and body over and over again; it had become the voice that had taken over me. But how could He, who now holds my daughter, expect such a difficult task from me? Does He know something about me that I don't know yet about myself? That is the question that has been lingering in my heart to this day.

After it happened, my husband came out of the shower. "Wha—" he stepped into the room. He stopped and went back into the bathroom. He thought for a second. He paused, took a breath, and stepped into the room in his bare feet again. "What happened here?" he asked after he had taken a long, deep breath. His chest expanded. I could see his body rise. And for the first time in his military-controlled mind, he ran to me in a childlike state in disbelief.

"John! She's alive! She's alive! Gaby is alive! She was just here!" I screamed in disbelief. After my mind settled down, I told him the story.

"I believe you," he said, hugging me in surrender.

Self-Redemption: Messenger of Good News

Within the breath of man is a silent grace; it is a glory of everlasting wisdom. It is the living energy that powers the body; it is the breath that makes love arise out of the unconscious. It is the eternal force that comes to transfigure a soul from the flesh, to make self, rise as a human babe, to learn the strengths of its feet, to stand straight in the grace of its knees, as it walks amongst humanity in the quest of its secret light. When creation in the vessel dies out of humanity, it is so his spirit may transcend, to rest, and experience its divine beauty, a body of living spirit and the light of everlasting love. He awakens from his own journey; in birth on earth, he is made flesh and called a human babe. But in dying of the flesh that he rises in spirit and once again is made pure light of conscious breath. He is love. He is pure. He is God's. In love and light, He is the haven of all eternal peace, the heart of our awesome and infinite refuge and safety.

—Evangeline

Self-Redemption: Love beyond Death, Time, Body, and Soul

A few weeks after we had buried my daughter Gaby's body, I was all alone. My husband had to resume work on the mainland. I was at the graveyard every morning and afternoon to tend to what I could touch, which was the newly spread pieces of green grass that lay on top of her plot and a piece of four-by-four-sized paper that gave her name, the date of her birth, and the date of her death.

One afternoon, I found myself crying again. It is not having the ability to touch and hug my baby daughter because she's beneath the earth; it blanketed me in great emptiness. I felt cold and so alone.

"Stop it, Mommy!" suddenly ordered this small light that hovered over me. She was all smiling in the shape and character of my Gaby.

"I'm so sorry," my spirit replied quickly.

"Mommy," she smiled, "I want you to meet him," she said and pointed to another smiling spirit that belonged to an old man. "Mommy! Tell that woman over there"—she pointed to the crying woman at the next gravestone—"that he is all right. She needs to know, Mommy, that he is here," she ordered me.

I walked down four gravestones toward the only other person in the garden at the time. "Excuse me," I pardoned myself. "Who is that you are visiting?" I asked her.

"My husband," she replied, wiping her tears.

"Does your husband? Ah… when you last saw him, did he have two missing teeth from his left upper jaw and three gold-plated teeth in the same jaw that shined when he smiled, and that's how you knew, even from afar, that it was your husband smiling at you?" I asked her all at once.

"Oh, yes." She nodded. "Uh-huh, that's him." She smiled. "That's him." Then she stopped and asked, "How did you know that? Did you know my husband?"

"No, ma'am," I answered. "I apologize for coming to you. I know it must feel like an intrusion, but I am just taking an order from my daughter. She has been appearing to me in spirit, but for the very first time, which is now, she has brought a friend with her.

"And her friend is a man of old age, about seventy-two, and he's wearing a yellow shirt and brown pants—"

"Yes, that's my husband's favorite attire with flip-flops."

"Yes! And he is now with us. Well, his spirit is with us here in the garden now, as well as my daughter's spirit," I explained.

The woman wailed in her tears and disbelief. Then the old man's spirit spoke, not in a language but in the form of a movie screen, which my spirit understood, and my tongue voiced out. Before I knew what was happening, I had described his life story, which had matched her life memories with him— the story of how they met and how they led their lives, including the time he stayed in the hospital, where he died. His message was for her to let go of the guilt, that he loved her, and that he hurt seeing her in pain and in a self-punishing state of grief and depression. He was with her now to let her know he is not dead and his love for her lives on. He was all right. He was also with her sisters as well as his own sisters, who had all passed one year apart from each other. In the end, he wished her happy birthday and happy anniversary, which he would be part of since he was with her all the time, watching over her and keeping her company, especially at night.

The old lady became a close friend of mine as time went by. If she had some issues about her forty-two-year-old son, she asked her husband in heaven what he thought. I found myself delivering messages back and forth, over, and over again.

My daughter was and still is very kind. I felt she was so happy and eager to keep me busy. I found myself dreading to visit her memorial garden if I only had an hour to spare out of my day because just as I saw her spirit, I also saw her friends, the other spirits who were already fixated on me with their smiles as they stood on their own gravestones, waiting for their living husbands or wives to arrive.

The spirits knew I would help them and make their living spouses the recipients of good news—I would be their voices and give them a kind and gentle assurance of love, as they were eagerly and excitedly given to from spirit to deliver. But their love was not just ordinary love. Their love, which they illuminatingly and passionately shared, was continuous and ever-living. It was no different than the love of Jesus Christ—a love that had defied all odds, which defied all the suffering and the finality of death, which I have come to experience.

I had not witnessed the Man of Peace in a body on earth. I cannot confirm the history and make certain He died on the cross and ascended to heaven. But here now in my life is a Man of Light and Peace, a comforter to the grieving mother. He is a giver of a new breath. A giver of a new heaven, He makes the door that makes spirit from heaven open so they may come in full light and glory of pure love. He had come down from His white and light-filled sky and brought within my heaven His peaceful heaven so He could deliver the living, joyful spirit of my daughter back to me. I had gratefully witnessed my daughter's spirit descend, deliver her love, and be comforted safely in His arms as they ascended to heaven lovingly. I lit up and was made strong by encompassing compassion and true love and mercy that came without having needed to earn them.

Every visit to the garden had become a heavenly place of rest. Time stops when I am there. I feel alive. I forget about my sorrow. I find that when I am carrying and sharing the burdens of others, my sorrow subsides. More and more, I find that my time has already been prearranged by someone I cannot see, but I know is of the light of heaven. The force is all-powerful. It can make earth's sky move in accordance with the purpose of love, which is being bestowed from the heart and light of this secret, unknown, yet kind heaven.

I frequently find myself being a visitor to a new, bright, and light-filled loving space. This garden is hidden but all-encompassing love it illuminates immensely the secret caves of heaven and the universe only to find I am there to see a spirit who is in dire need to give me a message for a loved one, so he or she will know that the spirit of the one who has passed is all right, with no physical scars, just an emotional concern for the one he or she left behind. When heaven and earth move, I only have to obey, for it is in doing that I find my purpose. In serving others, I am basking in the heaven of light. Here I am safe. It is a temporary source of peace, which has served to be the greatest and lasting tonic for my so unrecognizable, punctured, heavily scarred, tormented, bitter, and often very cold and lonely, soul yet with a desire to be a kind and good mother of a heart.

Such is the reality every mother and father who has lost his or her beloved child or children has to learn to live with. It is the most unnatural existence a soul could ever face, to have to swim out of the raging water, for every day has turned into a river of survival where the water is deep and rough; yet darkness never surrenders. The only way to float is to swim all alone, against the tides of the norm, armed only with unseen hope and faith. In the dark bubble of grief, I am not allowed to get tired. I must always stand watch, or the unmerciful and demonizing power of grief's tormenting waves may once again take hold upon my weak soul. It had already plunged me upside down and thrown me into a ruthless and cold dungeon, where even I could not hear my own cry, where I was blinded and could not see my own self, and where, most of all, it had turned me into an angry, strange soul who had become irrelevant to anything I once called life… my life.

Ten

The Fifth Stage of Grief: Surrendering to Life's Course

In breath, you have your being. In your light, you are spirits of eternal love that give rise to the conscious force, which charts the depth of the purpose of human existence. You are the light that comes to govern the infinities of creation. You are your heavenly Father's spirit child.

—Evangeline

A decision to live for the two of us as I learn and allow my child's love to carry me through gives me purpose.

I did not know whether my misery was coming from losing my daughter or losing the life I used to know. Both, I suppose. But there's more. I was too angry to face the truth. I had no control over life… my life. My life without my control had no meaning. Everything is gone. Meaningless. To make sense of it all, the night I wanted to commit suicide, I thought about what my daughter would feel if I had pushed the gas pedal in my car. I got scared. Then I thought about what happened to people who commit suicide.

According to Catholic teaching, they go to purgatory or hell but not heaven. The thought of disappointing her ate me up inside. It was then that I decided to contend with what grief has to offer; I must live life by fighting the best way I knew how. Now I hurt. An immeasurable pain I embody for missing my daughter. This is how it feels. I cried. Cried, I did, until I could gain the strength to think. I drove myself home, still crying; yet, something big had happened inside me, when I decided to listen to myself hurt that night. There was an inescapable silence that accompanied me home and brought me to a calm sleep for days on after. Accepting life on its terms, but not mine, had suddenly, to my surprise and disbelief, expelled me to a new space of being where I could feel free, breathe, and finally just be me, myself. I hurt, but it's okay. There's no rush. Everything is gone. No one cares. I heard my own feelings. I found I am in here, with me. Within myself is my breath of compassion and love. Not out there needing finding or saving. I need only to be here. Let go and breathe. So here I am all along. Here I am free to expand in thoughts. I am a space, conscious only to breathe an ever-expansive love and light out of this magnificent and ever sacred calm of darkness. Here no voices come. Only my own heart speaks without a voice, yet my thought is the entire body in space in myself and the rest of the universe. I feel all that is calm. I hear what is the silent serenity of love. So I breathe the sacred empty and calm space. I can hear all that is nothing. Space is peace. I am in peace. I am the breath of peace.

    I woke up sensing that in myself, I am outside of any mankind's created reality. It was the first time in a long time that I felt peace hover over me, and somehow it hasn't left me. Every day since I learned that peace comes only when I accept that life is perfect in its design to give and support life in a pattern, nature will consciously manifest it. *Life is a season of love, no matter the time, and my struggle is in my dilution that it needs saving.* Love, I understood, is perfect in all its intention and meaning. But Father Pedro forgot to mention this truth when I was a child, lost and afraid, searching for the meaning of my life, searching for a good God, to give answers to my questions. Why? Why did God allow me to be born into a frustrated, angry, and always hungry reality, where everyone is pissed off and afraid? All the women around me were all postpartum depressed and short-tempered. The men went to the fields; all day long, they could barely converse because all the self-conservation needed that day was spent in silent thoughts under the sun in the fields. So I went to God's house. I searched for God there, but what came out was God's guy. I needed an answer. Taking a long deep breath, I knew I was hungry and depleted. I was so hungry for loving and compassionate guidance. Out came Father Pedro. Kind. Well-meaning. He was certain he knew me at the age of eight. Then I realized there were many Father Pedro's in my world. I found that Father Pedro had so many brothers with the same uniforms. Whenever I happened to find God to answer my questions, all I heard and saw from all the thousands of masses they gave was one thing, I am guilty. My priest and religion said I needed saving. Father Pedro's brothers were certain that something was not right with life and me. Life and I needed saving. It is in guilt that I found where my ancestors' cause of poverty lies. I have lived life looking for someone to tell me I am innocent. I did not commit any sin. So I had been looking for me ever since. My ancestors did not know me. My church said they know me. Father Pedro lives but could not answer why I am me? Why I live? Why did I hurt? Why am I lost? Why am I called a sinner just because I am a child of Adam and Eve?

Driving home in silence and in the darkness came the spirit of light. The light gave me the answers to the questions I had asked when I was but a child. I learned that life is my child Gaby. In loving her, I see my worth. Life is the children in all of us. It is the light that shines brightly in my daughter's spirit when she comes to get mad at me for being a stubborn-minded creature that was going to give up my love when sentenced by grief, even though I was raised and governed by fear. Life is when fear was banished away. Life is when she blasted me in full illumination through her effervescent presence, shining her pure love. Life is when I looked up at the open heaven of light that she came from, and all I could hear my heart utter is the light of truth. Every *man* is a *spirit*. Every *spirit* is *light*. Every light is pure radiance. Every ray in full illumination is an extension of the body of the light of the eternal spirit, the Holy Spirit. Every child is a child of God, a *God of love and peace*. And certainly, after Father Pedro died, it was his angels, Christ, and my daughter's spirit that made sure his spirit awakened to the same light. He is love, and he needs not saving, because in love, Father Pedro's spirit, and all children of the world, are pure in the heart of his Father, our Father in heaven, and our God of love, our eternal and forever home, the heaven of peace, the life that gives beats to our human hearts. *Pure in light, brilliance in love, we are the children of God of peace and love.*

It all made sense to me why there is the need for Father Pedro to tell me his truth. Religion is human-made. It is of earth's mind's creation. It is not perfect. It was for me, very convictive and condemning. Religion itself will never know me. It will never know Gaby nor the billions of pure spirits of humanity on earth. It will never truly know Christ unless it knows and accepts the Holy Spirit's unceasing essence of the Father's light is pure mercy, an amazing and eternal grace. Religion continues to condemn the spirit of the Heavenly Father in all humanity. Religion will survive with any man's mind and pride. But religion rooted in the love and body of compassion, peace, love, tolerance, acceptance, and forgiveness rather than the law of business and fear, gives life and sanctuary to a kinder and gentler heart of the lost spirit of the billions of spirits of the whole, united families of sacred humanity. I took a long deep breath. I heard a fatherly, gentle voice from heaven, "Eat of all the trees and fruits of the land. But the fruit of good and evil, do not eat of it. Or you will die."

"Shit!" I cried. All my life, religion told everyone and me that we are children of good and bad! That's why I was angry. The assumption that everyone is bad, and self is good, has divided the heart and mind of humanity. The truth is, we are each love no matter where we are born. No matter who our parents are. In spirit we are one light. In spirit, we are life. In spirit, we are peace. Oh my God! Have we all been duped by the religion of good and evil? The fruit this garden that has given even the pure in spirit the ability to forget itself and serve fear, anger, and death. We are the light of love. We are a brilliant breath of peace. We are eternal life having been blessed by being bestowed by our Holy Father to be given a body through making love of our parents. Our very foundation in the flesh and spirit is love. Oh, my goodness!

My daughter died not because she is a child of Adam and Eve. Our ancestors and loved ones before us have died, not because they were evil.

Gaby died not because I am bad, not because I am a sinner, not because I am her mother.

"Child, all humans are birthed from spirit. Every human child will come out of its sacred mother's womb, will grow, be made strong in season, to create his humanity. Once the spirit work is finished, the created soul and its body is to die. All human children are birthed out of love of creation… Child, as spirit, you come to create good and kind humanity through the blessed mercy and season of the sacred flesh, the human body. It is the spirit's law to create love in spaces your consciousness has chosen to be a part of. It is the law of spirit's breath to love and to light all spaces with peace in full glory, with every breath you take. You in spirit are light. You are life. You are to love your self, mind, body, and soul as one whole being in order to experience the journey of true humanity. But if living on earth and in the body is suffering, and suffering becomes living, it is the law of love that you do not serve the entity of human minds. Fear, which is not yours, nor shall you serve any human diseases of misery. You are children of love. In my light, in my arms, you shall come home. My heart is love, and heaven's arms are your haven of light. Your peace, which is your being, is my peace and my heaven."

A week later, I saw my daughter's spirit and heard her get mad at me for wanting to give up. I prayed that Jesus would show me a church where I could honor myself and be myself in peace and unspoken prayer, so I could hear my good emptiness expand. I found St. Christopher's Church in Kailua. I go there in peace. Not having the need to find who I was. I come in peace. I go to serve my love, give myself time to align my being with the peace and love of Christ, Heavenly Father, His Holy Spirit, the angels, and our ancestors. A spiritual union, in my peaceful surrender.

Love is self, one with its maker's substance. Breath and love is every child in each sacred human suit, our body. Mankind, though the vessel in the brain and body of man, though it may be protected by the ego's blind eyes, sheltered with the sting of religion's condemnation and judgments, though made known to be a sinner, humanity's truth reigns above all creation; humankind is a divine child. It is a spirit of love and the breath of peace.

—Evangeline

Heal. Let go. Write what makes you willing to surrender to life's course: Being a child of God. I want to surrender the fear in my heart. I want to trust God. My life is precious.

_____
_____
_____
_____
_____

Looking back at your life, what are you grateful for?

_____
_____
_____
_____

Eleven

The Sixth Stage of Grief: The Demeaning Power of Depression

Don't Let the Power of Grief Take Over
Your Body and Breath of Love

"Mommy, love is more potent than grief. I was watching you when you and Daddy buried my baby body. You see? I am not dead. I am spirit before I came into the body, which your womb had prepared for me in eight months' time. I am the spirit that gave life to my body. I am the brilliance that lit my smile. I am the radiance that wells out of my eyes. Light is the Father's love and body. Light is Jesus's heart and body. I am the same. I am light. I am love. Just like all the angels and all human families in space, you call heaven. We are the hearts of true life. We are love. Love is light. Love is the food of light. Light makes all darkness vanish. Mommy, I am who I am. See me for who I am. I am where you are—always in your love. I am who cannot vanish. When my suit died, I am that who left the flesh. I was freed from my pain. Jesus and the angels came with many children. I rose with Jesus. We came home to the Father. Now Jesus and the Father are with me. With the spirits and the angels, we are the space. We are always with you in spirit, in thoughts, and your love."

—Evangeline

I came to terms that grief is of "no other man's land," a place all to myself. While the city and life buzz with the busy domain, though I may be in it, I hear nothing; I see nothing. It was my own island of existence. I wanted no one to come to shore. "I know what you're going through," a lady told me. I thought to myself, *"Believe me, sister. Unless you have been there and truly understand what I am going through, then you would not be saying such words."*

Only another mother who has buried her two-year-old child would recognize the language of my unbearable pain. Such mothers who have gone through the same trauma can only cry this kind of sorrow. This form of agony is not torture known to any humankind, but a deep, hollow, cold, sea of darkness that kills the light of the spirit, paralyzes the breath, and ends the life of the soul, while the heart still beats. "My arms are tied, my mouth is frozen, and I have lost the ability to speak. But I appreciate your effort to comfort me," I said.

But in the back of my mind, I hurt. I had wished that her compassion would have been enough to make a difference, to console my motherly soul. How I wished the pain didn't sting so much, to walk again. The truth of the matter is, there isn't a word out there that can make any difference because the only medicine for my broken heart is to have my daughter back in my arms, alive, happy, just the way it all was without the pain, the way it all should be as every mother holds their children at these very moments.

I heard once that life is a decision. *"So everything in life must come with a decision to live,"* I thought. Without wasting any more time, I decided. I do not want to surrender to grief. I don't want to die that way. I will not allow it. I have to take action. I have to fight. I have to put my life back in order. I cannot let my daughter lose the battle of life a second time by seeing me suffer. I cannot give up! If she sees me die, all her dreams and hard work die with me. I cannot let her die a second time when I failed to rise above grief and did not aim to live her dream for me to be alive and happy, which I knew she carried for me.

For days, I was delusional and dazed. I knew I was unstable, but I knew I needed to move on for her. I thought of her smile. I found it was powerful enough to fuel my days ahead. It had become my pillar as I reminded myself that I am the sole carrier of her dreams; that is why I had to find a way to move on and not let her sweet smile fade away with the dark winds of grief and loss.

Two weeks after my daughter was buried, I was back again at Tripler Hospital for grief counseling. During our conversation, my therapist stood up because a lady knocked on the other side of the door.

"He's gone!" the lady whispered.

"No," my therapist argued.

"He did not make it out of the emergency room. He's gone! Just now," the lady's voice said again. My therapist sat down, red in the eyes, with a stone-blue face, quiet.

"Is everything all right?" I asked her.

"One of my patients, a father, just lost his boy three weeks ago. He had refused to eat or drink anything since. He had been in and out of the hospital. He was brought to the emergency room. The doctors had been working to save his life, but he finally gave up… completely," she said.

Upon hearing the words, my heart sank. "How old was he?" I asked her, now in tears. How painful to see someone go through what I was struggling to get out of, and yet see them lose. I couldn't blame him; my heart yearned for Gaby's warmth and sweet smile. My heart hurt.

"Thirty-two, I think," she answered.

"Too young," I whispered. My tears fell because I knew everything the young father felt and why he did what he did—to be with his son. For a second, I thought of his joy of reuniting, holding his child in his arms. I smiled inside, but quickly, I cried. I wanted so badly to be with my daughter. In my mind, I thought he was brave. I was a coward. I cried not so much for him and his son, but my tears fell because I knew my daughter would be so happy to be with me as I would be with her.

I had to stop and reason, see the truth. Something inside me knew how hurt Gaby would be if I had not fought for the life she could not have. If I fought for my life, then she would see that time could heal the wounds of my spirit and this was the only way to heal her pain. If she had seen me fight to laugh one more time, then she would know the reason she wanted to be born to begin with, and she would also have her laughs through my experiences. If I fought so her daddy would not be alone in grief, then she would know I was aware that if she could have fought for her breath, she would have done everything she could so her daddy and I would not be in so much pain.

But she was only two years old. Her body was weak. And believe me, she fought every turn she could. Now it was her turn to see me fight for the two of us and for the sanity of the rest of our family, who suffered so much loss when she had to leave her body.

I knew it was not a coincidence for me to be at the hospital and learn about the death of the young man who could not fight. I knew it was meant for me to hear and know exactly how powerful and deceiving grief could be when it creeps up. It takes over the entire body and soul as if no one ever owned it.

I felt so many times that my spirit was being held by my daughter's string of love. My body, however, was yet another story. My heart would palpitate so often as if it was telling me it was throwing a fit because of its loss of joy. Doctors had done what they could and saw nothing wrong with it. But when I had an episode, it would hurt so terribly, squeezing hard, literally stopping the normal flow of the blood to my limbs. Then the rest of the day was a struggle. To stand up was a struggle. To pick up anything from the floor was painful. To do chores around the house was such a fight.

So despite the fact that I was lucky because just as the man who held my daughter said, I had been given a gift to see the truth, as I do see my daughter, and my spirit acknowledges she is alive and well in her spirit body, I became aware that my body has its own hunger. My uterus would throw a fit by cramping and twisting inward as if it was looking to sense her presence. It would push my brain to think of her and ask where she was. Then my brain would want my arms to feel her and hold her in order to experience what it had always been, complete. Sadly, when I could not deliver, the battle began—again. I felt powerless over grief.

SHINE LOVE, JOY, AND PEACE!

So I decided that the only way to be is not to give up. As the spirit of my body, I have to be courageous. I need to heal my body by taking ownership of the responsibility to nurture my feminine self. I can never have Gaby's body back. But I have my motherhood body to heal so it can give life another chance by healing my mental body of grief. In mind, the heart is broken. But in love, the heart and mind can learn to heal again. As the mind heals, my body will be encouraged to get back to wellness, existence.

Heal. Let go. Write in words how your grief is manifesting in your body now. What pain do you begin to feel? What parts of your body are hurting? Remember what Jesus said: "All feelings have words. All words are feelings." Write your pain out of you. Cleanse your emotional house. Now give your pain a voice so you can heal your heart, mind, and body:

_____
_____
_____
_____
_____
_____
_____

How do you plan to heal your mind and body?
The spirit is holy. It is love. It is the pure light of kindness.
The body is the vessel; it is a suit for the spirit.
The mind is the emotional body of your heaven and earth, human experiences—love, pain, joy, dreams, sorrows, grief, are housed within the mind. Take the sorrow out of your mind. The body's pain will be healed. When the mind is kindly healed and honored, the spirit will once again dwell in the body. You will know that you are a child of love—a breath of peace.

—Evangeline

Twelve

The Seventh Stage of Grief: Learning to Understand, Life Goes on, Love Keeps on Growing, Love Will Keep on Shining

Be Happy for Me, Mommy; Love Me Now for Who I Am

Before there is garden earth, there is the spirit of heaven, where love is light. The spirit is love. The spirit is the breath of peace. The spirit is born from spirit. The spirit must return to its Spirit Father and Mother—the spirit family of love and peace, the source of life, and the breath of humanity's family.

—Evangeline

I watched her die. I buried her body under the ground, yet she comes out from the door of new heaven in the pure luminosity of joy. Her new body is radiance in pure light. She is whole, brightly shining. She is contented. So free. So bright. She is always at play. She runs infinitely without tiring. She flies to the sea of universes everlasting. Her human pain is no more.

—Evangeline

One day, out of the necessity to survive for my husband and my family, I discovered a space outside that is also connected to me, where I sensed a beam of light shining on me—life rushed through my entire body. I seemed to have stumbled upon it when I finally acknowledged the truth. Since the first day of her death, my daughter was free from the bondage of the pain that had robbed her of a normal livelihood. I finally accepted the truth for what it was. Just the thought of it made my spirit smile. But I just had to hear it to feel complete, hear my tongue say it out loud so my ears could deliver it to the rest of my body, so my brain could believe it when it heard the words. I cried out, "Now she is flying free! Now she can talk! She can fly! She can be anywhere she wants to be! That is why she was involved in my daily life; that is how she has become a coordinator between heaven and earth."

Without question, she had worked so hard to let me know she, in spirit, is happy to be free, a freedom a mother could not give her child, but was all possible from the mercy of the divine alone. This truth I was assured life is founded on. My spirit was lit up by this truth. And every word the spirits have uttered in light have echoed through my veins, enlightening my entire body, nourishing my poor soul to life again.

With this in my heart, days, weeks, and months went by as I lived slowly regaining my senses. I began feeling the warmth of the sunshine again. Her spirit keeps me company still. She came and went with the wind. I got used to her spirit as she was always smiling. I began trusting the existence I could not see, for it was all right not to see where she headed when she disappeared from my side. Though it was too good and too weird to acknowledge her new form—her energy and her unbelievable light—I was forced to know it and slowly accepted that it was truly there. Such occurrences cannot be taken lightly. It was the only thing that made sense.

One such day happened three months after I buried her body. My heart of stone had been softened, an invitation for me *not* to live in anger. She taught me how to open my eyes to see her new world; the ears of my heart were forced to hear her shouts, not to deny her, but to acknowledge her new existence—alive and whole in the spirit.

I will never forget that day. I was driving one morning, and all of a sudden, it hit me. She was gone. She will never come back. I cried so hard that I did not realize I was on the road, driving carelessly. Then I heard a scream. "Pull over, Mommy!" she ordered. It was such a demanding force of energy coming from her as if I was the little girl, and she was the mother. I pulled over to the side of the road. I looked around after thirty minutes of wailing and saw I was parked on the side of the school playground. She stopped me earlier at the corner before I'd reached the point where children often cross the intersection. "You're going to Daddy, Mommy," she told me.

In her stern voice, I knew she loved me. Then I remembered when I thought my life was complete. I remembered how it was before she came.

We were stationed in Marine Corps Base Hawaii when the visitation of Mother Mary, who told us something would happen in a year that would cause us to move out of our home. Sure enough, after the visitation, I had gotten pregnant and was told at five months' gestation that her heart did not develop properly. We were ordered to relocate to a hospital that would perform her much needed heart surgery. It was October when that spirit of a kind and ever-loving sweet lady appeared; as it stood in time, it was October the following year that it was fulfilled. On October 23, we were at the airport, leaving Hawaii. I was seven-and-a-half months pregnant, bewildered, afraid, but I had to be strong.

My husband had to get the only available job in Pax River, Maryland. To keep the job and stay in the Navy to support ourselves, he drove fifty miles to work and fifty miles back home daily. At eight months' pregnant, six weeks after we moved into our new home on Biltmore Avenue, I was induced a month early on December 4, 2002, and gave birth on December 6, 2002, in Bethesda Hospital. A day after, an ambulance transferred our newborn to Philadelphia Children's hospital, only to be told there was nothing they can do for her. We were told to take her home. Give her a quality of life. No one knew how many days she would have. I knew she had a purpose here. I knew she was meant to be born and live, for whatever reason I respect to know. We kept asking, looking, searching for someone who had the answer to her heart's anomaly. Three months later, we found Dr. Henly, from Lucile Packard at Stanford, in California. He was the only heart surgeon who was able to help her. She had her first surgery at seven months. We went back to Maryland and came right back to Lucile Packard for her second heart surgery when she was seventeen months old. It was Dr. Henley who told us that she needed six heart surgeries by the time she reached the age of twelve if she was to survive. After the second heart surgery, we went back to Maryland to recover. But the winter months were really cold. Quality of life was hard to come by when we were both cooped up in the house all winter. So her dad and I took her back to Hawaii. She died fifteen days later. Though it was hard on her father to leave me alone after her death, we did not have a choice. He had to resume work. He went back to Pax River, Maryland. Now it had been a few months; her spirit was telling me things I couldn't understand. But it kept on happening, anyway.

"Your daddy is in Maryland," my spirit answered. "I can't leave this island. I can't leave your garden," I cried to her.

"I'll take care of my garden," she demandingly insisted.

"Oh, dear God, I am going crazy. I am seeing things! Help me! Please help me!" I cried.

I drove to the beach and thought hard. I contemplated suicide again. *"How easy it would be,"* I began thinking, *"to be with her, to hold her, to feel whole, to feel complete all over again if I died. If I died, I believed that all the unknown depth of the great dark abyss, the infinite ocean of emptiness that was wrapped and flowing through and around me, would disappear."*

The thought comforted me. I felt empowered but so empty and depleted after.

Then without further ado, the phone rang. My husband was on the line. "I need you to pack your bags now. It's three o'clock your time, I got you a ticket. Get to the airport, all you have to do is show up at the counter, and they will issue you a boarding pass. You leave at ten this evening," he said. I was speechless. I felt good inside. When I closed my eyes, I saw my daughter smile.

Suddenly, I could understand why she had to be there. My husband was worried about me. In a way, I was thankful that she was there during my breaking point, as I was consumed by a whirlwind of an absolute world of strange emptiness, self-pity, and helplessness; it was the toughest moment of great poverty. I could feel my body deteriorating slowly. Already, my mind too, had begun its journey to wear my spirit's hope down. Despite it all, it dawned on me that even in spirit, she was protecting me from harm. *"Its time,"* I thought *"I would be a complete fool not to listen to what she had to tell me."*

What followed after that event was shocking. Gaby's spirit was determined to carry me out of pain to show me that she knew everything that was going on in my life. Indeed, she knew more than I could ever understand.

When I got to Maryland, my husband met me at the airport with such kindness, beyond the kindness I had ever received from him. He spoke ever so gently, held me close to his seat when I sat in the car, and eagerly talked to me about the house we were going to where he had been renting a room. He talked about many things, again very gently. I knew he was in pain, grieving in his own way, but it was something we must not discuss—anything about Gaby, or we might face danger, never to get up from falling into misery once again.

The first week I was there, I felt tired. I could not speak. I was very weak, not just my body but from within the core of my spirit. My mind was exhausted. I was lying in bed one night, half awake and half asleep when I saw a luminous light again. "Mommy, I am coming back to you, don't worry." She smiled and disappeared. The second night, she appeared again, smiling. "Mommy, isn't it nice? I am coming back to you," she said.

"I can't handle caring for a sick child again. I am afraid my heart could not take it. It would explode. It would die," I said to her.

"No, Mommy, I'll be very healthy. I promise," she said and disappeared.

The third night, at about the same time as the previous two nights, I was half asleep. The voice of a young lady called, "Mommy!" She was all grown-up; from a toddler, she had grown into a thirty-year-old woman of graceful light. Her energy was gentle. She glowed in front of me. She sat next to me and caressed my hair. "Mommy, don't worry. I will come back to be a mommy to my two boys. You see, that's why I will be very healthy this time," she said.

She showed me a glimpse of our future together: me in my late sixties, with gray hair, and her, now a mother, with her husband, walking close to where we were both standing at the beach somewhere in Hawaii.

Later in the scene, two blond boys following their father's footsteps came running toward us as they called my daughter, "Mommy." After she delivered the scene, her spirit kissed me. Then she disappeared as mystically as she had appeared. I cried and cried for the rest of the night upon receiving that news. It was, for the most part, a cry of thanksgiving. But I could not deny that my tears fell because I could not comprehend the meaning of the message. Surely it was to tell me about the future, to give me hope. But I struggled so much. For what I needed was to have her back—the Gaby I knew, my tiny Gaby, my baby Gaby.

Six weeks after the vision, I went back to Hawaii. I went immediately to the graveyard in a taxi. The following morning, I went back to the garden, as usual. I changed the water of her flower vases and sat. Suddenly, I looked up. The sky above me came down. Out came a Man of Light, in a dazzling white gown. "It's you"—my heart bowed— "a man of peace, a man of love and light," my heart spoke eagerly.

This man, with a body of brilliant light, breathing a breath of brilliant peace, came to me when I was a child. I was eight years old in the deep boondocks of northern Philippines when he first appeared to me. Our unexpected meeting had caused me to question who I was. What I was. And what my relation in life was. Why was my world filled with poverty, struggle, suffering, while a shout of deep and innate yearning white fire burned within my being, urging me to keep on looking forward to finding something great, something that is me, yet I did not know what it was?

I was born in the Philippines, to my Mother, who had been divorced from her first husband in Pangasinan. Grandpa was a heavy drunk, and in the height of his drunken stage of being had forced Mother, thirteen years old at the time, to marry the son of his friend. The man Mother was forced to marry was forty years old. The marriage was abusive, emotionally, and physically. Mother was granted separation from her husband. The judge ruled Mother to be with her eldest child, her son. And the youngest, her daughter, was ordered by the court to stay with her husband.

With her five-year-old son, Mother left the province to work in Manila, where she met Father. A year later, they got pregnant with me. They both left the city and came back to Bulacan, where Father was from. His families were farmers. There, they worked the farm each day. Mother helped Father, and she stayed home with me. Mother became pregnant four more times—all boys. I was the only girl. It was the fourth pregnancy after me that she was rushed to the hospital to give birth to my brother, but during labor, she suffered a heart attack. Father was made to choose who he wanted to live, Mother, or my baby brother. He chose Mother. My brother died in her womb during the C-section. Mother stayed in the hospital for three months. We had no money to pay the hospital, so she wasn't allowed to be released without money. Mother and Father borrowed money to pay the hospital bills from my aunt, in the promise that when she recovered, Mother will be a housemaid and a nanny in the city to pay her back. After her recovery, Mother left us to pay her debt, which left me to take care of the rest of the family. Father took us to Pangasinan to the boondocks near my mother's family so someone could look after us. Grandma, mother's mother, was busy. I was left to care for the boys at age nine. Father had to stay at the farm in Bulacan, five hundred miles away. I had to be a mom and a dad, most of all, a provider for my brothers. I got it done, relying on wild greens and fish from the rivers. I was alone most times in this struggle. It was in this ordeal that I had encountered something amazing. In the boondocks, on my way from fetching wild greens and fire wood from the jungle, the river water rose very quickly as it often does during rainy monsoons. The gushing flood water rose up chest high, very quickly. In an effort to get home, I decided to cross the river to get home before the sun came down, but in the middle of my swimming, a grass wrapped itself around my ankle; it pulled me under over and over again.

"Decide to live," I heard a voice say. Deep in the murky, swirling water, I saw the light above me come, and from the lit sky appeared a man with a bright white light body carrying a cross. Floating above me, he shone brightly. He reached his right hand down to me. In an effort to reach up to him, I kicked and fought to get up above the water. When I surfaced, I saw the eight-yard-long grass float away from me, while a yard-long one, all twisted and broken parts of the rest of the grass, surfaced next to me and was dismantled and broken. The salmon grass, which got a hold of my ankle, had twisted itself around my legs, catching me. With the violent force of the river water, it had begun to submerge and drown me into exhaustion. As the broken salmon grass moved farther away from me by the floodwater, I blacked out. When I came to, I was naked but alive lying on the side of the riverbank, on top of a mound of bamboo roots. I was exhausted. I dragged myself home in darkness. It was the beginning of my search for the answer as to who was the Man so kind, with the body of pure grace and light that rescued me from drowning. He was there when no man could see and hear my needs. He was there when I needed saving. Without his hands, I knew I would have been dead.

Many years passed; I left the jungle life to go to school, but life was tough for me. Still, I couldn't afford fourth-grade tuition. Proper education was a luxury made only for the rich. But I knew I wanted to go and finish. It was a struggle. Mother and Father fought constantly. I ran away at the age of twelve to get a job to help Mother and Father pay bills. I became a nanny in the city. I walked each day, confused at my suffering. I survived with much prayer. Church visits were a daily routine to ease my anguish. I was lost. But I was in search of someone or something that could lead me to the spirit of the Man of Light, who floated in midair holding the cross as he saved me from drowning at the river.

He comes! Life Goes On. Love Keeps On Growing

Truth Is Light That Shines on All Darkness Above and Beyond Time

While I walk the roads of mankind, I forget myself. I see and hear the pain of my own mind's insecurities. In the road of my forefather, joy comes few and far between. Yet as the cave of my mind dawns, I discovered another world before mine. In the light is another heaven. Its wind is peace. Both substances are in the spirit of each child of man, no matter the time and season of his journey. Each man is the breath of peace; he is the bread and body of love manifested on earth.

—Evangeline

When I was seventeen, a year after I had met my husband, I had a dream that I came up to a mountain that appeared from the side of the street that I often walked to get to work. The sun lit its presence with morning glory. Eager to not miss a thing, I ran fast to get up to one of the tallest mountains, in which the sun was shining brightly. When I got on the tip, there was the same man I had been looking for; only now, he wore a human body. He was five-eleven in height with glowing tan skin and about one hundred sixty-five pounds. He wore a white tunic and was surrounded by many sheep. He was a shepherd, carrying a staff as he stood by a lone tree overlooking the earth's surface. He was waiting for me. But before I could be with him, the sky rained an ice-cold shower and drenched me clean; every part of darkness in my entire being vanished and in its place was my brilliant body of light. Then he made the sun dry me. I felt new from within my entire being.

"Come," he said to me in a gentle and kind voice. "The Father waits for your coming." I looked up where his eyes were fixed. Up above the clouds was a huge castle. Its gate began to open in the sight of me. When I woke up, I felt comforted and knew I had entered a real-world that my eyes could not see, but my heart could remember and know and feel was real. A sense of overwhelming belonging made me feel at peace.

I knew that the dream was not just an ordinary dream. It was a blessed experience.

Six months later, after the dream, John, who had recently joined the Navy, had asked to be stationed from Guam to Subic Bay, proposed. We married in the Philippines in 1988. After three years of being stationed in Subic Bay, we moved to Japan in ninety-two and left for Hawaii in July of ninety-seven. We got pregnant in 2002 and gave birth to our daughter, Gaby, who died and was buried.

Risen

True Love Sees the Living Glory of the Heavens

When a child is born, it's not a miracle; it is divine grace. But when a dark and ironclad heart sees love, when it learns to be governed by such substance, it is the greatest miracle that shines beyond the hearts of all creation.

—Evangeline

On the third day after her burial, my husband and I were together in bed. He stood up to go to the bathroom. I stayed in bed. I was depressed. I sat up on the foot of the bed. It was still dark outside. Even though John was with me, I felt so alone. I was lost in the dark. I did not know that I could be swallowed by the darkness of complete sadness, that even my husband, who was next to me, could not help me. I cried, burying my face under the pillow so John couldn't hear me. I did not want to see him cry. I didn't want him to see me cry. As I recall, it was in those sad and darkened times that my perception between life and death changed forever. It was dawn. The sunrise was about to break. I went to Gaby's crib, thinking she needed me. I realized Gaby is not home anymore. She is not with us anymore. I felt an empty ocean had struck me. I cried. On my knees, I fell as my mind reminded me that she's buried underground. "Oh, my God!" *"She will never be with me at night to sleep. She's not here with me every morning when I wake up,"* I thought in sorrow. I wailed, tucking my face in between my knees.

Suddenly there was light. Then my apartment roof disappeared. There was a bright living light above me. I blinked. A bright heaven of light came down so rapidly that when I thought I was going to explode, I was silenced with awe and peace instead.

"**Woman,**" said the Man of brilliant light that the new light-filled heaven had ushered in above me. "**Cry no more,**" he sounded stern. "**You have been given the gift to see the truth. The truth is before you. Do not deny the truth,**" he spoke, and the brilliance of his body illuminated the entire heaven, which he made come down to light my darkness. His being shone away every suffering I had known.

Then, there was a great brilliance that sat on his right arm.

"Mommy! Don't cry!" She clapped with joy and pointed at the head of my air mattress bed. She was an all brilliant stream of white fluid radiance, a flow of abundant life and contentment was screaming, beaming out from her entire being. She was illuminating great health, and utter wholeness was streaming from her being of complete satisfaction, even the heavens, which ushered in her presence, were dancing in morning glory.

"Mommy! Mommy!" called my Gaby, who now glowed in her brilliant body of light. She was filled with joy.

"*She is whole. Glowing. Healthy! Smiling! Happy! She is so beautiful! She is a spirit full of light. She is gleaming with a bright life!*" My heart admitted.

"Mommy, don't cry! Because in these many months"—she counted her fingers, thirteen times— "We have a gift for you," she revealed. Then an awesome vision of an infant child was being handed to me. I knew the child was a girl. She was covered in birthmarks on her tummy.

That was the first, but not the last time, this man has come to me. The heavens, which is also the spirit of heaven, follows and obeys His presence. When He comes, heaven is open.

Heaven above the Graveyard

After a bubble of light appeared, His spirit came down from it. Now He stands before me with a child in tow.

"Woman," He let go of the three-year-old spirit of a little girl to come to me as He stood at the foot of my newly buried child's graveyard. The spirit child ran to me. I found a light within me, the light that shines like His body was in me. This brilliant light moved and reached its arms and embraced the spirit child. I noticed then that within me, my spirit moved without having moved my physical arms. It was my own spirit that embraced her with gratitude. Yet I was deeply humbled. He went back to His sky alone. My sky, the physical space that I was in, remained still after He drew His spirit away. My heart knew I was being comforted in spirit by this Man of Light, who brings forth the breath of calm and peace during my frail heart and mind's wicked sea of dark sufferings.

Heaven Knows My Needs

When I am all alone, there, you come to give me a new breath and a vision of a whole new and morning-filled life.
—Evangeline

Six weeks after His visit, immediately after He gave me the spirit of a little girl, I started feeling sick, much of it had to do with the pain in my stomach, a young Navy doctor was happy to break the news to me. He grabbed his rolling chair and sat in front of me. "Well, we have a good reason you're feeling queasy." He gleamed in a gentlemanly manner and said, "That's because you're pregnant." He stood and congratulated me.

My husband, John, was overjoyed after he found out that I was pregnant again. After one year of being away from me, John left Pax River, Maryland, and was stationed back in Hawaii to be with me. After being in the MILITARY for twenty-seven years, he was nearing his retirement. He wanted to retire in Hawaii. With Gaby being buried in Hawaii, there was no other land that would give us a sense of being family other than Oahu, Hawaii, where we bought a house. John was there with me every step of the way during all my hospital visits. A sense of purpose began to light his fatherly heart again. He went to work doing what he does best. A good leader, a Navy lieutenant commander, he showed up and served his country. He fixed problems at work. He came home each day tired, but there was a sense of satisfaction at the end of each day. He was excited to be a dad again. We both needed to be strong. We knew it's not the end. In our own ways, we still hurt inside. He couldn't hide from me, the times when he went to work in pain, but needed to be strong. I tried my best not to miss Gaby so much; I kept myself busy. But I was deeply mourning still. For months, I needed to see a doctor for heart issues. It was PTSD.

It was during my second pregnancy that communication with my first daughter's spirit slowed down drastically. And when it did, I felt the light of my spirit slowly dim down. I could barely see. I began losing the faith that carried me, the new world I was just beginning to learn to live in; my brain could not explain or understand. The little memories I had yet thus far, hid from me. I went to my second pregnancy in great turmoil. Alone and afraid. My human mind was weakened with anguish. My heart was drowning in a great ocean of misery; it ached for my beloved Gaby. I was torn. I was mad.

Three days before I was admitted to the hospital to give birth, I was in my bedroom, having such a hard time falling asleep. I was overwhelmed with the anxiety of natural birth, uncomfortable with the size of my humongous belly, and the baby inside me felt as if she was in a soccer tournament every thirty minutes.

Then, at three in the morning, the rhythm of my breath was interrupted. All the discomfort about my body had disappeared. I found myself staring at the bedroom ceiling, which was no longer a ceiling but an open sky. There was that "bright light" man standing before me smiling, wearing a dazzling white gown, who said, "It's getting close." I was looking for Him to show me my daughter, again, in His arms, just as when He appeared to me the very first time with Gaby. But He never did. He was alone this time. His presence, however, left me the comfort of knowing I would be all right.

Soon, I found myself in the hospital. I was induced three days earlier than my due date. My doctor was going to leave the island; I did not want another Ob-gyn to assist me. I checked in on January 4. On January 6, I gave birth to my sweet, healthy daughter, Isabella, born weighing seven and a half pounds and twenty-two inches long, with massive and strong legs shouting at me that she was healthy and strong.

It dawned on me that Gabriella's birthday was December 6, because she was a month premature. Isabella was born January 6, a birthday Gabriella would have had, had she been full-term at birth. Was it a coincidence? It does not matter. "It is what it is," as my husband said.

"Here comes the blessing!" I smiled, tiredly at him. At that given hour, a great unseen river of compassion overflowed from my being toward my sweet, sweet husband, who had been in deep turmoil since Gaby passed. I knew the day she died in the Tripler Hospital Emergency Room was the very second too that his spirit and soul was injured, as a man and as a father. The very hour that Gaby died was the end of his knowing of perfect innocence. Never would he be the same again. Everything was now altered. As she closed her eyes and never opened them again, the whole father that he was just an hour before we entered the room of the ER had ended. Immediately after Gaby's death, I watched him pray, looked, and begged the gods of the heavens to return her to him. For hours, over and over, he kneeled and begged and stood and cried. Silence remained. The cold wind persisted. He stood up. He came to me. "Please… Please tell me, honey. Please tell me this is not happening," he begged me as he touched our daughter's cold body, while I embraced her. I cried in return because I was silently pleading that he tells me to wake up because it was all just a nightmare. I hugged my daughter's lifeless body. It's completely empty. There's no one home. She's gone. What's left of her? There was nothing there that I used to know. Where there was joy and warmth, it was a strange wind that greeted all my senses with vast oncoming emptiness. My comfort and sanctuary that she was, her yelp, her smiles, her gleam and pure joy, were now all are gone. No trace to be had. Her body was now a hollowed shell. An abandoned space, it was a strange dark cave belonging, not to anyone, not even to the lost. It was cold. Harsh. So unresponsively quiet. It blasted my soul to a deafening abyss of firing anger. *No! This can't be. This couldn't happen. This can't be… Please!*

I begged that cold and alien wind of death till I couldn't blink until I couldn't see. I lost my ability to speak. My husband turned his back from me and went back to his corner of the room, where he'd been praying. He went down to his knees for the twentieth time to beg for her to come back. When he stood, his knees were torn, bleeding. My heart cried and screamed its loudest. Some loose pebbles had dug themselves into his skin; some were lodged deep into his flesh. He couldn't feel them. I could. I wish so badly that I did not know the kind of pain he was feeling. But my beloved husband's agony mirrored my all—my spirit, my flesh, my soul, my mind and my heart, the heart that promised to love him for eternity. I promised then that I would protect his heart. He will not hurt and be lost like that again, ever.

Fast-forward to the present. Now my sweet husband smiles. He holds in his arms our second child. *Our promised gift had come.* He is a father again. I was awakened within. I felt my breath rise and saw the bright light of heaven dawning and brilliantly lighting the room. My heart rejoiced for him. I could see the light dawning on us.

"A surprise!" my husband proudly lifted his second daughter and cradled her in his arms and cried. My eyes and heart had longed for such a scene, a father holding his daughter for the very first time once again. A moment I thought would never be, a chance I couldn't believe I had been given once more. It had arrived, and it was what it was, a blessing.

In my spirit, I understood then that time had all along been coming in secret, so that this moment may appear its present gift to me as a mother. This very hour had manifested to reveal that time would bring darkness into the season of my life, though it may have passed; yet in passing, another time came to bring light and new promise. Time, after all, was kind to me. I was glad I waited and did not commit suicide; that night, I had fallen into the deep trance of great sadness and misery. The night I wanted to drive my car off the cliff. Awakened and somewhat sober of darkness, it was made known to me that despite Gaby's death, love beyond the space of my mind, body, and soul is another heaven, and it had been looking out for me. I am humbly grateful that it exists. I am honored to confess; I don't know much about it—this new heaven and its love. But I am grateful that I am alive. I am eager to learn its secret while I am still living.

In my husband's new smile as the gift of our daughter arrived, I saw my husband's light again. Love is, after all, a divine destiny given on earth. I looked at my husband and sleeping, newborn daughter. I could only say thank-you to the eternal essence of love, love that is of heaven manifested on earth. I thank that moment for having given my husband's joy back once more, which was taken after being lost at Gaby's passing. I thanked the time. I thanked heaven for my husband's birth and presence in my life.

It was time that brought forth my partner in this life. It was divine love that has maintained and kept our friendship together.

My Best Friend

The Navy Is Our Family

Regardless of your vessel that grounds you to earth's life, know you are the meaning of love, family, and life. Life is with you that keeps on moving. Life is eternal, as it is an external love that keeps on expanding beyond all spaces and beyond all times. From heaven, you have come. On earth, you have come again. Yet this time is the only time that matters. You've come to be my best friend, a gentle father, and a kind husband.
—Evangeline

My husband was born in Ohio. He was the second child of four siblings.

His parents separated and divorced when he was eleven. He joined the US Navy when he turned seventeen. He was stationed first in San Diego, then went to Guam, and eventually the Philippines, where we met in 1985 and married in July 16, 1988.

From the Philippines, we moved to Japan, and seven years later, we moved to Hawaii. After five years in Hawaii, John was able to transfer to a shore-based unit and would not deploy for at least three years, and so we decided to get pregnant with Gaby. After all the hospital travel, John had never questioned what I could do for him. John is a loving, kind, and awesome father and a husband. He was a great enlisted chief petty officer and earned a promotion to an LDO officer in the US Navy and was always looking after his young guys' well-being and future. He saw himself in each young man he worked with on or off duty. He was always asking for permission to give them a place to come to during the holidays, all through the times we were stationed overseas.

"Honey," he came to me three weeks before Thanksgiving of 1996, "can we invite my guys for Thanksgiving this year?"

After a bit of running in my head how I was going to arrange a two-bedroom apartment living room furniture because the base housing didn't have any room for kitchen table, I replied, "Of course, we can."

"Yeah, I'll tell them I'll pick them up with the van. I may need to have other guys pick the others up."

"Other chiefs need to help you? Why?"

"We've got about seventy young men in our squadron," he assured me.

"Hmm," I paused.

"We need to ask the entire family of officers to share their meal. I'll have to book the high-rise party room so we can have Thanksgiving with your men."

With the help of the other chiefs' wives and some officers' wives who gave up their quiet dinner with their families, who gladly brought all their meals to the Thanksgiving table to share, we managed to have the longest tables and fun Thanksgiving I have always cherished all my life.

I am blessed. Life had been a life of being alone and surviving since I was born. Then the time came and brought my beautiful husband to me. Poverty gave me misery. Though I sought and did not give up, I was sent this amazing man. The search was long over, but now was knowing of the world for what it was, a blessing to cherish, as long as I have him to smile and share life with when it was bright, when we stood to immerse in joy in the birth of our children, when we must kneel and pray till we lost ourselves, even when the death of our Gabriella, our very first child, came to make us feel forsaken and afraid. We cried and morned together. I was not alone. He is with me. He is my blessing. *(He is my heaven on earth. Shhh, he doesn't have to know that all the time. I don't want his ego to think he is perfect.)*

Now we both are given a chance to hold another child for another time. We will keep the dream as parents. We are once again a family. With struggles and trials, time gives us the joy and love of family and parenthood. That is the greatest gift of love and union; so long as we know we are blessed to have this time and a second chance to see us through—I must hold his hands. Today a new journey has just begun.

The mind would want to give up when its heart is broken, but the time comes to bring good news. This is my good news. To see my sweet husband smile and hold his baby in his arms after watching darkness come the day we buried our first beloved child. All I want is this moment, to see him smile and fulfill his fatherly purpose—to love his children to the ends of time and the world—no matter what. It is why we must keep living and being here. Humanity is beautiful when the heart of a father is shining in full love for his children.

Heal. Let go.
Write what you know and understand about your own compassion toward loved ones, others, and toward life as you heal your grief:

_____
_____
_____

Who are you grateful for in this life? List the name of the person or the people that you know who have been there for you all your life. Write how you feel about them. Write what you are looking forward to experience with them once you heal your spirit.

_____
_____
_____
_____

Thirteen

The Eighth Stage of Grief: Healing; The Physical Manifestation of Fear

The Rise and Fall of Hope

In my human world, a deep wound rose from my heart. I felt it tear when my child died. I felt its cut everywhere I turned. But the blood of relief never flows. So I hurt through the bones and burned in the flesh. My tear ducts remained dry. My emotional tears never welled up, never spilled down my cheek to ease the pain of my deep sorrow. My mind was numb through it all. The only medicine that can cure the grief of each man is to allow the light of His spirit to come; for in His full radiance, He is the glory of His eternal love, sprang forth as ever-loving waters from the fountain above, where His divine understandings and compassions endlessly flow.
—Evangeline

I found that once a mother loses her child, life is destined to be painful at every gate unless something miraculous took place. It took a lot of strength for my spirit to be strong. My soul was always restless. My body hurt. My heart was always hurting. The mother in me was in a silent struggle. My soul's light was my child's presence. My comfort in living was to hold, touch, and feel her back in my arms, next to my heart. That is a yearning that this lifetime may not quell, except by faith in eternal love's presence in my current life.

After I gave birth to Isabella, all the connections with Gabriella vanished. It was then that I found myself no different than the waves of the ocean. As I see its tide rise and fall from morning to night, there was my emotion. I struggled to keep Gabriella's spirit alive in me as Isabella's demand for my love increased. With Gabriela's spirit, in my vision, I could fly like a bird, with expanded wings to kiss the edge of my heaven and beyond the higher heavens, I could see. It is true that love conquers all. It is beyond powerful; it's unlimited. That's what I have. That is what she taught me I am capable of achieving through spiritual understanding of humanity's divine life, and its immortality.

Without Gaby's presence, however, I shrunk down to the darkest pit of helplessness. I could not understand why the communications between us had to stop. There were so many nights and days I would wait and pray for her to come to me again, just the way she used to show up, all joyful, brightly smiling, and carefree spirit that she is. When she was floating around me, everything that I am was new and alive again. Even the sky was happy to see her.

I waited. But there was nothing. The sun did shine, and the black-and-white clouds were sometimes pushed through by some energy, but it was followed only by silence and stillness. Her spirit, which many times before had powered the wind in front of her, never showed.

Shortly thereafter, about six weeks into her spirit's absence, my ability to cope dwindled slowly with each passing moment. I fell into a deep depression. Simultaneously, I was put on two types of antidepressant drugs. When I took them, I felt the stem of my brain light up as I became disconnected with everything in front of me. I did not care when my second daughter, Isabella, cried. I was numb. I was not the same, not there. The medication was useful only if I was finding a way to escape the reality in which I was living. But my purpose in taking it was to be aware of what was in front of me. I wanted to be a good mother to Isabella as much as I was to Gabriella.

The inner battle was hard. I found that my body, the one part of me I must come to know, would drag me to the oblivion of misery if I did not fight it with the strength of my spirit. I was afraid to go outside the house. I sat holding my Isabella in the rocking chair from sunrise to sunset. I was safe in the chair. I was in control. If I changed the scenery, it was because I went outside the bedroom door. I would go into our living room, only to prove to myself what I already knew—anyplace other than the rocking chair is a place of immediate threat, unsafe. So I always ran back to the safety of the rocking chair, a ritual not to be broken for months and years.

I thought I had won the fight against grief. I thought I was going to be different, but no. It was ruthless. Even the littlest strength I wanted to keep, it took away from me.

When December came, the month of Gaby's birthday, my world became senseless. I could not feel anything but fear and darkness. I could not think. I mourned all over again. I remembered all her sufferings, my own affliction, and what I could have done to keep her alive. Oh, the agony, all the events that unfolded the day she left me—the hour, minutes, every second of her death. There, yet again, the insurmountable pain. As cruel as it gets, my mind became my own enemy. It took me to the place I avoided at all costs.

Against my will, it took me back, back, to the emergency room. The difference then was the events went very quickly. I did not know what had hit me. This time, however, when the memory came back, it slowly haunted every inch of my soul with a dagger, rewinding every event as it opened all the sore wounds until they bled again. Playing the entire experience in slow motion, it paused, highlighting the most painful scenes over and over until I became crazy, exhausted, and numb inside.

Time and again, I felt helpless. No one knew what was going on in my head. No one could rescue me from such torment. *You are not a good mother for not saving your own daughter from dying, from her pain,* my mind would echo. There again, the internal battle began. My body and mind would defy my soul. The negative force was too strong to overcome. I wanted to escape, to die again. On the day of Gaby's birth, instead of celebrating her birthday, my spirit would freeze. It could cry every day till the last day of December would come to pass.

I had migraines. I would often feel dizzy. I had muscle cramps from my shoulders to my toes, often interrupted by spasms around the muscles of my eyes and cheeks. I was too weak to brush my teeth, too tired to bend down and tie my shoes. I could not sleep at night. It was horrible. I could not swallow. Every time I put food in my stomach, it would cramp endlessly. Regardless of what I consumed, all food tasted all the same—bitter.

The only relief was to vomit all the time. I would cradle the toilet bowl tighter than I would a best friend; it would provide me such relief, which I needed so often. It took only the first time to see how bad my life was. "Not only my body, not only my mind, not just my soul, but now I have to meet another enemy, the month of December!" I cried. "I can't win!"

I have dreaded every December. For to this day, it brings to me not the joy of Christmas, but a dark force that speaks its own language. "Ah, I am back once again," the torturing voice would say. "It's that month that brought you that one special day. Do you remember? You must not forget that day. The day your daughter left you, I hope you haven't forgotten a thing. If you did, don't worry. I brought back all the right ingredients, so your mind, body, and soul would remember exactly how it was."

Immediately after the warning, the punishment began yet again. Just as the moment my daughter, Gaby died, the entire scenario would unfold.

I was repulsed at the reality of seeing myself submerged in the pit of darkness for so long. Suddenly, I knew why some chose to die rather than be exhaustively brought to death so many times without a say. The pain of not being able to hold my sweet Gaby, the misery of missing her, and not knowing where she'd gone was the hardest dungeon to get out of even with hope. I don't know how other people do it.

"Maybe," I thought, *"that is when one needs to be blind-sighted, to believe there is a higher power. If there is a one true God, He, She, whomever, or whatever name fits, I have to believe you exist. I believe my own worthiness, for my creation, had taken place, and now here I exist, guilty of loving my child Gaby beyond what life could comprehend, beyond what it could endure. Please… it's time for your force to take over. I surrender. Carry me, for I am too weak and too broken to stand up. Carry me so I may gain the strength to carry my vessel. Give my soul*

its purpose and help me gain the strength to embrace others... until we hand, in hand, raise our hearts up to you."

—Evangeline

Even in that state, however, it was all too painful to feel I had not gone crazy.

It was a pity. Though heaven dawns, the mind does not know it. It knows only sorrow. In the mind is darkness. In the mind, grief was too big. It was better to accept its deafening clouds that blanketed my being than fight it. Its silent waters would seek even the little secret crevasse in my soul. There this toxic water nests and grows in silence, until I couldn't move, until it was painful to breathe. Now it was easier to accept that I had gone mental inside and out. It was hard to fight what I couldn't name. It was agonizingly painful to be the subject of its tormenting grip. I supposed everyone who hurt so bad for losing their beloved child would so desperately be in dire pain, but I knew I was not alone; there were others before me. How did they survive? Sadly, I know of no one who did not succumb to suffering as I am in the soul. I searched for answers. There's nothing to be had in the present. It was all in the spirit of the past that I found the miracle of my own life.

Gaby's Miracles and Visions

If you see that before you are spirits of love and peace, disguised in the vessels of humanity's body, there will be no suffering.

—Evangeline

I recalled a few months after my daughter died, she appeared with the wind. She took my hand. I went along with her. Well, my spirit did. She took me to space; it was a garden of light where a little girl was playing by herself. Once we entered the space, my daughter let go of me as she joined the little girl. Together, the girls sat on a chair and played with some colorful Legos and other toys lying on the toddler's table.

Aside from another grandmother's spirit, named Vivian, who sat while she hummed her way to combing her shoulder-length silver-colored hair, there was no one else around but another, older lady, in her late seventies, who was a guardian to the little girl. The old lady's name was Josephine, and the little girl was named Sara. Gabriella was happy as she and Sara played together. Sara was full of smiles. Josephine was so kind. She was gentle. She was a very caring spirit. She spends her present existence looking after little Sara as if Sara were her child. She welcomed Gabriella's visit with a smile, exactly how she welcomed me.

I thought it was just a dream, not real. The spirit world was as gentle as the wind; it was nothing like the physical world—tangible and vivid. I could feel the spirit world with everything that I am. It took a lot to see it with the eyes of my spirit. It felt as though my mind was fooling me. But there was a knowing in the spirit of my own consciousness that it was valid, and it did exist. So I did not dismiss the vision.

One day on that second month, after my daughter's burial, it was late February, my husband's teacher from the University of Maryland sent him an e-mail. She was sorry to hear about my husband's reason for missing his winter semester test. She was sorry that our daughter died. She went on to write that she, too, had lost her precious child. Then she sent a picture of her sweet angel. Shocked, I fell on my knees, crying. The little girl in my vision was the same girl in the picture. It was Sara. Suddenly I could piece together the puzzle my daughter and her friend had in common. They both suffered in their sacred bodies, immensely. There it hit me. I was not alone. There was another woman who bore the same pain I have.

One morning I had the chance to hear from her. But the longing in her voice pained me; I knew it was still the same depth and agonizing tone she cried the instant she had lost her child. It was all too familiar. The unspoken voice of her silent despair tore at my being. Her welling heart shattered the ears of my motherly soul. Her pain was too much to bear. I knew I was not far away from where she was, deep in sorrow still. It had been three years since her daughter's passing, and still, she moves in mourning.

I got scared. I feared that I too would morn so long I would lose who I am. What if I went insanely crazy and lost myself? I would lose the rest of my life. What would become of my husband? What would become of my Gabriella's dream, that dream she counted on me to continue to live, the promise I held on to keep, the dream that would fuel the rest of my walk, the promise that made it all right for her to leave, just as long as she no longer suffered in pain? Suddenly I had to ask myself, "What would become of life without me in it?" The unknown bothered me.

As long as I could remember, my biggest fear as a child were people who held the Bible in their hands as they stood on the street corner shouting at my face that I was not good enough. "You must repent! The coming of the Lord is at hand. Repent, little girl!"

"Repent! Save yourself from sins. Repent!" To this day, I despise it when a person comes to "enlighten" my lost spirit by quoting the Bible. I am not a Bible person. I will never be. I believe it is here to tell me the ancient times of hardship, of miracles, of trials and self-doubts, just as humans experience them today; and just like my ancestors endured, so shall I. I must do the same, with the faith of the good of creation, empowered by the silent and humble power of true love, I must persist, be persistent in finding God's reason to bless my family with my daughter's birth in this life. But I knew instinctually that this book was not written so strangers could excrete all the scary passages and throw it like a loose dart at me until I "repent!" I believe the spirits of the countless known and unknown authors of the Bible across time, shared the same purpose, to give me one message—to have hope. I too, will get through anything life throws at me. Even my grief shall pass me by. When others feel I must repent, according to their take on the Bible, I think their belief in the pure grace of God is not clear. The message of the Bible to me is this—not to hate myself more than what the book has already made me feel, and already does. The sorrow of the world already does that for me—automatically.

In the same set of eyes, I was made aware that I was crying for myself. I was so hurt, so broken in many pieces emotionally, spiritually, physically, and mentally that my entire being ached in all degrees. I cried beyond tears can allow as a mother of Gaby in the flesh. It was because I knew the truth. I see the truth. I feel the truth. I understand the immensity of love, which I will no longer feel as tangible as I once did—the way my Gaby delivered it to me. In light of that, I remember the value of being human, made known by the Catholic Church that Adam and Eve existed, and they pretty much screwed me and all children on the planet, innocent or not, for being born, for having fallen to sin by eating a freakin fruit that to this very day, no one soul gets to prove what fruit it was—apple, figs, or dates? Who knew? No one knows. Despite the gnawing questions that don't make sense, I was blessed enough to retain some stories from the Bible. Why it matters? Because what has been happening in my life cannot be explained by anything I confide in, decipher, touch, or even read to make sense.

During my depression, I stumbled upon a scene that revealed a close explanation of what I have experienced in my daughter's spirit's presence even after her death and burial. It soothed and enlightened me a bit. In one of the stories in the Bible, the morning following His death, Jesus's disciples found His body had disappeared from the tomb; and when Mary went outside, Jesus, who was now in Spirit, wearing His new body of light, spoke to His disciples, "Why look for the living amongst the dead?" He said to the women who came to prepare His body with oil, "Do not cry for the living, but rather, cry for yourselves."

A Soul in Affliction Can Be Healed by the Spirit of Courage

Courage brought us to earth as a child of man; but love—the love inherited from our present and past ancestors' lights, kindness, wisdom, cultures, solitude, stillness, and quiet works of nature's intelligence—is always humbly existing in calm and harmony while we are being fed by its innate language. True love is quiet and kind. Likewise, mankind must learn from the love that nature exhibits. The pattern of love is stillness. It is never boastful; it is solitude. It is an honest teacher of humility. It is life. Life comes to ignite the hidden seed of light through the surrounding degrees of depth of intelligence, powering the living vibrations of peace on earth no matter the seasons that cradle us. Nature waits in many ways to guide us when we arrived, yet it seems that love is limited by complex and very low expectations of humankind's mind. The mind will trade and bargain to no end. But the spirit of man, which is immortal, breathes, for it floats in peace, is quieted and calmed by its teachers, nature. Quietly the nature of our spirit is always at work. For it is casting love into its world where the mind knows not to exist. In heaven or on earth, we are the spirits of love that must govern the peace and stillness of our minds as nature governs its gentle and life-giving winds.

—Evangeline

To go on living after Gaby's passing was beyond impossible despite what came about after. My soul couldn't get on without her presence. I hear my heart say; I need her back just the way she was. The emptiness within my soul was breathless. Space is empty, dark, and cold. I see no one in this space. I was alone. So cold and so lonely. I need my daughter to hug. I know she's wondering where I've gone. So suddenly, I vanished. She needs me. She is waiting for me. Her life is over. She had died. Her dream and my dreams are both over. Everything stopped. Life stopped. The thought of ending my life became an automatic yearning as her mother. Yet in the consciousness of being a woman, and a spirit, I was fantastically conflicted. *"How do you ease this type of internal pain?"* I asked myself.

I had to question the meaning of my life since childhood. I had to ask why we are born. What are we living for? In my village, everyone lived to pray. But they often were hungry. Starving, the elders knelt at the altars to offer prayers morning and evening. I did not know if it was to beg for food or to appease God with worship. There was hardship between them, but it was often not due to misfortune from nature. The jungle gave everything we ever needed. The suffering was because everyone was busy thinking in their head, but took for granted the awesome comfort of being with solitude in nature. It is in this state that I see the cause of someone's emotional decay. When family or friends' corroded attitudes are their mental passion for bigotry, judgemental hate based on religion, politics, and even indifference towards other humanity possessing different colors of skin other than theirs always made life difficult for others who are kind and humble.

Outside the human mind, even as a young girl, I saw calm. Outside the house, nature's truth awaits. In nature, everything thrives; yet decay of everything in nature happened whether a tree was strong or whether it was fruitful. As for humanity, which surrounded me, children are born to age and to grow. In the end, they get sick and die. The flowers arise from bushes outside our house. It grows. Has fruits, then a day comes when it wilts and dies.

But prayer kept on while this event took place in turn of all seasons. Prayer was the only thing constant. The spirits of those who recited the Hail Mary were contented, even quieted. And the man on the cross where everyone goes to church each Sunday to pray to is still hanging in the center of the many church altars up to the days I left my country. Where I stood, I felt I was in between the worlds of the living and the dead. I knew I couldn't live like my praying ancestors. I could make myself kneel. I felt I could never rise on the church pews, for the judgment of being Adam and Eve's descendant was harsh on my lost, little girl's mind and heart. I could not find the strength to walk outside the trance of submission.

I was angry. Angry at myself for not wanting to be separated from my relatives' mindful experience, but I must step away, in order *not to submit* to the crime I see projected unconsciously all around me. It was a crime against my spirit to accept my grandparent's idea of being a good human being. To be good is to surrender to the church's teaching that suffering is part of being alive. Being poor and being treated less fortunate was a space my ancestors' religion boxed all of us in. I was angered by such expected and automatic demand. The church doesn't know itself. It didn't even know I existed. Yet it judged me a less fortunate, impoverish, and a separate being. I was called the poor. A lower-class compared to the men of "God," the priests, the chosen few.

I couldn't submit to guilt placed by the judgment of my religion that humankind are born sinners.

Where prayers were a recital of the old tongues, it was dauntingly foreign to my searching and curious soul. I was so hungry for truth. The vision of truth was not present. I was hungry to make sense of my disorienting daily reality. Clearly, the reality of my land of birth was not for me. It did not belong to me. It was the prayer from an old book taught to my ancestors. I came to know life. I wasn't old. I was but a child. I know I came to reap the silence of the stillness of truth. I came not in the contemplation of the inescapable struggle of poverty.

I looked out. I saw what was still and silent before me. It was not the prayers of my grandparents that I was being sustained at the moment; nature's silence supported me. The wind of the stillness is always gentle and kind. I found refuge not in recited prayers of human tongues, but the fresh breeze of silence outside my house. So I couldn't kneel as my ancestors did. I had to remain outside the house. Into the jungle, I went to play. In nature was the absence of judgment. I was who I was, a child. Everything around me thrives. Every tree and bush, the soil and the rains, the sky, and the birds—all did not question who I was; they embrace me, as I am in spirit, mind, and body.

Yet when I go back home, there is the hanging man. My struggle was poverty on many levels. His burden is suffering. They called that man Jesus. That was my world, a religion-based existence. Suffering in this state of being is an offering to this unseen "God" that wanted me to come up with money, so I deserved to pray in His house. I had nothing to give. I felt guilty. I was pretty sure I was not going to this "God," heaven. And I figured that was okay. So when everyone went to church, I did my house chores. I stayed to myself, mostly watching everyone who went to church badmouthing each other, behind their backs, yelling, pointing fingers at each other, and accusing one another of being Satan and Judas.

That was when I was a child, but when I got older and married an American man, I saw something a lot different. In America, there were no hanging men in churches. But there were plenty of Bible people who say Jesus is coming because He had risen. But I had a hard time understanding why they were always yelling and hard at work, convincing me I needed to be saved. It was so condemning to witness such authoritative men and women claiming that Jesus will come soon. These people are sure that before Jesus comes, there will be the end of the world. Nature is kind. Religion? Not so much. It was too much to choose between a hanging vision or the end of the world.

My illiterate brain wondered what type of Jesus was the man they say will save the world. I began to wonder whether the story of the risen Jesus was true. Because the Jesus I left on the cross in the Philippine churches is still in dire agony. To this very day He is haunting every little starving child who couldn't get out of the punch of poverty but would have the courage to want to save Him. I was angry that I couldn't protect any other kids from feeling guilty and shameful from the vision of church Jesus, whose image is still trapped in time in constant and undying agony. I couldn't save Him. I learned early on that it hurts to care. The world is already struggling and hurting. If there is an end of the world it had to be the end of the hate world in the heart of many men who think everyone is a sinner, but themselves. I can't relate to the hanging Jesus. I am lost with the Bible Jesus because of the very pain that subjected and accused me of being a sinner before they even knew that I walked barefoot on many barren fields since a child, fighting for an opportune moment to grab the strain of rice dropped by farmers during harvest, before birds got them; I had to spend all day barefoot trekking the vast sweltering field just to compete with the birds for rice droppings just to have food that evening.

I've often wondered for as much as many people, and churches that say they know a Jesus, with supposedly so much love and god-fearing people there are, why on the planet earth is there so much starvation going on? Why are these "loving" people quick to judge others who do not agree with their beliefs? My deep sorrow is in seeing poverty claim millions of lives' precious existence by the presence of constant hunger. When it is a common practice that churches collect tithings to feed the hungry.

In my world, integrity did not belong to the poor. Integrity is for the rich. Happiness belongs to the rich. The rich deserve to be happy, and the poor deserve to remain impoverished. In my world, poverty was a mirror that shouted at the world that one is a sinner. Poverty is associated with sins committed. Yes, going to the field in the heat of the sun and pick the leftover rice grain purposely left for the birds to eat was the work of a sinner.

Deep in my heart, I knew that poverty exists because there was no compassion to be had when I needed someone to include me in their prayers. Poverty shows when there is a lack of love. No one is deserving of lack of love. According to nature's pattern, everyone is love. The love I know requires a fertile ground of peace to blossom. How can I, a child, be at peace or know peace when I am already judged a sinner by my own religion before I was even born? A child is not Adam or Eve. When I see an infant, my heart says, "a child is precious." Every child is innocent of sin. Every child is a spirit of love manifested into the flesh, a body of an infant. Each child is born a gift of life, to bless all mankind with their remarkable presence. Every child is an extension of their forefather's life. Every child gives pure meaning to love; contrary to many mongers, the power-hungry universe of religions who believe children can buy their entry to heaven by going to church. That was how I was made to feel. For me, this internal argument was beyond real. It caused me to have post-traumatic stress disorder.

Now. More than ever. I can only focus on my issue. The visit of the Man of Light was dear, kind, and graceful. It was peaceful. I am still alive, wanting to love even more because of such visits. He holds my daughter's spirit in His arms. No one else on the planet could give me that vision but Him alone.

When I am too tired to think, His light beacons. The visits and all its loving glories—of my daughter's smiles and joy, her lights, and wisdom, her illuminating strength that lights the way of the spirits, lighting the ways to my own heart that calms my bones from aches and pains, releasing my mind, soul, and body from the guilt of sin. What if God is not one of us? What if God is all of us humans united in spirit, mindful of the purpose of why we are given a sacred body? Would religion become a space only for the union of one light? Would all hearts speak one desire, of unspoken language of all-inclusive and all-giving, merciful, and kind, nonjudgmental, selfless, and undarkened, no-sinner, mentality? Would that existence be called one heaven, where all is love and love is all? In nature of spirit, are we just like everything in life? Are we patterned by a group in pursuit of a higher purpose of survival against all the odds? Where a father and mother, brother, and sister are the body of one family? Love is the glue. Spirit is the light. Dream to love all is the cause. Our union is the desire. To multiply is the dream.

Nature is simple. It is the existence of selfless love. In the spirit of nature, God does not exist. A father's love shines—a mother's light comforts. The entire family is sustained. Brothers and sisters multiply. All grow to repeat the pattern of their family's legacy to sustain the dream for present and future humanity. To love, live, multiply, and shine that dream to be accomplished mankind is life. The rest is the human story of the adventure of self-perception, mental creativity, and spiritual and physical sense of union, a self-evolution.

How could I live in darkness when vividly the visits of the Man of Peace brought so much light into my life? This Man of Light ushered in the new heaven of white brilliance. No darkness may hide its luminosity. He brought with Him stillness beyond all worlds, a space of love that no words created on earth and in heaven may describe. In the silent calm, the spirit heaven that beamed in utter illumination of shimmering wind that is not from earth hovers gently, anytime a spirit is in need of good news. *A space of no religion is love. Its light shines in the darkness.*

Living Father. Living Vision

In utter quiet and stillness, He shines on the entire space where He stood. The wind and white light that surrounded Him is not of this world; it is the kingdom of its own silent wonders. The kingdom that treasures not gold or diamonds, but pure light of love, the breath and heart of the living spirits called children of peace, humanity, the divine family. The molecule of peace and pure warmth governed by pure light is the substance that His light body gives. He is the source of the brilliant and infinite grace that seems to exist on its own without ever slowing or stopping. When I breathed the wind, it was a kind of oxygen that could fill a giant lung to have a new life after it had lived many thousands of lifetimes. The light, the pure luminosity, the morning brilliance came before me, and all I could know in my heart, body, and soul is the inner knowing that it is always ever-flowing, unlimitedly cast all over the earth. If only we could admit that we are its breath. If only would we look inside and see that this bright light is the power that makes the beats of our hearts thump, the power that makes us grow to dance, so it may well from the heaven the breath of life, which is sourced from the radiance of the Living Father being, which is on the light throne beheld by countless crowns of living angels floating above the heavens in complete surrender to His splendid, light-filled grace, the living brilliance of pure love. He is light. He is the source. He is love. He is the Father of peace. His essence is pure and bright. His breaths light the calm and peace of all spaces. It is His majesties essence that now engulfed my entire being. It is His wind that has made everything of earth disappear behind me. He is before me now. He delivers her back to me in a new body of light, which my once-dead child, whom I had buried in the flesh, awakens to full life, to bathe in immense brilliance so she may possess joy and wisdom beyond all human's understanding.

Before Him, yesterday is the earth's dream. Tomorrow need not come. Here, now is all that exists. In this ocean, my daughter's spirit is smiling happily before me. It is this brilliant vision that ties the stories of the old generation to my newly encountered reality.

I cannot be called a child of man unless I have experienced a form of internal turmoil brought about by my ancestors' religion.

—Evangeline

Having been raised in the surroundings of religion-loving people who are nice one day and torturous to an innocent soul the next, by being denied water and food to eat, which came as often occurrences, have surely banished the trust in me to believe that what religion teaches is kindness to everyone. I know that my religion exists due to its own fear that one day it will not survive because its subjects will know and embody the truth that peace comes from the heart of one's spirit. It is not a person or thing. Peace is an unlimited ever-flowing divine grace. A force that no religion may endow a living creature, for it is the light that gives all creatures their very being, which governs the very essence of the spirit of one's very existence.

The Poor's Easter

All death by nature is an elegant transition for the spirit. It is not to be a projected and perverted sanctuary for the mind's illness, nor should it be externalized as a jail for three thousand years of the soul's darkened cages of internal suffering.
—Evangeline

There were so many times I wanted to find refuge in the church after burying Gaby. But I couldn't make myself feel safe even in the idea that it was going to aggrieve me when I showed up for Easter mass. Back when I got pregnant with Gaby, I was joyful when Easter came. It meant a new beginning. It was a celebration for the first time. Mother's Day of 2002 brought me a sense of happiness. I was congratulated by the choir group that I sang with, and the priest because I was pregnant. The joy was temporary, of course. I gave birth to her, she fought for her life, and now she's six feet under the ground. I couldn't get to her. When I dug inside me, I found the little girl that I used to be. I was eight. I was confused. I wanted to know what the meaning of Easter was. As a little girl, in my country, I dreaded Easter months. The weather became scorching hot. The water wells dried. Easter meant the vision of the suffering man again. Easter meant suffering to me. There was the black-and-white image of a man on the cross, hanging, over again in the movie played by my mean aunt's television. Every single Easter, as I fetched water from her water pump, I felt guilt and shame. I have had the privilege to peek through what was being played in her entertainment hour. The man who's been judged a sinner is hanged to meet His excruciating death. I knew then that religion is something I should steer clear from. It felt so wrong to see such an image, yet there were no words to describe the unspoken fears that haunted the eyes and weakened gaits of those knees who surrender their trust to the pews and waited for their hearts to fall in dismay as they wait for God to rescue them from agony. Upon the sight of the cross and His suffering, guilt and shame rose from within me. Even if I wasn't the one who put the man on the cross, I'd wondered what suffering was about and why it was allowed to exist to be contained within the breath of our birth in humanity. For me, it was the eerie darkness that came and churned me to numbness. And when I came to, my entire senses were governed by a dark and encapsulating bubble of guilt. Guilt was a new discovery for me as I saw the man hang to His death. Though I know I did not hang Him myself, His pain, which my heart perceived as frozen agony, devoured my senses from seeing the light of hope. This man's suffering on the cross mirrored my own confusion. The knowing I did not kill Him, yet I was taught that I did, was a tormenting discovery. My grandparents' religion formed my sense of shame before I was aware of the meaning of religion. Shame and guilt were religion's gift to me. Seeing the man on the cross was an unnecessary privilege that haunted my dear child's soul for as long as I lived.

Even if I wanted not to see, the season comes. Every Easter for the rest of my years growing up, without a choice, there was that man on the cross. His story, the image of afflicted wounds, that never-ending suffering, broke me to have faith in any religion that would scare the shit out of my child yet fully formed little brain of understanding.

While the April moon would forget the rain that it needs to water the rice patties all around me, the heat would come in a fury, demanding that I get some water to drink, when even the water pump almost ran dry. In my thirst for water, it would be revealed to me that the image of the Man hanging on the cross will not die anytime soon. He won't be out of my mind's vision. His tortures were an eventful story on my neighbor's television screen. Over and over again for seven days, the movie played. It was to mark the season of gratitude for the sins I was made to believe I committed. It was awful to feel guilty when I did not know what I did wrong. Everywhere I turned, I saw His suffering. Everything I did, there was that image of the man being beaten mercilessly. When I was hungry, I saw Him. When I was afraid, I saw Him. When I was sad, I saw that He is suffering worse than I was. How could I find strength when I was hungry and having a pitiful spell? The man on the cross, hanging lifeless, reminded me that my own suffering was justified by His image. Whatever I was going through, He had it worse. In spirit, we were both in pain. In poverty and hunger, we were the same. The wound of my inner turmoil to obtain peace never ends as His cross hangs continuously in my mind's eyes. Every day was the culmination of damming voices of guilt, sorrow, and fear.

Now that I've grown, I'm profoundly troubled and disappointed what had been the gift of my childhood was justified suffering, from the image of the man who died in agony. It was frustrating to look back at my childhood without anguish. Instead of education, my manna, my inherited treasure to sustain my soul, the rest of my breath, was an unsated hunger and that tormenting vision of the man on the cross was an image that religion planted in my surrounding to forever haunt me.

I grew even disappointed that now, not one scientist can prove that a man named Jesus, who was crucified over two thousand years ago, truly existed. I wanted to know who the suffering man was. Why such a vision had to be part of my innocent youth; since I was a child and knew nothing. But the message of His suffering spell has cast an eerie, psychotic, and damning spell on my entire life. Despite the advances of science and theory, the existence of the past story of the man who died from the cross, I cannot prove.

I would like to be giving scientists a chance to explain Him. But of course, the scientists will explain and theorize the man on the cross's life by their own understandings, by how it all happened in their own mind and the mind of the authors who wrote the tale of the man on the cross.

It is sickening for me to know faith can be so contradicting. It was to help me. Yet I was tortured by the vision it projected into my child soul. I knew something was off in religion's expression of what it wanted to teach me. It was cruel to fill me with the idea that, as a child, its tormenting vision was what I needed to awaken into in order to be encouraged, that suffering of the man on the cross would teach me how to survive, without feeling anxious. Religion has misunderstood me, even before I was born. I needed love, I was named a sinner, a child of Adam and Eve. I hungered for a kind guidance; it gave me damnations for being a helpless child. My humanity's faith was passionately governed by the Catholic Church's order, which gave me the hanging man. It made me feel it was my fault that He was bleeding in agony. Yet I could never bring Him down from the cross, because it is not my church. I am poor, I am to remember I don't belong until I have enough money to put in the collection box. That is how my young soul processed the image of the man on the cross. His accuser is the source of my suffering. He was misunderstood. I was judged a sinner for being a child of my parents.

Now that Gaby is buried under the ground, my soul wishes it could go to church to cry. But my guilt does not want to go back to the church in fear that I will hear from someone that the reason she died was something I had done. Sadly, the grown-up in me knows to have faith in other men and women of the church. That there's a chance, it will not happen. But the little girl in me who is terrified is afraid I would be judged harsly as before.

But now that my heart is torn, oh, how I wish that while my Gaby is sleeping and in rest, under the ground, that my kneeling at the church pew, lifting my head to the altars, and crying out what's left in me would be enough to comfort my tired soul, my broken heart. But guilt stopped me from having faith. My faith in my daughter's smile, the way she was in her light has cast doubt in my heart that what the church has taught my ancestors is true faith, freedom, and love. The church's image of the hanging man had caused me to suffer at heart, even when I was but a child. The church without compassion, for me, is a source of my human suffering and pain, the cause of my ancestors' thousand-year-old insanity, which I happened to inherit. Life doesn't make sense. Now that Gaby is dead, I yearned deeper. This life is but ideas of belief and chaos. My spirit can't rest in any man-made rules and its reality, as my soul, spirit, and breath rest in my daughter's laughter, joy, love, and the light that she illuminated in her presence into this mighty self-loathing reality. When I thought of my daughter's innocent love, her radiance, I knew I could not—in any reality—forget the delicate and soft essence of her spirit of truth; humanity is love.

Mourning Since Birth

The world projects wealth and poverty before me. The truth of the matter? Both realities care not if I ever existed. So I cry. In my soul, I begged for validation that despite richness and poverty, I am never lost. I am what I am. I come as I come, to love all spirits, all souls with all my heart, with all my soul, and with all my breath. My mind shall abide by my spirit's will. I am born to illuminate the secret code of the spirit. This, I shall teach my newly risen soul.

—Evangeline

Now that Gaby was gone. My joy has dimmed away. My refuge was gone. All I could see were the leftover memories of the past. The memory of my own life as a child seems to be calling for me to be acknowledged. My childhood's light and its darkness are beaconing. Its courage and its frailty call yet again. Here I am this child that seeks a place to rest. Now that I am a mom, I am back once again asking where do I belong. I can't follow my daughter to sleep, six feet under where I am sitting above her grave. My soul is not ready to take a chance to forget the reason for my own birth. I cannot acknowledge my human reality and give up on the very reason for my own existence. Now I am so lost. I seek where I belong. Where will I rest my head at night? I am unwanted. Each night since her birth, I used to rest my head next to her pillow. Above her head, I lay mine. I slept in comfort, watching the rise and fall of her chest. I used to sleep at ease at heart, mind, body, and soul. My motherly spirit had rested in the expectation of her future, her bright dreams, and promises. When she came, it was okay that I did not have a light of joy in my childhood. As a child, I was like no other children. I couldn't play. I was always disappointed in my surroundings. People were struggling day and night. There was no sleep, no quiet, no privacy from anyone. There was no order. Rules existed only to be broken. Poverty's souls are governed by unrest. Some children cannot see the pain that I see around me. Other children could sleep where the sundown reaches them. I could not. Poverty has a delicate stench that twists at my gut. When I see a hungry face or I am in front of a broken family, surrounded by naked kids, I sense the unspoken agony. I see it, touch it; I feel it, all day and every night, every second and every hour. When I'm tired, sleep is not my savior. Wandering to a secret place where my expectation of life is caring, where light fills the sanctuary of wholeness, is a delightful escape. Where children are cared for, educated, not hungry, they are sheltered in homes, not filtering the loitered streets in the middle of the night, just to make sense of an existence without the rules of time. Some naked. Some happy. But on the same note, they are all barefoot, with no one watching over them. I yearned for a place where I could hear and see happy, healthy, well-honored kids, with education shining on them as I dreamed it at heart. I yearned to sleep where there was peace so I could dream, without the silent echoes of pain from humanity's children. Not kept awake by empty gouges of punching hunger that bellowed on my soul a smoke of constant desperation coming from a deep well of hunger for validation of my surroundings—the poor children's starving eyes.

Now that I am no longer a child, I am glad that I had become not just a mother. But Gaby's mother. It is my daughter that gave my childhood suffering its light. She was the reason I had to endure. She was coming, so I had to be strong. Why then did my daughter have to die when her chance of living better than I did out of poverty was fixed? There is more opportunity in America than in the Philippines. She was born in America. Her future was blessed with the promise of boundless possibilities. Unlike America, where children are likely to have good schooling, poverty was my schooling in the Philippines. I was pleased I gave birth to her in America. It was to show my daughter that her life would be better than I had begun mine. It's not fair for an eight-year-old to have often felt that birth to this planet is such an ordeal to behold as I remember feeling all my childhood life. Like it did me, impoverished children are not treated kindly. Children are lost even before they can understand who they are in this world. In America, children are seen, but maybe not all are heard. In the Philippines, children are not seen. They are not heard. The spirits of children are not acknowledged. In America, it's not perfect, but they at least see some children.

One day I promised to teach Gaby the truth. I promised to tell her what the spirit of children had taught me. I wanted to teach her that despite my upbringing in poverty, the love of her father saved me. Poverty released me when I left the land of desperation. I found love. I left the land I was born into because of love. I married her father. I wondered why all my life, no one took the time to love me or see me the way her father's heart saw me? I wanted to tell her that the day her father proposed, I found who I was missing. The ways the heart and eyes of his love see me. That was the day I found what I couldn't make out in my mind. I needed to see the value of my life as a young girl. I needed to honor my life's purpose as a young woman. It was the very essence I was searching to understand. I wondered what drove the heart of her father to take note of me. Then one day, I saw his eyes look in mine. I was able to see what made the Philippines' impoverished children so beautiful. In light of poverty, children are the truth. They are pure love, light, joy, a new hope, new life, and new breath, an eternal promise, destined to rise and blossom into the womb of humanity. I wanted to teach her that the gift for all parents' dream is every child born on earth. I wanted to tell her she didn't have to be a grown-up to understand. I saw at a young age why I was full of dreams, why I saw visions of infinite possibilities. I had to dream even for my parents to get out of the grip of poverty. I wanted to tell her that children are the spirits of new earth regardless of what planet they are from or what religions they were born into or what laws and rules they are guided by. Children are love. I wanted to teach her that the land where I entered was not different than the land I had left. My new land, which her grandparents followed to respect, was accepting because it was outside religion's reach. It was allowing and not condemning. I became aware that freedom from poverty is never that one is free from the experience of getting hungry again. Freedom from sorrow and poverty is learning that one is a self, full love. It is her father's love that saved me. I wanted to show her that yes! Many will be born in the flesh of hunger and diseases. Yes. Often children were not seen though they filled the streets with buzzing echoes of the spirits of play and joy, even cries and terrors. Yet in the deep ocean of poverty, the spirits of the children shout louder their unconditional light that poverty cannot take away. I wanted to tell her that my dream became true. Children of poverty taught me that my heart's dream is real. Laughter, love, and joy are eternal substances that give life. And thus, this is the reason the innocent and pure are born into poverty. Poverty will never know love and joy without these divine essences of pure spirits of courage. I wanted to tell her that I learned that the greatest dignity belongs to the impoverished land. Any land without the joy of children is impoverished. So any land that is broken and torn needs the love of these children in order to find its purpose. I wanted to teach her that children's presence brings forth the light of the eternal world's blessings. Children's presence is the essence of each spirit, which poverty of the earth's rules and any man-made regulations may not reach to pollute. The spirit of every child, of every breath, is pure. Its unconditional love that shapes in the soul of man, vesseled in a grand suit, in humanity's uniform called flesh. In my hunger, I see the dream of heaven. Children's spirit is heaven within each breath. Heaven, it comes from; heaven, it will return in full light. Though I was scared to trust, I learned to love because I found that I am love all along, only no one knew me. I wanted to tell her that her father's love saved me from poverty of the knowledge within my being. I am a spirit that wants to shine only what is the truth.

    I sat there above her grave and told her, "I so wanted to tell you that despite your age of two, and one day, and I am now in my forties, you and I are the same. I wanted to teach you when you grew up. To see everyone before you as a spirit—the beautiful gift from God. Likewise, you are beautiful, no matter what the world says, no matter what you have and don't have. You are a child of love in spirit, even when others' eyes are blind at heart to see it. My daughter, now even that your body arrives in its eternal rest, you shine a perfect love as I see you, despite the faltering of your flesh. Though the aging of your begotten suit, your flesh never came; in the womb of time's changes, you live in joy. Remain my free spirit, child of light—dance when I cry. Sing with the wind when I am lost in worry. I hear you when my ears refuse to listen. I see your smile when I close my eyes. When I should give up because I am so tired, you dance above me. Thank you. Your voice remains a voice in the wilderness to echo joy onto my struggling world."

Now that her flesh sleeps, beneath the gravesite I sat upon, I see her spirit in my heart and mind. She is free. Her spirit has not changed. Her light is still the same to me. Her joy is where I can rest my head at night. Not at church. Not in my house, but in her truth. In her radiance. In her spirit, I rest my soul until the poverty of my soul, from wanting to hold her, cradle, and kiss her, is released from missing her so much. When will that be? Only heaven knows. Now I am here because of her father's love, her sisters' joy and dreams and unconditional love keep me. And I am aware that her spirit is guiding my spirit, comforting my soul when I am too overwhelmed. My mother heart is still here wanting to teach her my own humanity's discovery. Each day, I am my own evolution. I am rising because her spirit is shining her love still. Why do I see what other eyes do not see? Heaven, after all, is not real to the world of the flesh. Heaven is only real to the spirits whose love can only shine without the darkness and chaos of the mind. Heaven is only seen when the spirit is no longer in the shadow of the hidden cave of the flesh. Now I know the greatest lesson this world has taught me. It is love that saves the world—not economy alone, not religion alone, and absolutely not money and wealth. Love is the savior of any world that finds itself in darkness. Love is the truth. Love is honest.

Love on Earth Is the Light of the Heavens

Heaven is love; love is the light of all the heavens. A child is the body and promise of eternal love, shining in the darkness of the creation of mankind. This is the reason children are birthed is to open the door to life on earth. Each child's dream is the door of light and love. Children's love is the true secret light of heaven's infinite wisdom.

—Evangeline

In the eyes of my heart, I can never explain the beauty of the lights of the garden of heaven, which I began seeing more and more after my beloved child's spirit left her body, after the Man of Peace, whose body is light came and brought the mouth of the heaven down to me. Heaven is a vast space. It is uncontainable. Love is uncontainable; even the universe cannot behold an atom of its light. At times my breath stumbles. There are not enough words to describe the incomprehensible. The only way I can understand its existence is to know the purpose of my own birth, as I see and honor all the children's purpose on the planet. In my present, vision is space. It is brilliance. It is light-filled. No darkness. Before the throne, the light shines. Heaven is peace. The light that governs that peace are families who have died of earth, yet now they live as bodies of light, love and harmony, before the angels and the throne, which Our Father oversees in all ways. Spirit of love and wisdom is the light of our bodies. That is who we all are. Regardless of our circumstance when we arrived on earth, rich or poor, in spirit, we are the breath of love. Eternal love is the light body of each child. But as a child, religion had forgotten to tell me who I was and failed to tell me what substance I am made. Why did I exist when I didn't even know my name? Why was I able to reason when I could not yet speak as an infant? Why did I demand love from the world? How was it that I expected in my heart more than what I can explain? I am more than what the world can tell me. All the times I managed to go to church as a child, I felt I was surrounded by limits; and the only force that can silence the nagging limits was to play lifeless and lightless. Rather than illuminations of love to children, our church rules controlled the light of these spirits with judgments. Poverty killed my joy to be a free child. I was not alone. I am every child born in a land that many foreign powers have controlled and subjected. Instead of courage and encouragement, the joy of each child around me was raised in its darkening control, through hunger. My church, which promised God would come, pretended I did not exist. In its very eyes, I was not there.

I was one of the faces of children raised in the bed of insecurity and uneducated circumstances. Before children know from right and wrong, for some children, such as I, life was a land mine of bombing judgments of hell and transgression. I knew I was not guilty of sin. I knew I did nothing wrong. Nevertheless, I was treated as the embodiment of misfortune by the church, by relatives, and by life's circumstance. My grandparents didn't believe in the power of education. My father was never supported to go to school. When I was born, my father had no clue I wished I could finish school. I wish that all children finished the discipline schooling has to offer to prepare every child for its new world. Without the means of education, I was an outcast. Yet I was not shaken. Even when everything around me said I did not belong, I heard my own voice telling me who I was. I was myself. I was a child. I was innocent of sin. Wherever I walked, I could only wish that each child be welcomed with open arms, to be guided gently in spirit and soul, with the comfort of a gentle embrace when they are afraid. I had wished I was encouraged to learn from my mistakes, with the ultimate embrace that knows not to falter despite my failures. I wish there were adorations for each child's spirit of truth—compassion, honesty, and hope that lasts for eternity. I knew what it could be. I remember what love was like before I was born. I could not understand why it was no longer there when I opened my eyes and grew up as a child. But I know I've come to keep and remember that love is free. Now that I see heaven, my expectations had a source; for this is the will of our Father in heaven when He sends the angels to usher in the spirit of a child to manifest in the sacred body to give parents the hope and reason to wake each morning to face and courageously embrace time, which dawns ahead.

My Spirit Cares

Countless times, the new heaven came down revealing itself to me. A garden of light spread itself beyond what my eyes could perceive. This time is yet another revelation of good news. Two mother angels afloat were holding a spirit of a babe. "Tell the mother she will get pregnant tonight. Here is the spirit of her son. Her daughter will come in two years time,"

> *The angels of life and love are with us to usher in heaven on earth through the birth of our children.*
> —Evangeline

All children are pure love. These are the spirits of pure innocence. Now, I must care. I must tell the truth as given to me. I must proclaim as the Man of Peace and the spirit of my daughter reveal that all children understand they are not guilty of any sin. All children are blessings to their families; they are the new guardian and caretakers of this planet. They are not the future we wait to come in our dreams. They are the new breath of now. They are the future of our today. They are the body of living peace. They are to be embraced and loved now through kind teachings. They are not rough. They learn only through soft guidance. Children learn in the spirit of kind images of gentle wisdom. We must care for their lights, that their spirits be tended kindly if they are to shine brightly. Teach and guide them how to be good souls, teach them how to be kind to their minds, how to prepare the land to nurture their vessels, their bodies. Shape them how to be the kind spirits in the human body. Because our children are the light of our world before they are even born, before they were conceived as our children. As we guide them, they guide and strengthen us. Because of them, we are better vessels of the universe's peace. They are new vines of the new vineyards of this planet. They are the new gardener of peace, of love, of light. Compassion they come to learn to give to the world. In one glimpse, our children can mystify us with their smiles, with their innocent wisdom. We have to be like them at heart. Though I struggle, that is my life's mission, to see children in spirit before birth. I see their love. I am revealed their dream and mission on the planet. I see them in spirit light before their name is revealed at birth. There is no reason to shock our children with the vision of the Crucified Man. All children, each boy, and each girl, are bodies of the spirit of compassion. They feel suffering at its root. We must not hold them responsible for religion's lack of understanding of the true nature of the kindness of all children's spirits.

My Soul

> *Come, oh, spirit, come... come, and heal your brokenhearted and bewildered soul.*
>
> —Evangeline

When Gaby died, something in me, the strong woman in me that once was, disappeared. I died. The mother of Gaby in me died. So it is my truth that now, I cry for myself because when my daughter's temple was taken from me, I knew it was laid to rest to completely surrender its future to dust. To dust! To think that everything I loved—her hands, her feet, her face—will, all in the end turn to ashes. The horror of that inevitable reality kills me. I cried, for I knew I had to face my weaknesses, face my fear of coming to terms with living this life without her. I was afraid; I couldn't look at the future. I couldn't see it without her, not the way she was once, just the way I had her in my arms and the way I had dreamed of her future life—healed, healthy. But not dead! She's not gone!

My poor helpless soul was numb. Thank God for my spirit; for deep within its riverbed, it is at peace. It knows the truth. It is well aware that her spirit, too, just like that man of pure white living vibrant light had held and brought her back to me, she's been shed of pain and now gained her healthy, pink, radiant body, her body of light, the same body she used to have before she was born to me. And though it hurts and throbs, my heart never has and never will surrender its love for her. Here it is still; I carry all its pain if that is what it takes to carry on with life's dream for my poor soul.

At times, I wish I had buried my heart along with her body. Perhaps the hurt would finally end. Because it is still beating, I am left with its often-unexpected tantrums. It is still here, cradling all that I am made of, not giving up. It's carrying my body, unconditionally accepting the rise and fall of the battering effect of my estrogen-driven mind. And above all, I noticed how forgiving my broken heart was to the mistake of my sometimes foolish, naive, and irrational, compulsive self; that part of me who cannot help but be paranoid, always afraid of something it cannot understand. I have come to know that, despite the flaw of my foolish soul, there still is my beloved heart, the first part of me to be happy when a vision flashes within my creative mind. Its beat is the force to give my body the fuel so I can rise and meet any occasion that will come. My heart, even when it had been torn, still beats for me, supportive, to my often strong, hopeful, and dreamer of a soul.

I decided that sometimes because I am human, it is all right to battle with my body when I did not want it to hurt. I know it was human to make an enemy of my mind, turning one side as the devil's advocate, those critical times when I gave in to fear for allowing myself to be that little girl who screamed and kicked until her flip-flop had flung off in a different direction for not getting what she wanted at that specific moment she wanted it because she was certain she'd die.

And there is the other me, who stands behind my head as I rationalize that life is short, while I take bite after bite of the not-so-good-for-me piece of Double Dutch chocolate brownie, despite the knowledge that when I eat it, like a balloon in midair… up to the open sky I will float, because I was too fantastically bloated. Then I can, for the thousandth time, prove to myself that I am allergic to gluten.

Then there is the fighter in me, when I need to be, the disciplinarian when it is called for by life—the giver. The one who understands, the lover of truth, and the provider of love once again, it exists because there is my heart; it beats, for it is carrying me and everything that I am. I decided I could not make an enemy of it for good. I acknowledge it and embrace its goodness, accept it for what it is, the way it beats with happiness, in this case, even the way it mourns with life. It aches for the way it was, to love like a mother who so loved her child. It's well of love was opened the day my daughter was born. When she died, my heart was still wailing its love, but to whom and where would it flow? A question every parent has confronted when he or she loses a child; only now, it is my turn. I am aware it is I who must seek its healing as my heart carries me through time, in its quest of my soul's fulfillment of purpose despite life's rules. Life and time, I found, is the canvas to my own deeply rooted yearning. Life in its terms of the season is the decision I have come to, as my daughter and all spirits have come to shape and behold the quest to the answers that await in the coming of each sunrise. Life is good. The spirit of life is kind. The circumstances that arise as a matter of the heart is another story.

I found I can reason with my motherly soul, but I cannot reason with my heart. It loves the same regardless of time. Now that it can't express itself for its daughter, it is lost, full of sorrow. It was not done loving her child, but everything in life said it was over and finished. It is misplaced, suspended between the world of the living and the dead; it is alive, yet struggling very hard to survive. I don't know how, but in light of darkness, I am still here. I can hear my spirit voice despite the tired tears. I realize that my motherly heart, as much as it carries me, I must, in turn carry it in everything it is going through. I must look at it just the way it does me, not a burden but for a purpose.

I was left, confronted by the fact, that now I must learn how to live with a heavy, bleeding heart that feels at times like it is hooked on a thin string; indeed, it feels as if it is detached from me, for I am dragging it six feet behind me. Every time I take a stride, I feel its agony. It seems to hit every bump on the road and react to the slightest nick and bruises as if it is being impacted by newly opened wounds. Someone told me once that it would get better. Sadly, it hasn't, despite the time. It cannot be fooled.

I waited each day at the idea that somehow, my daughter would come back again. *She'll be back again.* I heard my spirit say. When I hear my spirit speak, my heart is able to move about with life's call. It beats for me; it moved my motherly soul, despite the sorrow.

I remember it was there to protect me from being hurt over again after my daughter's death, even though life is disappointing me at every turn I make. It carried my will to strengthen me when I needed to stand up. I remember the day I decided to take Gaby back to Hawaii, where she was conceived. I did not worry where we were going to live when we got to Hawaii. All I knew was that she needed to see the sunrise and play by the ocean as she heals from heart surgery. I begged my husband to take two weeks off from work so he could help me deal with all the medical doctor changes; from Walter Reed Hospital, we needed to transfer all her care at Tripler Army Hospital. My husband flew with us to Hawaii and was due to get back to work in Pax River, Maryland, two weeks after we arrived in Hawaii. The first week was spent on hospital visits to meet her new cardiologist, her pediatrician, and went around Tripler to know the staff who would accommodate her if she was to need oxygen. We got to Hawaii with Gaby on November 22, 2002. We had no place to go but the Marine Corps Lodge in Kaneohe Base. We couldn't stay on base for long. We looked for a room for rent off base. I prayed that a room by the beach would be available for us to rent for six months so we could wake up in the morning and let her play by the shore. After looking through the Sunday paper, I found a lady who had a studio for eight hundred and fifty dollars. We went out of the base to Lanikai in Kailua to check the place out December 5; and we decided though it was a block away from the beach, it was close enough to walk her to it every morning. Because we had no money, I paid the entire six months in advance using my visa card. I figured we would pay for it later, somehow. By the following day, December 6, it was Gaby's birthday. I noticed she was still running a fever; we opted not to celebrate by going out that morning. But we planned that when she felt better, we will go to Sea Life Park, to watch the dolphin show, and for her to enjoy watching the other marine life there. That same day of December 6, we needed to move out of the lodge so my husband could be sure we were okay before he had to leave in three days back to Maryland.

We moved to the Lanikai Studio that afternoon. That same evening, Gaby was restless, and by the following morning, she died. John left me alone in the studio to get back to work. I spent much of each day on her graveyard. After six weeks, I got awfully lonely. I wanted to be with John. I went to the landlord. I asked if she could return the three months' advance rent to me that I gave her. She could keep one month to give her time to find someone else to rent.

"No!" she argued. "You signed a six-month lease! I can't give that money back to you. You can leave early, but I won't be able to give you the money," she sounded alarmed and defensive.

"She told you what?" my husband yelled angrily at the phone. The following morning, he was back in Kailua, Hawaii, at the front door.

"I am finding you a house! You are not going to be treated like this," he said to me. Off we went with a realtor for house hunting. And by April 5, 2005, we got our house key. We have been living in the same house in Hawaii to this very day.

Ever since we moved, this house has carried me in strength, in joy, in misery, and darkness. It is in this house that I found how darkness can vanish; and how prayer may also change the course of darkness by calming the chaos of the mind.

One night, as my last resort, in an effort to find relief of my heart's pain, I went on my knees and begged that someone responsible for creating life save me. That someone Jesus talked about—the Heavenly Father, the creator of all that is, to give me a reason to live. I had begged for Him to show me why my daughter had to go through such pain. What was her purpose? What is my purpose? I pleaded, "Please tell me!" I cried. "Tell me what I need to do to make it, and I will obey," I promised. "Just don't let my broken heart and its pain make a mockery of my spirit for the rest of my life," I begged. "I will not kill myself. But, give me a reason to live with your mercy. Give me a way to grieve with grace, just as the mother of Jesus, Mary, had when her beloved Son was taken from her." I cried with everything that I am. Deep within, I am well aware that just like everyone before me has sought a world that is kind, my destitute heart would know there exists a world of myth that cannot be tested by science; the God that Father Pedro's Bible tried to explain but could not prove fact or right by adoration of religion, a belief that is a beaming projection of an inner quest of lost self, in its conflicted yearning to trust life, despite the image of war within that shines on all the deep struggles of mankind, between loving and embracing all, or judging and shunning those who are not in the same faith as they; the God that, since childhood, my grandparents bowed to—that someone powerful who they have sworn exists, I was assured now that I am mad and torn, now that the church cannot cure my bleeding soul, that He will come and take away the very pain my heart is in. I waited when my heart palpitated because it wanted to tell me it misses its daughter. I waited when my cardiologist told me he sees nothing wrong with my heart, but it hurts badly. I waited when the pain of misery was so agonizingly deep, I felt I was going to pass out, so I went countless times to the emergency rooms so doctors could prove through blood tests, over and over again, that nothing was wrong with me. Each time I walked out of the doctor's clinic after each test, they'd say, "See, nothing is wrong with you. See, it's all in your head. See, you are not having a heart attack. You don't need our help. But I am glad you came. Nothing's wrong with you."

Every single time a doctor tells me nothing is wrong with me. He/she failed to see, hear, and touch or examine me. A little bit of compassion would have guided how I could be cured. But not one doctor looked into my eyes. No one heard the voice of my heart. The doctors are void of the silent languages of healing spirits. I was alone. Completely alone. Quickly I found out it is in aloneness that the soul begins to die. When a healer's heart is hardened, when their ears have turned deaf, and their mind is closed, for compassion is voided, the patient is lost, the suffering soul in need of caring hearts are cast out of life's love.

How do you process the rise and fall of your grief? Was your caregiver accepting and supportive of you emotionally? Did you feel cared for? Explain why you feel you can survive the loss. Explain why not.

_____
_____
_____
_____
_____

Where I am, there is the Heavenly Father's conscious heart and light, consoling me to His spirit light, truth, and reason. Here, I am only to be still and breathe peace. I am a force in the light of living glory, for the Father is my light, and His breath is my peace. He is love shining in the darkness of all human trials.

—Evangeline

Fourteen

The Ninth Stage of Grief: Let Go of Control over This Earthly Life. Let the God of Love and Peace Come. Nature and Love Will Take Care of the Rest in Time.

> *Rise above suffering. The spirit will come to save its soul from emotional decay. Allowing the spirit to speak its eternal love is a man's true purpose in life.*
>
> —Evangeline

> *Humanity is a child of man. But the spirit child in every man is always pure in love and its breath of peace. When a man is in fear, his mind is not in the breath and shadow of light. The spirit must yearn louder to ask the mind to move away, so the breath of peace and the body of light, that is the true creator of love, may shine through and breathe out peace into the world of the soul. In the soul of man is darkness. In the spirit is the heart of man. It is the pure brilliance of the innocent and all-encompassing breath of peace. Here all creation is honored. All darkness is made light.*
>
> —Evangeline

The Journey of Self-Healing after Any Loss

Living waters from above flow, continuously nurturing the brilliant light of the spirits with eternal love and everlasting breath of peace.

—Evangeline

Man and His Medicine

We are eternal. We are light. We rise to heaven, to rise in love; we descend in the physical and material universe as its conscious force, needing to love brightly; without end, we transcend in spirit to behold our eternal bodies of light, but we could never, ever die. We are love. We are the breath of peace. We descended on earth to give life, to give purpose to humanity, in the creation of love.

—Evangeline

I often ask myself when life seems overcast. What is a vessel without a spirit? What is the mind without a vision? What is the heart without love beating and flowing through it? What is the earth without heaven? What is life without a dream? What is the end without beginning? What is grief without compassion and light? Sorrow. Sorrow is where there is no birth and death, no darkness and light, and no beginning or end. Oh, my spirit, shine your love, breathe out your peace. Make sorrow vanish from itself; for such eternal glory is the highest dreams of the universe, in order to shine back to the heavenly spirits, the goodness, and sacred purpose of humanity's journey.

—Evangeline

My Soul's Rude Awakening

Doctor, oh, Doctor, as you heal my fleshly wounds, don't forget the pain of my soul is also waiting for your spirit's voice of validation. Look me in the eye, so I know you are with me in consolation. Through your care,

SHINE LOVE, JOY, AND PEACE!

I know our Father's spirit in heaven is with both of us this very second. When you keep me safe at heart, I am healed in spirit, body, and soul.
—Evangeline

My spirit is healed each moment I see heaven open, of those many times loved ones come to deliver light of comfort and love to those left behind. My spirit is lit up when the Man on the Throne comes to comfort His beloved children. My soul is learning to contend with life as a human being, without Gaby to hold. But my body shouts in pain still some days when it aches only to embrace her. My soul misses her so much. I kept strong. But despite the ordeal with my body, which I knew I was willing to address, I could not rest as Gaby's mommy. Something in the mother in me wants more; it wants her dream to come again, back to the way she was. In this dream, I can't give up in search of my soul's healing. The pain as a mother who misses her child but could not hold her was persistent.

No one can help me. Healers and doctors can't give back what death has taken away. Then, as usual, doctors would sign me off yet again while I got that silent treatment, that sideways gaze that told me, "You're just paranoid. You're going crazy. Go home!"

I would go home. Yet when I wanted all the pain to go away when it appeared, I'd go back, hoping that when I did again, my daughter and that God they talked about in the Bible was going to heal me while I sat at the ER bed. But despite that wait, I remained a cycle of seasonal aches and tears. My body's agony of wanting to be with Gaby, but could not had taken over my soul. Something was wrong. Other mothers lost their child too. What are their states now?

What do I need to be all right? What will end this cycle of suffering that I am under? I realized I wanted to be validated. I needed to know that I, as Gaby's mommy, will be all right. But how? I found that most of my heartache was that no one in America wanted to talk about the dead child, my Gaby. Everyone around me was busy or too hurt to talk about her. No one was willing to hear me. Not even my brain. Why? She doesn't deserve to be forgotten. I hurt because no medicine could take the pain away. I needed comforting as a mommy. It didn't need an herb that will cure me. I just needed all my doctors to know that my heart is broken because Gaby died. But that's crazy. How can a heart be broken? What is the fact in the eyes of man and his medicine is not a soul matter, nor is it even a spiritual fact. Medicine is a bodywork. It is a physical exploration of what can be seen and touched. It dawned on me. My soul that hurts doesn't exist in most doctors' eyes. Because this kind of pain cannot be seen or touched, and to everyone around me, a mother's heart and soul, the spirit that breathes within, is unseen; therefore, I do not exist. Only my body does. I am not physically bleeding; I am okay. My heart and mind are broken.

Healing the Unseen Spirit in Each Human Being

When you love your spirit's light, the troubles of the mind will vanish. The pain of the soul will be healed; the body will be washed clean and be made new to become a living vessel from which the living water of truth will come and shine peace into your world.

—Evangeline

Yes! When you mourn in grief, like me, the blood test taken by doctors will not show how broken your soul's heart is. The EKG will not explain how it's bleeding because it watched its child die in the emergency room after all types of needles went in and brutalized her tiny body.

The CT scan will not have explained to the neurologist that you went mad, you had forgotten how to form sentences because your brain was shocked, it stopped communicating with your tongue since your beloved child was taken in the emergency room to get help to breathe better; instead, she was intubated, electrocuted, and pinned, not gently but aggressively by the doctors you were taught all your life that their job was to save mankind from dying. The MRI doctors will not tell you the reason you feel at times like you are being electrocuted due to the leftover trauma of having held your breath for so long when you watched strangers, the hospital staff, take your beloved to the morgue, all alone, in the dark, in the freezing cold, in the company of frozen dead. You were left to contend with your arms screaming to hold her, keep her warm, and cradle her to comfort her, but instead, you can no longer do so.

When you mourn, you die in spirit. When you mourn, your spirit's light vanishes, the soul that makes you a mother, a father, or that person that you used to know existed, who you used to be, the one who embodies your name becomes so lost, so alone, so outcast. The body that governs the soul slowly deteriorates. Without the light of the spirit, without the breath of spirit, the soul is depressed. To breathe is a struggle. To walk, even in the imagination, is forgotten. To dream a dream is nonexistent. To mourn is to die, of life, of promises, and of good visions. The ability to weave light-filled dreams is no longer life's part. To mourn is the sensation of self and of the world to have forgotten you ever lived.

Solutions

Take Care of Your Spirit

The mind will tell the soul to be afraid. Because the mind does not know that the very breath that powers it to being is the spirit of love. It is the spirit of light that powers the truth of life. The soul will believe what its mind says, while the body demands to be soothed, as the mind struggles to see its own love, its own light. These patterns are the cycles of humanity's survival. When the spirit's light of love comes, the soul is awakened from thousands of years of ignorant trance. It is in the love of the Holy Spirit; it is in honor of a spirit child's love for his and her father's heart that the sleeping spell of humanity's painful and destructive creation is broken.

—Evangeline

Doctors are for healing the bodies. Psychiatrists are to heal the mind's subconscious expressions within our souls. Yet it is love and compassion that heals our hearts. When you suffer a loss, give yourself the compassion and love you need when you hurt like you are going to die many times, yet there is no cure at hand. You hurt at heart. No doctors will be there to tell you how to stand from grief. Because doctors have not yet validated in the field of science that you are a spirit, born a child of man, who must wear a suit, called flesh—having been categorized as a female or a male body, you've come as the love and life of the body. In the eyes of the world's creation, you are different masks. In the eyes of a merchant, you're just another business to conduct and provide services for the continuance of survival of supply and demand. For a doctor's system, you are another number to add to the list of patients. To a religion, you're just another Adam and Eve who is suffering because you must have committed a horrendous sin before you were born on earth, so you must join the order of the church to be saved, and don't forget you're guilty, you need saving to go to heaven, and the only way is to pick a kind religion, or else you will not make it to heaven.

Father Pedro would lecture us again to believe that his God exists, but you must pray hard, if not harder because maybe his God is busy tending those who have a cleaner heart than yours.

The Point?

All these services are essential to keep you a living child of man. Doctors' healing is derived from the Heavenly Father's heart to heal the complex mechanism of our magnificent "suit" called the body. But what happens when your soul is so lost in the darkness of a pit, a dungeon that appeared after the death of your child when you could no longer see the smile and feel the warmth of the presence of your beloved light. What happens when the life of your love vanishes?

I asked myself why. Why did I feel so alone all the time when I was surrounded by so many doctors, things, and more late-night products promising I will be a better human being if I have all these things in my armors? Why have I not been comforted by those who I know exist to help my grief? I realized that there are no doctors, no priests, no ministers—who didn't want money, as 10 percent seed—who stopped and told me about the beauty of my own spirit. Perhaps

I thought no one wanted to let me know even if they knew. Grief is a matter of a spirit, not of the mind, not of the soul; above all, grief is nothing any material object can quiet. But rather, it is a deep yearning to be with the spirits of full consciousness of light and of love that the light and presence of our children alone may give.

The Encounter of the Holy Spirit

He is the God who never was to be made bound on earth, but a Father who sustains all to full illuminating awareness where the self is no more, but the spirit of love, kindness, compassion, mercy, and grace are all there is in heaven to flow everlastingly in the hearts and being of His children on to the garden of earth. For in love, we are His body. In His breath we are one life.

—Evangeline

In my daughters' death, as I have shared before, heaven came down shortly after. In the center of that heaven is the man who opened the heavens. But the heart that from which all heaven's light comes is another man. He is a kind spirit. An ever-living brilliance of a Father. Only this loving Father of peace, of light, the governor of all space above the universe, the Father of heaven, the humble presence of solemn glory to all that is, He who sits on the throne, who gives rise to those we buried in recent and long ago in death, those we dearly love; the Father who is not a God of fear, but a God of heaven and earth. He is a spirit. He is the father of mercy, of light, who is Holy in spirit shines the softest brilliance that can make the angels and all the unseen world care and serve our beloved loved ones in their rest. Now His presence shines gently upon us who seek Him, those who are ready to know their own spirit. Those who are ready to walk the spirit path are welcomed by His loving heart and compassionate arms. He has come to gently guide and care for those who are in need of His embrace.

His way is my spirit's rest. The narrow path leads to the silence of the yearning of my human heart. His will has not taken anything away from me. His light has always bestowed a radiance that sustains the love that governs my breath as a human being. Even when my mind has shut down, my inner voice spoke louder. The heart of my spirit cannot deny His presence. I found that my consciousness is always seeking the truth out of every step I make. It was there yearning to experience right no matter what drove my soul mad. My spirit, that part of me that knows the beauty of love, I learned is my conscious self. It was the kind voice beneath my mind. It was that voice under my breath that makes my brain illuminate with light-filled visions. Yes! It drove me crazy when it demanded I not give up seeking peace no matter what doctors have to say. It knows I am suffering in my soul. It knows I am grieving and needs to seek the truth. Where has my loving daughter gone? I went back and forth to the doctors in the aim to quell the pain of my lost mother's heart, seeking comfort from anyone I thought qualified to give it. When my soul got tired, I felt it rise and told my soul what it knows. When someone we love dies, it is not the medicine that can alleviate our broken heart's pain. It is compassion. It is knowing the truth. We are spirit. We are love itself. We only need to know we are the vessel of this gentle force so that when we are lost, and in the dark, when we can no longer feel the love of our beloved ones, it is our light of knowledge that must surrender from the chaos of life; we must die of the want of what the world is projecting in us, to need, to want. We must in spirit surrender time to grieve. In grief, I found my daughter's true voice. Her spirit comes. She came not alone, but with the Man of Peace, he ushered in the door of His heaven. As with the Heavenly Father, who sits on the throne, so does the Prince of Heaven descend and transcend to bring our eternal peace without dying in the flesh. It is in love that He comes in spirit to shine the depth of our consciousness. But never alone; rather, He comes with our loved ones' spirits in tow right beside Him.

> *You are me. Grief is a trial of our spirits to acknowledge its eternal substance that shines love—compassion—peace—forgiveness—the breath that heals the lost hearts of humanity. Love is the way to our truth. Compassion is our heaven of*

peace. Each man is a divine child of love. Do not deny that we are the breath of eternal and infinite space of peace.

—Evangeline

In dealing with the Man on the Throne, who is the Holy spirit, the God of love, the God of mercy, the spirit Father of humanity, the Father of Jesus—His loving son, the Messiah of our Father's peace onto our humanity's family, I learned that my spirit has guardian angels as spirtual guides. You have many spirits guiding you too. But often, it is not the man-made guides that we need to encounter when we just lost a loved one from death. In mourning Gaby, I learned these truths from the spirits of our loved ones.

In the flesh, you, just like me, are Adam or Eve. You and I are made of matter. Matter is what science can detect. But science is also the only field that if it can't explain what it sees, it doesn't exist no matter how real you are. But just like my broken mother soul, the door of the church is wide open, and the pews are down waiting on me so I can kneel and ask to be forgiven for the sins Adam and Eve did before I was born, way before I even knew I existed. Yet again, as always, no matter how much I knelt, I was still troubled and lost; not even priests would say to me and you, that we, matter because we made it here. From pure spirit, who is love, we are finally given a beautiful body. We are now grounded in human reality, and we are called humans. No pastor has explained to me that my soul is in the dark and hurt because I am broken out of love, lost as a spirit without such love.

I was all these when I buried my beloved child. In my grief, everyone was too busy to even look at me in the eyes and say something without making me feel like I'm wasting their time. There's that "oh poor you" look, which I can see as pity, yet hiding like a giant elephant in their eyes.

I am taking my time to say now what I know all souls need to know as the Holy God our Father descended to open to me. Take heart. When you lose a beloved, know you are loved and are always being guided. You are guided and cared for not just by the Holy Spirit but also by the spirits of our loved ones in heaven as they work together with the angels. Why? Because we are first, not a body, but a spirit family. Our true home is the infinities beyond the universes. We are the light of love, the light of compassion; the breath of peace is within us every second of our lives. We are so much more in eternal truth. We need not believe. We must only experience by giving compassion and embrace wherever the opportunity calls our presence. Whenever we use this energy, we will encounter who we are within in spirit. And when we find ourselves, so too do we find that we are not alone in this universe. We are in the care of the angels and the love of the spirits.

Doctors of the Body

The body is built in the womb, nurtured by minerals and essences of the planet's garden waters. Yet the flesh will not rise when its light and its love refuses to inhabit this fantastic and remarkable nature, sacred, and spiritually blessed creation. The body of all spirits is of the earth. Yet without spirit, the body knows not of love. The spirit is of the heavens; it is the living generator of love and peace. Humanity is the spirit in the body, and its intelligence is sourced in the mind of the universe. Still, its consciousness and its love shines from the brilliant light of everlasting love of family, which powers the love of our Our Father on the Throne, who is the God of love and mercy. The grace of our Holy Mother's mercy, illumined by the Prince of peace, who is Jesus the messiah, the son of the living God of Compassion—our spirit brother, in the union of our spirits will to achieve the goal to harvest our humanity's ultimate desire to fulfill in time all our sacred masculine, of everyman's spirit divine virtues, him, the force of the tree of life-brotherhood; in honor of the sacred feminine, of every woman, her, the spirit divine's womb--sisterhood. For in truth, life is both male and female. In heaven, the two are one body of life; of equal force in spirit radiance. In the universe, on earth, both are equal, yet sacred divine powers of the holy spirit's body, who both transcend the physical tree of life's creation to its ultimate beauty, of man and woman. He and she, male and female, the spirit's masculine and the feminine are both the living breaths of the divine tree—the sacred family—humanity.
—Evangeline

SHINE LOVE, JOY, AND PEACE!

The greatest gift of medicine is learning how the brain processes information from personal and environmental experiences. Psychologists are great with the mind. They will guide you to talk. Be mindful that there are ones that are compassionate, and you will feel better in their presence. Not because they heal your brain, but because they validated your presence by being merciful. When someone cares, your heart is soothed and comforted. Your soul becomes calm. You feel good because you feel safe. When you feel safe, the brain calms down. It is then that the light of love comes through. True healing is first a matter of spirit, before it is the heart, before it is the mind and body.

However, there are those therapists who made me feel humiliated by the five extra minutes it would take for me to catch my tongue to find the strength to form a word before she stood and said time is up. My copay for that one hour is twenty dollars off of two hundred and twenty that were billed to my healthcare provider. And I must not forget to pay before I leave the building.

So with love, when you are down, gain the mental strength to choose kindness wherever you seek care. There are those who know the language of the heart. Your Spirit Father's love is in them. Your human ancestors' eternal guidance is shining through from above them. These are the faithful servants of meaningful creation. They are angels on earth, sent before you were born, to be there for you when humanity's darkness befell your path. Find them with your heart. They want nothing from you. They are only there standing by to guide you out of the darkness. They are there to make you whole, so you may light and shine love again. Their presence alone can make you remember how loved and blessed you are, despite the pain. Take your time to search. You deserve it. The latter part is no fun.

Knock, Knock! Who's There?

I was there, but I was not seen. I've spoken but was not heard.
—Evangeline

When you lose a loved one, plan how you are going to grieve. No one can do it for you. You have to decide to do it. But do it. Grieve in the grace of truth. Don't get stuck as I was. It took two years for me to realize I was dealing with the same words over again. "Come back and talk again." My physiologist reminded me. Having to remember and repeat what the pain was like was extremely exhausting. Unfortunately, for me, that chain that governs the memory of joy and who I used to be is forgotten; for the very nature of my human brain when I could no longer hold and hug, hear, and play with Gaby's hands and body had turned the life off of its light. Even on a bright sunny day, my brain and heart rejected joy and remembers and records everything it perceives as darkness, pain, and trauma. It was a deep sense of being lost, but like anyone who now grieves, I don't know why. I was not afraid. But I know I was too numb too lost, but I was alone, floating in the ocean of strange darkness.

My brain could not protect me not to make the same mistake again the next day when I got depressed. In grief, it was grueling to be so sad but I didn't have the energy to be happy. It never ends, what I found was me, lost in time and concern of money as well, because I had to come up with a copay that came as multiple charges of twenty dollars. I was concerned about where it was going to come from, water and electric bills, or groceries.

What to Do Instead

The Father of love created loving hearts to shine and breathe peace in the depth of all darkness. When the mind of darkness comes, seek the light of your Spirit Father. See your own light within that shines your thoughts and love. His angels have already surrounded your presence. When the angels of light comes they shine compassion and refuse to ask anything out of the darkness of the mind. They come to deliver your light back to you, which humanity's pain and fear, hurt, and anger have taken away.

—Evangeline

Look for a kind Mental Health—doctor. At least your money will have bought a sense of warmth. Don't rush. Breathe. Don't be like me in the beginning, to bet your bottom dollar for copay will have long dissolved and yet your grief remains painful. Even your wallet will have forgotten itself before you ever feel you mattered enough not to keep repeating the same story of your pain. AARGHHH!

I finally came off it and said to myself one day, "So you can go in circles until you feel that every day is a groundhog day in your black dungeon of grief." Only to be amazed at that silent nudge, even you believe that you are absolutely mad and you want to end it all, something in you will keep asking to feel better, so you go back to the psychologist and talk some more.

Remember: Don't Believe It! Know So!

Your brain is shocked and injured when you lose a loved one. So you can't count on your injured brain to save you. And when your brain does not talk to your soul to tell you what you needed to hear most, how precious you are as a spirit child of love, that you are pretty lost, so will your phycologist tell you how precious you are. You just have to know you mattered enough to be trusted a gift of a divine child, wife, husband, friend, family, such in my case, my Gabriella (Gaby).

One Language

In moving, we heal our body; in loving, we heal our broken hearts. Embracing others even when our arms are weakened, we find our inner strength; and in demanding that our lungs take a deep breath, to open our minds unconditionally, that we understand and offer compassion when we are lost and afraid. This is how we summon our own consciousness to rise and project to all spaces of heaven and the universe, our eternal light. Our presence is the breath of divine courage, on this fragile minds, of the so ever-gracious garden earth.

—Evangeline

In mourning, you are me. My language is yours. Yours is mine. Mourning is one stumbling language of endless pain, no matter what planet you go to. It is a universal language of deep loss, a deafening loud cry of darkness, a state of feeling that you are numb, in the abandonment of still muteness, a shell walking with no place to go, but in circles, you keep on turning with days on end until there is no more movement, yet here you still are, your feet below you. You still exist to feel the pain.

Be still. Remember that you are a spirit, the being that has come to give breath to the soul, to your name, to your flesh, your body. Tell your soul you are a beautiful spirit of light. The brain will light up. You will feel in control. You will feel your own darkness shift and move away until it gets your attention and tries to communicate its pain to you. When you look at the pain, it is a silent plea. Your soul will find its way to order; even if it has a hard time doing so at first, your spirit will be lit up to take charge and help heal the pain by being in tune with the current solution.

Breathe. Thank your soul. Love your spirit. Watch the heavens light up above as you see your own radiance illuminated from within.

No, You Are Not the Solar Systems

With the Heavenly Father's grace, I found myself traveling in the universe called the mind in a dream after I asked the Heavenly Father why He forbids me to seek the fortune teller in our town that everyone was bragging about. While dream traveling in the universal mind, I recall a lesson which He gave me not long ago. For two weeks, He sent me fortune tellers from all over the planet world. Some were men and others were women. They read to me. I felt entertained but became more anxious as my spirit felt empty and tired. I noticed I was not being fed spiritually. I missed Him. I was missing His gentle and Fatherly presence. I missed His care. I felt guilty for all the money that He had to pay each of the fortune tellers. I was ashamed because of the two weeks of what could have been a precious time, I lost without communicating with Him. Now here

I was in a foreign space again. In my dream travel in the universal mind, I noticed that the sun does not light this space. There was the absence of light. No sunshine. It was a deep void. It was dark but I could make out the empty spaces and some soul images in front of me as I traveled further upward. There are many beings there. There were disembodied human gods. One human god was in his seventies, a Chinese-looking man. His friend was a lion god standing next to him. He had the body of a lion. But, acts and talks like a man.

"Do not go to her," they both said to me, looking down on earth right below them. A fortune-teller lady on earth is dealing with her tarot cards.

"We are helping her to make a living," they both admitted caringly. They look up above. There was a light shining softly from outside this mind world. "Child get out from there!" The Heavenly voice called from above the universe mind sounding His concern. It is the old man sitting on the throne, watching over me and the conversation.

"You belong to Him. Go to Him. You are His." They sincerely respected and honored the old man's presence. I was amazed that they were cautious of their domain. But the Holy Father did not judge them.

There are many realities within what's seen. Just as there are many in the unseen. But the spirit of the Holy Father is the watchman, above all these realities. He is the light and love of all creation. The greatest creation is His spirit of love, His compassion, and His kindness.

You Are Not the Mental Universe

Astrologers and the cosmos think they know your mind and makeup. Religions believe you can't live without the cross. Politics and policies demand that you are its subject. Child of humanity, behold the light of your spirit, so you can make the cosmos, religions, and the laws of man conscious of love and peace, which is the true playground of meaningful creation.
—Evangeline

You are not the moon. You are not the mental mind. You are the beloved conscious spirit that does not die but shines to love all. The magic is in the instant realization that you have the power within to change how you feel. When you can acknowledge that you are powerless over darkness, you stop trying to fight it. You stop going after it in circles, hoping you know where its tail ends. In dying of darkness, you stop existing in it.

Darkness is fear. It is an illusion. It does not exist. Rise from the darkness of your mind's fear. Turn it off. Only love is real. You are love! You are conscious. You are real. Worries are mind made fears—not real. You are a real living child of God. You are real. You are alive! Touch and feel you self. You are real. You are living light of intelligence. You are smart. You are born from the Holy spirit who now exists on earth because you are breathing His breath out into the world. You are the embodiment of the spirit heaven, birthed in the vessel of our ancestral tree. You are the breath of truth, a vessel in a newly risen vine of the new spring of seasonal flesh. You are the life, the spirit, the caretaker of this living, beautiful, and only one real planet—Earth.

Rather

You let go and begin the journey to rise above suffering. The instant relief is in your secret power. Your spirit power is to light the darkness. No man can take that destiny away from you. You are born to make a choice. Serving darkness and suffering is a choice. When you realize, you no longer need to suffer, you can take action to let go and break away; you choose to move forward and discover a life without that limitation. The death of darkness out of you is the birth of light in you. This is the highest journey. You allow love to become you. You become the body of love. Here in the light communications begin. Divine guidance comes through and manifests as your spirit transcends higher in evolution.

Stasis creates suffering. Conscious movement creates space for love, so peace may dwell herein.
—Evangeline

In grief, let go of yourself. Come out into the world and serve those who are suffering, for they too are in the dark. In doing, we heal. In loving others, we find ourselves. Because you are free, though you may be with those who are suffering now, though those who are in pain may be distant from yourself, they are in need of your kindness. They are in love the same with you, close enough to lend a hug. It is in this simple secret domain that you blossom in light; your light will come out, your spirit will shine. And heaven's spirits will be drawn to you, help you, manifest love, wherever you go on, doing good in service of others.

There is no hurt of the body, mind, and soul that eternal love cannot cure. In love, all is well.
—Evangeline

I saw him come out of the heaven of light. Then when I looked at the mouth of heaven, which is a peaceful sanctuary of shimmering grandeurs, a beautiful whirling tunnel formed. It is a kind tunnel. It is gentle in light as His body shines the same. I see that the tunnel's door opens and closes as He stands before it. I knew that the tunnel is the way to heaven. He is the door of heaven, and the heavens obey Him. And all the spirits that come out of His door have died from all ills of the minds and have passed through all excruciating pain of all diseases; yet with Him, they live in new bodies of white lights. They are the pure brilliance of sweet grace. From His heaven, they come and arrive at the door of my vision. They stepped into my sky. They come in absolutely brilliant smiles. They come shining in full love. They come to heal the ones left behind. The brokenhearted are embraced with a soft, yet warm glow, of radiating union, of pure compassion. It's not in words that they are healed. But it is in the presence of the light that their hearts are made whole from brokenness and suffering. Now that the heavens have opened, at last, the suffering of the mind and heart is no more. Darkness is no more. In its place is a gentle and loving light of peace and love.

—Evangeline

As I learned, in the dark energy of grief, you will hurt like you could die over and over again. Your every organ feels like it is being torn out of your very soul. You will feel the rise and fall of the pain, different organs taking turns to scream each day, till you crunch to the fetal position and throw up till your intestines hurt. Your knees will bleed like never before because you pleaded and begged, but no one stopped to listen. No one was listening. Your brain would snap. Your anger will growl louder than those savage cats in the hellish wilderness, making you burn in the fire with each bite, as you feel you are screaming lava and seeing red, to fight, but you can't move; in fact, you haven't moved. Everything you are seeing is created by your mind of fear. You have gone mad and surely will rest only to find yourself crazier than the last time. In it all, you are alone. No god in the flesh knows your soul's pain exists; not even doctors of science. They will gladly put you in the ring of medicated state, so now you can be officially and legally be called crazy, to be put on Zoloft so you cannot feel the darkness, but you feel like your entire brain is being fried with bright light, and your insides feel like you are being gently electrocuted, and all you want to do is scream, explode out of your own skin, but all you hear, is "That is just the medication's side effects, it will go away."

Three types of medication, as I was on later, you feel like you have been turned into a boulder, a giant stone, only now you are in the middle of a dark forest, all alone among tall fine trees that keep on chattering some foreign language you cannot understand, only to get smacked with a speeding white light that tells you, you are in your doctor's office again.

For some but not all:

SHINE LOVE, JOY, AND PEACE!

If you are not in front of your doctor right now, you don't exist. As my suffering was consistent, not one word was uttered to describe to someone what I was going through—such agonizing pain. No one understood then and now, because no one gets it except for those who have gone into the dark abyss the hour their loved one died.

Fear is never a true happening reality.
—Evangeline

Grief is not a reality that love makes. It is the sensation and perception of a soul in the pit of darkness. The soul is not the flesh. The soul is a creation of the senses. Our human soul perceives the world through the five senses. Taste, feel, hear, speak, and see are all senses. The mind is the main body of the sensory department of the soul. Fear is the creation of the mind. Only it doesn't stop *consuming* the *emotional* body of the mind, as it piles up worries to the entire being of the soul. The brain is always neutral. It will serve all the senses of all man-made fears, its emotional memory of creation. Likewise, it serves love and peace, the spirit creations. When one fears, all the senses play their parts to feed it—fear, anger, guilt, etc. Fear builds and constructs a reality within its emotional body in the mind. But it's not alone. All other emotions build their parts. They are all there. But no one can detect and test that it is relevant, because it is not seen by a monitor, not seen by the eyes, for grief is a broken pain my mind and my broken heart carries. It did not own my body; it is what had taken over my emotion of joy. But in the end, it's not all bad. Why? The light from eternal love came and shone its greatest inside and outside of me. Grief, no matter how dark and heavy it is, in this life, it can only be cured by the light and love of our spirits and shined by our loved ones who passed. I learned that our spirit does not die. Even if the worlds of the earth stop. We survive as bodies of love. For even after death, those before us are with us in spirit. They come in pure spirit after they die in the flesh. They come to comfort and light up the hearts and minds and souls of us who are left behind. Love is the light of the body in itself. Compassion, the everlasting brilliance of this light, heals all darkness. The everlasting light eternal is the love that embraces and heals our hearts and our souls when both are broken.

What Is Death

In a vision, He appeared in bright, white light, sitting on His Majesty's throne. On his palms are nine young marines. "Child, I have them," He spoke in a great caring voice. He is solemn as I was. "There were twelve. Where are the others?" my spirit asked. "They are down there," He answered. I knew the three may still be conscious in the water. I looked up and was broken. I knew that He grieves with our humanity's loss. I woke up from the dream. An hour later, the news revealed two helicopters in training collided in midair. I looked up and knew I was no longer dreaming, for the Holy Father was before me. His spirit is on earth. I see His heart. He hurts for the parents and the entire community who are heavy at work, trying to find the survivors of the helicopter's crash. Now He reveals himself in a brilliant image upon the ocean where the crash happened. Up in the sky, above the seacoast, His palm cradles the nine young marines, whose spirits ran straight to Him upon leaving their broken flesh. His heart is illuminating warmth. His light is comforting to all nine spirits on His palm. His entire being beheld them with His fatherly love. His light illuminated the earth, the waters, and the entire shoreline where the helicopter crashed, where the bodies had rested underwater. He sends His son Jesus to bring a big boat to collect the Marines' remains and the two helicopters, two and a half miles above the harbor, which lay in darkness under the trench waters. Under the trench, He showed me where His heart watched; two helicopters are next to each other— one was 45 percent compromised, and the other was less than 25 percent, with its roof and window damaged. Nevertheless, I knew He blessed the site, for He made it sacred with His presence. With these innocent children now in His palm, He summoned the hearts of His other children to find those who are on the waters. He told me about His plan. He celebrates the courage of these young Marines who sacrificed their life in support of service to protect and to shine love.

SHINE LOVE, JOY, AND PEACE!

But before doing, He showed me that He would calm the sea from hurling winds; the Holy spirit made the sunrise new and bright, He placed His index fingers on the mouth of Kilauea volcano to silence its fires. He cleared the smoke from the sky, so when the time of surrender came for the families on earth, a graceful ceremony He established to celebrate the life and courage of His twelve young children who died in training on how to save other men or women in the face of trouble. He is there at the ceremony. Below Him, the earth's wind and the unseen bodies of loving spirits have prepared both heaven and earth to celebrate courage. For these spirit, angels' transitions to His heaven of peace, which His heart illuminates in eternal love and grace, is now upon the earth as well as in heaven.

—Evangeline

So I am awakened to discover that death is not a matter the flesh can withstand. Death is an illusion of the mind of fear, of the mind that knows not of the true body of pure love. Spirit has no end. It has *no* beginning or end. Though it will enter a creation of time and season of birth and death, it is always the light and breath of love. It is the body of love forever. It is the heaven of peace where all creations rise and where all creations end. Death is a journey of release from a cage of grounding limitations called bodies. The body is a gift to all spirits. The spirit is birthed to come into the vessel, which is the flesh, to project love and joy in an everlasting illumination of eternal brilliance to all on earth. In the law of spirit's nature, death is not the end but a transcendental ascension to love. It is a transitional process of change; it is a release, an entry to the ultimate divine conscious self, where the vessel is let go. What remains in the heart of mankind is a divine treasure of remembrance, a memory of life's domains, in light of conscious and sometimes unconscious actions to create as begotten souls here to discover who we are in light of these beloved gardens. Families. Humanity's family. Humanity's spirits. We are memories of love. We are the love that we create. We are the presence that the light of our own legacies celebrates. It is a life lived, a dream of heaven fulfilled on earth. Though upon death, the body is put to rest. Though it surrenders to dust, our emotional works of love, darkness, or light is a world that awaits the yet unborn. From these legacies, the highest is love. When we work in the emotion of love, fear is forgotten; only so when it surfaces, love must come again. For even fear itself thrives not to exist but to bathe as bodies of love. Thus when a father or a mother loves a child, it creates the true home of the child. The spirit's home is our spirit of love. It is unseen. Unlike the house made of matter is seen. Love is the creation of the spirit. A house is the creation of the soul to house the body, to shelter it from dangers and all elements. But no matter how big the house is built by any man or woman, it will collapse. Because it is the law of matter that all buildings that are made must all collapse and be bulldozed to the ground. A building belongs to the laws of creations. The law of the universe. All creation will rise. All creation will cease to be after its purpose is done. Yet within a man and woman is yet another house. When a man and woman love, they create a home. It is not a building that makes a couple. It is the unseen home; the emotional works of love between a man and a woman is the house of their spirits.

Love, respect, equality, honoring each other's individual gifts, encouraging each other to grow are love molecules that build a true home for the spirits of the unborn. It is what gives comfort and light, dignity and pride to all their children, whose emotional homes of love are made secure before birth. The spirit of the parents' love and awareness is the emotional home that gives kind guidance and true teaching of peaceful creation to all spirits of children to come, experience the soul's journey, to grow with dignity, and in peace in light of conscious creation while on this beloved planet.

Fears are not of heaven. It is the emotional body of our ancestors' reality that we are born into to inherit. Thus, suffering is still on earth. These emotional fears that our forefathers have fought and won, lost and won again in the name of man-made countries, man-made religions, and law-made politics persist to exist for the unborn spirits, to inheret and pass on to their future descendants, the incoming generations, to keep the sufferings as the main roots of the new soul's controlled and programmed identity. Our ancestors' war never left humanity, even though they've died in the flesh thousands of years ago. Fear is a belief. Like religion and politics, fear is an emotional need to survive in the arms of humanity while its soul keeps on seeking where the light and love of its world is in order to live. Why does the soul yearn to seek the body and breath on earth?—its love, its breath, the simple truth of its being, a transcendent light of its own consciousness. Every soul yearned to find itself. It is love. It is peace. For it is a spirit in a man. Yet children will be born to the world of unconsciousness of the truth, for the emotional creations of our forefathers have forgotten to entrust us with truth and love of our own spirits. Children are being born to remember who they are and light the emotional tragedy of its world. The wars of each man are the war of the emotional body of the mind. Here, no one's thought ever dies. All legacies of birth brought to end by death remain a reality to the minds, the tragic histories of mankind. These wars of mankind are the creations of fear by the past lives of humanity. Even when the earth, the begotten garden of the spirits of love, give to mankind the spirit, the spirit has come and gone in time, yet what it had created is a mind of fears for all to embody. The mind is a creation of man's egos, beliefs, and fears, insecurities, and struggles. It is not a work of the Holy Spirit. For the works of His bodies of love and peace have remained in solitude, stillness, and harmony as the nature of life gives it to mankind. Mankind's creations of fears will not end unless its true body of love and peace is lit up in him. The greatest creation is spirit rising in love to shine through the heart, to give the order of peace into its created mind. The spirit is the love of man. The spirit is the breath of man. Peace is a heavenly wind of divine breath made conscious by its holy and eternal light. Thus, the beginning of a new life in the world of our families in the spirit realms is made open for the spirit to enter in. In the world of spirits, of the unseen heaven, the spirit transcends to full being, after it had created the mind and in the body, after the body is shed. Regardless of creation, regardless of death, new life experience in spirit begins for all humanity. In these transitions, the spirit's journey to healing begins. Healing of the ones left behind on earth must also begin.

Suffering No More

To the souls who do not understand the reason and nature of death, death is perceived as unspeakable suffering. To the soul who does not know the way of the spirits, death is an experience of silent agony. To the mind which knows not of the power of its own spirits, when life, as it knew it with their soulmate ends, the darkness lingers, and sorrow is the life of the world.

What Happens After Death?

As the body of the dead is entombed or burned to dust, loved ones tend to the demand of legal matters to make sure every law regarding that person's identity is finalized. This law is man-made, which the collective mind has created in agreement to create a civil existence.

This is to ensure his material possessions, from which his own soul has worked to gain his money, he may will to its inheritors.

Meanwhile, in the nature of love eternal, the dead rise in spirit. The dead are governed by guides, spirit energies that teach and preserve the spirit's illumination to power up again with brilliant dreams, of love, of peace, of divine union with its original spirit family in heaven, where light is home, love is a green pasture of peace. This is rest. All spirits must rest from all creation. In a cocoon of peace and love, it shall return. Here, the spirit is transfigured to an image of a spirit. But it is not until it is in front of its Holy Father, the Holy Spirit, that this spirit is aware that he and she is a child, divine. Here it is an innocent being once more. In the Holy Spirit's arms, the child breathes pure peace.

Without the love of spirit family in heaven, as it is on earth, the left behind becomes lost—because the sensation of joy, hope, and dreams are no longer being delivered by laughter and visions of the person who passed on, whose spirit had just left the body void of consciousness and have transcended back to its natural state of being, the light, the breath, who is a weaver and a deliverer of God's love on earth. The spirit, the child divine, our eternal body, our eternal love, which is holy, holy as our Father in heaven is holy, returns to the source where it was nurtured and loved as bright sparks of life before being born to human families on earth. To him, every spirit who knows its body, its light, and its truth rushes back to its home in a blink.

Family and the Meaning of Life

From heaven, He descended. He quickly stood floating gracefully before me. In His right arm is a toddler spirit, "Woman," He called out as He released the child to me. "Here is your child," He uttered before He flew back to His eternal heaven. My third child was born soon after.
—Evangeline

Family is not first a physical experience; it is a spiritual manifestation of love from heaven to earth. It is a knowing of a feeling of safety in every step of our growth as souls. Family is warmth and care. Family is light that illuminates within our soul's daily evolution toward conscious awakening as a new soul, a child of man. When we unite and commune in one presence to serve all nations, all hearts, intentionally with love and compassion, when we guide as we embrace unconditionally, it is the highest and most sacred creation in all humanity. Together, we plant love. Together we grow strong. Together we grow in courage to learn to forgive each other every day, so we can reflect and learn from our mistakes, only to keep on making dreams so we can love even bigger, dream higher, more than we could have done alone.

A new beginning is born to humanity; each child is given birth. Through birth, the eternal cord of life, we extend our own purpose as healers, caretakers, and servants of love in the womb of time.

In each birth of a new child, a part of our light is given more strength.
—Evangeline

The Birth of Infinities

Each birth, we come to create. We commune to validate that our love can grow bigger, infinitely more to give us purpose to be here, so we can live again another day after the sun disappears to honor us to rest, and awake after; for another dawn surely has to come in its new beginning to awaken us in light of our own brilliance.
—Evangeline

Grief Is a Belief: It Is Not the Light of Truth

Do you know that when your soul is awakened from the dungeon of sorrows, which grief itself gives, the spirit of love in you will shine?
—Evangeline

Grief is not a matter science can cure. Grief is a matter of lost love, a belief that light can vanish, a primal fear of man that love can die, and life can be turned off. Grief is a process, a cave of darkness created by the mind. Because the mind is governed by the complexity of the human brain, which is designed to survive the primitive processes of the fight-or-flight response within the emotional mind of each man.

The Greatest Machine Ever to Be Created

As it is in joy, the human brain is designed to serve its host, the spirit. So too that it serves the human soul's emotional body of fear, where the brain processes the depressed state of the unlit, empty passages of broken dreams, which the mind has made in the state of life voided of the flow of happiness. Yet when the mind is touched by grief, it is now unable to know joy; for the experiences are halted by a sense of great loss that can best be described as an endless void within the sea of the unknown existence, a great space that is fueled by the power of dark fears and the soul's ignorance of the beauty of its own remarkable light of spirit, which is love.

The Mental Universe within the Mental State of Being

Only the broken mind demands the incomprehensible manifestation of assumed and expected tragedies.
—Evangeline

The human mind is the invincible web of collective forces floating within a secret space of belief and experiences. It is easily persuaded and governed by myths and made-up regulations. It is a universe of minds. It is chaotic. Everything in it is a self-regulating character within its own dark universe that must survive only by service of a slave that is willing to be governed by self-serving avatars.
—Evangeline

Unfortunately, even after I knew my daughter was safe in spirit, and now healed as a human soul, my sorrowful brain served me still and haunted me with more visions of past sufferings. It was part of my brain to feel I was in the midst of darkness. It seemed grief within me was fashioned with this broken mind in it, and I had no control over it, just as the brain cannot object to what it will follow. But my spirit decides to love my soul by healing the heart of my mind.

The Spirit Does Not Give Up

True Light always lights up brightly.
—Evangeline

The mind of sadness lays dormant even when I, the spirit, chose to be happy that day. If I allowed it, it would create visions of realities I cannot control. In its height, the mind is made by the human psyche's fears, consistent seasons of tragedies; which, puts the soul on the edge of life, where existing is a struggle and living is suffering. Sad as it is, neither the brain nor the mind know they both exist, and yet coexisting, they both serve the soul in its daily quest to experience the tragedies and blessings of humanity. As the soul evolves, its job title is found, its roles and its focus to fulfill what it had promised to overcome in this plane begin to manifest, therein lies the purpose of the spirit and the soul; it builds itself in order to serve humanity.

There yet again is the irony of being human. We are a complex being, but we only acknowledge the body and not the soul's ability to express itself with grace, its love, its dreams, that shape the very core of our humanity's souls, to light our spirits with their presence. Grief can be cured by visions of warm and brilliant embraces of light that love alone gives after peace is ushered in, and all-encompassing smiles with the silent embrace of one arm of our father through the compassion of our fellow brothers who feel our pain, that our soul is awakened. In being one with compassion, no matter how deeply broken we are our mind, in the soul, in the body, or even in spirit, love will come. Only through divine compassion, which our spirit breathes and shares to the world, will the matters of the mind, the brain, and the body will disappear, and even grief will vanish. Immersing our spirit in the light of our divine spirit love and trading our troubles with compassion, all poverties in the world will suffice. It is in the spirit, the core of our being, that we can be healed, before the brain, the soul, and the body heals.

Spirit Above All

In this heaven, which my heart sees. Above, below, inside, and all-round me—all spirits float. All are lit up. The spirits light all darkness. Darkness is not here. When I looked down, the spirit on earth could not float because they are grounded by the sacred flesh of Adam and Eve; so the spirits in heaven must light up to give all those in the flesh below the love and light they need to rise above the darkness of the human mind.

SHINE LOVE, JOY, AND PEACE!

The mind eats at the light of the spirit. But once the spirit is lit, the mind's darkness is no more.

—Evangeline

The Shaping of Our Souls Gives Us Mankind

On the soul level, we are man and woman, a boy and a girl body, but we are a child of man nurtured by our mothers and fathers. In their presence, we are shaped. Guided with what they were themselves taught. As a soul grows, from infancy to youth, we learn to speak, think like all humans, shaped by our religions, humanized by our cultures as a tribe. Strengthened, we grow more until we think like our mother and father, we reason like grandpa and grandma, we solve our problems the way Dad and Mom solve obstacles as they deal with the environment and the world. We grow. We find that half, the opposite force of our love; we get married and have families, and then we have children of our own. We dream of the job we wish to serve humanity with to contribute to our economy, to keep the circle of life going to sustain ourselves in order to live. But most importantly, to be here, for everyone we love, every single hour of the day, warming, lighting our smile, our embrace, our joy, fulfilling our dreams to grow a bigger web of materialized dreams, all for the sake of our humanity.

In the soul, we are all servants. We live to serve the peace and heal, make whole what is broken in our family of humanity. No one soul does nothing. Even the homeless teach us not to fear. Some of those with brain injuries still survive living the feeling of the highs and the lows, in order to serve all of us, by showing us not to f——k up our brains with drugs. And those who are in transition for losing everything reminds us to get a better job, to put our passion into it so anything we touch will have been touched by love. We know to be careful how we spend the little money we have to afford a roof above our head so we can legally say, "I'm paying for this space. Leave me alone. Don't take my home from me. I'm paying my taxes." On a soul level, what we see and project as good or bad in everyone is the collective mind's creations of what life is to be. However, above and below, life is love. The spirit of who we are is the very essence we have all come to birth each day to the best of our soul's ability.

Our soul will not stop going in circles until our spirit owns itself. It must light up.

In spirit, everyone is the light of the soul, the conscious lamp of our begotten humanity of the earth, and the eternal glory of the heavens.
—Evangeline

In the flesh, we are our souls. In the simplistic nature of our spirit's hearts, we are complete illumination. Man is both soul and spirit. Yet it is in the light of our inner spirit, that we are peace. In peace, we are the body of compassion, we are grace, we are the breath of kindness, we are light, and we are the love that our light shines through all creations. When we don't shine, we struggle. Our soul becomes the vessel of repetitive cycles of suffering. Shine your light by loving. Shine your light by doing what is good. Think with the emotion of love. Heal your soul. Claim your breath of peace from the suffering of the mind. Own your peace by teaching the mind to let go of chaos and fears. Tell it that you are spirit. You are its light. You are the force that governs the infinite.

The Breath and Light of the Soul

The greatest journey of man is to seek the light and peace of his magnificent body, the light of his heaven, which surpasses the universe; for his own being is the power of his divine spirit, his breath of eternal love.
—Evangeline

The Man of Peace came and took my hand. Above the space beyond all spaces, we transcended. In the sea of all distant yet very closely, blossoming orbs of lights appearing and dancing and disappearing at once, He spoke, "Our spirits are the consciousness in the science of this magnificent universe. In this pure state, we power the soul to be shaped in the language of the five senses, which our brain fires up from the outside environment and expresses the sensations throughout our organs: to taste with our tongue, to feel with our touch, to see with our eyes, to hear with our ears, to smell with our nose. But it is in love of our eternal breath, in light of our soul that we will live in peace while we are in this creative egg of beautiful creation, we term the *universe*—the ocean field of all living creatures and creations."

The Eternal Grace within Our Spirit's Forces

Deny the man of his body, but he remains conscious of his light, so he rises to claim his ever-yearning desire to eat with humanity and drink the divine food that humanity served. For the spirit is the body of courage and humanity's secret peace, and a weaver of eternal and external love which the spirit itself must keep moving and tending to garden that light within him until he experiences itself as the ones among infinite trees of life, which have undergone a season of full blossom, bore fruits and scattered the seeds to bloom on the soil to serve as living water to the garden of Eden, called humanity.

—Evangeline

We are the reason life exists. We are making conscious the beauty of life through our senses. We, in spirit, in our truth, are the reason we can testify that life is beautiful. Thus, we are born to manifest our self, conscious of human experience—through our laughter, our joy, our pain, our dreams, our visions, and expectations. We evolve as conscious spirits while we manifest ourselves—from a child to youth through parenthood; all the same, it is through life's challenges and seasonal changes within the environment and within our soul's evolutions that we are to be strengthened.

Strengthened like everyone else before us, we must shine in spirit, after a death of any dream, for in our soul's journey comes an internal clock that ticks in each move we make, as each day rises, as we breathe each breath. In each soul, an internal clock burns where we must rest of being complex humans and be at peace again in spirit. When we stop moving, to the brain, all functioning is all over. To the psyche's mind, the party is over. To the body, it surrenders to dust. To the soul, it stops and heals out of the darkness of the mind. To the conscious self, it is transmuted to perfection, preserved and restored in light, to love and shine in radiant peace. It is in being spirits that all man can rest. So the earth will come in its season, call upon its spirits to come in the cycle of creation in the womb of time, so in being one again, the garden will have its gods of lights rise from the dust as the Adam and Eve to create in love until once more the light calls for its child, to rest and move about the infinite heavens and dream over again until we shine as spirits of the heavens to give light to the dark space of the created body of the universe below, and around us.

—Evangeline

When the Mechanics of the Brain Stumbles

In the beginning, it is the pure breath of consciousness that descended on earth to be in the body of a babe. The spirit of consciousness powers the brain, to govern a new babe's soul's purpose as a human soul. But both the consciousness and the soul will not be without the mechanics of the brain. For without the universe of the brain that governs the mental attitude of the physical universe, both the spirit and the soul will not experience the perceptive state of creative mankind, which is one of the self, in all of humanity. The body, the mind, the brain is the soul, and the soul is one with the whole spirit. In the heaven of the conscious mind, all is one.

—Evangeline

I learned that our brain is constantly working to serve our spirit. Our spirit that feeds the power of our soul's purpose to partake in life never dies. Only our soul suffers when the spirit is interrupted in fueling the brain to full expressions. This happens when the heart is broken when sorrow sets in. Our souls hurt, lost in the dark. Yet until a spirit of eternal ones comes in full bloom, bringing over the light of our love, which is our conscious body, our spirit, the child divine in us that knows peace will struggle to make sense of life's presence. The soul may not know itself, but the spirit will not forget its divine dreams to light up and banish the suffering of the soul. However, the spirit and the soul are both at the mercy of the mechanics of the brain. I learned with my own suffering that it is in experiencing death that the brain's mechanics could be altered greatly. By grief, the brain itself forgets its own processes when the heart and the emotional body are overwhelmed. And that's what made it feel crazy, in great disorder, and intoxicatingly maddening to even the kindness of spirits.

When my daughter died, darkness collapsed upon the only world I ever knew. I felt the shift inside my brain. The second she didn't take her breath and express it out; my soul was shocked; my spirit disappeared. I didn't believe it could happen. My brain was still pumping my soul with the sensations of life while they were working on her to breathe as she was being resuscitated. A part of me was feeling the love of my daughter. I felt the eternal warmth that kept coming; my brain felt balance; I felt alive; I was radiant in beautiful imagery of visions with her presence still. And so still, I was still filled with her laughter.

Minutes went by. It took the feelings of her cold feet, sensing the absence of her warmth, smelling the wicked scent of dry alcohol and sterilized cold emergency room filled with machines, seeing her purple lips, her cold frozen stillness, kissing her with my nose to feel her breath, but her breathless, lifeless body was all that remained. She was hollow, when her breath was absent. When her body remained cold, that was an event that created a hole within me; the death of my daughter Gaby was an assault to my being as a good mother. My mind broke; my brain was altered. But it was my heart, the love of my heart for my daughter that kept me moving. So the mental collapse was a state I knew was happening, and to survive, my heart conscious of love had to take over. That is when the spirits came to help me tend the light and wisdom of what remains after a death experience, the love of my daughter.

The Mind Snaps, the Brain Keeps On

A mother's brain is to give life to a soul, to nurture and to love forever till the end of her own life. But when the mind falters, and the brain gives up on the colors and memories of love after the death of her child, life calls for the mother's spirit of mercy and understanding. Her spirit may rise and make sense of the limitations of the brain. It is her spirit that must rise above the cry of her own soul's broken heart, so in full consciousness, the mother within her may walk again, restored by the power of the love of her divine child.

—Evangeline

The hour my daughter died, I heard my mind snap. I felt my brain halted from the pain of my heart. The brain wanted to give me something that was no longer there. Even after holding her for hours, my brain froze, waiting to ignite for my soul. It couldn't stop to accept that she was gone; her spirit was gone. The big part of my brain functioning—which was made alive by Gaby's energy, her presence, which governed my senses as her mother—had become hollow. I felt the soul of the mother in me vanish the very second that the energy that was being given to me by my daughter, the force that made me a mother other than just a woman now, was inexplicably absent. I felt everything stopped. Everything vanished. I was dead as a soul as Gaby's mother. My brain stopped creating the very fuel that made me whole, safe, and glad in the presence of Gaby. Because I could not feel her warmth, her joy, see her smile again, etc., my brain struggled to function without her light. I was a broken woman. No longer a mother. I had died as a soul—Gaby's motherly soul.

No Stopping

The eyes of grief are darkness. Its heart is a world of suspended existence. The soul is neither here nor there. Not standing, sitting, or walking, it floats in the ocean of the lost space. It is then that the spirit of the lost soul must come and take away all the mental darkness of its own mind, to make the spirit transcend above the pain, to rise outside the body, which houses the well of grief.

—Evangeline

I found that our body contains its own mechanism of survival—the human brain. Our own emotion is the vessel of all recorded experiences that the brain must express. Yet our spirit is yet another brain, with its own sight, with its own yearning, with its own conscious dream and desires. Though death comes, and the brain suffers in darkness through emotional grief, it is in the body of our spirit that we can be healed and can be made conscious. When I see the spirits in heaven, they are whole; they are not suffering like us on earth. They have no pain because, in spirit, they chose to claim their true identity, which is the light of the world. They are living because they are in constant light to love, no matter how dark the world is. Love is the way of the spirits. Spirit is who we are. We can be healed in spirit. We can rise above suffering if we are willing to love again.

Our force cannot die. It is the same essence that this planet is secretly and powerfully sustaining. In every breath, there in us is a silent yearning to keep seeing the light that we have been secretly immersed since birth. However, the spiritual nature of us was and is denied by human regulations and creation. The work of the mind without love and compassion is not of the creation of our conscious spirits. As beings of light-filled love upon sight of dark and cold spaces, we live aching to fill that empty space, that which gives us the unsettling feeling that things aren't quite right. So we come as a spirit to be birthed on earth as a child of man. Upon birth, we give earthlings a better future through our help and service. The trouble is our ancestors have been struggling to gain their unlimited spiritual light due to poverty and control of the mind's fears and its judgmental tendencies to harden the hearts of those it protects.

Contrary to the grief of our emotional bodies, we are in spirit the life and light of our flesh. When I saw that the Heavenly Father is a spirit, and all the angels and our loved ones all now in heaven are lit up in the same essence of light, and with all my being, I see that eternal love is their breath, I knew then that everything I am in man's eyes is not the truth. Love and peace is the truth. And this very truth is the basic sustenance of all beings both in the universe and the heaven of infinities outside of its creations.

So my heart is ignited to light before the living spirit of the Father on the throne. My broken brain struggles to gain the usual processes that Gaby's presence once created, but my spirit's heart and mind see only love and the light that surpasses all seasons of deaths. Though after her passing, my brain gave me the sensation and the feeling that the world had no color and daily existing was constant misery, I found that the brain knows not of love. It is a machine. It hears nothing, sees nothing, and feels nothing of love. Because Gaby's presence is no longer being seen by my soul's eyes, my emotional brain and my human body had to depend on my spirit to heal both body and soul, to learn to rehabilitate the human brain again from its tormenting darkness.

The Spirit and Its Eyes

When darkness came, when my brain began to malfunction with sorrow, everything was dark and foggy. Even my breath was altered. The only thing going was my tears. When I sensed deeper, I realized there was more in me. The love of my daughter carried me. My dream to be with my husband carried me. Even when I was plunged into darkness, something in me persisted. I knew this is the spirit from which love from above flows. It is inside of who I am. It is a part of me that still remains. That part of me that is aware. I knew this essence made everything alive in spirit even after the bodies of humanity have died.

Though in the darkest world that formed all around me, I became restless. I heard my deep silent yearning to seek, to keep on, never to stop. Never surrender to the broken visions that my brain and my emotional body were giving me.

Then in this silence, there came a peaceful darkness. It is a night sky. Still. It is a restful void. I felt whole and very calm as I ascended upward. When I arrived. My feet were cradled by a soft, green grass with morning dews still on them. I suddenly saw the lit world, where Gaby is alive, and there was a man and many shining bodies of people in the shape and image of everyone I ever loved and known as relatives who used to live with me, those who have all died. Now, they are living, smiling, and by the way, their new breath and intention, though no longer with human bodies, in their new form, bodies of pure bright light, they can come and go whenever and wherever they wish.

> *Love cannot be limited by any space, nor can it*
> *be contained forever by the womb of time.*
> —Evangeline

In their spirit existence, there is no noise. No language, no plane ticket, no need to have homes, they are home; they are stillness. They are consciousness in the spaces that embodies life. They are life; they are the light; they are bright stars in human form. As the garden also lights, their lights govern all the infinite spaces all around them. A garden where it never rains, the living trees that need no watering surround them. They are the lights that shine on the moon. They are the lights that embody peace. In their presence is the breath of care. Their full intention to light me up with absolute light of pure brilliance illuminated me to come to stillness and peace.

Then I saw the truth. Our spirit families and us now on earth, we are the truth called love. In spirit, we are the eyes of truth. Our breath lives forever. We don't need the sun to shine. We are the lights of the chosen garden we walk. That is why we can never get lost forever. We are the living forces that are awakened by our innate ability to choose life, no matter the state in which we find ourselves. Our soul may choose to live in the spirit of love, so long as we still have the breath of human life, to partake in our mission to dream and start over again as we walk the soil of this very sacred garden called planet earth.

When we choose to live, I find that the brain remembers to light up. Yet again, it will wake up. It will begin processing all the sensations of being human in an updated version of the current happening in the nature in which we now live our lives.

On a soul level, after darkness, we come to find ourselves the same as before—tired, trying, maybe wanting to live, but maybe not, but maybe still reluctant to give life a chance; yet while the mind and the ego seek a deep sense that we are another spirit within, it yearns to fill a space and goes on calling for our consciousness to rise. This gentle expectation is the call of the spirit to breathe again. Breathe the heaven that is born to ignite the source of divine love into the world. This call doesn't go away. It will not go away. From a pure state of existence, which is love, light, and peace, we are drawn to exist, to have life no matter where we are. We are spirits. We live to love forever, beyond time. When we love, we experience the truth in us. We are the source of bliss, joy, and courage. We are endless. Our breath is the body of forever. The very purpose of knowing who we are as fuel of love is in our manifestation as a human being in the womb of time; it may dwell here in the spirits from heaven to breathe within a circle of life, of the family of souls, in celebration of life on the most sacred garden, which the universe has birthed for the time we have chosen to visit.

Birth and Death

We are the light of our birth. We are also the bearer of the path of death, governed by positive breath, magnetized by the space within our souls' yearning to manifest the experience through time and physical reality, so humanity itself may evolve in consciousness. As a society, we are struggling. But as souls, we all yearn the same. We have before birth dreamed one dream. From heaven, we dream of seeing the planet and all its inhabitants at peace. So we come. Birth manifested us here. Now it is our journey to yearn the peace that we know has dawned, for many of us have come to be birthed here to breathe peace and shine love to our current humanity. We, as a society may make being on earth a serene experience for all lives to live in peace. There are no other caretakers for this earth, but we and its newborns are here counting on us to remind them the light and love of our spirits passed on by our ancestors' commitment to planting consciousness into this earth world called humanity.

We shall remember that in spirit, we come to be the gardeners of peace. Season's calamities will come to balance the ecosystems. But humanity is the calamities' healers. We are here to heal the cancer of the planet's trauma of past injuries, both physical and emotional. There are no other species, who destroys the planet's reserves as much as humanity's fears and destructive creations, which is war and discontentment, unrest, and disrespect toward another being.

But it is also us who can heal the mind, heal the land, restore the garden to its vital state of health. In the eyes of the Heavenly Father and all the children of the Holy Spirit and all life, we are peace. This planet is the only garden in the universe for us humans. This planet is it. This garden is all. One planet. One earth for you and me. Now is the only time. There will be no other life as important as this. This life is the only life that counts: you, your life, and your presence in humanity. Now wherever you stand is all. Choose to give peace. Choose to do good. That is who you are—a child of divine peace.

Family—an Earth's Gift

Heaven is not enough to live on in spirit. If we only knew the beauty of this garden's gift, we would come not once but live many times over and again. The garden welcomes and teaches the spirits that it is the breath of both the external and eternal. In its descent, the spirit wills it to be human; and in its ascent, it wills itself to be the light of all the universe as His spirit source powers the universe. In spirit, the Father and the spirit child are both creators. Together they are one in peace, as all is one always.

—Evangeline

In love, we make families. In the family, we are governed by our cultures and our religions, which make up the shape and form of our souls. When cultures are taken from even one man, humanity's core strength of peace, its eternal light vanishes for both humanity and spirit.

The highest religion is love. The greatest dream is harmony.
—Evangeline

When religion is denied from one soul, faith in humanity vanishes, the soul's self-worth, its spirits breath is denied, its peace, love, and hope are no more. The soul dies. Religion pushes us to search down the path of fear, a form of limitations that our spirits of love cannot be eternally bound. The religion of man is a push for our spirits to dwell in the light of eternal love. We are beyond any religion. We are the love that religion is trying to imitate. We are the light and power of our families. We are peacemakers. A concept that religion cannot control. Light can only grow when treated gently. All light outgrows religion's limitations, when it embodies its breath, its compass, a compass of eternal love, a body of self-radiating essence of illuminated peace, a mind conscious of weaving calm and serenity into its own heart, a heart that never asks the world of its gifts but a heart that embodied and projected serenity into the world, through the silence of harmonious being.

Adam and Eve

The greatest poverty of my spirit, mind, and soul is to be born in the mental universe of bad and good ideas of the mind's projected expectations of purity that beacons humanity's reality of past, present, and future's never-ending self-ordained struggle. Born spirits of blessed human vessels, Adam being the masculine and Eve being the feminine spirits of the human bodies—the flesh, in the union of love and in peace, the two birth out the tree of the human. This true creation of humanity is good. For, the spirits that dwell in love and peace are good. Yet the mind does not know the heart of the spirits. It refuses to see the purpose of the spirits. It is in the mind's belief that Adam and Eve are deemed the sinners of humanity's creation; now, because I am born, I am to be judged a sinner.

The greatest tragedy of creation is the judgmental attitude of uncompassionate minds. But the heart goes on giving love, order, and peace to the minds of lost creation.

—Evangeline

Ever since I was a child, the only people that I was made known to exist, other than the humans around me, were a woman and a man who "pioneered sins," as my ancestors proclaimed with their mouths every day of my childhood life. At an early age, I was told of Adam and Eve's sins, every single time I questioned the cause of people's suffering. I was informed it was these two creatures' fault that we are all hurting inside. It is Adam and Eve's fault that food doesn't just drop from heaven when I'm hungry. It is their fault when my neighbors have to tell lies in order not to get blamed for things they did wrong. Adam and Eve are the reason we are excruciatingly tired and hopeless. They are the reason death happens, and we are their offspring. It was so condemning to be part of this myth. Even my eight-year-old brain could not believe that was the cause of my never-ending hunger, the cause of my young soul's poverty.

I was taught that Adam was a man, and all men are Adam. So, I decided that Father is Adam and Mother is Eve. As a spirit, I was made into a child, who had turned to Eve. Things did make sense very quickly. My parents loved me with every inch of breath they could give my brothers and me. I learned later on that I am a woman soul. My husband made me a wife, but my daughter made me a newly created woman, a mother. John, my husband, became a new Adam, not just a man, now a father. Both of us, in the presence of Gaby's spirit, we are made a family of souls. And the very hour that Gaby died was the end of that first family, both our souls had come to dream to expect to last until we die.

Meanwhile, as expected of all children, our daughter goes on, as her internal clock as a soul runs with passion and determination, for she is strong in spirit.

Instead, the cycle of John's and my family ended quickly before it had begun. The new religion, which we began to shape for our new family, vanished. The new culture that we began to create with her stopped. All humanity within our soul stopped existing. We died as Gaby's family when she died. Both in our silent ways, we deeply suffered. Individually we were forced to feel forsaken. In the name of religion, there is a sense of shame that I failed my daughter. My guilt in living while she is no longer here is impossible to erase—guilt and shame echo in the back of my soul. Though I know I did not commit a sin, Father Pedro's Adam and Eve's sins still echo in my being. As if my mind, my soul, and my all do not know any other way to look at death as my own ancestors' religion's take on my daughter's short life. Somehow that big silent elephant in the room has imprinted a pang of never-ending guilt, an automatic assumption that I caused it because I am a descendant of Adam and Eve, a sinner for having been born. Yet again, I am not just Adam and Eve's descendant. I am a child of the Heavenly Father. The Man who sits on the throne, as he gives and illuminates from all His being eternal peace and love. And before Him, I am no man's tragedy but a spirit child of love who is eternal in-breath and harmony.

Coping Mechanism

The mind will be entertained by the ways and demands of the world while the soul will keep on as the mind perceives and dictates to the soul, but the spirit is shunned away by the mind and the soul. It is in the mind state that a man can be broken as the soul is broken. Yet summon the soul's conscious spirits to come. Both the mind and the soul will be mended by the love and wisdom that the spirits of compassion and mercy that heaven's breath gives to every soul with the mind who breathes the wind of love for humanity now on earth.

—Evangeline

John, my husband, was able to get busy at work immediately after our two-year-old Gaby died. Being an only child and dying so soon had left such an ocean of emptiness in both of our hearts. In order to survive, when loneliness, guilt, and powerlessness became a night-and-day struggle for both of us, I grieved in silence. John had to be strong. He had to support our family. He kept on with his job and showed up for the military's demands. When he came home, he had to escape his mind to survive. He had to dull the pain of his emotions. He drank his bottles of wine daily for years until he suffered painful attacks of blasting, electrocuting pain of trigeminal neuralgia.

After a neurologist told him he had trigeminal neuralgia, he sent John away and was asked to come back the following week. When John came back, the neurologist was no longer at the hospital. He had been sent to Afghanistan.

John and I were on our own. Instead of being listened to, the system of Tripler Army Medical Center failed to listen, guide us; and even when we were so lost, they failed to listen to us. A neurologist was what we needed. Pain doctors took hold of John and gave him unnecessary surgeries, which didn't help the pain. He was getting worse by the day. I was powerless. He was all alone. Watching him suffer made my life a debilitating ordeal to which I must contend. There was no place to run to feel safe.

Again when we asked for a neurologist and an MRI, but no doctor gave the request; no one listened to us. For three years of agony, John was given five different opiates, all of which were administered by different doctors at the same time within Tripler Hospital.

I managed to get busy by educating myself on trigeminal neuralgia. I couldn't be afraid because I knew he needed care. When I couldn't help him, and no doctor was willing to order an MRI, I lived trying to fight the thoughts that I was living in man-made hell. It was not a joke. It was happening. I couldn't move and get him help because he counted on the doctors to know what they were doing. I became far more lost each day as my own husband, the man I loved for his ability to be so caring to everyone, would face me and repeatedly lie as if I was stupid when I told him his doctors were killing him.

I was taking my husband to the emergency room twice a week. Two years went by after having lived in the hospital in supporting him through unneeded surgeries, which doctors swore they knew what they were doing, which had proven a waste of time and money. The unfathomable struggles my husband went through daily was shocking to watch. It tormented my brain to see him drugged up rather than valued and cared for immediately when he needed medical intervention the most. "This is America?" I thought. This is medicine? I wished it was different. The reality was heart-wrenching strife to my already broken soul.

I watched helplessly as my husband would stand but barely able to walk straight. Medical doctors had proven to me that they were there to shut my husband up. That domain, they accomplished, as they made me powerless over my own husband's care. I was seen but not heard—more frustration.

The grief of losing Gaby was put aside. I was in turmoil over my husband's suffering. When I spoke to doctors, they did not listen. I felt degraded. I was just a wife. I wasn't some military personnel. They made sure I got the cue; I didn't have to be listened to. I'm not the patient.

Caring for my husband had become deep suffering on my own. I was overwhelmed by the disjointed yet well-meaning service of our military medical system. I knew I had to help John not die from addiction. Emotionally he needed to heal from grief; biochemically, he needed to recover from addiction from all the opiates and alcohol his brain demanded from him. Physically he needed a neurologist, a surgeon, to heal his trigeminal nerve.

I learned that it's one thing to be in pain, but it's another to watch someone I love to be in so much agony, I never knew if it was going to end, yet I had no power to ease his suffering. I couldn't do anything about it. John had to be in charge of his body. He had to own his well-being, not the doctors and not the Army medical system. But John's spirit was barely hanging on. His spirit of consciousness was taken by grief, pain, and fear. My beloved husband felt like he was not present to enjoy life with me and our children.

For years, I watched my husband suffer physically, emotionally, and spiritually and knew from the depth of my consciousness I was all alone, for I had already lost his soul.

Physically, his liver began to show distress; he had accumulated water in his legs. For years, he slurred when he spoke. He was so high on pain meds—a cure that silenced the brain from thinking, a suffocation of the soul to govern its spirit. At a later part, he began peeing blood; I knew his kidneys were being damaged. He was afraid but too drugged up to think right, too tired to even eat right; he was constantly craving sweets and dairy. If it was bad for him, he would eat it. It was absolutely maddening. It was mentally impeding him, but it was keeping him alive. So, we went in circles because I love him. I stayed and watched for his spirit to keep on—until he wakes.

My husband, the man I so loved and cherished, was no longer there. What took place was the disease of the mind. His soul struggled. His spirit, I knew, was weakened by the desire of his mind. Yet in the same, his soul as my kind husband, his spirit as a man suffered. I had to keep him safe from himself and the medical doctors, who think they know everything, yet they fail to look at his eyes, fail to listen to his silent plea, and see what was going on. He needed a doctor who cared. No doctor was willing to listen and provide help without resorting to pain meds as an only option.

I was frustrated. It was an insult to ask for help from doctors who were trained to help, yet it was evident that they were serving fear and limitations rather than being able to open up to the possibility that if they listened to my husband's plea to get an MRI and have a neurologist take a look was an act of crime. John didn't want to be on pain meds. No one knew the answer to his well-being; we kept coming back to doctors to help because, after all, aren't they here to serve those of us who need healing? In John's case, doctors had failed him, and the system failed him.

Every night was a nightmare. I dreaded waking up the following morning. I was afraid I was going to find a corpse. I knew that with so much medication in his system, his body was going to give. I feared he was going to die from addiction and organ failure, a common death to the addicted soul.

There came the hour where my tears and frustration kept me lost. On my knees, I begged, "God... I know you exist. If you can heal him, make him live. If you can't, take him... just as you have taken Gaby." I cried on my fallen knees.

The answer came so calmly in a soft wind. A voice from above the sky came gently down and, like a soft wind, danced upon my right shoulder, and the soft voice whispered ever so gently, "Inner Balance..." I looked up to see who the voice belonged to. It was from the light that dawned above me. It belonged to the old man who sits upon a white throne who was wearing a soft, silky gown. I stopped washing the dishes in the kitchen and ran to the living room on my computer. I googled the words "Inner Balance." And sure enough, it was a place of healing for John. It was a rehab in Loveland, Colorado. I learned that they could treat John, but he had to go and fly there. Although there was not an immediate room for John, there was one room that was about to be open two months later. I hesitated at first because to secure the room cost $18,000 dollars. And the entire thirty-day treatment would cost about $50,000, including airfare. "Take him!" said the Man on the Throne. He was so calm. His voice was certain and straight to the point. "It's already paid for," He said, comforting me. He cared so deeply for John and me. I could still cry. His presence never left me. He is a father. A loving, gentle, wisdom-filled Father rescued me. When humankind couldn't provide, He comes. He came to helped me. John had checked in at Inner Balance on August 3, 2011. Forty-five days later, John was sober from alcohol; and the staff at the wellness center was able to get him off of all five opiates. He was given a tool that money and grief cannot earn. He learned to listen to his emotions. When he's sad, he has to cry. When he misses Gaby, he has to share his feelings with me, talk about her laughter and all her bright light, and all the gifts she brought into our lives until his longing passed. He is to honor his feelings when they appear.

When our emotional bodies hurt, it is a call to our higher consciousness to allow the feelings to rise. Our spirit is to stop doing what it is busy doing. Our soul is trying to tell our spirit its hurt. The spirit must honor the feelings that arise from our souls no matter what it may be. Being alive means, we are the vessels of emotional bodies of energies. These energies come in sequence to help us feel life. They are sensory languages to the emotions we are experiencing. These emotions are our tools to express our take on humanity and life. Joy will fuel us to bright life. Sadness and longing will come reminding us where we've been. It surfaces to remind us we are still alive. It shows us sadness, followed by wisdom; both come hand in hand, just a reminder to honor our growth by acknowledging how far we've come. Grief and sadness will appear. We must acknowledge these emotions, for in doing so, we agree that we are its witness to life's experiences. Without judgments, we must thank their presence; their winds will come to assist our soul in being awakened. When their job is finished, these winds will disappear on their own and set our soul free.

The Tragedy of the Mind

The mind craves all things, good and bad. When it's hungry, it eats not of the bread of man; rather, it eats at the soul. When it becomes comforted by addiction, it steals the body, kicking the conscious spirit of love from its home, its human brain. The spirit of man is fragile and gentle. Give it love, and it will reign upon the mind of the universe. Breathe in it's peace, and it gives purpose to the sea of life, which for eons have been open for all spirits of love to dwell herein.

—Evangeline

It is in grief that we are lost. Yet the mind will want to adapt and live for the sake of the soul. However, it is in grief that the mind of a drunk breathes belittling words. It speaks degradations. It breathes anger. It shouts endless pain. It breaks everything it touches. It destroys hearts. And when it is silent, it breaks the spirits of others, for even it squandered its own life through the absence of compassion. This is the mind of addiction. It is psychotic in behaviors as it sees life as the existence of great, happy, and rightful, and destructive acts of distortion. The diseased mind not only lies, but it believes it is powerful and has the right to own everything in the world. It gambles the house, the life, family, and it even gambles the future of the spirit and its soul by lies and more lies. From a brokenhearted mother to an abandoned wife, I had become mad by grief but made vicious by the snare and powerful punch of opiate addictions precipitated by ignorant doctors who's lack of conscience, reasons, and absence of feelings, of the breath of compassion toward my husband, myself and my children. As a friend and a wife, I was reduced to nothing of value by doctors and alcoholism's futile, absolutely cunning, and demonic tendencies. After I lost my soul as a mother, so too did I have to mourn my soul as a wife, a best friend, a lover, and a family. I was but an imprint of a wife, left as a name and idea to my husband. The love we had shared was dampened by anger and cries, diminished by his belittling lies and selfish behaviors. My spirit comforted my soul, comforted the angry wife in me, by learning to pray that I may not be the tragedy of the broken soul because I promised the day I married him that I would love him with all my heart in bad and in good. My spirit is bound by such a promise. I knew that bad or good people made it in life. And good and bad people's relationships recover. Why? I asked. Well, look at grandpas and the grandmas of the world. They make it somehow. That's why they grow older and have many grandchildren. No matter what, they make it. They make it because good and bad; no one quits on loving. They keep moving. They keep dreaming. Until their years add up, they keep loving.

So I gave up life, as I knew it; I learned to trust the honest whispers of silence, which taught me to listen to the quiet unspoken light of the voiceless truth. I am the spirit of love. I can never be reduced to anger, never to be known to the world as a a servant and a co-dependent of a wife. I am a spirit. I know and will forever behold the truth. I am love. No matter what John did and what doctors did not do, I am still the love that John had and will keep having even after I die.

My husband's alcoholic mind will never remember my spirit, for it has not known me. But my spirit knew my husband before he was heartbroken. I knew his joy when we first met. I knew the brightness of his hope when he told me about his dreams. I knew his smile when he turned into a childlike state, corky, and yet he was that young man who was kind. So when I looked at the empty gaze from the eyes of his body and saw the surface of the shell, his demeanor, and his soul's pleading distress, his arrogant drunkenness couldn't hide, I knew my husband—the spirit that made me smile, the spirit that loved and gave me hope long ago—was buried way beneath and could not surface. He was in there somewhere. I knew that like me, in my secret suffering, he was fighting to come up, fighting to breathe and struggling to surface so he could own his mind and take care of his body, to honor his soul once again. So I watched him cry, hide in the closet, he did many times, because he was confused and very afraid.

After years of medical doctors' abuse, I feared that my husband was going to suffer a heart attack. The fear of him dying, the fear that I may have to see my children live without a father broke my soul. It troubled my spirit deeply.

I threatened to sue the medical establishments if they did not honor my husband's cause of pain. Four years later, they finally listened and took an MRI, which enlightened them to send him to a neurologist surgeon, which performed the much-needed brain surgery, which should have been performed four years back. The pain left; my husband's biochemistry was all dulled by pain meds. It took that prayer in the kitchen to get him to the right rehab. It took divine intervention. It took the Man on the Throne. He is not a god but a Father of that everlasting peace that makes heaven exist in harmony and peace.

The day my daughter died, on December 7, 2004, my husband's soul as a father died; as his soul as a husband was hijacked by medical doctors through pain meds, following alcohol abuse and medication, which altered his behavior, so have I felt an utter sense of aloneness that cannot be described by words. The abandonment was beyond life's suffering. The sense of ever-flowing cold, dark abyss was continuously appearing and I was the only one in it. I couldn't surface; I couldn't swim. This entity had no water, no edges, no light, no breath. It was the ocean of everything that is nothing. It is a space where every molecule flowing was a massive river of no movement that spreads a whirlwind of lost and toxic elements of silent mental agony that no eyes could see, and no ears could hear.

Meanwhile, deep beneath my conscious self, my spirit, my soul wanted to come out of my skin.

Each day of watching someone I love dearly succumb to the disease of the brain, his mind had become but a speck of lost memories. He had forgotten me, and everything about me was blurred. He could no longer remember how our love used to be. Because his brain was being drugged, I saw, felt, knew, tasted, and embodied my husband as a walking shell, while his addiction fed him lively dreams to own cars we could not afford, spending money like he had plenty of it. He went to work drunk with opiates in his system because the doctor said it was okay.

His spirit was shunned, and his own soul had forgotten that he is a loving spirit. I felt the only way to survive was to float above the darkness constantly. I knew I couldn't fight the disease. I couldn't fight the sorrow. But the only choice I had was not to fight it or run from it. It was there to tell me something. I had not denied its existence. It was as if it was allowed to exist, so I could tell myself that it wasn't right. I had to accept its manifestations before I could tell myself there was a way out of it.

Addiction was hostile in domain yet silent in words. Yet it was eerie at the same instant. The only relief was to ground me in my truth. I went back to myself. My spirit was untouched. The memories are there for me to go home to the truth. My soul may be so confused and frustrated and angry, but my soul, my love, refuses to forget who John was and who he truly is. Not just as I remembered him but how I knew him. Despite life's glory and its entire struggle, I always knew he wanted only to love me.

I knew the spirit of my husband would never want to hurt me; I forced myself to remember how kind he used to be. I made myself remember his spirit's language when we were newlyweds. I pushed my mind to its deepest recesses to see me young and in love again, with this young man who was full of life and promises. He crossed the Pacific Ocean to find me. When he did, he left but only to cross it again countless times to be with me for good.

My spirit, my heart, and my soul as his wife remembered who he truly was before the death of Gaby, before the alcohol, before medication. I knew the breath of love that fueled his kindness, his smile, his dreams governed my soul to remember to see the truth. I know the very force that fueled his light; his kindness still was the spirit that made me have a meaningful existence. He loved me unconditionally; he took me for who I was. Then he loved the world and took it for what it was. The way he would cash his only last twenty dollars so he could give it to the homeless and give them food, so they were not scouring the garbage cans on the street that he often walked home from work. He showed me the bright light of hope in lending a hand to those in need, waiting for mercy; it restored the faith in my heart to understand the purpose of birth—my humanity. Despite the addiction of his mind and altered state of being in suffering, I know his spirit that is love was with me, seeking to be whole—desperately.

Adam's Sobriety Is Eve's Peace

The Man of Peace came. He took me to the garden of heaven. Here there is a pure light garden. Spirits that are husbands wait for their wives' death so the spirits may come to them from the earth; in the same, wives wait in spirits for their husbands to come from the earth. The love between the two remains bright and strong no matter the time, no matter the experience of death. Then when both husband and wife are done waiting, they hold hands and shine peace in silent contentment as they walk in the heart of the garden of the heavens, new life, where the light of all love is sourced and never dies.

—Evangeline

Addictions and pain had taken a big chunk of time from my husband's internal clock. Though I could not say it was time wasted, I was aware I had lost a quality of life that others may be experiencing at the moment. I lost myself. My sense of calm was altered. My sense of peace was often tried. It had subjected me to the depths of anger and total abandonment as a woman. I was as I watched in agony a lost soul—an angry wife, as he struggled to listen and find a way out of addiction. It's been years of fighting to save my husband's spirit. I know that like me, from the loss of his daughter, my husband was never to be the same again. Mourning our Gaby had altered the state of peace, hope, dreams, and love in our breaths. The pain of the true reality that she had died and is no longer here had both ruined and injured our souls and made a mockery of our spirits, mind, body, and had altered the current state of living. Our marriage was a struggle to keep tending with hope. My spirit yearned to know how marriages, which are created by God and sourced in divine love, manage to survive this human life. Somehow our ancestors had loving marriages on earth. How? I wondered. I understood now why people give up. Some must, in order to survive. One must let go. In order to live. In order to walk and breathe again.

In April of 2011, I needed help saving my marriage. To make sense of it all, I needed to remember how God—our merciful Father strengthened me with His visit. As I washed dishes, I begged, "Father, I saw you before Gaby died. You were there. You guided me. I know you exist. Please don't let alcoholism ruin my spirit. As death has already cast me to die as a mother, please… Please don't make me bury my husband. If you will heal him, heal him. If you can't heal him, take him! Just don't make a mockery of my being. Please heal him."

As instantaneously as I prayed, so did a soft, silent wind swiftly hover around my ears and shoulders.

"Inner Balance," the calm wind spoke; my mind and heart detected its silent peace. I was awakened with light from within and suddenly at peace.

I ran to the computer and typed "Inner Balance."

On the front of the web page was a video link.

"We help people detox!" the man in the video spoke firmly.

I explored further and was made known that Inner Balance was a rehab center in Loveland, Colorado. I called immediately and was made aware I needed eighteen thousand dollars to reserve a room and would need fifty thousand dollars to complete a one-month program, including airfare.

My heart sank with disappointment. I had only thirty thousand in life savings.

"Take him," said a commanding voice from the Man sitting on the throne, suddenly hovering gently above me.

"Take him. It's already paid," He said ever so sternly. I was filled with a fresh wind of strength and comfort.

By July 27, my husband and our family gathered to celebrate his thirty years of Navy service. It was a long thirty years, yet the most trying of those were the last four years. In his retirement ceremony, he slurred through his speech and spoke disjointedly, having forgotten to thank my parents for being there for us whenever he needed them. He was high on opiates. My heart broke with compassion for him and my parents. Addiction had broken our family relationship. We were struggling spiritually; we needed help. It was a help no one on earth I knew could give. We were all lost. We were all suffering. And no one else could reach beneath it all to stop the pain.

Three days after his retirement ceremony, he checked in at Inner Balance. The staff weaned him off all meds the whole time he was there, through detox. They taught him how to care for his mind. He learned to eat healthily and be mindful of his thoughts. All was possible due to the detox the center performed the first twenty-four hours he arrived at the center.

"Thank you for loving my son," said my father-in-law. "I decided to pay for the rest of the treatment," he shared kindly.

I cried with relief as I braced myself with gladness. That was the promise made certain to take place by the Holy Father.

"Hon, I can't come home at the beginning of the month," called my husband a month later as I anticipated the day of his release.

"Why not, honey?"

"I had a hard time weaning off Klonopin. They need me to stay for another two weeks. It will cost another fifteen hundred," he revealed, sounding fragile.

Before I could worry about the cost, I heard, "Don't worry, my mother and stepfather paid for it already," he comforted me.

With the help of family, my husband came home sober. There began the work again of learning to trust, of learning to forgive, of learning to listen to my spirit to seek kindness no matter what, to learn to love again, despite what my fears, despite what my hurt feelings said.

A week later, his pain broke; his addicted mind said his body hurt. When he told the doctor about his pain, the ignorant doctor who lacked compassion, unconscious of my husband's soul's sufferings, who refused to think, refused to honor my family and my husband's hard work from rehab, happily gave my husband an opiate patch to kill him again.

From which began another vicious struggle to get him out of an addicted state of being. He is currently in deep emotional trauma, afraid to let go of his lifeline, the medication. He is still being governed by another kind doctor, "because of pain," as he says, with a daily dose of five ml. of methadone.

Blessings

The birth of a child calls for a new beginning. Its presence is a fulfillment of another blessed, sacred, yet a newly dawning dream, risen, awakened in truth—humanity.
—Evangeline

Even now that my daughters Isabella and Michaela had been born, sadly as it is, they would never know the true childlike light that once radiated out from their father's illumination as long as his brain was governed by medications that altered the state of his senses. To feel life as it is being given now, in every moment that comes, as blessings and joy would require great awareness. Yet in the brain that is governed by medication, the altered state is merely a way in which the soul and the man in him live in the body, but the spirit of awareness, the spirit of love and joy, is a substance that will be shunned by his tormented brain.

To that, I am deeply saddened. I mourned my daughter Gaby, but my focus is to gain the good health that my husband used to have. I am mourning the life I used to know of myself. To love so much but not be acknowledged is the loneliest place to be. Now with my husband's program with Alcoholic Anonymous and the 12 Steps, sobriety is achievable. With God's help, we can move forward and continue healing as a couple, and pursue our commitment to be loving parents despite the hardship at times.

As a mothering soul, as Gaby's mother, I had lost the wholeness of myself when my daughter's joy in her body died. In that space took hold "fibromyalgia," as doctors would call it. I call it pain and sorrow, the natural state of yearning for what was, the knowledge that could never be quelled by life ever again. The feeling of being whole and innocent of death cannot be rewound, for such knowledge belongs to the years before my daughter's passing. My soul, as Gaby's mother, longed for the feeling of wholeness that I once was, in innocent joy, the deep trust and faith within that I assumed and deeply trusted that life to behold for me. In the sorrow of my loss, such wholeness would never come again. For life with my daughter as I knew as wholeness could not be repeated by the womb of the progressing time. Yet again, it is in a new time that a realization comes. My spirit that is whole in light beckons above, watching and enveloping me with its unconditional and gentle radiance of utter illumination.

The courage of the world is self-love, mercy, and grace.
—Evangeline

When was the first time you heard your spirit speak its truth? When did you hear it comfort you when no one else on earth could? List what you are grateful for your spirit when it saved your soul from being in the dark. What of your humanity was a blessing as your spirit shined on it?

_____

_____

The spirit is the dreamer, the mind is the fuel, the body is the vessel, yet it is the soul that must manifest both the spirit and the kind and gentle whisper of the mind, through the works of the hands and the action of the body.
—Evangeline

Fifteen

The Tenth Stage of Grief: Acceptance

Acceptance. Forgiveness is accepting the light, love, and peace within self and shining these lights out to the world everywhere consciousness finds itself present.

Acceptance to death and loss, failure, and sorrows can never be imagined by a condemned soul, but the spirit of man may learn from all the miseries of the mind and heart of mankind in order to forgive the ills of grief that were endured. Peace of the soul is love. Love is the light of the mind that shines forgiveness on all created and yet uncreated manifestation. When mankind shines its love on to life, eternal breaths will flow out through him. The universe of peace manifests itself. Man is the love and peace of the universe.

—Evangeline

Divine Intervention from Spirit of Mercy

One September evening, in our house in Hawaii, a few weeks after my surrendering prayer, I was restless. Like most nights before, I sat sadly, lost in a silent sea of agitated meditation, struggling, waiting long and hard for me to come into a space of gentle calm, in prayer. It was midnight. I was alone. I was exhausted, but I could not sleep. I was lonely again, but I could no longer cry. While my newborn Isabella was asleep with my husband in the downstairs bedroom, I found myself meditating as I sat quietly on the couch of our upstairs living room. The coolness of the night began to relax my body. A gentle gush of air filtered through the living room jalousie windows and enveloped me. Yet, I was not at ease. I wanted to be. So I found myself in a space where I was floating. Finally, I came to a blank space. Here, I wanted nothing. I wished for nothing. I thought of nothing. It was a vast space of kind infinities; it was in me and outside of me. I was in a womb of safety. It felt good. After a while, I could hear the trees outside while their leaves were being caressed by the wind. Back and forth, they twirled gently, prancing side to side through the air.

Right after, I became aware of a presence in my living room. When I looked in my mind's eyes before me, there was a shimmering soft light. Before long, it had turned into stronger white energy, in the form of a human. Suddenly there He was, sitting on a chair, an older man, in his ageless fifties, glowing in fluid form. He was kind, and more than thirty feet tall. He was smiling as He was gently glowing more and more as he breathed. *"He is just a product of my imagination,"* I thought. I shook my head again and again. I touched my eyeballs through their lids.

No matter how hard I did it, when I opened and closed them, He was still in front of me sitting very still, comfortably, gently smiling. I looked at his eyes and face; I could not see through the luminous shadow. He was glowing with soft energy overpowered by His gentle smile. I thought, *Maybe I should just run away.* But I couldn't move or stand up. I was paralyzed by sweet calm as I was surrounded by so much peace from His love.

"Oh, my child… sit down," He ordered in a very formal, yet reserved, accent. Every word He said afterward comforted me. "I want to tell you a story," He went on. "But, you must record this story so you will not forget." Then He disappeared with the wind. I was left bewildered.

"I am just tired," I thought to myself. "I am finally going crazy… This has to stop," I ordered myself as I stood up and began walking away from the couch. Baffled and confused, I went to bed.

Though still in wonder the following morning, I felt at peace. I could not decide what to make of the old man. I went on with my daily chores with Him in mind.

One afternoon, a week later, as I began to put Isabella down on her bed, a kind voice said, "It's time, child." I was amazed. I shook my head, blinked my eyes, and stared at the form before me. There He was with his long gown again. He sat slightly reclined on his floating chair, smiling. Immediately, I was hypnotized. My hand had turned the computer on and started punching the keyboard with my fingers. Everything in me wanted to catch up as I tried to put words to the visions He was showing me. I began to see pictures as if I were watching television. I began to feel everything in the story, guided by His wonderful light-filled visions, of heart-to-heart, unspoken voice; He narrated in soft white light, illuminating a paradise reality, so brilliant, so calm, solitude governed my whole being.

Before His throne, a green garden revealed itself to me. Suddenly I was in it. I entered the castle's gate. There I saw a little girl, surrounded by three mother angels with wings. Brilliant light rejoiced around them. The light, the garden, and the angels were focused on what the little girl was describing. She was talking proudly. She was telling them all about her journey—about the earth, about her dad… about her… mom… me! It was Gaby! Then she talked about her grandma—my mother. Then she smiled as she talked about her grandfather, my dad—the people who surrounded her from birth to her death. She talked about her experience in the hospital. She smiled. Then she danced her head side to side and talked some more. Amazed, I could not understand how a two-year-old child could be so joyful, interactive, and intricate with her conversation with the angels. The angels were fascinated as much as they were interested, passionate, and devotedly loving toward her. They adored her. *They admired her. They cherished her.* The spirit of children is missed when they venture out of the heaven of light. My heart echoed in revelation. I left them knowing she is loved and cherished as much as I love her as a mother. My spirit saw her strength. She was not alone.

Now suddenly. I was lifted above another scene. I was higher. I was above the castle. Then another vision revealed itself. A two-year-old little girl runs to the garden from the inside of the castle. An old man runs after her. She giggled in delight. He was honored and glad to embrace her pure innocence.

"Let me take care of her now," His heart echoed, awakening the sleeping heart inside of me. "Take good care of yourself," He insisted. He laughingly embraced her and sat her on his lap, joyfully and contentedly. She played on His lap. She was contented. Joyful and carefree, she glowed freedom. She leaned her head to His chest. She went to sleep on His arms. He fell asleep on the throne, with her on his lap. I was at peace and in awe. She doesn't know I am there watching. But the love between her and the old man was mutual. She was glad to be home. He was divinely at ease with her company. He was at ease in having her back. He waited for her return. I know that all around the castle was peace. Where there are movements, it was a subtle echo of music filtering through the air. I went higher to the other side of the castle where the music was being played. Here angels were coming and going, serving everyone around them with utter and full and undivided presence. Children were gathered by angels and cared for with much passion and devotion. From infant to toddler, there are angels all around communing with the gift of each other's presence. Each spirit is of light and love. Each is cherished for their light and wisdom. Here angels shine to light the heart and spirits of human light. In light and eternal love, no spirit is left behind. All is light. All must shine; the light is home. The light is love. *And love is safety*. My heart spoke its revelations.

Then I looked above me as a fantastic yet soft brilliant light beaconed. It called me. The light shines in the garden. The garden was floating above me. Soon I was invited in. Here all human spirits that once were ancient healers on the planet were busy working with female angels. Though the main work is a leisurely pace of being present at all times, looking after little children and cherubs at play, every spirit is busy tending others. *This castle had many levels;* my heart spoke. *In each floor are many gardens serving one purpose—to be the living presence of eternal refuge, the kingdom's hearts are the spirit bodies of radiant compassion, that shine and give light—to love all children, to embrace and comfort, to shine peace, nurture to a new life all children of God, to unite as one all humanity in the warmth and love of the living Father's arms, the God of peace and mercy, the God of light and new life, to make whole in consciousness what is broken in the mind, to resurrect in spirit what death had surrendered to its God—its living children—the holy family of God—humanity's spirit of love, compassion, and mercy—the gods and goddesses of the planet earth.*

Heaven's Many Secret Rooms

There are many secret rooms. This castle has many hidden secret rooms that lead to a multi-level of breathtaking nature escapes of light-filled gardens. It is always a morning-filled brilliance lighting everything and everyone. I backed out and floated above and looked all-around at the castle. It is a castle of light, peace, harmony, and a divine solitude only found by a secret path that has been laid hidden to those who are outside the castle. Then I saw another hidden level of the castle, where angels and babies sang divine music, lullabying all the newly arrived baby spirits to a restful sleep after a long, long journey from the earth. Outside the rooms, many mommy angels would take turns as many infants and toddlers needed care. Toddlers, babies were surrounded by young boy and girl cherubs that help the mother angels babysit.

After three pages of writing the visions before me, I realized that the visions I was writing about were of a little girl who died. Her spirit lives and is loved. Her body was buried and remained on earth. I know. I was there every step of the way. Though death was the experience, and though it is now part of the past, it is still my life's fuel in my present journey. In writing, I realized that time is always present. But the space that my daughter should have made filled by her human experience remains empty. Her human future is absent. Her future humanity is a space no longer part of my human story. The present had stopped giving me the gift of Gaby's life on earth. Rather it plays in my mind only glimpses of my life's memories, of joy, fear, and sorrow, of love and sweet blessings in the company of a newborn little girl, my sweet Gaby, who was then a toddler.

Her spirit then may have been tiny, but her radiance was immense. Her life story was of great trial. It was short. Her birth was a race to keep her living in the breath of life's possibilities, only to end so soon to her death. In the heart of a mother's memory, everything is past. There is no repeating the same experience. She came in the womb of time, and time kissed me with her love. Time brought her, and in two winter moons, then took her spirit back. She was my life's innocent spirit of glory, grace, and light.

Now in this garden of a new life. The womb of time may not reach this light. Now it is yet a new present. Time cannot know its beginning. Here the light of a spirit has no end.

Her new reality is no longer a memory. She is the light of a new home. Her light is not the true light of my planet earth. This light that shined in the heavens was her love hidden by the flesh. Yet in spirit she shines in full love and wisdom. She is now a spirit. She shines among the living. She is a compassionate, ever-living, forever loving body of a luminous child of a conscious star.

Next I arrived in a deeper space. A man floated in a tunnel of light. In his arms was a little girl. I saw her light, the very force that made her alive in the body, lifted from the earth, and began traveling in vast spaces with much excitement, without tiring as this Man of Light held her. How is she not alone? She is embraced by a pure white light in an image of a brilliant body of the spirit man. With a spirit of Man holding her, I looked down at where they had been. I saw that she was first on an island on earth. It was in Hawaii. Her spirit was playing by herself. I knew she was in a trance. Meanwhile, a six-hundred-pound woman sat leisurely as a boy and girl toddlers, ages two and three, climbed on her belly fold, up to her left shoulder, and slid down to her arm and gently landing on her left hand. They climb on her with glee. With much joy and satisfaction, the children played. I couldn't help but look at the woman's attentive focus. It was toward this little two-year-old girl in a trance. I knew she was being kept in a trance for the purpose of waiting. Then a white light tunnel descended. The woman picked up the child and handed her to the Man of Light, who just arrived. The child came out of her trance and happily ran toward him.

Within a blink, the tunnel that took her disappeared, and out they came to a new garden. A motherly woman was waiting. She was a graceful mother. She took the child from the Man of Light. After a quick rest. The Man of Light took her. Within a blink, they came to a beautiful garden, where three motherly angels were waiting. She remembered every one of them. They embraced her. They missed her. They carried her to the castle following the Man of Light. In one of the rooms, the angels tucked her to rest and sleep. And when she awoke, I found her in the garden talking to three eighteen-foot-tall mother angels.

The more I entered this mystical world, I knew that the little girl was Gaby's spirit. And what I saw through visions during my writing was her journey as she transitioned to the spirit realm. As I wrote, I was being illuminated by warm white light. The brilliance was enlightening. I was comforted. I forgot my sadness. Every vision was filling and answering the questions I had asked as to who was taking care of my daughter after she had died.

Now I got to see how her death and burial were not her end. What might have been an accidental death to my experience was her being released from the experience of pain and limitations of the vessel that incased her beautiful, perfect, joyful, bright, precious and loving spirit.

Even when the body is not perfect, the spirit of my child's perfection shined compassion toward me and the earth. She came. She came and filled me as long as her body had allowed. For such a gift, I am forever changed. I am more than I can ever know as a soul, as a spirit, as a mother. It is not because she was born that I find myself more. It is in her death that I find the meaning of my own existence as a girl, as a woman, as a mother. Life on earth, no matter how joyful or dreary, is a divine spirit descent to a new beginning of a soul's life to shine on all. Heaven is the light and world of pure spirit bodies that fuel love. All love dwells from the eternal heaven. It bares pure spirit divine in grace and mercy, illuminating only peace to all universes in all degrees of existence, both in the world of the external, the seen, and that of the eternal, the unseen. The spirit of each child is a transcendent force. It comes when it wants, and it goes where it desires. The time it does not know. For it is everlasting. It is forever. The spirit is everywhere; it finds itself loving. When a child is born into the world, it is heaven giving earth a new spirit, to light and guide humanity to love as spirit love, eternal and forever.

Heaven and earth are one in the same dream. Both give their best for true, kind, gentle, and loving creation.

—Evangeline

The Process of Birth

The mother arches her back and lifts her spine to raise her head. In deep groaning passion and force, she surrenders herself to heaven's brilliance. In her kiss, she knocks at the door of the heavens. And when heaven's door opens, the Father looks down to the door of earth and lets the spark of His breath flow, to swim in the river water of the mother's sacred womb. The spark of life between heaven and earth ignites. A new light awakens. A new heart beats at last for the first time. Mother Earth creates a vessel, a sacred body. A new soul is made. A new name is drawn from the heavens. The spirit comes with a name. Now the spirit must come to dwell in life's new creation.

When a spirit leaves the heavens and enters its mother's womb, it lights the new suit of life; a new baby is born, giving birth to a new soul—creating a new and vast universe to a father's and mother's heart visions of a new humanity. When the spirit comes to dwell in the flesh, it is a new creation. It is a new soul. Every birth brings forth a new and loving pure child. In a body, it will be human learning all human insecurities and its imperfections, while the spirit in a body is the love and the light of its sacred force, being illumined and powered by its own riverbed of eternal heaven, the light, the love, its true home.

Everyone—no matter the color of their skin while on earth, no matter how backward or forward the culture that beheld each birth, every spirit is driven by silent conscious knowing that it is simply passing to plant love into the world of man. For everyone who starts the journey to humanity will see darkness. But darkness called for such light to burn in love, so darkness may know its divine purpose. Darkness cannot exist without light. The light must come to save darkness from itself. The light is love. Even darkness must call for the light to transform itself into love. In the silent wind of the universe, darkness is the bed of love. And light is its heart, conscious of pure love.

—Evangeline

Now she transitioned to the light; I saw that there were pure bright light gardens where all spirits go. Different levels of gardens existed. Some are hidden in the brilliant light. The light garden is stunningly beautiful, so pure—the wind is so clean and fresh my lungs could breathe and expand beyond all worlds. The grasses were so green; the morning dews were sitting on them while the morning beamed softly on them. Everywhere I looked was so brilliant, I felt whole. The light is the truth. Truth is peaceful and life-giving. It is a green pasture for a new life. Suddenly I knew that all things past belong to the time of one's imagining. In the figment of the imagination, the image is kept as a glimpse of the creation of life. Life is a story. It will come into being, and it will go. But heaven is light. It is pure love. Love, where it is true, lights up the eternal world, and here peace reigns above all. Where peace shines, love alone is real. Love is forever and ever, with no beginning or end.

All creation will have ceased to exist. Yet it is its love that will never cease to exist. For when all seasons have passed, love will remain conscious of self. Love is self, and love is the light of all that exists.

Then the womb of darkness and silence called for me. Time whammed itself gently through me. Three hours later, the door of the heavens closed; the vision stopped. I could see my feet on the cold floor. I am in the body. I looked up. The door of the light heaven is closed. The old man was nowhere in sight. *He only came to deliver a part of the story.*

I read the first paragraph I typed. It dawned on me that I had begun writing a secret revelation of a space no human eyes can detect. I wondered what its purpose was about other than to comfort me. I mattered despite my loss. I mattered enough for the gentleman of the throne. Sparks of light will greet me when I can't sometimes breathe for missing her. In the light, I see her on His lap as He rests. That was a sweet vision. Even after her death, my daughter's glory, He wanted to share with me. I knew He didn't have to come. But He did. I didn't know what love was, somehow I now know love is all there ever was.

The love of a father's spirit is eternal. The love of a child is eternal. The love of a mother is eternal. Love is it! The rest of creation is an explanation of this eternal and yet unspoken love. It is all that there ever was, is, and will ever be!

—Evangeline

Eternal Love

The universe is the heaven of earth, the human flesh, and its mind. Yet hidden from the eyes of the universe is another heaven. It is the heaven of pure light, where the substance of the heart are sourced and illuminate. It is the living heaven, where pure love flows; and all forms are contemplated before it is to manifest in creation. All hues of colors originate here. It is here that colors return. In the same, the guardians are from this light. All sizes of angelic beings and humanity's family are birthed here in spirits; after the journey in the universe, it is in this light that all spirits of consciousness must return. The heart of heaven is the Father of love. The Holy Spirit is the heaven of all spirits, from which all living water of life's grace come.

—Evangeline

For many months, the old man's spirit came and went with His sweet and gentlemanly manner. His presence is infinitely bright. His kind demeanor matched His soothing yet nonverbal words of an accent. I had grown accustomed to expect His visit any time as I went on with my daily chores. Out of the blue, when I was done with one chore, when it was a good window to take a break, He would show up just the way my daughter used to show up with the wind, gentle and smiling with peace. "Come, child," He said every time, "it's time to write."

Two years after my second daughter was born, He kept me company; and the story He delivered in glimpses for this book that I wrote in between cleaning my house and feeding my newborn child had finally been recorded, but the story was nowhere finished. His visits were filling the great hole of my aching spirit with so much substance unknown to life. His very essence and presence brought hope for my evolving soul, the light of my hungry spirit, and the love that I am awakening to find each day as I rise on my journey as a child of man, a girl, a woman, a mother, a sister, a wife, and a servant to all brothers and sisters of mankind before me.

The Language of the Spirit Is the Unspoken Words of the Heart

In heaven is silence. The purity of the light is His holy grace. The heart is the entire body of brilliant mercy and solitude—the Man of Light. The body of complete and utter pure and brilliant luminosities that govern all creation is the living force of pure love, to which peace is the order that governs the bed of all creation to dream, to rise, to labor in the spirit of love, before one is bound in comfort, to return where it had begun.

Before me in the light, He spoke just like my Gabriella did, with His mind, through the light of His kind and loving heart. He would provide me with luminous visions complete with every silent conversation that had taken place within this story. His presence could not come more perfectly. It seemed when I needed help the most; He was there.

Has this Spirit, this Father being always been there with me all along? Was He there when I gave birth to my child? Was I ever truly alone in this human journey, or has He been part of me in every breath I took as a child of my human father? It seems He was there all along watching me, guiding my spirit to light when my soul was sleepy and tired. It is His guidance and light that brings forth the vision of creating the right choice. In Him, humanity is not complicated. The choice is simple. It is to choose the light of the heart, and the light that powers all the spirits. Love no matter what the circumstance. There were many days I couldn't imagine how I would survive grief at all when everyone around me was clueless about how to reach out to me. But love made me conscious. I searched for my own love. I found the edge of my light. When I dug deep through my own being, I saw my own light; I forgot the sentiment of my human mind and its mental conflict. When I searched in the heart of my grief, I saw the light above me. In the light is heaven. Its body is peace, and its throne is a giant spirit of a Father who lights up in loving every one of His spirit children that he lets go in the universe to power the new light and breath of spirits' creations called humanity. Earth is a new and sacred creation. Mankind is a new creation of spirits. Humanity is a domain of the spirits. Love is family. Earth is one family in spirit. It is compassion, grace, and acceptance. It is one light shining on the darkness of the souls. The spirits of each man are light. It is love. Love is one big family. Humanity is a sacred and loving creation. Everyone is in it.

So the greatest revelation is before me. My soul is new. It doesn't know that my spirit is conscious of right. Righteousness is a light above all darkness. My soul as a child of man has been searching for what is right. All along, it was above and inside of me. My soul doesn't know how to bring it life. It is hidden. Life is a struggle if love is hidden. The search for love is the journey as long as it needs to be found. I tried my best to do the right thing. The right thing in fear is never enough to quell my longing. I remember after giving birth to Isabella when I fell ill. My doctors had associated my pain with postpartum depression. As I recalled clearly, I was already in the past been issued two types of antidepressant drugs, both of which numbed me from the reality I was fighting very hard to be part. But once again, my doctors tried to help by giving me another type of medication to combat the struggle of bloodless yet dull, paralyzing numbing ache of my body. When I took the meds, just like before, I could not move. I did not have the ability to respond to my daughter's cries, no matter how loud they were. It was pure hell to want to take care of her, but the medicines had turned me into a zombie. I could hear her cry, but my body's motherly instinct to hold her and comfort her had been shut off. My mind was detached; my body would not move when I wanted to hold her. It was frustrating.

For a while, in a medicated state, when the old man would come to visit me, I would see His presence and smile, but we could not communicate. I could not hear or see what He was trying to tell me. The story was halted for six months. It was then that my numbed brain and my miserable soul had experienced complete hopelessness, which felt like an unwanted and unexpected death once again. The ability to feel and connect failed me. I felt lost, alone, and confused, even more than the day my daughter died.

Having experienced the grace of His soft nonverbal, yet loudly radiant comforting voice, His presence alone illuminated a soothing essence of calm and safety. I awakened to a deep knowing that I was a newborn infant, being cradled in the light of pure warmth of love. I was safe. The world and everything in it were suddenly okay. I was never to be just a mother. There was a deep sense that the best of who I am to be was to come.

Days passed. I found that I could not live without the old man's kind light. Without His visits, my world was gray and cold. My life was filled with worries. I could not live alone. Without hope, if I could not have the visions of His presence, and without the sacred glimpse of the light-filled story in my heart, my life had no meaning. My cloudy mind was its high mountain that had stopped me from seeing the radiance of heaven's light.

I decided to find a way out of that unwanted depression in my life. I had to do what my body was good at doing. I resorted to waking up at four and five in the morning to work out in order to wake my body up with all the sweating and movement from running. I would drive to the gym for twenty minutes. It was during one of those drives through the quiet and desolate road that I discovered I could communicate with the old man. Then and there, while I was behind the wheel, without the pills in my body, I could feel and see Him. He always came with such a loving presence, again calming and nurturing me with all light of grace. I was safe. I was going to be all right. He is with me in everything that I do. I have to open my heart and learn to allow His love and presence to be the focal point of my daily existence; His presence in my vision is a sacred meditation.

After three months, before I knew it, I had gained the strength I needed in my mind and body without the aid of any medication. My brain function became normal again, and communication between He and I resumed with great understanding, again without spoken words but light to light, heart to heart, intention to intention. Writing again was the main highlight of my days. The more I wrote, the deeper in the light garden I went, the more spirit beings I saw. When the lights of heaven open, the spirits are lit up and rejoicing that I have come. They talk to me with their whole body. Light to light, they radiate in loving peaceful intention. All are one in the light of His loving presence—all respect one another as vital light of the entire whole of existence. One spirit is not whole without the respect of the presence of the other. I feel all of them are connected. If one is not lit up, so the rest will not also be. The heaven garden will not be. There will not be life. That is the vital role of individual spirits. One is the whole itself with the Man of Light as my guide. He alone opened the door to these hidden spirit gardens. "*This is the secret of the eternal world,*" I thought. "*Everlasting love is the door that leads to this divine garden.*"

Family: Love is Forever!

I communed knowing that the secret I am placing into words are for all human families to drink and eat in the pure spirit in order to be blessed, in order to truly live, and be sustained in peace and love while on earth. Here every human that has died shines on the living. They are all our families of beings like those on earth; without the flesh, they are more, for their lights from heaven feed the purpose of the universe. They are all the spirits of our ancestors and loved ones who we thought were gone—dead. They are those we have buried underground and those we turned to ashes, in the past; those we have bid our goodbyes not long ago. They are those who we have mourned and worried for ages fearing that their imperfections in the soul would have made open the gates of hell, in fear that they have succumbed to the pit of the finality of the end. But it is not so.

As energy they are all loving and true love, they come from heaven smiling. They were beaming in pure excitement to show me that in spirits of humble hearts, they are still learning the secret of humanity's lessons. Even in heaven, they are excited to grow in light of righteous beings; embodying a deeper sense of light-filled gratitude and meekness. As vast as the heavens above, the universe below is but the size of a small baby's brain; I know for certain that spirits do not disappear. As love evolves, so too is the soul of each human. They transcend higher and higher than their last experience of life on earth. Now, before me, they live; they are living bodies of pure kindness, of pure love. They are lovingly radiating with gladness and calm joy. Here they are, the lights and peace that makeup all the living bodies of families, whom we thought we had lost to death on earth. The more I allow the light space to open around me; I learned that I could communicate with these endless and loving spirits only heart to heart. Surely there is no tongue needed for the purpose of spoken words.

Spoken words are the voices of the mind. But love is the ever-present domain of silent calm. Here is a space of brilliant joy. Here, pure grace and pure intention is the lamp that shines out of all divine spirits. To the human mind, filled with human rules, this heaven is absent; for the heart is closed. To the heart that is open, and to the soul that is free, heaven is the light that gives glory to an open and allowing mind.

—Evangeline

A Divine Discovery

Heaven is a space of personal communion with the spirit of love—our families who have died, are now are living in full light on the spirit garden. The Father's throne shines the brightest above all created gardens. He is the body of bright and pure love, the peace,

SHINE LOVE, JOY, AND PEACE!

and the light that is feeding the purity of our families' bodies with the same radiance that His heart, intention, and glory illuminates in graceful presence, powering the light bodies of our ancestors and beloved families of loving spirits. If there is light in the deep sea, His throne shines it. Where there is calm in the wind, His body is illuminating it. He is lighting the entire heavens with the substance of peace. The Spirit Father and our spirit families' form of communication was vivid, clear. It is the language of pure love—the language of our hearts. The light of our divine being, our deep and pure loving intentions, and the unspoken brilliance of our lights are the languages of true essence that are softly vibrating through all of the unseen spirits' hearts. In our spirit heaven, from where we came, light is the radiance that speaks. Like a movie, their presence is in sequence, illuminating my spirit heart with the pure white light of truth. The light gave me its true story. I lived every second as if the plot was the blanket of my own breath. In heaven are heavenly bodies of light. Their life is love; our breath is one substance as their being. The spirits of our loved ones are one essence within our being while we are living in the flesh. They are the pure spirit of love, bodies of pure consciousness, aware that all is love, in spite of tragic human experiences of sorrows that were surrendered in the history of time. In heaven there is no time. Now is an ocean of the infinities. It never moves. It never changes. It never left. In this ocean of peaceful sanctuary, all float. Yet all light is one, grounded by one substance of love, called compassion. Always is the essence of this heaven. Now is always peace. Now is ever-living grace. Now the smiles are forever. Now is all innocence. Now, is all. Heaven is the being of safety. Everyone is one pure radiance. These radiances are being welled from the purity of the fantastic glory of love and grace. Here, compassion is the living water that brings solitude to rest in forever, to cradle all spirit beings to be one with the supreme radiance of light, whose body and breath power all to know only love. For, when a spark of light nests in a soul, it comes to purify a land within a universe, to awaken to peace. Upon its birth, it shall light all creation.

In the light ground of the gardens of heaven, I walked. Here, all-loving spirits are the least of what is grand. The purest of all love

I find is the space itself. Every space is vibrating in immense purity of ever-loving, endless cocoon of pure glory of sustaining creations of all forms. Peace is the breath that makes up heaven itself. All is light, and all is peace. And peace is love, for the King and Father of the Holy Spirit is love.

In this brilliance, I heard the darkness of creation call. I thought of humanity. I felt all of the heartbreaks of the earth. I find that the energy of life-giving earth is nestled in the divine power of subtle vibration of peace, just as the heavens have trees and valleys, so is the earth, trees, and creatures, oceans, and mountains are cocooned in the womb of peace. Peace is the bed of all life. Peace is the riverbed of all that is seen and unseen. Then a light grander than all that is above and radiantly comforting all the oceans that are below beckoned like a kind and gentle lighthouse. He is a giant, soft, and gentle body of luminosities, lighting the dark space with harmony. The ocean of life became an ocean of solitude. All are becoming a body of grace.

Peace is all being. All humans are spirits of peace. Each human spirit is a kind and gentle power of truth and love. The rest is creation.

I looked up again when the luminosity wanted to say more. I saw the truth. The source of the peace of heaven, the power from which all spirits shine as rays from His giant vibrating body, is not just a light. I found myself looking at the Man of the throne, all-loving. Life-giving. Surprise. He is not a God. He is a giant tender-loving and kind Father to all spirits, to all angels, to all infinite wisdom of wind of consciousness. You are the dream of birth. You are the destiny of humanity. He is the dream destination of love for sacred humanity. He is a creator to all that is. Seasons come in a cycle to honor His glory. The ocean sings its tides rejoicing in His creation. Life above the grounds and creatures below are one in the breath of joy and peace.

I discovered the plot it contained was a living waterfall quenching the dry and thirsty veins of my lone human soul. In witness to the truth of who we are, and what every child of this Father spirit on the throne has prepared as our destiny and future for all of us His children, I finally was put to ease. I am never in control of life's design. I am only given the power to love despite the choices of experience I have will to partake in the creation of love. In this light, part of my broken self was slowly being put together piece by piece as I gained hope. Like a puzzle, one piece at a time, I began to slowly feel whole again as the story answered all my yet-unasked questions. What happens to us after we die? Where do we go? Why are we on the planet?

Time Heals

The womb of time is precious. It dreams. It builds. It manifests. It destroys and self-destructs where there is no light, where there is no love. But in the power of love, it heals the broken and begins anew.
—Evangeline

In June 2008, I had gained my strength back, though not 100 percent. One afternoon on my living room couch, I was resting, when the beautiful light-bodied man who appeared before me in the beginning, holding Gabriella in His arms, was again in front of me. Just as He appeared to me in 2005, holding the spirit of a child, "Here is your child," He had said as He let the child come to me. The visit was a gift, two months later, I had gotten pregnant with Isabella, my second daughter.

Now, yet again, three years later, He came for the third time. He came down from His heaven, and quickly before me, He stood. He showed up bearing good news once more. "Woman," He said as I took note of the soul of the child standing, resting the weight of her body against His right leg while He held the child's hands. He continued, "Here is your child." He then let the precious spirit come to me. My spirit embraced the child gladly to welcome her with my love. Six weeks later, I found out I was pregnant with my third child, Michaela.

When this book I was made to write was completed, the old Man too left me, just as my daughter did. I cried for two weeks, mourning a loss for the second time. I missed Him just as much as

I missed my Gabriella. I often asked myself who the old man was. Why did he come to me? Was He an angel who heard and saw my desperate plea for mercy? I do not have a name for Him. I had forgotten to even ask. All I have of Him is the comfort He provided with His presence when I needed a friend, a Father, a confidant. He was the pure gentle light in my darkness. He was my refuge when I needed a warm and comforting shelter.

How could I thank Him for the visions—the story? All I know deep in my heart and soul is that writing this story of the spirit world in glimpses carried me through a different reality for which there were no words yet invented to look within my own soul's intention to live in peace in order to match its amazing light's grace. The light world, this evergreen pasture of a light-filled garden, was a powerful shimmering radiance that cannot be summed up by the word *glorious* alone. All words have not found this realm. Each light prism had carried with it energy unseen to the eyes, but its language was beyond words. It was a succession of miraculous potions administered within the core of my conscious spirit to awaken slowly to its original strength, my once-so-miserable soul. This hidden world is the world of pure love. It is a reality only real to the spirit of pure peace.

Whatever His reason for revealing himself to me, He knows His love saved me. I cry still from missing my daughter, but I have the strength now in my body and soul to be happy for her and respect her faith—that in the spirit life, she could live without pain. She is no longer suffering. Now I don't just wish she was in heaven. I know deep in my heart that she is home—back in the arms of the Father, the one, the only being who could love her more than I ever could as her mother.

PART THREE

Sixteen

The Man on the Throne

The Conversation

Remember, there is neither birth nor death in spirit. We are life, and the force of love sustains us, for we are its body; therefore, it is the natural cycle of our spirits in motion to emerge with time, into our sacred vehicles called flesh. Adam and Eve, male and female, we rise in a suit. We come to know who we are in life as children of man. We come to acknowledge the existence of suffering, as female and male souls. In our soul is our emotional body, which is the house of our feelings. In love, we come to validate life's source of darkness so we may learn how to let go, as we transition from one reality of understanding, in order to move to the next, in the continuous adventure of our infinite intelligence, as conscious, divine beings chartering the depth of the universe, lighting every path with love, and light of mercy, with the calm radiance of our eternal body of wisdom, our divine breath of peace.

—Evangeline

"Sit down, child," the Holy Spirit, Father ordered. The vision is always here, playing in my heart again. Once again, as the first time, I looked up at Him in wonder and daze. Amazed, I fell on my knees. *"Who is this man, a kind body of light and grace, oh so loving, so gentle, so careful of my spirit, who answered my cries when no human mind understood, and no human heart had opened when I knocked, and when*

I begged on my knees, no eyes saw, and no ears heard my silent plea?" I thought. Feeling important that I matter to Him, I willingly sat and listened to what He had to say. "I came to tell you a story, a story you need to know," He said in gentle words. I respectfully nodded. "You must record this story and remember it in your heart all the days of your life," He ordered with such a commanding yet loving tone of voice.

Though I didn't know how the story would come about in words, in His perfection, I was aware that my human mind as a mother was broken. Though I had lost the ability to think, I could not speak, I was made aware that I was gently being treated as if my heart was very fragile. For once, there was kindness. Everything around me could not show kindness. I couldn't believe it existed, that kindness was not lost in death and the pit of darkness. That instant, I was in an inconsolable state; yet the human nature within me that was sad, angry, afraid, and forsaken was surprised. I couldn't believe who I was speaking to. I hurt, but yet all that I've ever known of pain's distinctive voices were instantly gone. All that I was as a punished and deserted human being vanished. Intuitively, I found I was not alone. I was with Him. The part of me that He called a child, His child, was not the human child that I know exists, but my spirit that sees and knows Him. How? What? How is it that I see Him and He sees me? It is the part of me that sees Him, who He called a child. Inside of me is the part of me that is accepting of Him, knowing of Him. There is inside of me an awesome wonderment that is in great awareness of His silent mercy. Instantly, I was awakened by His truth. I am as every child on earth, as every soul is in every mankind, is a spirit in every breath. My breath is His to claim a child. I am, in essence, fathered by a great brilliant and kind, awesome, and infinitely merciful spirit of grace. I am His spirit child. I am a part of His spirit's heart. As every human is His heart's radiance, I am as all humans are—bodies of constant awareness of love. Love is the breath of His light. Light is the brilliance of His love for me and humanity. I thought beyond reason. *We are the light consciousness in the sea of human experiences. Humanity is our eternal dream.* We are spirit families having chosen to manifest in the physical matter of the universe's suits, called the human body. The sacred duty is in our will to create good out of the grace of all the seen and the unseen spaces' of manifestations. Out of divine love from our Holy Spirit Father, to every one of us, His spirit children are born human, so we may rise as spirits by claiming our pure body of consciousness by cleansing and shining our love into the life we choose to create. Every child of the spirit is in charge of its dream. The dream is a desire to create a conscious, loving, and peaceful humanity. My being human is my dream. My being a mother is divine grace. Though I am in the flesh, and He is the light of my spirit, my love is His love, and my life is His life. In the breath of love, we are one essence. Just as I cannot be a human without my mother and father, I cannot be a spirit of consciousness unless I am being showered by the soft and gentle grace of His conscious existence.

Before Him, I am in the spirit safe. I cannot continue to exist unless I am one, of the purity, of His light's brilliance, His Majesties' amazing body of grace. Broken in spirit, I cannot remain unconscious. In my daughter's death, He came to make me conscious that love and spirit do not die, nor does it disappear. Death is only an idea to the unconscious. All death in spirit is simply the end of the experience of a known form. A form is a sacred flesh and divine grace. In spirit, death is a release from form—a body, a vessel. It is the expansion of the spirit to full consciousness. Humanity may be broken in the mind, for suffering is of the mind's ego, yet in spirit, I may not stay the same. I am as every human is the essential body of the Heavenly Father's ultimate purity of grace. My well-being and glory is His full illumination within all beings, light, love, peace—no matter the degree and depth one finds itself in this divinely inspired tree of life called the universe.

It is in utter darkness within my soul that I see the one true light shining in all peaceful darkness.

—Evangeline

Seventeen

The Father's Presence

He spoke no words as He glistens, smiling humbly before me. The king of all kings, a Father of all fathers, He shines in the wisdom of no beginning and end. His light is soft, shimmering, gentle, clear, smiling like a child, pure light embraced and enveloped me for eternity, as every prism of His intentions had enlivened every cell of my being, changing and erasing all the ills of my past painful memories as a hurt, abandoned, injured human child. His light in full bloom, every ray, was love going through me, giving me a whole new breath of peaceful calm and easeful rest. I am at peace. I felt love. From within, I was glowing in brightness. I was the embodiment of His warmth. For the very first time in my entire life, I felt I had all the reasons to live. I am the joy of His light. I am the light of His presence. I am the body of His love. I am; because I am everything that He is in love and everything that I am in every breath.

Then when I thought He was no more after his kind and gentle smile enlivened me, within my visions, He remains. His mercy is forever. It is the only essence that remains when everything of creation has passed away. The imprint of His loving and graceful, yet ever gentle, presence has become the living light within me, consoling me to peace, calming my heart to ease. And to all my surroundings, a complete and utter surrender, because His heart of serenity governs both the silent power of the heavens, making the wind of earth humble and in gratitude of His brilliant presence.

Amazed, I had forgotten the world. I had forgotten I belong to the world of man. For all the pain in that instant was dissolved. Suddenly, I was more. I was more than just a woman, more than a mother. I am a child, a spirit, a woman, a mother, in mind and vessels of humanity's experiences of realities on earth; here still with a second wind of breath, as His child, I am who I am in the spirit, a child of love. I am still to blossom in full. I heard my heart announce, *Even death has its purpose*, after all of the darkness in me, vanished.

> *When death comes, the spirit rises! The spirit that powers the life of heavens must come to claim what is of the heavens, which is love and breath of His Majesty's spirit. I am as the Father is—eternal and everlasting. I am the light and breath of my body. All my brothers and sisters are spirits in the bodies. We are one light family vessel in nature's purpose to create its humanity in the spirit of love and in peace.*
>
> —Evangeline

Illuminated

> *Birth comes. Death comes. Both must come in order to pass away. Love shines. Peace shines. Both lights are one. In a loving and kind humanity, it stays.*
>
> —Evangeline

In His presence, death and darkness are past. In the darkness, my heart and mind cried their tears. Now that light has come, and its source is a gentle and loving spirit of a Father, I am aware that I was only to live the rest of my days with the understanding of the true purpose of life. In my spirit's eyes, life is of great meaning. To live aware of the unseen presence of our spirits' heaven is the only way life may prove to me its gifts.

Before I knew death existed, I was in mind, body, whole. I trusted life. I trusted the world. Though I died as a perfect mother of

Gaby, in my spirit, I am still here. But I know I am never to be the same as I had felt. I am not helpless. I am to breathe only peace. I am peace. I am love. Love is the foundation of all life in heaven and on earth. It is love, the highest of all substances, pure and bright, is the secret life force of all creation. Its vessel is every humanity, every child, every soul, everybody, every heart, mind, and spirit.

In that one silent and cool night, I would come to know once again that joy, happiness, and light truly are the way of true peace; the eternal and unseen love of this kind One, He alone illuminates as the light force within and out every breath I take. Through all conscious love I give, He is with me. In His presence, in His light, a lost, lost child, I will never be.

His presence is light. He is the throne of love. Love is gentle. He is love. I am but one stream of His infinite ray governing the breath of conscious awareness. I understood His unspoken whispers. Truth is the silent, infallible light of gentle peace. Peace is holy. For its body is the heart and breath of all creation, from which His entire body, heart, and mind bestow upon all creations. The Holy Spirit is the brilliance that never fades or ceases. He is there always, watching life from a light-filled throne. He governs the entire body of the universe with mercy. Above the universe of creation and within all creation, His will is the source of the infinities of all seasons' great wonders. His spirit never ceases to guide His children with His love, with His light. From the works of darkness and chaos, He saves them who abide by His light and respectful of His gentle power as a divine Father of humanity.

Everything passes, yet it is His light, the source of the body of our own consciousness, that stays. He has come. He comes in my rest. Gently He comes as soft wind beckoning me to be still in the space of silence. Here all I am is the breath of truth. True creation is love! True harvest is peace. True light is wisdom. Heaven is the spirit of life in the love of peace. Everything else is creation, making sense of chaos in search of its higher self—love, and peace.

—Evangeline

Creation in True Light Is Not Born from Humanity's Mind

Gentle love is the breath and conscious presence of all human souls, for, man is first a spirit, and it is first a holy breath bestowed on earth from the heart and mind of the holy love whose being is truth and body is light of the heavens' heavens.
—Evangeline

Love is the Holy Spirit's light. This light is sourced from the Heavenly Father's entire being; it is His entire consciousness, heart, wisdom, and brilliant body. Love is the essence of our human spirit's light. We are light of consciousness before we are given the infant body that our mother's womb has sacredly built. In pure consciousness, fear is nonexistent. When consciousness enters the body and finds out it is in the flesh, the first experience of fear is created by the infant mind. That is the first of human fear. It is not created in the heart, but in the thoughts of the mind. The mind does not have an off and on switch. It is always working. Love is easily forgotten by the human mind. For the mind is not a heart. The heart is pure love. The mind is of the domain of an insecure universe of a lost soul, abandoned and unheard. Here the mind is but a sad feeling, a sensation of a lost self which is deeply governed by disjointed thoughts, trapped in the deep waters of forbidden shadows of dry, sharp crystals of untapped and forgotten brittle tears. It is that sensation within that is not aware of the presence of time. It is in the mind that the self is hurt, and a victim of the unknown caused. It perceives itself as alone. It is in the mind that the soul's perceptions are altered, away from the true and current reality of life's present gift. It is in the mind that self has manifested as awakening the body of ills and achy, hurt, floating in the womb of the endless depth of the infinite ocean of the forbidden and unknown universe, void of any light. It is in the mind that the child is in darkness, for the spirit of love, which is the highest self within in the beginning of its creation, is absent. The bitter self is the byproduct of an injured mind, which is manifested through creative works of lost and wandering souls. It perceives. It reasons. It learns to survive. It learns to fight. It learns to feel strong and important. It is a body of expectations left to fend for itself as an orphan, due to human fears. The collective mind is the creation of the soul's alter ego; it exists in the policy of mankind's rules and regulations of controlled survival. It's inherent as our forefathers and mothers built it as a survival house when they were humans on earth. The mind is a created reality. What goes on in the mind is the realities agreed upon and collaborated with other minds. Therefore, it is not a true reality of the heart. It is not a reality of which the spirit is in charge.

Even all ancestors have died from all suffering that they had endured, the oppression and heartache turned to dust so that they may hurt and yearn no more, for they have ascended as the light bodies of eternal truth. Every soul will rest from the creation of the mind, so the spirit of consciousness shall rise to be free from the mind-made realities of mankind, where suffering is the norm and fears are self-embodiment. A light body of wholeness becomes their bodies, and light is their being of breath and love in the heavens of the spirits. Likewise, though we are contained in a colorful and intelligent body, we must in spirit shine peace in all our domain on earth; for which always we are secretly and invisibly part and have our being in purpose to exist within creation to experience human love, which is invincibly bounded by our beloved brothers' and sisters' lights and breaths. As the universe is our universe, so is the planet's spirit is also one in love, which is one substance in spirit regardless of what colors of the vessel that the Holy Father and His angels have chosen to dwell the spark of His holy breath. All men and all hearts are spirit consciousness that powers all souls. All spirit is divine in the breath. The source of that breath is the Holy Father. Not a god of mankind, but a Father of grace, a Father of love, a Father of peace. If we love all humankind, regardless of the color of their skin, we, in turn, respect that we are, in essence, the love we have come to illuminate on earth. "Love one another," says Jesus.

That is not an order. Not merely a wish. It is the *secret code* of humanity and all creation below the heavens' feet. We are spirit first before we are given our bodies. When we love each other, we shine the light of our Father's spirit through the eternity of spaces. One earth, each spirit that practices compassion, shines the infinite force within him that originates from the Holy Father's heart and body. As His Majesty's heart, mind, and brilliant body are on the throne, it is so to shine above all true life. He, above all creation, is light and all creation exists because He is the purest of all light. The purity of His white light's luminosity gives spirits to all other colors below Him. Yes! All colors in the heavens, the universe, and in all creations are sourced in the purity of our Father's heart. All colors are vibrations and all vibrations are colorful. Yet it is sourced in the pure white light of our Heavenly Father's being. Life is a tree of love.

The most brilliant of all energies are white prisms casting out from the Heavenly Father's being. Its name is *compassion*. This pure brilliance is eternal. This absolute and fantastic luminosity is pure love. Kindness is eternal love manifested as the language of truth. Peace itself is the substance that binds heaven to existence. It is peace that powers all creation, order, and renewal of life. The changes of varying seasons and continuous cycle of creation within the body of the universe is driven by the presence of our Holy Father, the Holy Spirit, and our own spirit's journey to seek the light of peace out from the darkness of human mental minds. It is in peace that all spirits of the heavens may come to be conscious of life itself in mankind's reality—family. It is our being at peace that we may build and dream the highest of all dreams. In the spirit of love and peace, we descended at birth in search of the truth. We yearn to know humanity as a kind, loving, and worthwhile experience. Though it may be so short for some of our families who have gone too soon, we are rooted in the same eternal tree; though our loved one's body dies, it merely is one leaf falling from its magnificent and invincible branch of life to touch the ground with its essence. Yet the tree of love, that our loved one so shines in his or her life is only strengthened; for the internal essence of our loved ones are concentrated in the root and trunk, the core of the tree of life, that fuel all the heavens with the pure, and all living radiances of love and peace.

> *No matter the season, the essence of love*
> *within a man is radiant and pure.*
>
> —Evangeline

The Mind of Grief

    Grief is one of humanities' heartbreak's fruit. In grief, my mind was ill and paralyzed. It was a daily and nightly experience of fears and tears. Fears were so harsh on my soul. It denied my spirit's ability to speak. Its built-in catastrophic magnet of flashing realities from all the news of the world never leaves the heart of the mind of my fearful and lost soul. The mind that governs the thoughts of chaos was out to drown my spirit in darkness. I knew at last that since a child, I feared because I had reasons. The mind of many man-made realities never treated me kindly, because I also was part of one collective mind that is governed by tragic histories of humanity, the past and present wars within and of the world. The human mind was not kind to my spirit. It abused my brain with constant chaos and dark visions of being lost in the jungles of angry people, hungry children, and countries that thrive on politics of the perfected imperfections, of policies of the politics yet collectively formed. The mind of the world was my humanity. I was always afraid. My mind was constantly processing painful and tragic scenes from the past world I knew not existed, and adding only to the trauma was the daily world news, my present world's constant deaths and hunger being flashed by the television news. In my mind was my daughter's death. Her absence in my mind of sorrow holds dear, all the way down to the sea of bottomless longing to see her smile again. A longing that I know will never be in the laws of nature's order. The collective mind that is of the world was there, fueling my pain, filling me with energies of consistent trauma, as my brain struggled to give myself the order and sensations to breathe again as I behold my daughters in my arms.

    The mind of man is the chaotic feeling of constant survival and the urgent illusion that one is destined to suffer; therefore, it must always be on guard. That tugging notion and failing expectations that there is hope is simply a delusion of the mind. The innate trust that life is good, and birth to it is to acquire order, never seems to manifest without a trick. The creation of the collective mind is a war against peace. Every mind is afraid. Every mind is under attack by forces unseen, which never ceases to echo from the subconscious voices from thousands of years' of sorrows of being human. The tragedy of collective minds is the creation of fears. It is grief itself. In grief, love is nonexistent; for the mind and the brain, there is no rest. There is never peace, never light, never hope, and most of all, never mercy. In the collective humanity, all hearts have been broken, all minds have been hurt, and all humanity is in turmoil. Yet, everyone must survive.

True life is the world of peace, created by the spirits that know heaven is self in the body of action and motion.
—Evangeline

Let all breakthrough be the means to an end of all wars of the universe's minds, a man-made creation; but let it be the spirit of peace that brings new birth and a new beginning to the breath of the newly awakened mankind, for it is in the haven of the hearts that all live and serenity breathes the wind of unspoken freedom. All spirits yearn for love and peace, for it is only the invincible haven where terror and war may not reach, and death shall never dawn; in truth, heaven is not on the soil of the earth; it is the breath of man. And in his allowing heart, all existence may experience the ultimate love of being divine in each breath he takes while in the grace of the most sacred and blessed flesh—humanity.
—Evangeline

I learned that the spirit is not the mind. When the Heavenly Father on the throne appeared to me in His visit, the bright, pristine heaven that illuminated around Him revealed itself as the sanctuary of ultimate peace; for the light that governs the garden and heaven of peace is beaming from His entire body, making all unknown and known vanish. Love is light. Pure light is the world. Compassion, mercy, and glory are all there is.

In His presence, something inside me surrenders in peace. I feel safe; my entire being is no longer just a body, but I feel lit up. Everyone who has died on earth, all human beings who are now with Him, are shining in their own white and pristinely conscious beings of full light. They are in the pure state of the human spirit. I saw what makes each of them living. I know the eternal fuel that breathes love in every one of these human beings' mercy and grace alone. In this truth, I've come to light within my spirit. In their presence, something in me stopped being afraid. Now, as I stood before the Holy Spirit's throne, the new heaven, which speaks directly to my heart without words, revealed itself wider and bigger. He is the light beyond heaven and the universe. His presence is the grace and purity of eternal light. In His love, my spirit is awakened to pure kindness. I am, as every human heart, each human being is His divine child. We are the eternal breath made souls in the flesh. We are the spirit that loves within the flesh. We individually are important beings as His children; every spirit is His child, and all the dead rise beyond earth's gravity and come to Him. All the living yearn for His presence because His Majesty is our spirit home. He is the goodness I long yearned. Now I know that in spirit, I am a child of peace.

Though I am a mother in human flesh, a mother as a human soul, in spirit, I am still but a helpless child. No matter how old I become as a child of man, as I am a being still governed by the brain and the collective minds of my own evolution and of the worlds, I am still one that searches the truth; I am the breath of peace. No matter the flesh, no matter the brain, and no matter the chaos of the mind, no matter the domain of the universe, no matter the science, and all of the matters of the world, in His presence before His throne, in His love, I am always but an innocent child needing His care. The light of my soul is His love—love is illuminated and recorded as the story that serves as a beacon of light to my desperate soul. His illumination is the great white light that shines beyond all spaces. He is a body of light. Even His throne obeys His peace. In His Majesty's presence, grace is the world in Him, through Him, and before Him. In these lights, our spirit is life. And the earth, in His brilliance, floats as the perfected host of life—as the universe has cradled its creations in humble order, through all mankind's existence.

I've come to know love. But it is not in the love of man alone that I will live, not death alone that I die. I live because I am a child of the Father. In my Father's love, I do not die. In His spirit, there is no death.

I rise from darkness in order to be a child of peace. In peace, there is no death; my spirit declared before His presence.

—Evangeline

How could my heart deny such grace? His guidance and light, His presence alone gives. No man except in His will may govern peace as He illuminates it to power all the good of creations. And to all that is unknown, we are to rise above ourselves yet again, higher each time, so even the recesses of the universe will come into our presence. Creation is fixed in its journey, but mankind's spirit, in consciousness, is to rise higher than all the heavens, back to the source, where our families are rooted, where our ancestors' arms of love and light await us in our rest.

—Evangeline

Eighteen

Rise: The Gift of Heaven Is You

What the eyes see, the soul can explain; what the spirit sees, the eyes and the soul can't see. But the heart sees the Holy Spirit, illuminating within all spirits floating in the womb of darkness. The heart will always breathe in silence and harmony of love, as the universe is governed by the still vibration of pure light to power all life's realities within the multi-body of the universe.

—Evangeline

Many months came after the death of my daughter. My soul was lost in the ocean of grief. I was alone in the darkness. I was so afraid. There was a pain, a deep longing in my being I couldn't reach to turn off no matter how hard I tried. Every day, my heart couldn't keep up with the rules and human limitations I was demanded to belong as a woman. Yet, I was not honored. I was not heard when I told everyone I hurt. I can stand in spirit and know in the love of truth that in all things, humanity embodies kind and gentle solutions. My job is to ask for the way and find the courage to go and seek that solution that I know is set to come.

Life sometimes is overwhelming and proves to be difficult. But it will *pass*. I see that our Father in spirit, of heaven and earth, is not a God that destroys, as I was made to believe as a child. He is the Father of peace. Gentle and loving, He shines His light calmly. Humbly He watches, yearning and wanting only to be acknowledged that He is the love in us. He is that part of us needing to be loved and cared for. He is that light in us that wants to manifest for all to see, especially when life at times feels unfair and difficult.

There are times after the visits of the Man on the Throne, I still find myself in the dark. Sometimes I find that my mind has forgotten all the light that gave my life excitement and laughter, yet there is my spirit lifting my soul, to see and not give up on the brilliance of light that seizes to rest as nature gives in cycle despite the faltering attitude of my human emotional mind. Fear projects limitation and darkness in all minds that see it. But the mind needs to know we are spirit. We are not a vessel in the mind. We are the true life of love. The mind is of the world. It is not of the gentle truth of the spirit or of the heart. Broken, the mind projects itself as mankind's eternal world.

The universe of the mind is a belief, a fear, a control—chaotic, suppression, limitations, imposed and projected in multilevel broadcasting on others from the ill gods and goddesses of psychotic disorders within the creation of a lost and insecure, unloved, and depressed man.
Let it be known that the spirit of man is the light and love of the man, even when he is in the mind of darkness.
—Evangeline

Nineteen

Breathe

You are a beautiful life.
—Evangeline

In love alone, I found I can do all things good in spirit. I can choose to get up and help life be kind to me by being kind to everyone around me. Though there were occasions that my mind got tired, and everything about my surroundings became dull, I hear the gift of silence. I feel the calming stillness in my soul. Even when my brain does not want to cooperate, even when it seemed numb, and life does not make sense, such as when I could see people open their mouths to talk, but I could not hear what they were saying. I see them laugh and run, but I couldn't discern any feelings of joy. I knew that my mind was overwhelmed. My emotions were exhausted. Even when my brain, too, was becoming tired while my mind was already the first to forget that I am a spirit. I am in the soul still. Still here fighting. But when I let go and allow life to carry me for today, I can breathe again. I see a glimpse of my daughter's laughter in my mind. Suddenly I can feel my yearning for her. But honor that I must stay to see the sunrise's brightness.

I fought to keep finding a reason I should live and have a life again. That is the way of the spirits. Our spirits do not know how to give up even when the world and everything about the world have all turned to dust. Even after the rest of my children were born, I was still sad missing Gaby. My love for Gaby still lives on in my spirit. My spirit sees her smiling and dawning at me, at our family, when I least expect, when my mind forgets. At times, as a human mother, my soul is struggling. Each time I think of her, a sense that half of my being is greatly missing became a reality, I had to learn to quell within me. There are days I see the world, but inside as a mother, half of my universe has dropped or has fallen far, far away to a place unknown, a space of nothingness. My soul is not whole. But that is the language of being Adam and Eve's descendant. Life is difficult, and when I couldn't understand what was going on, it was easier for the mind to go back and hear the echoes of our human ancestors' condemned voices and assume I must have committed a sin to deserve the grief I was experiencing. I learned that I could never trust the mind. The mind is mental. It is lazy. It is crazy. It is always afraid. But it takes a conscious spirit to train and govern it with peace and love. So, though it is there for me, I taught it to remain open to Gaby's memories. Her love. Her nature as a pure spirit. I reminded it not to forget Gaby's smile. I demanded it cherishes the innocent joy Gaby still illuminates in the spirit of my other children who were both born after she was freed of her body. Though sometimes I need to cry for missing her the way she used to be. My spirit is raised up. My mind is open and alert. So when the spirit heaven comes open, the Father and His son, our beloved spirits, may dwell in our being as we partake in making a kind and loving, whole family.

Twenty

My Soul's Discovery

    Because my heart lived for Gaby, I hurt and fall on the ground still now when I think of how much time I have lost without her with me. I hurt just the same at the beginning of her death if I allow ignorance to run my days. I fall in tears, always feeling like I was a train wreck. As her mother, I struggled to survive. But as a spirit, I rose, I reasoned and found a deeper purpose to make life a better place for my husband and my children, my family. I need to be part of life here on earth. Each time I would get carried away by sorrow, I fought to get back in the present. It was not easy. I struggled to do the simplest task as going out of the door to breathe and even think. I fought until I was tired. I wept until I could no longer remember what true tears were. I was crying without tears because it was my sadness and loss that had come over the rest of my being. Over and over again, it manages to steal the light of the present. Yet I learned that when I look up to pray, I was reminded to go outside myself. But then again, out into the world, the echoes of life all around me—joy, laughter, dreams, and promises I couldn't hear; and when I use my eyes to see life, I see life's bigger impending wars at hand, brought about by politics of the world. When I teach my eyes to see the mental world of the news, I see children dying from wars in Iraq, Syria, and Afghanistan. My tormented eyes see the problems of my current world. I know how death feels. I was feeling it not just for myself, but for anyone in the whole world who has lost a loved one too. I learned the mega truth: it is in love and loss that we are all connected, as much as we are one family of humanity connected by the one dream to exist in the harmony and silent breath of peace. As a mother, I am everyone who is grieving the loss of her child. Like everyone who has experienced a death of a child, after the burial of my child, the purpose of my present was dusky, frail, and, most times, an uncomfortable, eerie echo of the great deep of bottomless stillness that light cannot see.

I tried to be strong, but I couldn't without help. The only way I would get out of the trance was to flashback to an important event in my life when I encountered a vision that would heighten my human perception even deeper, beyond words, beyond all souls' experiences, a heightened awareness beyond earth life's hearts and minds in struggles.

Brilliant Plane: A Higher Plane

Light begets brilliance that ignites love to flourish into the bosoms of even the most barren of hidden wilderness.
—Evangeline

In pain, when I couldn't hear and see the joy and purpose of the world, a new light world began to slowly open and reveled its presence around me. I discovered the space of total silence. A space of non judgments, it is the world of fine energy of unlimited space where all heaven is the continuum of the same journey of expansion. Though I am floating alone in it, I am not lost because I am still contained within its eternal fiber.

From this perspective, my human mind sight vanished. My spirit's heart sees more than my eyes. In the spirit of life and humanity, I see another layer of a hidden world; it was a perfect world of harmonious stillness, where all tragedies have a purpose and contained within the purpose is the meaning of self-growth and expressions. Beyond days and nights, I began to be immersed in an ocean of silent calm, a sensation that is unseen to human senses, but my spirit dwells in it as the only safe haven that is open and willing to contain what is left of my conscious soul. It was not a place; it was an invincible presence of subtle reality, a sanctuary of light, a sacred space where all healing originates, all silence flows, and a sense of wholeness is contentment and peace as a total illuminating embodiment of complete being.

The Visit Was the Teaching

The door is the spirit. The man and His love is the light that makes visible to the heart the unseen world that makes earth, galaxies, and the universe float in the infinite sea of life; love eternal is true life. It is an abode of peace; and, of awesome brightness.
—Evangeline

I was at the Kailua Beach Park with my eleven-month-old Isabella (my second daughter before Michaela; my third daughter was born). Isabella was barefoot on the grass, trying to learn to balance her strength while she tried to learn how to stand up alone. She crawled till she found she could stand before she discovered she could walk without holding on to my fingers. Every time I stood her up, she would want to run excitedly. It was an exciting time and invigorating feeling to see her try without being afraid.

It was not easy for me to see the contrast between a heart with anomalies and a healthy and robust heart. It was heartbreaking for me to know what I saw. Gaby's difficulty was in her breathing and in her effort to walk before running out of breath. Her struggle was a painful ordeal to behold as a mother. It was experiencing what we take for granted with Isabella, yet automatically not to be done at ease with Gaby; that made life both rich and a blessing, but at the same time a painful and challenging encounter.

Discovering the beauty of the human body in a child was the moment I quickly remembered how hard it was for Gaby all her life to sit up or stand without being braced by the side of her crib or without placing both hands under her armpit. For Gaby, life was a lot of work. My tears fell. It took Isabella to see. I saw what I did not know to be hard because I had nothing to compare. To stand up took a lot of breath from her. All she could do was smile in joy and dance her head side to side instead. But for Gaby, it was all she had. She gave it all. Even when she could not walk, she smiled, she glowed, and she celebrated. Her flow of joy never ceased; nothing stopped her.

The more Isabella advanced in months, the validation of how physically delayed Gaby was when she was alive tore at my soul, while my spirit embraced fully and gratefully Isabella's health. I wish so much I had taken her pain away. I was in tears. I missed her. But I had to be strong for Isabella; inside, I was also deeply longing for Gaby's presence, as I was being immersed in the shadow of her pain while she was with me. I fought it but to no avail. I wished as a mother that Gaby could walk and run around at the park with me to watch Isabella walk for the first time. She would have loved the experience to see her baby sister happy as she took her first steps.

Twenty-One

The Man of Peace

"Woman, know thyself. You will know you are the light and love of your world, for your Creator's heart is your breath, from whose power you rose consciously that you are a spirit of love before you are given a flesh and born a child of man, who comes to give love and life to the spirit, soul, mind, and purpose of a family in humanity."

—Evangeline

My mind would want what it wants. It didn't honor the spirit's blessings. I knew I was a blessing in spirit. My mind wanted only to see Gaby. It wanted to make my arms feel Gaby, not just Isabella, but Gaby. It was in that deep inner turmoil that my heart was screaming. To know I have two children but can only be with one and not be with the other was a sudden punch. I encountered how painful it was not to hold two of my daughters at the same time. The disjointed reality for my mind was too much to bear. I felt my soul cry. I couldn't stop my eyes from crying. I could not stop my heart from hurting. It misses Gaby in the time and tomorrow that I knew would never come. I realized I had to contend to what was in front of me. Yet still, I struggled. My mind was so distraught; my spirit was in darkness, and my soul was so broken. Yet despite the crowded park, no one could see my struggle.

Helpless as countless times, post-traumatic stress disorder would take me to the numbness world again, where I couldn't feel or see the gift of the present time. Again, I lost all my senses. Yet in that darkness was the restless knowing that it is not the end, but a discovery of something unspoken; way above my mind's depthless agony was another world of ultimate feelings and visions of the light world, a world where my heart automatically is drawn, where it need not speak, for peace is love it gives as validation, where it can hear the language of silence.

When a miracle happened, time, and even I cannot explain it. Silence brings it down. I remember before Michaela's birth, when Isabella was barely walking, a miracle came. So fast it occurred, yet so gentle it transpired. For weeks I had not slept. I was lost in missing Gaby. I was lost in knowing how to be a mother to my barely year-old Isabella. I had succumbed to fear. I was afraid to move. Yet I knew my spirit was doing everything to get me moving. I went to the park. I felt I needed to go every morning to calm my day.

Depression is an internal struggle within oneself. No one can see this darkness but the mind of the self. One can get so lost in it. But my daughter Isabella's needs to walk and grow was such a saving grace. I could easily have given up. But I stood and decided I was going to be a good mother no matter what the death of Gaby did to my heart and mind. Yes, I felt like the world ended, but Isabella's world just began, and I better be there for her as I committedly was there for Gaby. My mind was frozen, my heart—broken. My love kept on brightly. My body was confused. My brain was exhausted, so I cried. I cried for mercy as I walked Isabella onto the grass at the park. Tears fell as I felt my knees buckle. My mind was not there. It was not with Gaby. My body was tired because my emotions and brain were in constant struggle. When I was about to fall on my knees on the grass, a call of light flashed from above stopping me from fainting. It flashed. It was brought over by a kind being. What came after was something I cannot describe until the day I die. It happened. Bright light from the sky came down. From it appeared the Man of Peace. He was brilliant and yet silently dazzling in white prisms of living, pulsating, clear diamond light brilliance, before manifesting in a normal image of a man's slightly tan skin, golden and wavy hair to His shoulders, hundred and thirty pounds at first, before He completely manifested as one hundred sixty-five pounds, five feet eleven in height, in a linen tunic and a brown cloak. Compassion overfilled His eyes for me, yet the strength and certainty of my well-being governed His entire presence. He was young, as He appeared before me many times. He always treated me with equal importance, as if I was His concern. He was kind. This time He came with a request, just as the Holy Spirit Father demanded that I write.

"Woman." He hovered down to me. He handed me a golden pen. "Write the grief out of you," He commanded, handing me a leather-bound book. "Write, or this dungeon of miseries will devour the light and love of the Heavenly Father out of you." He sounded concerned. "How do I write?" my spirit asked. "I can't write." The thought of writing pained me. He insisted in His voice. I had to trust in His belief in me.

Speechless, I was shocked in tears.

"Woman, you must release your grief, for grief is a feeling of abandonment and fear. Grief is emotion. Emotion has color, and color is vibration. Let go of your sadness, this grief, for it is wicked of all darkness. Darkness is the body of the unknown universe of pain. It has weighted your spirit down. Decide to let go. Words will come on their own." He took my hands. Again, He said, "Your darkness is a paralyzing vibration, which has caged your spirit down. Release your soul from its tormenting domain, write your feelings, for it is a word wanting to get out of you. Well it out." He raised His energy body above the trees. I was mystified. He smiled. Looking down at me.

"Shine. Be free. Be the light of your Father again. Be the child of light again. Be His love again. You, every child, every soul born a man, are the light of the world."

A soft veil of light moved slightly. Before He went into it, he looked at me with deep eyes of compassion. He added, "You, the humanity are the spirit of light. You are the love that has come to light and give meaning and purpose to life." He dried my tears and went up to His silhouette, white, giant energy bubble and disappeared.

"You are love. You are the purpose of life," he added. Even when I could no longer trace His presence, I could feel His thoughts. He cared so desperately for me.

Immense love came over me. I wanted it to stay that way, but my child, who was now running on the grass, just fell, cried, and was reaching both her arms to me for support and safety.

Just like that, I snapped back into the present. I needed to survive again. My brain took over. He vanished. But my heart's eyes see Him. I saw His light hover above me a while.

In silence, with no words fitting to make sense of what I was revealed, I knew I am not just a mother. I am still a child to the One, to whom I matter, beyond the purpose of the universe.

I am a spirit. No wonder I am so hurt, so lost as a soul,
I am before life on earth a spirit that is cared for and
always loved by the force that is the source of love itself.
—Evangeline

In spirit, I know I am strong. Every human being is. That is the light of our truth. He taught me that I am an indestructible human being in spirit. So are you. My heart as a woman was being raised up above the normal capacity of human perception, beyond the body, mind, and brain. My mind was greatly being challenged to open up to the unexplained world unseen to the human eyes but brightly shining within every human spirit's heart. One day at a time, I am being summoned to evolve beyond limits. So I rise. One day at a time, I rise. I knew, based on the kind visions of this Holy, Holy, Holy Father of all spirits in an image of a purely loving and all-encompassing man, His beloved child has paved the way for Him. Into the human planet world, He comes in and out to deliver His Majesty's gift of unconditional love and understanding to those hearts who have yearned for their true light, the light of the spirit. The light of the Holy Father is heaven. It is a gentle and caring truth of kindness that powers all creation within the universe. It is this loving power that mankind's spirit is born. The spirit of love and consciousness is the child divine in all humankind. There is more to humanity in us than being a woman, a man, a mother, a father, and a wife and a husband.

There is more to all domains than that of humanity's belief and surrenders to the idea of religions. There is more to humanity's vision of the collaboration of governmental service for true justice of love and peace, versus an idealism of self-righteous governance and malignant power and control. There is a hidden world that is connecting with me. It is not a physical world. It is a world of instant speed. It is a spirit world. It is a world of love, of brilliance grandeurs, kindness, and gentle wind of rays of hidden and yet all true morning glory. This is the ultimate heaven. This is our spirit, abode. This is our home after humanity, for each of us at our different time ends. Home is light. Home is free.

When I am exhausted of being so exhausted and in pain, I am being comforted in spirit, being guided as a soul; yet all the same, as a child who lost her path, as a woman who keeps on stumbling in her own mind and fantastically demoralized by guilt and shame of my daughter's death and lost faith in humanity's ability to be compassionate toward me when so quickly they took her body from me an hour after her death, I was struck by deep darkness—of misunderstanding. In an alone and lonely pit, I lost my light. I lost my world. But in spirit, I was being guided to gain strength so I may walk again. With that, I had to command my soul to be at peace. I needed to teach my mind to be kind to itself. I had to order it to see the unseen good hidden in everyone who finds the courage to be kind and smile in front of me. In being so alone and lonely, though I walked in the land of a thousand people, I was not seen. I was being summoned to witness a stranger's smile, from a recovering alcoholic and a homeless old guy who stood up dragging his feet from the wheel-chair to the community beach park shower stall that awakened my eyes to see a huge light-bodied angel helping him in spirit, to reach the shower so he could rinse himself. A thirty foot tall male angel, with a living diamond brilliance illuminating though his entire being came down to me and said, "I want to hug him." He pointed at the man in the shower. I hugged the guy the next day when I came back to the park. He stopped and talked to me. The angel's body enfolded him with brilliantly shining and soft light. A healing love for his broken mind, body, spirit, and soul. The loving presence of the angel of light made me see the truth. The spirits of love are hidden from human eyes, but angels are always

SHINE LOVE, JOY, AND PEACE!

helping those who are struggling in spirit, mind, and body. I thought "I am still alive because I see the truth. Spirits of lights are always shining over and around all human beings." Where there is suffering, there are their lights. I know I am love because the angel showed me how he works in secret. In witness of an angel's unconditional love for a struggling human being, even the one who is unaware of his divine presence, has caused me to surface out of my sadness. In the time being, I felt my spirit rise out of grief and was freed from the grip of paralyzing darkness. Every day, Gaby's smile, and the memories of her soft and gentle warmth when I held her began to fade away. I hated it. I would hide in the cozy recesses of my dark dungeon of a mind and cry. Yet when someone smiles at me, I seemed to pop back out breathing. Then I see the light of the sun, the green trees swaying back and forth. The birds were chirping above my head. Nature is kind. Being at the park made people smile at me. So under the tree, I took my baby every day and waited for people to pass by and smile and talk to me. The kindness of the Man of Peace gave me a sense of worthiness I alone can acknowledge before it can manifest. He showed up to tell me what no human mind and heart may reveal to me. The secret nature of me is spirit. The mind can go, but my spirit, He proclaimed, is a light of the Father, His Father. It is not His presence that saves me. It is His care and unconditional remorse for my sorrow, His gentle compassion that drove me to be so drawn to nature's silence. His kindness is as gentle as the wind in a quiet tree-filled park. Being in nature helps silence my mind. Seeing Him appear gently in nature was the only true vision of the good that came to save me from guilt and shame of not being able to help my daughter live. My emotional mind was tragically broken in ignorance. It is the gentle presence of compassion that saved my spirit from insanity, making suicide an only option from so much agony after losing Gaby. Guilt and shame, the world and voices of the mind's judgments whispered often, but my spirit is soothed by the unfading vision of the light and body of the Man of Peace, whose presence and love I am made calm and still.

—Evangeline

I needed to honor the peace that came to give me a new whole life, a new second round of breath as a woman and a mother. I must honor the Heavenly Father's love and peace so I may honor my humanity as a child of my human parents and as a sister to all my siblings. The Man of Peace comes only to bring forth the Man on the Throne. The son makes way for His Holy Father. The son comes to give light to the souls so the Heavenly Father may find His begotten children in our darkness, to comfort and heal our hearts from grief.

Heaven is the internal abode for all children of consciousness. Consciousness is a body of light, generated by the love of compassion, courage, and kindness. Consciousness is the true body of all spirits; all spirits are born in heaven. All spirits come from heaven, where the Father of love and light, courage, and compassion reigns in full luminosity.
—Evangeline

Love yourself; you will find your gentle spirit. Love your spirit of peace; you will find your spirit's Father's arms. In His gentle glory, you will be made secure always. Here death will not be a pain for the heart to endure. In light of the spirit, all deaths will be of nature's gift to come and go in order that the spirit is released, freed, and guided back home to its Father, its Spirit Father, the God of peace and love, the gentle creator of the grand and immaculate universe.

PART FOUR

Twenty-Two

Fashioned in His Image

Before Him, I was awakened to my own humanity's beauty. A man and a woman are not just beautiful faces; within these beings reside the souls of manifested bodies of energies, a depth of multidimensional and multifaceted healers and creators of peace. They are the weavers of good. Within their souls are the minds, within the mind are the hearts governed by the gifts of intellect, the ability to reason and reflect on the gift of the world, which are both of joy and the source of sorrows, of the past and the future. Within their dreams are divine secret houses of light-filled visions; within these visions are their wills of both compassion and humble innocence, which are being manifested in time through the vessel of Adam and Eve, the equally balanced house called flesh. Their unconditional mercy runs through actions and speech through reason and creations in the womb of time. Adam and Eve, the man and woman bringing forth the love of the Father's heavens on to earth as their works and dreams are projected within the glory of the eternal truth.

To blossom like flowers is to create in love and to live no matter the space, for man and woman are the faces and bodies of the light and love of the heavens. All the earth is their transcendent breaths of everlasting consciousness, illuminating the secret light of all the spirits of life eternal.
—Evangeline

I now realized that there is an eternal world within our physical existence. My heart is the eyes of this light-filled world. In the visions of the truth, spirits lights are present in all spaces, outside ourselves. This space is called heaven, as it is being revealed to me. Every spirit is our family. Every angel and every child is our family. No one is separate. Everyone, including the animal kingdoms and every living thing on earth, is sourced from one body of pure light and a breath of conscious existence. In this heaven is union. Separation is not a thought to be experienced. Everyone is an important light of the whole. I know now that life is spirit. Life did not happen because I am born a child of man. Life in our beginning is peace. Life in the spirit is light. Life in the spirit of embracing the infinities of our love is the breath that makes heaven remain in stillness and everlasting harmony; heaven's space of eternity is the breath of compassion. Compassion is space in itself. Its life is us; for the children of love are the kingdom of humanity on earth.

Spirit Child Is Free

Before humanity was its world, the spirit is light. It is free. The spirit descends only to rise out of the womb of its mother in order to walk the land of man so it may make himself conscious of human life. The spirit is to ascend after its human journey and experiences are fulfilled. Spirit is free; it shall not be bound by the institution of a human mind's religion. All religion is bound by rules and order of tradition. But the spirit is unbound by the minds of the earth. Spirit itself is light. It shall light all darkness. It must walk to give love to the world. Spirit is not a religion. It is the body of love, shining in all creation. Spirit is the spirit of every child. Every human child is pure spirit. It is the pure light of love.

—Evangeline

I thought hard. I was made conscious. On earth is our struggle. But heaven is our peace. Why do we struggle in the flesh if we are spirits and breaths of peace all along?

In the spirit of life, this garden is sacred. Though mankind on earth will struggle in poverty, it is a poverty of communication, poverty of compassion, poverty in misunderstandings of who we truly are as spirit beings before we are human. Suffering is in forgetting that we are first spirits that are unconditional and conscious of only love. Suffering is in divisions of our spirits, divisions of our minds, divisions in beliefs. We separate our love from our bodies. Material wealth and disconnected is our mind's main domain. We must first, in our daily purpose, realize that our spirits, body, mind, and reason to live is so each, in-breath live to be kind souls in all domains that we partake.

Our Living Treasures Are the Richness of the Spirit's Light

A babe given its freedom to live in peace is as powerful as the entire family of humanity shining and existing in full grace.
—Evangeline

In the heaven of peace, there is no darkness. Heaven is a space of pure white light. Light is the breath of love that powers every living nature within and outside its space. The light of heaven is magnified by the loving bodies of every spirit within the light—our loved ones—the spirit of our family who had died on earth. Here, they live. Every spirit is light. The generator of life is their home. Home is light. Governed by the giant body of love, the Heavenly Father's ever presence, sitting on His throne. In His light, every child is a divine force, governed by the absolute power of His divinity. Before matters of the earth, before the human flesh, we are the true richness of life. We are the heavenly bodies of peace. In spirit, we are all love. We must not forget this truth. This truth is the core and foundation of our light, the radiance of our pure being. Love is the light that we come to shine on human creation in this human world. Just as the sun shines its light to the fullest to give life to all matters in creations. So its pure eternal light must shine on all the souls of the planet in order to feed love and make conscious all creations of the light's peaceful substance.

Sacred Birth

Each birth is sacred. Each birth of a child is filled with purpose. A child is a gift that this sacred garden of a world so desperately needs in order to serve the spirits with humanity's experiences. We must honor every child on earth. We must honor all of us that make way for them. In the eyes of the Father, we are His children. We descend in the womb, and come out as a child of man. Yet all must ascend to heaven when every creation ends. If one of us struggles, the rest is not at ease; the Father is not just concerned. He hurts. When we refuse to honor our light through love, when we refuse to acknowledge our true strength, which we are to be humble enough to create peace and compassion, which we promised to instill on earth, we abandon our own purposely given breath. In such acts, He is abandoned. The planet is abandoned. Pain will persist. I see Him in sorrow. He is lost in our domain. We stumble at heart. We are in mind blinded by fears. He is nowhere because we refuse to open our spirit eyes of love to see Him. He watches over the earth. Upon the throne, He sits in pain. Without love, He is powerless over our destructive domains. Without compassion, He is powerless over the outcome of the pain which our action produces. Through the disconnect between the spirit and the mind, our humanity is broken, and our souls remain in the dark. But heaven is within each spirit. Each spirit empowers the being of each soul. The spirit light must be summoned to ignite it from within us, as some of our forefathers, who were here before us changed the course of human consciousness into a more peaceable domain due to the embodiment of their eternal truth. They know that humanity shall be a peaceful endeavor to reflect the origin of the breaths of man's love, which is above. They come and change the world for the better than they found it at birth. Each babe at birth is pure. Regardless of our current age, in spirit, we are the body of truth. We are the consciousness of gentle and pure light. We are peaceful and loving beings. Before birth, we decided to come into our body to join the current experiences of humanity's reality. We come at birth with one desire to light our beings. We come to raise up the human consciousness to its Father in heaven. We shall make humanity the same as the heavens from which we come. Each birth is an opportunity to awaken in us the heaven of peace. We are here to make conscious of who we dream of humanity to be. Humanity is capable of being a space where children thrive in peace, encouraged to be who they are destined to be as souls. Children are blank canvases. When we shape them in love; they will be filled with love. And that will be the fuel they will project into the world. Shape them in anger and discontent; they trust no one and will likely project out onto the world what was deposited in their being since childhood. Our children will be governed by the light we shape them—good or bad. All children are born in fear of the foreign realities of being in the flesh after having been free children of divine consciousness, free to access the depth of a multi-universe within a thought. In the body, they will learn to survive out of fear. They will grow in the notion of good and bad. But as parents, as spirit caretakers, we must remind them of who they truly are, pure spirit bodies of love. They come to create good in humanity by loving and creating for the wholeness of the entire humanity. They come to make conscious of humanity's domain through the innate spiritual knowledge of the infinite nature of humanity's divinities before the earth. Children's love for humanity gave them birth here. Our love for our humanity can be planted within these beings. We must teach them love; we must support them to grow in peace by providing them a home, a country, a planet that supports the evolutions of their eternal lights.

The Source of Life of Humanity's Spirit

The Father of Compassion

"Father, don't cry, I will go down there in the garden. I will tell them about you. Your children will remember you again. Regardless of the continents below their feet, your children will know that in spirits as in the flesh, we are brothers and sisters, we are one. You are our Father, the creator of love and peace. The Father of the spirit of love and peace. Your humanity in all of us will shine. Humanity, your children, will

learn to love one another. They will learn to love themselves. They will learn compassion, learn to listen to each other's hearts. Your children will remember who they are in spirit. They are sent to earth to create peace so you as our Father will no longer suffer in sorrow as you see your begotten children divided in their hearts, tormented in their minds and lost in their souls. Father, as you see your children's spirits be degraded by the unconscious domain of divided minds, as they embrace the uncertain promises that create wars among brotherhoods to pain you, in your love for all of us, wars between the hearts and the minds will cease to exist. Peace and love is your humanity in us and through us. We are to mirror your creation of glorious heavens on earth. We shall in the flesh of the earth shine out your entire mind, body, and brilliance through love, compassion, and the peaceful breath of your merciful and ever-living presence within each of us."

—Evangeline

My mind of gratitude does not come through as often as I would like. When my soul is tired, and my brain is overwhelmed, the entire world collapses all around me. Yet then again, when that so often familiar darkness comes, I see the light come. I hear my spirit yearn to rise to shine on what my life had been founded on since my birth—love, peace, and my family on earth, and the yearning of the light of my family in the spirit of love and peace.

Humanity's Life and Infinite Blessings

Life embraced me in its cycle and gave its best to me. How I take this fruit is going to be my decision. I came with nothing. Life gave me a body that contains the force of myself, shaping me into a soul, fed by the gifts and senses of its religions, its cultures, its dreams, its cumulative bounties of caring souls; life gave me a mother, a father, brothers, sisters, and made me into a family. When I grew up, it gave me a husband. It gave me marriage, gave me a children, and I became a mother. Life gave me its land's harvest, nurtured me with its perfected seasonal winds, of hot and cold, comforted me with warmth from the touch of my child's soft tiny hands, beheld me as a woman from the nurturing care of my husband. It gave me strength and value, gave me the passion for learning to behold my families, and of all the love of others that I am giftedly surrounded. My senses as a soul mother were always filled before there were any short seasons of lack when my daughter's body died. But even then, the time came surely as the sun's grace rose every morning to deliver the spirit divine to comfort my soul to life again. The spirit of love and all creation overfilled me beyond what I had come to give it.

Even though my child went on out of the body, I can never rewind the knowing of the love that flowed out of my heart since the day she was born to me. Life, I realized, is not a tragedy. It is here to ask my spirit to come, so humanity's life itself may give to my soul its best bounties, for everything else of heaven and earth is already done for me.

—Evangeline

Love was already here waiting only to manifest with time when I was ready in years after it raised and shaped and strengthened me as a soul. Life I know is already here, so when I came, I only did what it asked of my spirit, to love, and to shine through all my breath of love, through humble compassion, no matter what war, famine, faith, even death would give and take, so my soul may know its secret code as conscious spirit divine.

I learned after loss, after death, love of life comes. Love comes despite all, as the sun shines on all to light everything that is life, the innate force that is carrying me to be conscious of humanity's true forces, its peace, love, and dreams to awaken my soul by its gentle embrace through its light *touch* and gentle guidance comes so that I can *feel* again, give me its latest culinary creation as it serves me the new bounty from its newly-risen vines, so I can *taste* its spirit's fruits again, be filled more than I did yesterday. It has drawn for me a new spring, so its pregnant flowers may awaken me to *smell* the sweetness of life's morning rain and wind, to inspire me to breathe again without fear, and to be free at last; as life would have me, give it all for my spirit, so when I died as a mother once, when I desire to open my spirit's eyes, it will awaken me to a secret horizon that human souls' eyes may not dawn. My spirit can see beyond what the mind creates. My eyes are open. The heaven came to ignite my new spirit mind to see the good visions, the smile of two little girls laughing and squealing before me have awakened that dull recesses of my brain and have turned the switch on of the mother part of my soul once more.

"Mommy! Mommy! Mommy!" they came and kiss me, so for the first time of the second awakening as a spirit soul, I know I am not just a mother of Gaby; I am also a mother of Isabella, and Michaela. For the first time, I can see, open my eyes, feel my heart come alive, and breathe in and out a mother's wind again. A gift only this planet can give me. I am free again for the first time in a long time. Though I was lost, I am given one new life to which I am to live.

My brain began its healing as the spirit of heaven was lighting it. I, just as my Gaby, Isabella, and Michaela, were given a body, and soul to fulfill the experience of humanity's gift to bare life, give life, and form and shape love out of the soul through the experience of beholding a family. Just as I am, every soul here that walks and tills the land remains a spirit, the light that came to shine, no matter how dark the world sometimes may appear. My love as I see heaven dawn, as they proclaim above me, is the light of my world. It is endless. It can feed a body to express a soul within humanity. Though the soul may forget itself, the spirit may come in full light again and teach the soul to live and have a life again, give life another chance, dream again until all the yearning to light the world out of its suffering is fulfilled. This is my humanity. I am building humanity as all my brothers and sisters are doing the same in their magnificent ways.

I am still here. I still love. And ever still, life is ready to nurture and embrace me, as it had yesterday, today, and will tomorrow, because I decided to be awake rather than asleep in grief, though grief demanded that I submit to the power of debilitating damnation. My spirit was called by the light from above to rise. So I rise. My spirit commends my soul to love again. I shall in soul, body, and mind, continue to emit love in, through, and out in time once more.

SHINE LOVE, JOY, AND PEACE!

Before the Throne, the Universe, and the Flesh

In the depth of darkness, I see the light. The light is the Son of man shining. He was looking at me. I looked at myself. I was transformed into a light brighter than thousands of full radiant moons. I discovered that I myself am a light. I looked above the Son of man as He hovers standing above me; a throne's light blasted a pure white radiance embracing me kindly with gentle and soft warmth. Upon the throne sits a Man of Light, lighting me. Silently He shone ever greatly. His presence comforted me to shine my light out of the darkness. I am safe. I am love. I am cradled by the breath of peace—I am no longer lost; I am found. I am not alone.
—Evangeline

I see the throne in the center of the wondrous infinity. Infinity is a peaceful space. Harmony is the breath of the Spirit Father as He dawns His peace at the vibrating universe below Him. The body of the universal existence is the harmony between all vibrations that govern the mind of creations into being of peaceful order's distraction and regeneration in service to life itself. The universe is perfect in its creative cycles of creations and deconstructions. Both rhythms are important cycles in favor of the guardian force of sweet synchronicity of silence that powers the universe's harmony. Stillness is the greatest work of dark matter's essence. It is a generator of life. It is a substance that is of a living compost, a glue; the most potent vibration that gives power to all life is this force. It is not matter; it is a cumulated source of a multiverse of all degrees of dense energies, feeding light to the source of all light in it and above it. Then I looked up above the universe and saw pure heaven of peace. The wind and light is pure light. I saw a man in heaven on His throne, floating in the infinite ocean of peace.

He is the peace that gives power to the universe's energy; His essence is lit up by the power of the universe. The universe and its God cannot have heaven without the presence of each other. The God is love; heaven is His peace, yet the universe is His mind of order—from which all cycles rise and fall within the womb of creation.
—Evangeline

But the mind of humanity is still lost of its purpose to create only in love by learning to let go of destruction, as the universe must do to its body to keep its purpose, to house the will and love of the divine spirits. The spirit of man must learn to evolve in kindness to keep its body in constant harmony with evolutions of the spirit's consciousness while a child of man. The mind of mankind is made to cradle fear and harbor the workings of humanity from thousands of years of creative unrest in the creation of images of wars. Yet the universe keeps moving as it teaches the mind to move in the spirit of love. Even nature creates in love, so the spirit must create in love. Love works only at present. It is the fuel of the present. It comes to teach the collective mind to evolve to its highest potential. The mind of the universe is the collective. The source of the suffering of humanity is in the collective mind, not in the spirit. It is not in love that the man suffers, but in its mind's fears and limitations. It is in conditions and separation. In the collective minds, everyone is its own domain. The spirit shall light the mind. Yet the mind is a filter. It separates and categorizes what it perceives. In the mind is the separation of mankind. The mind refuses the spirit. Yet in spirit, humanity is free. In love, mankind is the breath of the heavens. In his eternity, mankind's spirits are the lights of the universe's body, within all creation. The stars that govern the garden of the heavens is the love and hearts of humanity's family. The spirits are the living stars, the breathing consciousness that the universe must serve for the heavens to expand, in order that humanity will come to its own embodiment—as one kind family of human beings of peace, in the garden of Eden called earth.

—Evangeline

Before the throne, after my child's death, I found who I am in front of the man whose image is not seen by the human eyes and mind. The eyes of my love see Him in full image. The Holy Spirit is a Father. He is the heart and body of love. He is the breath of peace. The universe is His creation. The spirits within the universe and the heaven of peace exist because of His presence. All family within a human family is fashioned according to His heart. He is a father and all human children are His conscious spirits before they are born into a reality of the human mind. The mind should obey the conscious light of His spirit, but the mind only sees humanity's domain. Without the spirit's light, the mind is lost within the dark caves of emotional fears. Yet when the spirit is born again into the truth of its light, it sees its Father. It sees its home and the heart and spirit are at peace. The mind will be at peace. Humanity is an experience of grace.

This is who I am: I am a child of the spirit of pure light and peace. That is what the spirits of the heavens and the eternal world shine through all existence. I have come from grief to awaken again, as my beloved children came to be born for me so more experience of mothering may begin. The new day has given me fuel to seek the gift of life once more. I see that all spirits in heaven have died from humanity's dreams thousands and billions of times, yet they shine in light to cultivate the good of their creations, which is love. Likewise, I must live again not in the light of my soul alone, but in life's bounties of my fellow brothers' strength, in their passions to create, to embrace me with their soul's religions, to awaken me even when weak and in slumber, to cry tears when in pain, to rest when I am tired, to heal when I feel broken, to stand, rise, breathe, run, and live again—even when it is sorrowful, to rise and to show me to accept that I am not just a mother. I am a spirit in a soul, so I may learn to contemplate and pray that in the presence of both good and bad, they give me a mirror of myself, that I am also the embodiment and force of mercy. I am breath. I am the processes of human bodies through my brain's programming to awaken me to my own distinct, one-of-a-kind light, here to shine the take of my humanity through my five senses. I am fed by warmth and safety of compassion, nurtured by creations, and fueled by the illuminations of humanity's passion to survive despite famines, to rise and dream again despite wars and live again despite death. The same force that shapes the lives of my ancestors' spirits that power the life force that governs the cultures that also colored mine. The gift bestowed and planted by the breath of the spirits of their beloved ancestors, which is also fueling mine, as I am the embodiment of the mirror of time past that fuel the very nature of who I am still now, is my consciousness. I am the universe of the entire humanity. Humanity is me in life. The world is I, as my soul is within humanity, my dream is to see it in peace despite the seasonal struggles. I am a family. Never have I been once alone, because love is I in the spirit of life, and life is the eternal relationship of compassion and peace within the family of humankind. We are birthed in one desire to unite as one body of peace, no matter what religion, no matter the politics, no matter the economic background, we are one-of-a-kind human. We can only elevate our spirit to tend to our cause of suffering; we must rise above the gap of misunderstanding and unite in spirit as one body of light to illuminate healing within our souls' fears. If we stay true to our dream to bring peace on earth, we must rise beyond the minds of our humanity and claim our body as the vessel of spirits of peace, for we each are the light of it, as our Father in heaven is the same substance, living and casting love in pure spirit before and within all the matter of the flesh. Likewise, we are whole in spirit, giving breath, grounding, and providing purpose and life to the body called flesh.

Humankind is the spirit of love before the body, mind, emotions, and the brain. Mankind is the breath of peace before it is given a name, purpose, and a soul. Mankind is fashioned in its creator's divine image. It is the spirit of light. It is the spirit of love. Its spirit's breath of peace. All children of mankind are the children of the Holy Father, who is the love, light, peace, and grace shining light in the heart of all creation.

—Evangeline

Whole

A man who seeks God is lost in the creation of mankind's mind. A man who seeks love within his heart is found. Heaven of compassion is the true heart of man. Here only love for a father, our mother and love for all beloved brothers and sisters exist. Truth lives in the heart of man. The heart is one light of love, from which no other god, other than the love of a child for its father lives.

—Evangeline

A New Beginning

Heal. Let go. Write your understanding of the blessings of your life: who are you as a child of man? What do you know about your mind, your body, and your soul? Do you know that in spirit, you gave light to the heavens? Do you know that in the flesh, you give life to your own body and soul? Do you know that you are to heal your soul in order to heal your own humanity? You are the light of this world.

I am the love of my world. I am the peace of myself and the world. I am love. I am peace.

_____
_____
_____
_____
_____
_____
_____

Write your new life's purpose.

_____
_____
_____
_____
_____

PART FIVE

Twenty-Three

The Divine Child in Each Man

Joy is never of any world. Joy is of the spirit's heart. It is a pure brilliance of light beaming out of one's spirit. It is the pure blossom of divine love.
—Evangeline

Every child is the light of love and peace. It is pure and gentle. The fire of anger, thunder, and the storm may not put this light away, nor shall the mind of ignorance, fears, and insecurities hide it. Yet, if this spirit rises in a soft and gentle guiding wind of kindness, it will light the world above all storms, to make quiet all thunders, shine, and banish all darkness, before it is transfigured above the universe and becomes the stars of all the infinite heavens. Gentle is the wind of a child's spirit.
—Evangeline

Closure: Humanity cannot have closure. Humanity is a new creation. Until humanity as a whole becomes a breath of peace and one body of love, this planet will call for its gods and goddesses to be made conscious of its humanity's souls, life after life, time after time, dream after all dreams, until all gods have vanished, and love and peace rest in stillness as the pure light of human glory.

First Child: Pure Spirit, Ever-Living Mercy, Eternal, and External Grace

Languages of love are in every child: a spirit of pure, gentle, ever-living courage which is born into the human world; conscious of the purpose to light the world with compassion, empathy, understanding, acceptance, and tolerance.

Languages of self: the spirit of *peace* is the breath of light, the infinite wisdom of eternal knowledge of the truth that allows the union, harmony, solitude, quiet, and stillness to flow into kaleidoscopes of realities, expansive through the variability of expressions, to penetrate deep into the spirits of all existence, giving hues and complexity of the divine, creating the extreme beauties of a colorful life, to make flourish all that is living in time through endowments of kindness, gentleness, and patience, giving life, life-giving breath, of self's permissions, and all the allowing sense of infinite light, born as pure brilliance to blossom itself as castings of comfort and peace onto the world.

Second Child: Of Man, With and Without Faith

Languages of suffering: judgments, spirit, economy, society, souls, and family.

Fear, anger, shame, rejection, intolerance, frustrations, guilt, helplessness, sorrow, inequality, vengeance, and impatience. These energies are confused. They are the fuel of wars within the self that projects in thoughts and through all actions of sufferings onto the world. When any of these emotions are within a being, they suppress the spirit from thriving. This disrespectful force is stagnation of emotion. It turns every living thing into ashes and dust.

The Holy Spirit

Heaven

> *Luminosity is the light, love, and peace, shining its whole infinite body into the womb of all darkness.*
> —Evangeline

His Majesty sits upon His brilliant throne. He is surrounded by virgins of pure glory and peace. All the clouds float before Him, the purest of all lights, and morning glory rejoices in their pure light in His presence.

The brilliant space of creations spoke in delight in gentle calm. My spirit's heart is transfigured into a child. I am at peace.

> *My heart instantly announced: love does not concur. Nor may it exist to be concurred. Love is pure light. It shines on all. It embraces all. Love is the greatest substance that governs the infinite degrees of all existence of a man, universe, and the heavenly spaces. In light and love as one body of creation, love is one, and one is all. Love is the living vessel in man; it is man's lights, where the being is conscious of itself, blessed, yet humble that it has human life experiences. Mankind is of colorful prisms of the brilliant rainbows, infused in one luminous glory of purity in spirit, of love, of one light cell among billions of one body of the great source, a father's heart's light, shining through the divine wisdom of His spirit children called humanity.*
> —Evangeline

When death comes to the flesh, the mind of one's humanity dies. Its human experiences, the way everything was is no more; for the flesh that suits the spirit is no more. The soul's ego also dies, for the breath of man is no more. The soul that had risen from infancy, who learned to walk, learned to dream, as the child of man is no more; but the breath that came and made the flesh rise to behold humanity's family—that light and love, that humanity's light—is no more. The name of the child of the man is no more. His purpose for that given sacred and divine season as a human being has been fulfilled. Humanity of this beloved spirit has come to an end. It is finished.

Yet this is not the end of love for the spirit of life. The spirit that gave life to the body, that which breathed life and love onto humanity, is risen and awakens to itself, as the pure breath of consciousness. The breath of life awakens to the pure state of brilliance, its own body of light. The self's new eyes are opened, and becomes aware of its truth. Consciousness is life, and its presence is the essence that projects love on earth's reality. The super-consciousness is pure love. Love is the heart of the heavens of all universe spaces. Love is the light that shines outside the universe, making all heaven float. Love is but an innocent child of spirit who comes to manifest into the planet a divine dream and in being good, gives orders to all creation, that it finds glorious—the human family and its past, present, and future life. The love of one child's spirit magnifies its home, its Spirit Father, the Holy spirit's joy.

Everything lives because of the light and love of the super-consciousness, which we term the "source," yet the source is infinite grace of pure radiance; it does not limit His body of love. In His divinity, love is consciousness. In consciousness, God does not exist. Love is the only force that powers all life, as life powers itself with divine consciousness. The Holy Father's arms and heart are the heaven that our every ancestor comes home to, to dwell in peace after death. The garden of rest below His feet is the garden of an awakened being, a new life, after the arduous and sometimes very trying life on earth. Love must come to itself. In its divinity, all spirits are beings of peace. Love is one, for all life is one. The source is the light of eternal life of all. The mind does not know love. If love shines, the mind closes its doors to it, for it does not understand its substance. The mind is man-made; love has no beginning, for it is not created. Love is grace; love is infinite. It is heaven as the light and heart that governs its peace, and harmony is a Father so divine in wisdom and pure in white light. His presence surpasses times and minds' collective understanding. Above the universe, He dawns as the great light to all His children. Love is all there is; the breath of love governs the life of all humanity. The source of this divinity is a radiance, the essence of our Father's heart, which consciously flows through the living cord of our individual, unique in all degrees of prisms in spirits, but our breath, of life in heaven and of the earth, is family. In heaven, which is above, all spirits are life; and all life is one. As it is, above the universe is the heavenly body of the infinite space of brilliant soft light of purity. The center of that heaven is the throne. The Man on the Throne is not a god. He is a Holy Father in which all wisdom arises, and pure light illuminates. Below Him is a universe. It is a world of matter from which all spirits come to create. The universal light is the Holy Father's pure light of peace. Everything that matters in the universe works in order of seasonal creations. Here, the Holy Spirit may enter creations as the light of consciousness. By allowing His children to come to create, the spirits of His children become aware of their own body of light as they learn where and what they choose to experience. Humanity is the greatest and most sacred creation in the universe. The garden is the only garden where spirits dwell by creating. No one spirit may come on earth if it's not born into a womb of a family. Family is a sacred endeavor for our spirit. All family on earth is one family of love. In love, we are one. In the body, we are one wisdom, a creator, and a maker of humanity's peace. The most sacred work in the universe is not to create matter in order to survive. We come to shape our soul with the spirit of kindness in order to know the depth of our individual brilliance. The spirit must create in kindness. In kindness, one finds its own light. It is in light that one finds its eternal love. And when the spirit finds its light and shines it, peace comes into the world. Because in peace, all live. In spirit, all souls' consciousness on earth and heaven, are at peace. Humanity is a spirit of love.

—Evangeline

PART SIX

Twenty-Four

Shape in an Image of the Holy Spirit of Love

The spirit is pure white light. A presence of pure brilliant luminosity of love. A fluorescent human form, bright light shining before me, lighting purely within me. So far, yet so close. In the presence of His being, it had traveled through the speed beyond all lights. So pure. So silent. Space, above and beyond the cosmos, shine His pure compassion. Creation adorns Him with its infinite mercy. Consciousness surrenders their beings in pure glory of calm. Solitude lights Him. Time and space greet Him with infinite wisdom. Seasons reap in the full joy of His lights, serving Him the honor of abundant grace. Holy is the secret code of human spirits. The spirit of a human child shines from the heart of its Holy Spirit, its God of love, its breath of peace, its Father in spirit, its light in creation, its true home after all creation ends. This gentle and giant love shines in the darkness of creation, the eternal grace of heaven. From His throne, His soft radiance generates life to the universe's cycles of infinite intelligence. Such beauty He shines out of nature to feed the humanity that gives power and shelter to the flesh.

Bodies Are Sacred Vessels of Light Eternal

Brightly shining, they are all fluorescent bodies in the shapes of human images, beaming from the eternal spaces of rendering peace. It is a space that has no end. As they are the light of eternal lights, they have no end. I see them hover and float around and above me; the spirits are at play. But they come to show me that there is a garden where billions of spirits wait to be granted a body so they may be grounded in time to experience love on earth. They yearn to come to give back to humanity its lights. They wait to be born, to come, and to heal the ills of the planet's divided minds, which tears at the peace of this wondrous garden of a sacred and all-loving blessed world.

—Evangeline

The First Body: Love and Peace, Spirit of Joy, a Force of Consciousness

Child of man! Know that you are a vessel in the secret compartment of nature's function. One image of light vessels in multiple bodies within complex systems of the brain, the mind, the organs, and the heart. Yet know that you are not just flesh or just the mental image of the emotional body. For you are not just a name, not just the purpose of a soul. You are the spirit of light that makes the systems belonging to the mental universe and man's mind, the flesh, and the soul-conscious of love, eternal.

—Evangeline

Before the spirits, I see who we are in secret. It was a great awakening to know that my emotions, which had been my source of self, my own knowing, had gone awry the day my daughter died. In witness of her wanting to breathe, yet she could not breathe, was a struggle that prevented the mother in me to not feel the powerlessness. My daughter's spirit struggled to survive, yet to no avail, she did not wake up. What remained asleep was her body. Never would she awaken to sleep and rest in the warmth of my arms. Not to see her smile, not to hear her squeal in joy. Not to call me Mommy and inform me that life's discovery constituted finality. Her body is asleep forever. All at once, death blinded me. My eyes could not see, my ears could not hear, my tongue could not speak, my knees could not stand, and my feet could not take a stride. I was trapped in a paralyzing jail of dormant self-punishment fueled by my ignorant mind.

But now before the spirits, I am not an emotional body alone. I am not the same soul as I was yesterday. I am new in light of the light before me. Though I am broken in my emotional mind, I am still, in all degree, a loving mother. I am still here. I am still a woman. I am still a spirit that loves, despite the emotional traumas that the experience of death and loss have manifested in my emotional body, which is of my mind's perception.

I learned before the lights of love above:

The emotional trauma of loss is not to be housed by the vessel if the spirit of love is to live in the body. The Man of Peace came from heaven. He explained what it was, a feeling that wanted to get out of me. He gave it a word, He came and gave me the eyes to see, He opened the eyes of my spirit, and He brought the eyes of my mind to see love so I may stand. Though in my soul, I was quiet, though, in my darkness, I sometimes may have awakened, there in my heart, in my spirit, love is a self-knowing that I can be free again. I was to see. My spirit was burdened and buried by grief. I had a choice to well it out of me—by writing, by letting it go. My body is a sacred vehicle for me to be grounded on earth, so though I hurt and was lost in grief, I may stand and rise in understanding. I am still blessed, as all of us now on this planet, because we, all of us, are still here governed by our vessels.

My body, as is my daughters and all humanity, is sacred.

I am still in a body that allows the mother in me to be healed through the understanding of my own self-evolution. So it is their message of wisdom and light that I must not deny the rest of my life the truth.

Pain and sorrow come, but just as the wind comes, the pain will go, and sorrow fades away to make way for a better sunrise, a new outlook that comes to life as long as one is on earth. In life's gift of motherhood, I am still a parent and a woman. This immaculate grace of the divine gift is given only by life on earth. I owe these experiences to the gift of nature's feminine energy. I owe all that I am now to my human gift, my body, and my spirit's vessel. For such a gift, I am ever grateful to our divinity's creative expressions that have manifested and are being expressed throughout this kind planet, this magnificent yet only globe for humanity's home, Earth.

The Second Body: Emotions, the Recorded Feelings of Human Life's Experiences

Emotion is a system on its own, here to keep my spirit within the compass of life, but it doesn't know I am a spirit, nor does it recognize that I am the breath of light and the love of life. With my emotions as my guide, it is my spirit's duty to rise again after death. I, as the spirit, must keep going after disappointments. My heart and mind will see life and honor the love within all families until humanity as one rises from the darkness, as the spirits shall not surrender to the fears of the minds and cloudy shadows of painful traumas. I am a spirit. Every human being is a spirit, as our ancestors and loved ones are spirits. Spirit is to love and not to succumb to injuries of emotions from which all my sorrows of humanity's pain have come.

—Evangeline

Only after I wrote the painful, traumatizing feelings of grief was I was able to take a clean, fresh breath, which I had not had since the hour of my daughter's death, instantly, I felt lighter. I saw a morning sunrise come. A sense of a beaming white-light-filled green garden appeared. A new beginning is before me. It is not of a physical world. It is a lively world of lights. It is a world of the spirits. It is of peace. It is of love. This world is the source of love and peace within every human heart. This spirit world is alive. It is where all physical realities' pure goodness is rooted before every manifestation. It is always here coinciding with the world inside and outside of me. It is space. It's all around me. It is graceful, silent, and peaceful.

In emptying my emotional mind of pain, this garden made itself known. As if writing all the darkness came the unbelievable revelation that heaven truly is in the simplest form, a subtle force, of a kind love. The less I carried the pain of my emotional house, the more I released all the stuck feelings out of me. It is by emptying the trauma and fears that were inside, which the past gifted me, I found myself free to forgive. After releasing all the burden that I carried for years, I was a clear vessel. I was space within space. This state ushered in the light and space which is the way of the spirits, to commune with me. The encounter now had become clearer, brighter, as it had become often. I began to know the secret of my own humanity. I saw that spirit is not the functioning of the body. I learned I am not my emotions. Emotions are the feeling of transmitted reality from the outside world, projected within by my own experiences, of processing life's encounters, which is governed by my own human perception.

I learned that the spirit is light. I see that even light must choose what emotion it will feed the mind. Each day I must not forget the complex duty of my human sanity. My human emotion at all times is a recorder of life, and it was going to keep feeding me the good and the bad feelings of life's realities, whether I liked it or not. My only job is not to own its tragedies but to give it my spirit of understanding, my compassion, my eternal love by being aware of my own emotions.

Eternal love is the breath and body of the human spirit.
                                                              —Evangeline

The Third Body: Human Brain; the Machine of Life, the Processors of Emotional Events within Life's Orders and Disorders

I see her spirit floating above her body connected with an invincible cord of light that is hanging from her spirit body's umbilical cord, yet in the same, attached to her human body that is sitting on a rocking chair, is that cord of life. "You still have your body down here; what are you doing floating up above it?" I asked this eighty-two-year-old woman's spirit before me. "My brain is injured… it keeps making me drool, and when in my body, I have a hard time doing what I love to do. It keeps taking me places where I am afraid. I don't like being limited; I don't like being afraid. It's frustrating to be in that brain," she reasoned.

"What is it that you love to do?"

"I just want to keep loving. I want to hug my grandkids and float in peace, without struggle… Don't you worry, I'll get back to my body when it's time to eat my meal," she assured me.

The third body is the brain. It is of man, yet it is neutral to the spirit and the soul.

I learned that my spirit could communicate at a spirit level. Shocking. But it is what it is. Quickly, I learned that it was not only my heart that was broken the day my daughter Gaby died. My emotion that knew joy was no longer aware of what truly being happy was about. No matter how hard I tried, nothing was familiar, the way it was when she was alive with me.

But above all these tragedies, there was a deeper discovery. I learned that I couldn't count on my brain to keep me alive either. It was worse than my emotional heart. Like that old woman in her old body, my brain was distorted and frail as my emotions. I felt everything that made me who I used to be was no longer with me. The bright, all-happy kid that I used to be, the dreamer that I was, the whole person, body, soul, mind, and spirit, was no longer part of the present.

I struggled daily. My brain played a trick on me whenever it remembered Gaby is not here, but yet I am. Its unrest it has had, without help from my emotions, could quickly bring my spirit light out of life, out of peace, out of present time, as it had developed its own shutdown mode when even the slightest mistake comes in the day. It was still fragile, traumatized by the vision of my daughter's death. Out of my duty and purpose to be a sane and well-meaning mother, I had to consciously rise over my brain's fear in order to get through daily existence. There were many occasions when all it could remember was the death of Gaby. In an instant, I could flashback to the emergency room where she never wakes. Wait, no need to burden you with that.

Injured brain: I see the spirit above its brain and body. Yet the woman is unconscious of what its spirit is doing above its brain and body.

My brain fed the house of anxiety, mightily whenever it was triggered by anything in my surroundings that resembled pain. All I had to do was be slightly tired before I felt afraid. So little would take to make me feel powerless, alone, and all hurt. If I am not aware that my brain should and is supposed to thrive on kindness and orders of balance, I would not be able to see the light of any tomorrow. Just as my emotional body, my heart, and soul are hurt, so is my brain, it needs to learn to fear less. It needs time to heal. Time for today is here for such healing of the brokenhearted. But as the truth speaks, only love, eternal love, can quell such deep and unspoken yearning.

The Spirit above the Emotional Mind and Brain Is the Spirit of Love Alone

For the life of the brain, balance is kindness. Balance makes the brain function with fewer fears. Balance knows that I am a spirit of peace. I am not just my soul, not just my body, not just my mind, not just my brain. I am the spirit of consciousness living at the mercy of my body's miraculous design.

I live as a mother, a woman, and a soul, in service of my spirit to experience the jewel of humanity's passion for evolving in love and for manifesting peace, until heaven is experienced for the balance of humanity's emotions, fueled by the functioning of the normal brain's biochemistry. I learned that when the brain is injured, the spirit is not able to express its conscious light or express any uplifting emotion. But the spirit of our loved-ones shine through no matter what, for the eternal spirits of their wisdom are lighting and powering our self-evolution every step of the way until our mind is lit up in the loving joy of the spirits we so love.

Our brain is the only vessel that allows our spirit to express the emotion of love, compassion, mercy, and kindness for others and for humanity itself. For the spirit consciousness is a breath of healing and light on to earth. In the eyes of spirit, it sees humanity as one body, one spirit of love; and humanity is the spirit of divine courage where a dream of a whole family lives. I found that even the brain seeks balance in both love and peace.

Twenty-Five

New Eyes

In every child of man is his spirit, and in every spirit is the eyes of the heavens of love and truth.

—Evangeline

Because I could, I chose. I chose to teach my emotions to see goodness in life and the goodness that is making the planet a sacred gift of life to all spirits, to the souls of humanity. Earth is already rotating on an axis of peace. From above, the earth is already protected by other planets. It is, after all, a planet of life. Where then did the struggle originate? Where then is chaos's source? It is in the mind of the masses. Fear is created by the mental mind of not one but all minds on earth. It is heightened by belief in separations and condemnations. Judgment is its tongue. Separation is its refuge. Anger is its source. Anger is its projected world. This is not the work of the love of humanity. Humanity is in love with a child, a mother, a father, brothers, and sisters. It is the unspoken yet illuminated grace of light of our ancestors' kindness and graceful wisdom that we've come to own our light in the part of humanity's peace. Family's peace is the highest creation within the universe. Peace is a work of love. It is a work of the heart. It can never be the mind. For the mind will not exist in the power of love unless it knows that its heart is from the light of peace.

"Govern your mind with love and the mountains of fears will vanish," the Man of Peace and the Holy Father reminded me.

I stayed away from the news that projected disasters in the world. I chose to remind my brain to record the sound and vision of nature that surrounds me. I chose that my human soul sees kindness in each man. And even when my soul is tired, I make it understand that no one came to earth to suffer alone but to plant peace and love into this world. For that's just like my soul, and my spirit, every child, every human being who is born comes in full light as love. And as we become trapped in the mercy of a powerless yet full of radiating humble love of our innocent essence, we will rise in consciousness as a child of man, so long as our body is healthy. Our spirit must be guided out of the mental stress created by fear in our human mind. If we are to be shaped into good souls as each of us comes seeking heaven's essence out of the world, we must not be in tragic conditions and in urgent diseases of the mental mind, which is chaotic. Despite the hard labor of family to prepare in love our coming, we all come to experience compassion, understanding, and love. The arms of the spirit, the warm light of eternal love, we have all come to know how to project out into the world around us and embody while we are grounded by sacred matter, a divine vessel, grounded by the arms of our loved ones, our family, and our community.

Twenty-Six

New in Spirit

Reprograming of a New Brain

Who you were yesterday is no longer who you are this very second. Yesterday mistakes came. You learned from it. Now comes so you may know that you have the will to create a new spirit within your new self. See good. Do good. Think good. You are more today. In spirit, today is a new creation. Today you are new and whole.

—Evangeline

With much practice, I programmed my mind and brain to light up my intention to live a peaceful life. I told it to always remember the truth. When sadness came, it did not mean I am dying as Gaby's mother again. It doesn't mean something is wrong, that Gaby is dead again. Rather, the truth reveals itself; sadness is part of life. But it is in grief and sadness that we know we need to be in the light. We need to embrace who we are in spirit. Sadness is the world at times, but we are the spirits that may cure sadness when we chose to experience a higher expression of being human. Love is us. Our breath is love. Love floats. We are free in love. Our spirit is the life of the body. Our eternal dream is the fuel of our mind, which houses our emotions of joy and sorrow, but our future is to train our brain to ignite in love and make way to the rising of the consciousness of the body of peace.

Every child is a house and a channel of peace. These beings are the breath of true compassion, light, and wisdom.
—Evangeline

What dawns above sadness is the heaven of light, heaven no eyes of man can see, but the heart of a mother and the spirit child within me see. The world of heaven is hidden to the mind. But what is hidden in our perceived reality, our spirit's hearts and eyes see; these brilliant essences that sustain all darkness to life is made to reveal to the eyes and hearts of the spirit child that seeks it, a paradise of light, love, green pasture of eternal rest.

Before me shines white and gentle luminosities brighter than a thousand full moons and suns combined, it is the source that feeds love into the world. It beacons both on all the living and the dead. This heaven that comes down to touch my earth's heaven is as transcendent as my daughter's spirit. In this heaven, every soul who died in the flesh on earth is, in fact, not dead. They live. They acquired new bodies of light. It is a soft, gentle brilliance of white elegance and pure living light of all-encompassing peace. This light illuminates from the core of their being. Their hearts drive these bodies to shine a light of complete health, a light of infinite compassion, a light of illuminated grace, a body that is of the radiant breath of humble wisdom. They are the effervescent bodies of everlasting understanding of the innate power of simple love, and with great radiance, all live as love to self, as one illuminated vibration with all. They are the light stars that are of man. The spirits, our beloveds, are living stars of heaven. They are all sons and daughters of man. Each human and all creatures are the life of this magnificent garden. We on earth are the extensions of their living power.

Oh, my beloveds, let it be made known that the light of the living spirit in heaven is the same color of the spirits that is within each child of man now on earth. It is the same harmony that governs the very spirits of all creatures on the planet. We are one light of love. We are one ray of brilliant grace. We are of one harmony.

No Tears in Heaven

In each man, tears are the cleansing dross that must well out of the spirit, so the emotional body, the mind of worries and pain, and the fears and weakened light of the mental body is washed away and renewed. When all seen and the unseen bodies of self are cleansed, the light of peaceful spirit comes to flow out peace and love into the world once more.
—Evangeline

In heaven, tears do not fall. On this plane no disease forms. This light body cannot experience agony. The hurt of the flesh is never to be experienced. Here no spirit dies. For all spirits are its divine of light, and all is its love, and love is its eternity. It is the heaven that all hearts of humanity must come to after earth. But lucky are the souls who embody the essence of their breath, for the soul will breathe their light and spirit of love into the world and give to the world the amazing grace of love that powers all living to breathe in harmony. In our spirit, heaven and earth are one essence of grace.
—Evangeline

Twenty-Seven

Heaven on Earth

The spirits dawn on the earth's hearts and says, "In the garden is your heart. From above, you are our heaven on earth. Your hearts are our garden. We are at peace when every one of your hearts is in the grace of peace. Be at peace. Shine peace for you are lights. Shine love for you are the living stars destined to shine on the earth."

My daughter's heaven is filled with spirits. *Millions* in all degrees of different garden spirits beamed in full light. Of gentle grace, they are glorified in the complete and ever-living radiance of contentedness. It is every human child's heaven. Families on earth are from here. Love is here before the earth is even formed, before all spirits decided to carry over love, peace, and family on to the mercy of the flesh, a creation called humanity on earth. We are the spirits of life. We come to bring life and consciousness on earth, so we can make a heaven of peace within our experiences as earth's intelligent creatures. I knew that without the lights of our spirits, we are a lost humanity, always afraid, as we stumble in darkness.

I see the spirits' contentment in heaven. How they died is but a blink in the past—no need to mention how they passed on. What mattered is that they light and shine in love. So where there is the struggle in humanity, there are their lights. For they are still the light that governs our world as we learn to govern in peace in the physical world.

Without the love of our spirits, all domain that matters to our hearts will have become material-conquering endeavors that trap the soul from its innate light, in physical pursuits of perfection, leaving only our spirits famished, for our creations of wealth and power are of no substance in light to our wholeness, as divine bodies of love that behold the grace of our entire families.

True wealth is the silent power within to shine peace and love.

Spirits' wealth is love, grace, and light. No money is ever allowed to come here. Just as no money may quell the silent yearning of the spirit's heart to be whole in peace, while it is a vessel in a body, all money stays on earth. For it is made on earth. But love is love. Love is the breath of heaven, and all spirits live and have truth and being in its eternal essence.

—Evangeline

Before All Births

The heavens are always here. Though their spirit of love is hidden to the eyes of man, to the spirit of man, they are ever breathing. Like living rivers of pristine waters, they are flowing down from above as a spring of fresh breath—of life consciousness. Heaven's substances are alive. They are living energies of lights. They are spirits of subtle yet of the highest of all frequencies. So fine, they emit only the purest vibrational frequencies that power all the space to communicate through intelligent wisdom. Spirits co-exist in our human space. They are love. They are light. They are life forces, shining through within each soul. In all matter are the unseen magnet of life forces, which we term dark matter, yet these spirits are one ocean of peace that govern all life and natures' seasons to express life within all beings. The hidden worlds shall remain secrets to the human mind. But their living presence is the infinite door to the heart of humanity's spirit of compassion and love.

—Evangeline

Peace Is Humanity's Divinity

Where there is peace, heaven, which our ancestors are a part, is true life. In all creation in the universe and of heaven is peace. In all space, the secret forces of heaven breathe only this magnificent essence, which is the breath of the ever-living source from our Father's heart and devotion to nurture and love us eternally through the inner workings of our energy, which powers us physically and emotionally in our quest to understand the simplicity of our spirits' essence and our humanity's true divinity.

Because heaven is the light and love of the seen and the unseen, it is an essence even the infinite spirits may not be able to explain; for the Source is not a Father alone in being. He is the power and light of our home, which is governing all life, both the universe outside and the universe within the flesh, both in matter, and spirit.

Twenty-Eight

To Bring Out from Within Is Heaven

A second life on Garden Earth is a lifetime wish come true.
—Evangeline

The only garden for humanity's spirit is Earth. Earth, for all spirits, is a paradise of love. Earth is our humanity. Earth is our peace. Earth is our family.
—Evangeline

Embodying compassion, acceptance, and tolerance within our vessels for our humanity's nourishments is our being emotionally balanced. It is these substances that make life worth living while we are experiencing humanity's families of man and woman, young and old. We are life. We still walk on this beloved garden in the breath of silent grace of peace, not because we have earned it, but because we are children of divine mercy and love.
—Evangeline

Above Is Always Below

Look above. You'll hear your spirit yearn for your true home. Without words, your soul would ache for its spirit body of true love. Look below; you will hear the voice of your compassion speak loud as your love demands to embrace the whole world of its tears. No matter where you are, no matter where you go, you are the love and light of this world's heaven and earth.

—Evangeline

The unseen heaven is within us and outside of us. It is always in, out, around, below, and above us. When we focus on love and peace, we are its doors. We are the door of heaven as we are the door of the reality in the physical plane. When we breathe peace and love, we birth heaven out onto the world as the breath of the present world. We are the channels of peace now. We are the love that we have come to experience now. We only have to know we are the doors of the world. The world is already heaven on earth now.

—Evangeline

Holy is this time now, for you are conscious of your own body of light. Shine. Love and peace will become the world.

—Evangeline

Twenty-Nine

A Heaven within Heaven

Love within a man is as big as the earth and infinite as the heavens above all the universes beyond human's universes, for the fountain of His breath, is the heart of peace, the source of life to all beings. He who reigns with the full luminosity of brilliant wisdom, above time, higher than the main body of all universes, is a Father of all man. He is love, from which all spirits in creation are made conscious of His Majesty's divine and eternal substance.

—Evangeline

The self in each man is the brilliance of peace and light, of both heaven and earth. When the womb of time calls for a spirit to be born, it is so heaven's spirit, which is from the source, has come to transmute peace into humanity's world. For every child in spirit is the Father's extension of love to dwell as the breath of wisdom into all humanity's destined creation.

—Evangeline

Though children are spirits in perfection, humanity is a new domain. Teach a child to dream in good for each babe is good in spirit and perfect in nature. Teach a child to move and act in kindness, for he is kindness and light in spirit. Teach a child to be a peaceful human, for that is the reason the babe is born into humanity. The babe is the new lamp of humanity. For when a child dreams in kindness, empathy, com-

passion, and giving, there within the child is our Father's light shining upon those who are awake to witness the silent glory of divine grace. Shape a soul to dream good of the world. For in that child's breath is a secret, sleeping wisdom from the source, which is of the Divine Father. In a good dream, our families in heaven rejoice. Heaven's door of love is in the life of our bodies. The experience of humanity is an extension of the divine self to manifest a dream greater than that which was of the past. Building a humanity is a domain requiring a new and evolved soul. For those who are awakened, a new world comes. Peace, love, joy, and healing is being life itself.

—Evangeline

The greatest discovery of humanity is to see itself as one light with the heaven of all lights. Yet the greatest gift of humankind is the ability to will its mind, body, and its soul's dreams to walk in the spirit. For in spirit, each man is love, and its breath is of peace. In peace, harmony is the nature of the spirits, even when the seasons of calamities present themselves in the darkest hours of time.

—Evangeline

The Lamp

Oh, man, know you are a lamp of love. Ignite, therefore, your being so your light may fill the womb of time; in so doing, every season itself may know of its highest purpose. Love cannot be chosen, for it is always itself in full glory. It can only be illuminated so the world may awaken in full light summoning the spirits of heaven to shine through in each humankind.

—Evangeline

A lamp that gives light to all darkness is the spirit becoming a child of man. Love a child. For the child is a gift of love from the Spirit Father. Love a father for he is sent as a child himself to grow in wisdom so one day, like the Father in spirit, he may experience the grace of fatherhood, as a God of peace himself experiencing the joy of being a father.

Love a mother, for she is the living host of all creation, a bridge of life to all human life. She is the way to life. Generations she bore into her womb. As time prepares for the birth of wisdom in all creation, so is every mother's womb nurtured to give birth to new life to provide love for all seasons. Love every child. Boy and girl, love both equally, for both are spirits eternal light, a force that gives life to all flesh, which is the body, the light and weaver of the mind, and the soul that is created in sacred purpose to channel and transmit life's dreams through the expansion of the soul's love and peace.

Thirty

The Throne

As I focus my love on my daughter, I am invited to commune with the vision of the throne's secret jewel of light and life. The infinities of all spaces above the heavens and the creations below are governed by the brilliance of all-powerful, yet gentle illuminating force of light. He is the source of all perfected human spirits of love.

Below the throne above the universe, I have come to the light garden to embrace my daughter's spirit. I drank from her love and learned from her great joy, so in turn, when she admitted her spirit into the ailments of the human body's limitations, she shines through. Always smiling, her spirit is of endless expressions of truth. Love is truth. Here she lives, as all spirits around the spaces of this bright life also live in full blossoms of calm and serene silence, of complete and utter light-filled expressions of complete being. I've come because I was invited to see the divine light of heaven.

When the world outside is complicated, when tears have washed away all my mind's chaos, the gentle visits of these loving families of spirits is my gift. I am invited up to the gardens of heaven to transcend so I may know the truth. I am lifted to be at ease. In truth, my heart is calmed. In the gentle wind of this knowledge, I am made to breathe and be free. All fears leave me, for in its place is light and greater wisdom, followed by lit visions of what's to come in peace during the brightness of the morning light.

After all the tears are shed, a new beginning comes to flourish within the spirit of each soul. It is the eternal light within each man that governs all souls to love. Love is man, and man is love.
—Evangeline

Brilliant Garden of Heaven

Without the body, without the quarrel of the mind, here live the spirits that light up eternity in an infallible brilliant and soft, gentle and kind, harmony. These spirits of love live, in being the pureness of divinity beyond the thousands of lifelines that source the powers of human hearts. Here I see what is beyond all deaths. Eternal is all. All lights are one iridescent breath of peace. I see the infinity's boundless space. Love alone reigns here. All bodies are projecting from within the dazzling brilliance of love, which is not alone a breath, but of a full conscious body of illuminations. All human bodies are no more; all insecurities and thousands of years of old memories of traumas from wars and sorrows are no more. All diseases, big and small, have not been forgotten yet left in the memories of humanity's past, for all pain has been shed, and the human spirit is light itself in its entirety. It is in being of light that they float in peace. This is the secret that is within each soul that walks the earth. Man is the living vessel of eternal light. Peace is man's eternal and external breath. Humanity itself is light. Male and female are the forces that make the body alive and has its being in a full positive vibration. Male and female are the light of the love of all heavens. Both masculine and the feminine co-exist as one living dream—the light bodies of the begotten family of humanity.

The Spirit's Unending Love

Though they wear not the body that I have, they understand my agony. I can never say they are separate from me. They are before me because I am one with them in spirit; likewise, they are one with all humanity's love and dreams. Spirits are my future. The humanity that I am is their future; the spirit's humanity is the planet earth, and mankind's spirit is our holy families in heaven.

—Evangeline

Families dawn from the gardens of the secret heavens. The agony of my soul is like theirs not long ago when they walked our beloved earth, yet here they smile in full light, for they suffer and hurt no more. Long forgotten, buried in the dust of the earth's ashes were their fears, yet they rose above time and sun to dawn upon the earth's beloveds, yearning to fill every heart's crevasse with warm love.

"Death in all the mind's treasure is life to the spirit divine," says the spirit of Mother Mary upon my visit to her garden of peace. "Heaven is the spirit of each man. Life is his love. Breath is his light. Peace is his being."

I remember to look within my spirit's eyes. For in it, I am now made aware that I am a breath of love as all human beings and all creatures are. Within our spirit is light. Within our breath is peace. Heaven dawns, always, because we live in the grace of the unseen winds of both the body of light and its breaths of peace. We humans and spirits of heavens are the bodies of eternal love. We are the lights of the universe's realities and all human darkness.

Instant Ascent and Descent

How can heaven come down in a flash? How can its door be the body of a giant man that gives light to life? How can His love give *new life and new breath to a mourning mother, after her heart had died when her child died? "Because heaven is love. Love is always the spirit. The*

spirit is the light of space before there is any beginning or end to the universes that created the mind, the souls, and body of all humanity."
—Evangeline

The Man of Peace lit up, ushering in heaven that I can see. For He is living life of absolute brilliance, brighter than all the moons in all the known cosmos, pure white breathing prisms, pure peace, and life-giving than all the suns in the known and yet unknown universe. In His arms is my daughter. She is free, joyful, and so happy. In my daughter's love, I was able to obtain courage. In this reality that showed up, my beloved daughter is to continue on living, in safety, without pain, with the freedom to come and go, above the universe and beyond the blue ocean of peace, where I see her as one among the billions of light bodies illuminating in contented peace in the eternal world outside the physical realities—called the spirit world. This world that called my spirit out of sorrow; now, without a choice, I have become part. For as much as I know, I am aware that I exist, so are these beings before me, whose bodies are lights, whose hearts and intentions for being alive are only to shine the light of eternity to everything that is below and above. Their very presence surpasses all other lights that exist.

In our journey, we entered a world beyond the universal river, beyond the memories of the time. What there is, is nothing. Nothing is the absence of creation. I see that above the universe and time is the ocean of peace. No creation is part. *Heaven is a space for stars. The stars are of bodies of love.* They are the lights of all creation below. I was made aware that love that never dies is the love of our spirits. The spirits dawn on earth, always. In a still yet kind voice, they come. They guide our hearts to be still, to be calm, to remember to do good because that is the true nature of our spirit. They do exist, not in my human mind's understanding, but my spirit's heart's current ability to form a nonverbal discernment, a heart-to-heart communication that flows infinitely within a higher vibrational current that is transporting fine energies of visions and information into my all—spirit, body, and mind. All currents from their love behold only the purity of beaming white light dispersed into the infinity of peace. Their rays from their bodies are peace, which makes up the bodies of divine stars of eternal beings called our beloved families, our eternal home, the spirits. I was elated! I know that they are us in the future. But I know importantly that though we are in the flesh, we are now these lights and love in spirit. I knew that it is so temporary that we are in the body. Each day on earth is one day closer to this state of being. We are heading to our future. This heaven is still. It dawns in all hearts, and in each child of man. For, all man is a child of one family of heaven now on earth.

So their intentions are nothing less than pure, divine, and unconditional. It is to give us eternal love while we are granted the gifts of the flesh. Pure consciousness beyond the functioning and limited perceptions of collective human minds, beyond our emotional limitation, they are with us always. They are in each and every one of us humans, for they are the roots of our living breath. That which is earth is a gift of the flesh; that which is the mind, which beholds limitations and glory of humanity, is of humanity's fears of creations. But above all creation, both of heaven and earth, beyond the minds, is the throne of the Spirit Father, whose love is unconditional as the newborn babe, yet His wisdom creates life, breathe out love out of the dust of the soil, to create a divine suit for the spirit to create a divine soul out of man, to crawl, and to walk on to the planet's sacred garden.

Beyond the souls is our eternal love. We are one with our ancestors. We are eternal in our spirits. We are the glory of peace because we are the breath of peace. It is our spirits that are lighting all the darkness of the earth's emotional, yet joyful and creative realities. In our courage, they are with us. In our darkness, they light us. In our joy, they are within our hearts illuminating their eternal love, every thought, and every step as we walk in our experience as individuals yet one desire to build a safe and kind refuge for the now-born and the yet-unborn humanity.

Thirty-One

The Purity of the Spirit World

Man! Listen to your deep yearning. Open your spirit's eyes. See good in everyone and all things. What you will encounter is the pure love and glory of your own spirit.
—Evangeline

The spirit world is subtle. Bright. Always and forever is its substance. No darkness may dwell in it. Time is not present. Now, is always. It is a place of no beginning or end. In this garden of light and space, depending on what level I am invited to see, children and cherub angels are always closer to the throne. In a vast depth of multilevel realities, it is always governed by families and clans of angels with wings both in physical and pure energy bodies. In all cases, there are multiple gardens of angels serving our spirit human families that passed on. There are gardens of bright lights with angels and our loved ones' spirits, serving each other in harmony and light; of calm and peace, they are working to guide the lost, they work with our families of teachers, educating and cherishing the spirits of the unborn. For the angels, we are family before there is humanity. In spirit, we are shaped in consciousness by the angels. Likewise, in the truth of the angels, we must exist conscious of our dream to serve all life, nurture kindly while on earth, co-create respectfully with nature's exquisite universe, and evolve in the knowledge of the divine purpose of humankind's family—to rest without guilt and shame after all human work is attained—to unite as one light with the God of peace in heaven. Without fear, we think as the angels think and love as the angels' love, for they are our mothers and fathers, our guides, and our confidants, as our Father is the source of the love that they are teaching us to manifest in humanity.

Weather Spirits

> *Space is consciousness. It is our planet's home. Consciousness is intelligent. It feels, it breathes, it learns, and it hurts in discomfort like any human being on earth when its body's mechanism is in constant trauma and disharmony.*
> —Evangeline

August 2014, it had been so hot for weeks. The ocean water was hot. The ocean didn't give a breeze. The wind all over the island was hot. Children at school were in discomfort. They couldn't learn. I prayed. I was worried that the kindergarteners would not learn at all that day. The rooms were not air-conditioned. I ran to Target and used the money left in my bank account. I wanted to make sure the kindergartners didn't suffer. Then I thought about the other children's rooms. They are hot too. I got all the fans on the shelves. I dropped the fans off at the school. Dizzy and uncomfortable, I went to the ocean. I prayed to the Father: I looked at the horizon and space. It was telling me something. Then angels came down—thousands of them. Mostly children ages ten and fourteen.

It was worrisome. I thought of the tsunami a year ago. I was afraid that the heat was foretelling of what was to come. I asked the angels, who began holding my arms as they began singing.

"Why do tsunamis come and take away families by the shore? Why does heat care not if God's children are in discomfort?"

"Because I have cancer," answered a depressed and sideways-lying giant of a gentle Pillsbury dough-looking image of a spirit. His body was translucent. He was giant energy in the shape of a giant human. He was one body among many layers of bodies within the space of the universe. He bit his lip and cringed his discomfort. He hurts like a human. He had legs, a head, arms as every being does, only he is energy. Earth is one planetary system in his belly. His internal atmosphere is the galaxy's circulatory system. His intestines' pathways that run through his leg were covered in holes. It was scorching balls of fires causing him to twitch in pain. His intestine was bloated by massive typhoon cloud clusters circling hundreds of miles an hour.

"Where is your cancer coming from?" I asked him. He looked into his tummy. He lit up the earth's heated atmosphere. There are many fires and heat coming from the planet, causing the heat and disorder inside of him.

"How can you heal your cancer? How do we cool your belly down?" I asked him.

"I can't...," he answered.

"There are tsunamis in the last three years. You're killing many humans... most of them are not the ones who've caused your cancer. They are new humans. They are many children. They don't have anything to do with your pain. They are all innocent children of your God, my Heavenly Father."

"Don't take it personally," he said. My internal system will do what it takes to regulate its temperature... just like your body would do. I have nothing to do with human deaths. This is how I am made."

"Cool your body down. There's got to be a way," I told him.

"What way is that?" He said.

"Rain at night to release the internal pressure. Then make it windy during the day, all over the planet, to circulate your organs." I told him.

"I can do that?" He said.

"Yes!" I encouraged him.

"You must do so in order that your internal circulatory systems become balanced, so your systems do not unknowingly create tidal waves that cause tsunamis, killing human families."

"I can do that?" He questioned.

"Yes. Regulate your temperature so that your system does not build up and create an earthquake and tsunamis that cause death. We are the good bugs in your tummy. There are bad bugs too, but we're not that one. Don't take any more children. They are the healers of your cancer. Let them live. They will heal the planet, and take away the source of your cancer," I promised him.

My conversation with him made me feel hopeful. He understood. Millions of spirits of young angels came down and surrounded his massive body. They held my hand. They began singing. We sang to him. As the music from our spirit beings calmed him, the atmosphere, which made up thick and orbiting clouds, spun in massive scales like being vacuumed as the clouds rose up gently in his tummy, and the clouds began to move up to his chest. The notes of the music drew the typhoon clouds up to his mouth. He burped a good burp, releasing a giant force of the wind that would have caused multiple typhoons, deadly tsunamis, and earth-shattering destruction on people. The atmosphere outside his body shook. He was surprised.

"Ah... Thank you." He rested his head.

"You're welcome," I said.

The angels clapped. I took a breath of relief. Now I am back on the shore. The angels came with the wind behind them. The cool breeze returned. "The school children need you," I directed the winds to the classrooms all over the islands who were suffering from the heat.

The angels left me. I called the school.

"Did a breeze show up just now?"

"Yes!" said my teacher friend.

"Thank you," I said to the spirit. "Now that we know you exist, we have to make sure we are kind to our environment. We live in your tummy!" I was amazed.

"No fire!" he said.

"No fire. No smoke!" he insisted.

"We humans have to be careful at how we treat our earthly home. We live in your internal body."

"Thank you," he replied, now relaxed.

What happens on earth affects the entire cosmos. Humanity's choices to create in good make the entire universe a balanced space of human and other living existence... Yet when even one soul's domain is disruptive to itself, it hurts the entire universe. It hurts the world and all the spirits above the universe.

—Evangeline

In spirit, the breath of the mind and body is one force within all creation.

—Evangeline

There are angels of pure consciousness that do not have bodies. They have no shape like human spirits. These are nature spirits. These beings exist in the balance of harmony. In union with the Father, they fulfill and serve the light and well-being of the entire universe. They are pockets of spaces within the universe. All created systems of both heaven and the unseen forces that govern the perfection of the energy of the planet earth are governed by the consciousness of these mega beings. Earth is driven by a celestial power of calming essence between the vibrational balance of pure warm and cold energies. In these secret passages within the universe, spaces are pathways where angels and love—one's spirits—are coming and going through the web of time through these unseen forces. Angels come and go down to earth at all seconds to guide and keep safe all souls, whether we listen, believe in the spirits, or not. Angels are busy at work, serving heaven's righteousness. Angels, with our loved ones, shine on our families here on earth. With the exception of bodies, they are here coexisting in a vital yet fine level of reality that fuels human time, in support of the conscious experience of physical reality.

There are human spirits with the angels. These are ancient healer spirits that work with the angels. They are pretty much like us in the flesh. They work with angels to heal souls. As the angels are always existing to give love, supporting the life of all souls in those spirits in transitions from the earth plane to heaven planes and vice versa. Some human spirits must work with angels to serve kindness in all hearts and spaces as Jesus, and the Father always work at the same rate—always.

These healers are ancient in wisdom. Time is nonexistent to them. Their spirits have learned all that needed to be learned on the planet. They have no desire to live in the limited virtues of the flesh, so they choose to evolve in spirit, in serving the space, which we call heaven, as they come and go with the task at hand to return as a guide. In heaven, all light spirits are devoted to pure service of love. To give, to serve all spirits on earth, fuel their passion and devotion to exist as beings of full light and luminosities. The Heavenly Father is also in the same image in light of only peace and of the body of eternal and everlasting love, which we as children of our Father are fashioned and invincibly dwell in wisdom and spirits always.

In the physical bodies, these are one-of-a-kind blessed garments, so we may in spirit come. We explore the gift of creation, which are human families. For the greatest creation of the Father and all our spirits is the making of earth. Earth is our garden. Earth is our canvas to give birth to humanity, which means being born is to partake in the domain to cultivate love in this paradise. But we come not to plant trees and cultivate the land alone. We come to plant peace, grow compassion, cultivate understanding, till our hearts and mind with the breath of humility, until we learn to serve all life with respect and equality. Above and beyond, we must learn to grow beyond the limitations of our human fears, to grow our breaths of love. In so doing, we gain wisdom how to fulfill our works in action. For we are the vessel of peace; to water the garden with a drink, to know that we have come from the fountain of our Father's heart and love. We have our breath, for his love flows in each one of us.

Thirty-Two

Heaven's Bodies of Light

Deep in space, there is no mind that reasons, no words need to be spoken. All there is, is a rendering space of absolute brilliance of fantastic illumination that makes all beings light up in complete grace and everlasting wisdom. Love is solitude; it is the ultimate body of all consciousness, for consciousness itself is light in all spaces.

—Evangeline

When I first saw heaven. The thought of being human on earth is but a slide of sacred and divine memories, to *be cherished* and to *be embodied* as collective thoughts of past realities. Now all there is left is love. Before the throne are the green pastures, of all degrees of heights and grasslands that have no weeds. A golf course like green setting forever and ever. The light that governs all spaces is white space with no end. This light is the background of the infinite gardens with spirit bodies that are filled with fluorescent luminosities. I see my daughter's spirit busy breathing and pulsating in her bright shape of pure brilliant illumination. Her whole body is beaming in pure white light as all the angels and our loved ones in heaven do. Her breath is wisdom, which is not bound. She is of kindness, of calm love, of silent stillness, as every spirit and angel does. Everything around her is brilliance because she lights the space, as everyone we love in spirit does. Here, where the sun and moon are absent, the eternal light is the hearts and light of the pure essence of eternity, who are the bodies of our loved ones, no longer on the earth plane of beings. The light of heaven is the spirit's being. All spirits here are the stars of heaven; their complete illumination is pure love. The compass that strengthened their existence is the knowledge and experience of our own humanity. It seems that heaven would not be its truth without the physical haven called family. Family in the garden of heaven is life itself. There are no other experiences that are more important despite the universe's vastness below these heavens. The love that glues life in the eternal is the silent force that governs our inner haven, our eternal forces, our light, the unseen force that fuels eternal peace. Heaven's light is peace alone. Peace is divine grace. Only love grows here. In love is joy. In love is harmony. In love is understanding. In love is compassion. In love is kindness. In love is one. In love, everything is one. Nothing else.

The Universe of Life's Consciousness

Behold. The universe is a giant space of all creation. Here all matters are the vessel to all infinitely conscious forces of energies. Therein lies within the universe the lesser of creations—the universe of the mind, which humanity makes. The mind is not the creation of the light and truth. The energy of matter and physical called for the spirits of the heaven to enter the universe, so the mind that is mentally created by humankind in control and fears may learn of love—as the action of love is lived manifested through the working of families' communion to come to earth life after life. All human spirits desire to come on earth to build a graceful and kind, ever-loving, and peaceful families of holy humanity.
—Evangeline

All confusion and darkness are caged within the bubble dome of the universe, which is the center of all creative expression, fashioned by all spirits, which is all of us. We are in the beginning light of peace, but we, in spirit, come to the universe to explore the universe's expanding depth. The universe must expand to make room for creation. But it must do so in the conscious presence of its gods.

The spirits of love must come. We are these gods of conscious light that are born into human bodies. We must come to grow human love through our light. We must learn to breathe human peace through forgiveness and understanding in order to own the gift of our true humanity. We must grow our body of peace, because peace is what governs the heavens, and that indeed is the force that we are trying to plant the seed on earth. We planted in the past; we have come through times over and over again so we may keep the tree of humanity's peace growing, as we, souls of these gardens, evolve in spirit as our Father in heaven is the essence of peace. We come bearing the essence so we can testify that we are the body, mind, and heart of the spirits of our Heavenly Father's essence—love, peace, light, bearing an image and shape of a beautiful man, the King of all peace. And we are His children, divine in human love and in spirit, we are the same light. The beauty of the vessel of the universe is His fatherly heart that shines everlasting grace on all. Male and female, we manifest as spirits of love, to plant and govern peace on earth. Such is our true essence. For our true spirit is one with our divine Father's ultimate refuge.

Thirty-Three

Gaby

As already given, Gaby is not alone in the spirit realm. She is in the arms of the Man of Peace, in the comfort of many angels, in and around the boundless joy of children that went on forever in all degrees of innocence and purity of unconditional light's happiness, who in one glimpse alone, together they breathed in me the serenity and light of truth. And this truth is the abundant brilliance that shines out from each and every creature and man when they extend their being for others through love, despite the vessel which we are now contained. We are forces pure of light and truth. Love is the infinite body of our spirits. In true mercy and grace, we are conscious. It is in love that we are to be who we are as the Father is spirit and is a father. We are His children in spirit. We must remain pure in spirit light, despite the aging of the flesh. When we create in humility, when we humble ourselves to a child, we become who we are in simple truth. Life is simple. We are unconditional in light. We are love alone. As our Father is a Father, we are children that must stay pure in the substance of love. His is the simple love we call the light of the heaven, which even the Bible attempted to comprehend but man and priest in all the churches of the world fail to describe in full illumination until they themselves are called to remember that they are the peace in spirit. The Holy One may describe His presence as He wills it. The mind does not know the language of our heart, which is everlasting peace and always an eternal love. Our pure luminosities are the most simplistic act in nature—to breathe mercy is to cast love into the physical world, to know love is to breathe peace; peace is a breath of love. Churches have governed the soul with its rules and regulations. Unless we belong, we are outcast, called evil, judged sinners. The order of truth is peace. Peace is true freedom. Yet no institutions on the planet can dwell in the depth of truth; for orders are cast only by religion's perception to own the souls of humanity, yet it rejects the beauty of the spirits that breathe life to the soul and the flesh. Love is the light of all human darkness. Light is the consciousness of all human dysfunctions. Compassion, which is the breath of love alone, is the one and only cure for human sufferings due to impoverished sanctions placed in the human mind.

True religion is self-love. The self that is governed by peace does not serve and honor the eternal wars within the created mind of egos, which is fueled by a myth of darkness, a faith that honors the forces of evil and man-made God, the gods that control and reject the subtle substances that give life to all that is peace, love, compassion, and tolerance. These attributes of the spirits are the basic building blocks of life, family, which fuel both eternal and physical love. This is the subtle and quiet wind that comes when all thoughts, expectations, and subjugations of the mind subside.

Thirty-Four

Everything Birthed Must Die Before It Can Rise Again

Each beginning is drawn by the birth of a dream, yet even all dreams die after they are fulfilled. So once again, the seasons usher in time to come, greeting the dreamer to die out of the flesh, so in spirit, it can rise and live a new life of glory and expanded wisdom. After its gentle rest, in nature of the universe's time, even humanity may rest, for it is governed by the spirit of those who decide to leave the pureness light of love in order to come and light the place of the earth, replacing the space of those who are ready to bid farewell to humanity. They've drank the waters and cleaned the waters of life.

—Evangeline

No matter how precious creation has been, no matter how kind life came to pass, the ill of the minds are left here on earth's garden. In the passing of the flesh, the original sins of the minds are surrendered into dust as the flesh is turned to ashes. Be aware. Let the mind also turn to sleep. For the mind's domain may linger still through the works and minds of the injured souls. Know that you are the bridge of love. Teach the mind that our forefathers' hearts ache, their roads, and built models of survival shall be buried in the passing of their flesh. A newborn will create its own bridge of learning. The new human must learn but not repeat that which created past tragedies in its own ancestors' humanity. The newborn has come to clean the dirty waters that our ancestors' emotional inherited minds have swam in in their lifetime. All births, despite the terrors and horrors of the lives of our ancestors, shall come bringing new living waters of life and peace onto this planet earth. Here a new garden will appear for the new soul to walk. It is in this new drawn garden that a new experience of newly evolved humanity will rise to unite the divides of the minds, to transfigure all wisdom of the soul's spirit into one love-filled mind.

Living in Peace

The dead shall rise. In spirit, there is only space of peace. It is a space of light. There is no physical altar. There are our breaths, our spirit's heart, summoning my eyes to keep open to see that this Man of Peace is the light of the infinite brilliance that governs the eternal space of light and peace to no end. The brilliant light that governs all creation within the heavens' spirits and the universe's bounty, the source of all eternal and external love, is all there is. Before birth and after death, after the universe, light is home. His entire being is still serving all the spirits below and above Him in prisms of the everlasting and brilliant flow of life-giving breath of grace.

Thirty-Five

As He Comes

Demanding nothing of me but to breathe alone the light eternal, into our world, which I am grounded through the gift of my suit, my body, as does everyone here on the planet, is still manifesting from within. His presence demands that I come to my own light; I am to breathe only peace despite the brokenness of my hurt mind. This choice is a choice I alone can make, so I may experience knowing that on earth, I am a light. I am a drop of light, a breath of space, one orb among all the uncountable brilliance of the lights of the Heavenly Father's body of love, a breath of peace, conscious of the awestruck and endless sea of wondrous miracles of the Father's Majesty's and abiding creation.

Heaven Comes

He stood behind me as I looked at the children's pain and suffering. Hungry and abandoned children make up the world of my deep sorrow. Poor and struggling homelessness shouts and tugs at my heart. Gently and softly, He said in a whisper, "The world outside of man is chaotic. You wake up in this disorder in order that you seek what is within. Here you will find the love, the light, and peace of yourself. Shine! The outside world is waiting—to eat and drink the true bread and water of true creation, which only love and peace alone, have the will to always manifest."
—Evangeline

The Man of Peace, His Majesty's son, who came with my daughter's spirits, opened the mouth of the heavens. He came down, holding her contented and joyful spirit in the comfort of His right arm. Below Him, He delivered the gardens that contain the spirits of my dead brother; and my grandparents who passed on are all together and are surrounded by their ancestors who shine above me in light brilliance. Like the Man of Peace, who bears no name, befitting of His peaceful nature of pure light and breath of peace, every spirit here is one color of pure brilliance, of white peace, the bodies of our everlasting love.

Then the Man of Peace came and ushered me up to His light sky. A door that went on beyond my sky is His haven of the luminous garden of living grace. His ocean of light streamed from Him through the shapeless essence of pure substance of an infinite well of calm and solitude. Living brilliance danced in the quieted joyful peace, a space of no end, where the essence of love, that which powers the secret code of our families' hearts, the human source of blood, our divine code, our DNA, the spirit, soul, and body are raised up and now made illuminated.

Entering the Peaceful Ocean of Life and Light, the Abode of Infinite Source

He took me higher, passing through countless edges of hidden realities. There are many countless worlds we passed through before we entered the beginning of no end. There is a white space, and a giant throne governs its heart from above. On the throne is a giant man whose heart, mind, body, and spirit shine in full blasting radiance, of an absolute, pure ocean of endless peace. Grace beheld my all. Peace, I became one. I was transfigured as a child, a body of peace before the radiant Man on the Throne.

I was lifted up so I may be revealed the secret of my human existence. Before Him, all human endeavors, including suffering and darkness, have been left to a slide of divine memory. Left to the edge of humanity's man-made sufferings, left on earth of my own humanity, all sorrows are left behind on earth's gravity. Before Him, I was to know the full glory of my own spirit's substance. I am a being of peace, heart, consciousness, and breath. I am as He is in substance; only I am as all humanity is in the state, still a youth in the secrets of heaven and the universe, as He is the ageless body of brilliant wisdom, which no time has ever known. Before Him, I may never again believe what I was taught to believe as a child of my human parents; that all my humanity's disappointments will be solved and be taken away by some mysterious, so vindictive, and punishing God who wants me to give Him offerings, so I can feel good inside my churning stomach. My Catholic ancestors go to Church each Sunday and their god was very pleased to watch me be in agony from hunger while I watched, everyone I love goes hungry; because, the church that took our offerings was going to give it to the god that needs my few pesos. The god of the Church expected of me to be glad that I was hungry; because the priests of the Churches who are hiding behind the velvet curtains, the hungrier than I was of souls, the needy, will finally eat because I surrendered my own pesos that given day.

In truth, the priests were well fed, comfortable in their robes. They are loved and protected by the walls of the Church that made them priests. Even the priest could not reach down to me to give aid to my hungry mind, soul, and body. Sadly, I haven't met a priest that shared their offerings to quiet my hunger. In truth, I was, as all children without true love, the hungry one. I was famished from the day I was born; as a child, poverty raised me, and hunger fed me. With consistencies of man's failed promises, I woke each morning; but hope my spirit kept for me. Over and over again, I hoped. To this very day, hope is still the very sweat that is coming out from the pores of my skin. Yet I am also the sisters of the hungry boys who get hurt as I watch my family be so denied of basic necessities of life such as food; it was defining and tormenting to my little child of a soul to believe it exists as I exist. My humanity since the beginning of dawn was to awaken, so I may have watched those I love work the field day and night, yet still, they awakened to another restless night, hungrier than yesterday. In my world, another day has dawned, so the universe of man's limitations and lack of peace have too often come to once again greet us with the same serving of hurt.

PART SEVEN

Thirty-Six

Mind, Body, Soul, Spirit Purpose

"A doctor, a surgeon, a lawyer, a judge, a nurse—whichever you dedicated more than ten years of your life, you will become passionate," His presence revealed to me. "You will be so good at being a servant human. Then I will worry about you too," He said, sounding concerned. "If you become one of those who heal, you will be among those who suffer. If you become a doctor, who will do my job?"

"What is your job, Father?" I asked Him whose throne is upon me, His majesty, the Holy of all holies, the Spirit Father of all fathers, the King of all kings. So calm, yet so full of care and concern.

"I want to heal my children's hearts," He confessed. "My children give their lives to heal the rest of my children. I want to be with them. They have no one to turn to. They hurt too," He insisted in a soft-spoken voice. His eyes teared up with mercy.

—Evangeline

What I Learned: I Must Write for the World to Know Itself

The truth about human life is lived by each man before me, but the truth of the spirit within each man is not yet told in truth. I needed to know the spirit of truth since a child. My struggle was in wanting to see or feel it in the world around me. But I did not see it. I had a sense since birth that I was lost. Because of the constant embodiment of poverty I was born into, I was condemned by guilt and shame for being present in the world. But when I thought I was alone in poverty and hunger, so did everyone around me suffer. My suffering, after all, is not just for myself, but for all whose love and peace were judged not worthy to shine while some were encouraged to take over my birth-given space.

I have been mourning for the truth ever since the day I was born. I have not been living in light since I was a child. I was lost in darkness, trying to find who I was. I walked and ran, survived, and dreamed like any child. Yet through it all, I sensed, I was alone. Yet, I was conscious of my search for love. That force that I know is waiting for me to come. From the outside, there was a great sadness that overcame my being each day, telling me I do not belong to a religion, do not deserve to witness the suffering of my own loved ones' struggles; being alone, I was powerless when they were in tears. It was always confusing when there was a celebration of the rich families around us. We the poor were not invited to attend. It did not make sense to me that the culture that I was born into required the death of an animal for each celebration. It was a customary practice that a pig, a cow, a sweet innocent animal must die before every wedding, baptism, and birthday may take place. I was tormented by sorrows for the livestock's lives would end so my families could celebrate. I had to hear the cries of dying pigs, while an elder would slit the throat of the animal to take its life. I was troubled by such unnecessary practice. In spirit, I struggled for answers to my own life's ultimate question. Why do I suffer? Why do I hurt when I witness pain when animals have to be sacrificed so that others feel celebratory? I was haunted by all faces of suffering, even when others were drunk in temporary joy.

"Who am I?"

So now by the grace of the Prince of Peace who ushers in the heaven of peace, pure light came down, to shine gently on my dark world. His visits to me bestows the wind of peace in my senses, deep in the well of the life of my heart. I was made to light from within, soul, body, mind, and spirit. When my soul is in tears, my spirit is comforted. He breathes a lasting light that powered me to see the purpose of life itself. Eternal and everlasting, life is a humble breath of divine love.

Anger

The birth of man is restlessness; anger and fear, it is part of its humanities existence. Unless the breath of peace comes, it is lost in the wilderness of darkness, not knowing his secret strength. He is wisdom. He is born to rise, shouting Mercy! Mercy! Mercy! I live in Our Majesty's breath of love, which no man alone may give freely, even if his light is in the sea of great earth's wealth and mankind's intelligent abundance.
—Evangeline

Looking back at my own childhood, it was not that I was born poor that angered me. It was people who represented churches that angered me. The idea that I was a girl, and Eve is the reason I was where I was. I was taught that children are born in sin because Adam and Eve made it that way was a belief that gave people the right to judge why all children born poor deserve to be in the state of hunger and abandonment. I have awakened from a grand dusky spell of my ancestors' souls' belief, that a god who entertains suffering actually built a church, who bore many more for himself so pastors became wealthy in gold, steak, and butter while I suffered as a child soul, hungry, and too afraid to ask questions of the cause of my sorrows. Why is everyone around me suffering? Church, to me, was a house of welling out the unspoken pains that no drug could cure. The church was the final surrendering of all broken dreams that never manifested because no one was there to help ignite their vision. Everyone who entered the church, in my eyes, was finding a way not to feel the inner turmoil within their being.

Somehow my spirit needed to be in it to feel God. Yet though I waited, the priest—though I knew was a servant of Christ—did not see me. It is in church that I was made known to find God, yet it is cold, musty, and often filled with agonizing faces who were burdened in their souls; this was not heaven but a house of torturous agonies, and it left the traumatic imprint of pain in my soul no matter where I went, no matter how I evolved. It was a house where pain was put on the center altar, where my innocence was crucified, a house that would steal the light of hope in my heart, a house that served tormented and silenced agonies to my child soul, even before my mind could understand of the world's great pain, before my mind could form any reason. My parents' churches were supposed to be the Sunday rest houses for the poor like me; after long six days of toiling under the sun, on the seventh day, we were promised rest. However, there was no rest in my soul when we kneeled on the pew. For it was of worship in these houses that I had become lost to the meaning of my own birth. I was judged as a sinner. The priests' voices of damnation upon my soul cast an eerie pain in my heart before I could learn how to reason in my mind. I was lost. I was unwanted, way before I knew the difference between right and wrong.

When I came home, just like my ancestors, my soul was broken in faith, tormented as a soul, delicate in speech, frail in mind. I was depleted. It was in the church at a young age that I was given a sense of belonging to a group. They are as I was called—the less fortunate.

Eventually, I grew up. I finally found the truth. There is no god as the church had described Him! What brought me up was the breath of divine love within me. In love, there is never a heaven that demands from its creature's selfishness. In knowing of the spirits who come before me, God is not made in heaven. Love is made in heaven. God is an idea of a man, trying to explain the body of the spirits that shine the light of heaven's glory.

In heaven, there is no narcissistic god who could eat up all the gold and my pesos. We were the poor who struggled day and night to give to our church on earth. The idea that the poor give so the other poor may not miss a meal didn't make sense to me.

Heaven and in spirit, there is only compassion toward those who seek kindness and reason. No God that demands of me what it had demanded of my ancestors, a lifetime after lifetime of commitment that God needs offerings and sacrifices of alms so we may be deemed worthy of its praise.

Heaven, after all, has no church. Earth has many churches that I know are created for what it was intended in the beginning. Churches, I thought since a child should house peace, a house where the spirits may rest, yet I was tormented in my soul by the rules and regulations of those indifferences between the beliefs and orders of the people who run them. I used to wonder that if the church is to house god, why then when I entered, I was subjected to only believe the god that that church members believe in—the god of unrest and division—not the spirit father of unity and peace.

So I learned that many churches love their god. And I had the Catholic Church that loved for me to see the helpless hanging man on the cross that upon sight made me feel no one makes it in this world without getting hanged. I was helpless and dreaded going into my own church. But I knew I had to learn to be okay with the vision because I was not alone. There was always my group that needed to talk to God. And there has always been the poor me, and my brothers, who were too hungry to stand in prayer. Just as the old were weakened, so would the newborn become weak in spirit so we could kneel in surrender to the altar of mindful fears, of self-martyrdom, and judgments.

When I should have rejoiced and rose, I was as my brothers—given the long pew to be on our knees while we found, if any at all, the last strength in our bones to look up so we could stare and pray to a lifeless, deaf, and mute of a wooden man on the cross, bleeding, oozing blood in His head and side, who casted a silent dart into my heart, to stare at my already lost soul that said, "You did this to me. Because you are sinners!"

Breathless, as it did at age eight, so it is still, the remnant of that guilty wind that has lodged in my being to this day, which makes me doubt that this planet is finally at the dawning of peace. Even as I write this book, a part of me has been held hostage by the past. When I came out of the beautiful heavenly ornate church, I watched in silence my deeply meditated brothers, who were made weakened in the knees while they found the strength in fear to work the fields as hard as yesterday, because hard work meant you could make enough money to save that guy hanging from the cross, for not dying in hunger, for not letting him down.

So I watched my parents and their parents' labor. I watched them recharge on their knees. In the same, I watched their spirit cry for the end of meditative torture, of emotional punishment from the vision of the dead man on the cross, as they stumbled in yearning to come to an understanding of the true purpose of life and its suffering.

I mourned children in the streets who were being raised in hunger as I and my brothers were. I often felt hopeless as I was still hungry and even afraid that I had just been crucified in the soul and mind, as expected by the very beings who thought with their might that no one should forget the crucifixion of Christ. I thought the sanctuary I had hoped to hide from the children's eyes of poverty was the house of peace. Yet when I entered, I saw the image of the crucified man. In the church, I felt crucified. Outside the church, I couldn't forget the guilt that I felt for the crucified man. And when I went out in the street, the begging mothers, naked children, and the homeless families all around gave me the same sense of disorienting reality. In this world, I felt everyone around me was crucified by the church's views of true life and freedom.

Two angels arrived, followed by the Man of Peace. His voice so softly echoed, "My brothers' and sisters' souls search to end the suffering in their being. Remind them that the house they seek is their spirit—the bread and drink of everlasting light is their will. They are life. Let their spirit so shine, for they are love. They are the breath of peace. Their spirit of love and peace is the dwelling sanctuary of our Holy Father. He alone is our home of love. He is our sanctuary of eternal and external peace. He is that who ends all human sufferings within a man. Rise! Shine your father's love. Rise. Shine your Father's breath of peace, for you are as your Father is, the light and love, peace, and wisdom in spirit before there is the beginning of any man's humanity. You dwell in the light of your Father, and your Father dwells in your love. He breathes in your peace, making you conscious of humanity's eternal dream."

Thirty-Seven

Crazy, Mental Image of Suffering

In His wooden image of His arms stretched open wide on a man-made cross, all love that ever lived on earth died; and as darkness came, so too came the judgment of humanity ingrained forever in the minds of the ignorant and lost, fragile and winded hearts, where all the dead is to remain forever asleep in the cast cave of darkness. And all degrees and forms of suffering are always humanity's past, present, and future itself.

—Evangeline

While the wooden man hangs on the cold and eerie cross, the heaven above the cross, lit up. From it came down a living spirit of man. He is the Man of peace. He is radiant. Heaven's light followed Him down. He is a spirit of love. Heaven abides by His presence. He is the door of heaven. In heaven, all the dead have risen. All pain has been forgotten. All sins have been forgiven. Heaven is a light-filled garden. Here everyone who had been broken by humanity's ignorance is made whole. Our ancestor's humanity lives on, as they in spirit live on forever. Our spirit Father is their father, and the Man of peace is their teacher of kindness, love, and peace. He is our ancestors' prince of peace and love. He is their light out of all their painful and heartbreaking sorrows when they were afraid, abandoned, and lost, during their times on earth.

In His body of love, of His radiant light, a whole beginning of new abundant life of peace and grace is always the womb of our true humanity's heaven. Now that He has come. Heaven is on earth. Because He is light, so He comes to light all the souls' darkness; for His spirit, our Father's spirit, and the heavenly mothers and all angels are the innocent light burning in every spirit born onto the planet, and of every soul on the planet, in the light and purity of a child's joy, all families are reminded by their silent voice of truth. All humanity is one light. We are light. He comes to ignite what is heaven in all humankind, our ever-living love, and spirit.

—Evangeline

With much passion, the lost in darkness manifested an image befitting of eternal suffering, the image that opens the well, which forms the original roots of a guilty feeling, a well of great discomfort, from which poverty and fear have risen. Meanwhile, their hearts thrive in limited light. Having forgotten that love is aching to run through them from eternity, my suffering in the church was not just in the heart, but also in the mind. I felt everyone, including myself, was caught up in the mental control of a crazy meditative trance called suffering. A plank of wood and an image of a man exemplifies absolute death and suffering. The image displays all episodes of his poured blood so the new generations may know Him. Only in my eight-year-old heart, this suffering is eerily matching the suffering of every poor family whose day-to-day toil without a breath of fresh wind to summon them to be lifted off worry never comes; for, without hope of light to lift them off from hunger is projected by the lifeless image of the wooden man hanging on the wooden cross from a thousand years of this on going image of suffering and death. It is of no end. And when one is called to rest, the pews await. But, rarely does one find the strength to stand up and walk with dignity as they go home and light their family with the eternal light of absolute love as what a quiet and peaceful sanctuary should manifest from a kind and gentle God—the Father of Peace.

When I felt the need to pray to God at church, before I sat to kneel, the windows above the cross called out to me. I raised my head high. The pew strengthened me as my heart saw the spirit of the man above the wooden cross, floating way up above the altar, outside the roof. I learned that the living spirit of the man on the cross is free. While the altar was dark, His light is brilliant. Everything around Him lives.

His space is the spirit within the nature of calm. His peace is a space outside human pain and suffering. It is in His presence that I hear the birds sing. With Him, I see colors of all hues magnifying the unlimited bounties of nature. It is there that I finally feel at ease. The stillness nourished my spirit. My mind disappeared as all my questioning subsided.

Forever, it seems, the man on the cross remains an image of torture. Even He is, who has risen in spirit, hurt and powerless that a wood, so beautiful of nature's creation, is ingrained, created to magnify suffering and endless tortures that never to cease in the heart and mind of every human being that gazes at Him. No matter how far I come and go, I return to my grandparents' church; there remains His wooden image waiting so still. He is hanged in the altar of churches for every living creature to pray to. The heart of the child in me is torn. I often asked if anyone noticed at all that this wooden God my ancestors' priest wanted me to pray to is not living. And is it not evident that in His suffering and frozen state of being, the wooden man's gift to the world is none other than feeling the never-ending entrapment of everyone's mind who prostrate themselves before Him so in His image all is bounded by a silent mirror of pain, poverty and sorrows. This god that my ancestors pray to is ever-present to keep at bay the stillness of deep fear in my child soul.

How could I take a glimpse of joy in the church? My inherited life on earth depicts the death suffered by the wooden man who died on the cross. Why has the past not taken the cross away? Death had taken the hanging man away. When will my humanity be free from the frozen depiction of suffering and pain on the cross? I asked myself.

"Today!" The spirits of the heavens answered. "The Spirit of Christ lives. The man on the cross had risen in spirit."

"I know! He lives, loves, lights, comforts and guides the poor like me from life's pain and struggles. He came many times lifting me up from all troubles. With the heavenly Father's presence, and with the Heavenly Mother's comfort, He came and dried my tears away."

—Evangeline

Thirty-Eight

Heaven Has No Man-God

I came to earth to find the secret path to God. I found brothers and sisters, gods, and goddesses of wealth and mind's dreams. Yet when my child died, another secret heaven opened. I saw a brilliant man who is not a god. He is the king of gentle and compassionate creations. He is the tender voice of wisdom. He lights the consciousness that flows to and from all creations. He is the living spirit within all that exists. Above all, He is the soft and gentle body of a Father. Of gentle hands, and with eternal strength of compassionate arms, He is the ever-living body of comforting brilliance of love and peace, from whom each man's spirit beamed out in full rays. He is the source of all-white brilliance, the same substance that mankind will create in their life's quest, so the path within may be open. In the riverbed of their brilliance will every spirit come back to their Father again. He is the home all spirits seek to rest in the quest of the heart, life, and true origin of eternal nature of divinity from which the entire race of humanity is sourced.

—Evangeline

Growing up, I was surrounded by people that would utter, "With God's help."

So I knew someone was looking after everyone who says those words. I've searched for God since birth. In no time did I find one when I needed help most. Yet when I was willing to give up pain in suffering, when I refused to kneel before the altar of judgments, but willing to die, for my child had died with my love, in my misery, when no God came, new spirit heaven had opened. From its brilliance formed a door, a dazzling luminosity that transfigures to give out a pure body of light, ushering in the living Man of Peace. In His presence, He brought back my daughter's spirit—there, my child sits all joyful in His right arm, the source of my motherly love lives. For in His arms, my beloved child Gabriella is redeemed from time's casted death. The sting of death is no more. She has risen with the Lord. She lives in spirit. She is whole. She is shining in the brilliant grace of divine contentedness and ease. She is transfigured into a healthy and all-joyful and loving body of innocent and pure brilliant love.

My heart and mind confessed. Blessed is the infant vessel that bore you on earth. You filled me with heaven's glory, and, blessed the ground your feet have walked and ever gently cradled your innocent soul.
—Evangeline

The heavenly Father, Mother Mary, our ancestors, and Jesus with His angels came from heaven. They came to deliver her back to find my heartbeats, to give me a breeze of truth, and to nurture my lost soul back to life, so I may have awakened from religion's spell that the real heaven, from which all that is created have sprung from and have their being, is a haven of the spirits of eternal peace. It is not a heavenly decorated house made of stone, which I was made to comprehend as a child. And a human god who was made by human hearts has never comprehended this peaceful existence, for the minds and the hearts of mankind have worked for eons to entertain the newborn and its ancestors that its god is invincible, hiding behind the red curtain. He is selfish and always needing sacrifices, hungry, craves anger, vicious for gold, passionate for wars, and its roots of contentment is oppression and slavery. When I was hungry and tired, the altar of the human god openly greeted me, silencing my spirit not to shine, not to light. I was made to know since a child; this invincible god forgives only with the omen of human currency. I was not welcome by this god and its creator. I had no money. I was born poor.

I was unwanted. The display of the wooden image shouted loud who I am. In His house, I was in the cross, bleeding, left to die.

So I thought I would steer clear from the wooden man's sufferings. I tried not to go back to His house. Little did I know that even the spirit of the man who is called Jesus is not at the church altars. He is above the church. Waiting for me to come out of my meditative trance of sufferings in the church, rise out of the pews, walk out of the church, raise my head and arms up high to Him and walk into His garden of peace, where He can light the rest of my path until I find the strength to light with Him as He leads me through the rest of my humanity's experiences in search of peace and of love.

The Holy Spirit's and His Fatherly Throne

He and His children build a universe for a playground. "Go. Play my children. Be kind. Watch over one another. Remember me. Do not forget; I love you. I am with you always."

—Evangeline

In the heaven's peace is a throne, whom a giant ever-loving Father and a king of eternal grace in an image of a gentle, so gentle, and all-loving, all-understanding man. From within His entirety, mind, body, even in His light heart, is a living, breathing generator of the brilliant breath of infinite peace. He illuminates an absolute purity of infinite, yet so gentle love; the wisdom of light, He radiates in all His being. He is the vision of everlasting mercy, a body of divine luminosity. His breath is exuding the heart of brilliant grace overfilling all the spirits of living creation. This kind grace is the breath, that shines a silent wind that pushed all the raging oceans of pain as a broken mother, and banished the longing of the lost child in me once and for all, giving me the body that all the spirits behold, a body of peace, from which all wisdom of good creation rise to full illumination, casting all the darkness out of my being; from within, I illumined a radiant light that powered my lungs to breathe peace. Alone, I am inside and outside. I am one with life because I am its light. I am one among the brilliant child bodies that vessel His Majesty's spirits of consciousness and peace within the womb of life, the foundation of my own humanity's experiences.

Not a soul, not in the flesh, He is a Spirit Father. A body of brilliant luminosities of purity and truth, He is holy. He is love. Bearing in full illumination, our loved ones' new bodies, of light, of love, of peace, in all their hearts and their being is His holy breath of grace. The very essence that lights the new eternal bodies of our beloved ones who have shed their human suits, our loved ones now buried under the soil of the earth, who are dead in the flesh; yet now in an image of the Father, our Spirit Father, they are awakened in love, given light-bodies as Jesus lights in the state the love of this eternal grace. They are the wisdom that comes through our darkness. They are the love that shines in our weakness. They are the sweet and soft, gentle voices of courage through our dreams. As the Father, so loves all His children—us.

From heaven, our ancestors' spirits came down on to the earth in order to build for us the new generation, our human home. When all deeds were accomplished, they leave the planet, their bodies have died, in order that in spirit once again they may rise, in the garden of peace. For our loved ones who have risen out of human bodies, the creation of human experiences is no more.

—Evangeline

Thirty-Nine

Spirit of Light

Child, write your vision so the soul of man may usher into humanity its spirit of light, which is my body and breath of peace.
—Evangeline

In our ultimate light, we are the breath of our Heavenly Father's being. The spirits of our Divine Father is who we are. Each child is a child of our Spirit Father. A spirit of peace before we come as the soul, a child of man; we are an eternal breath of light, peace, and love; we are the spirit that powers the flesh of Adam and Eve. We are the breath of life itself. Before we were born to our bodies, we are whole energy. We are lit up, filled with His body of light and grace. I had forgotten, but now I remember the call. I remember when I was awakened from darkness by the light. As it was then in the beginning, so is His love, the son, the Man of Peace's voice still echos in my soul's heart soundly and ever so sincerely serene. "Woman, cry no more," He illuminated before me in pure white spirit light, making all darkness that devoured me whole, vanished within and outside me. When I came to, I was still Gabriella's mother. I was deeply aware that my daughter had already died, yet still, my mind could not explain how she was alive in spirit as she and the spirits of loved ones visited me often.

Here and Now

So here now, I am living another life. I discovered that the spirit world is a life no man can give, for it is not just of man's reality that we exist and breathe. We have our being because of light and the breath of eternal love. We live because we are the breath of the eternal and the external world. In spirit, we are the breath of everlasting.

—Evangeline

It is a new, whole life that heaven alone has delivered and bestowed so freely to me, even after having experienced the darkness that the death of my child Gaby gave. The brilliant spirits are with us when we are ready to understand the source of our humanity's spirit light, the core, and the foundation of our eternal love. When we surrender, we know that heaven can come down from the heart of the sky and change our world forever, as it did and does to me still. In light and His coming, the Man of Peace and His Holy Father who sits on the throne, our Spirit Father, have come down to illuminate their pure love and peace to strengthen me, to awaken me from agonies of death, to lift my spirit, to honor the light in my life by honoring their presence so I can gain the courage to write out from me the emotion of darkness that weaved, churned, and twisted by anger, guilt, fear, resentment, and all other emotions that swallowed me to succumb to a paralytic state of death, the greatest poverty of being a lost and wandering soul—called grief, a suspenseful existence.

In pain and grief, I couldn't breathe. Frozen, I couldn't move. Fragile, I was too brittle to open my eyes to see the color of the sun and trees. Abandoned, I was banished in the pit of endless darkness, all alone, dying by the hour of the days. In a body, in a soul, I mattered not. For in the eyes of those around me, I, the spirit divine am unseen. To humans, I did not exist. To the Holy Spirit of love, my spirit is light. In my spirit of love, I can fly beyond the skies. The love of the heavens powers my own breath, which is the source of all being in both the universe and beyond.

Forty

The Tragedy of Being a Human Soul

Through the eyes of man, in his peace, and his compassion, you will experience his spirit's love. Through his professions, you will know his soul as a servant of eternal love and peace. The body is only a vehicle for the spirit, which is serving humanity in an image of a soul. The spirit, the soul, and the flesh's foods are the substances of kindness and gentle compassion. The man is of earth's body, his mind is of earth's and the universe, yet in the spirit, he is a holy child, of love and peace. He/she is of the Holy Spirit's body of light, sourced in the heart of our divine Father, the kind King of all true and peaceful creation.

—Evangeline

In *grief,* no one could see my suffering. I must say it again. The greatest suffering that a human being can endure is not being acknowledged that I was hurting as a mother, a lost soul from having not the power to make Gaby live without pain. No one seems to acknowledge that in the pure state, I am also a spirit child, conscious, hungry for the space of compassion, eager to express my breath freely, so even in the death of my daughter, I once again in spirit awaken to illuminate in love. I existed yearning for how it used to be when Gaby was alive. Yet to the eyes of those around me, a mother soul, and the woman that I am, I do not hurt. I do not hurt, for I do not exist. No one could see the pain in my heart.

The spirits who came gave the mother in me a validation. I knew I have always been myself. But for the first time, I heard my own spirit's voice speak. I am a spirit, a mother, and through Christ's love, I am powerless over my child's body's death, but Christ is teaching me that I am a powerful spirit, to sustain one death to keep on living who, with the Heavenly Father's grace, can love again even after death's sting. I, as the spirits above me acknowledge through the Holy Families' presence and illumination—am the light of my flesh. I am which makes the matter of loving a child, shaping, and building a family happen. I am in the spirit that has consistently worked as all the mothers in the world do despite grief, wake up each morning to serve and extend the life of humanity to keep the bridge going for the incoming spirits of lights into this very reality called human family. In grief, the spirit and soul hurt. My flesh may not be bleeding. But my spirit and soul was in peril. I am a mother at heart, a spirit that loves, though I am—as every woman soul here is light of my flesh called—Eve. The only way I can heal is to be acknowledged as spirit, a sacred mother soul, in a sacred and divine body. Just as anyone who is a human, I can *be cared* for when I am on my knees through *gentle compassion*.

Forty-One

Surrendering All Darkness

To the mind, surrendering is the end. To time, it is progression. To the spirit divine, surrendering the works of the mind is truth. To self, it is letting go of a dream of a soul, which had been attained by understanding. To the conscious spirit, it is coming home to be in union with the stars; to be held and to be united in one body of love and to illuminate in the sea of eternal grace, from which its ancestors have been consecrated to a new life, must rise to rest from creation to light the heart of eternal peace, which is the body of itself and the light of its own eternal home. This is the way of the human spirits. This is the eternal code of humankind.

—Evangeline

In my daily walk of missing Gaby's presence, I would often cry and ask myself what she may have looked like at the age of nine, ten, and eleven? My heart as a mothering soul wanted to see, hold, and care for her during these stages of a child's expected human evolution.

My brain would hurt as it untiringly tried to make up images of what she may have looked like. To no avail, my mind was tired. As a mother, my heart yearned for such reality. Yet in the same note, I knew none of what my mind's wishful images mattered. In the heart of my human mind, Gaby will always be two years old. That is what I remember as her mother. My brain, no matter how, will abide by Gaby being two years old to process my entire needs to survive as her mother. Yet my emotional body holds the image of Gaby being a two-year-old child.

I would get depressed again and again. My brain was hijacked by dusky days, and my heart was heavy with the inner turmoil of heat and anger that went on days and weeks on a cycle that would come and go without mercy on my soul. If I allowed it, it would have kept me hostage, leaving me conscious only when my spirit awoke, that I have been a mockery of life's disorders, of consistent struggles.

With my daughter's spirit visits and the Man of Peace's kind encouragements and guidance, another thinking became instilled in my being. There is more to life. That is why I am still alive. My job is finding that which is more in life. I am here to find the secret of its good. I am here to discover what truly is the purpose of this earth's realities and its destiny to keep humanity alive. In that desire, I have forgotten my grief. In its place is deep passion. I see sparks of dreams. Visions with bright and joyful acts began filling my being. I am filled by white visions outside my mind and beyond the skies. When I see good, I hear joy. When I hear silent joy, I see calm. I am serene. There was no worry to be traced. Even when I felt disturbed that such instances I am part of, my spirit was always there to remind me to breathe. When I did, all the thick darkness hovering over and in me was poured and shed out. When I emptied my soul of the toxic gunk that I was emotionally carrying, word per word by writing, I felt another part of me, my spirit, rise; I surfaced, I began to breathe. Then I became stronger, thus making my heart expand and my breathing at ease, and my vision transcended brighter beyond what human eyes could see beyond what time gives.

A second chance in life is having the humbling vision of the unseen. In being aware of my human complexity, in light of a new happy start, a new life is making me whole. Not surprisingly, I found that it is both love of the heaven and the earth, is what I am made of, and thus in ventures of my own inner spirit's depths that I will be made whole.

Every child is a drop of a new spring's dew. Its spirit grows into a river; it turns into both an ocean of ice-cold and warm water. The sun watches its wave dance, move, and sing. The sun rises and shines its rays to nurture the light of this water. When its presence quells all the waters of the seas' wonders, the spirit dew's essence is quieted, the sun rays take it up into its winds, to dance and fly, in, up, and above the cosmos, only to light the heavens with its flickering wisdom, chanting the spirit, the spirit song of life once more.

—Evangeline

The Unseen Waves in the Mind

The mind does not know the love and light of its own spirit.
—Evangeline

A whole mind will create new and good dreams. The broken mind struggles to breathe. Survival becomes imminent. Life seems like it is on the daily edge of constant danger. The soul becomes afraid. It hides. To create any vision of a new dream is nonexistent. Therefore, it takes all the broken traumas it witnessed. Like a never-ending wave, it comes to rise and fall within the mind, creating a hole in its soul's broken heart. The brain will process the past, making it the present, so even when all tragedies have passed with the old wind, the waves of trauma are the brain's current events that will rise and fall for the soul's presence.

"Write out your emotions," the Man of Peace told me. But it was not easy. There was work to be done. There were clearing and making conscious of the time to do nothing else but utilize it for writing alone. There was my mind to conquer. I need it to obey. There was my body to keep still and my brain to be put to ease. Everything was a constant struggle. Yet I found that when I was slightly conscious that I need no more of life, I was instantly at peace. So I wrote. I faced my emotional rubbish. I did curse everyone who was ever mean to me in life. Then came the alarming truth. I was disappointed in myself. Surprisingly I was embarrassed at how ignorant my soul could get as a child of man by taking the time to be angry at what happened in the past. Then I felt bad for utilizing time inharmoniously when I thought of the past. I was worse than those who hurt me.

Forgiveness Is Kindness to One's Mind, Soul, and Spirit

All that I can ever be is myself. No one would ever know the depth of my essence. I only need to love, honor, and respect my spirit, kindly.
—Evangeline

I decided I had to be kind instead. I thanked the time for giving me the hour for recollection. I heard my spirit's voice. It constantly spoke through my entire being. I understood that my soul could be influenced so easily by many disruptive forces from outside and inside the world around me. In surviving, both harmful and wasteful energies coincided within my soul, I knew I must make way to be conscious of what I want to drive my life, as I govern the rest of my purpose. I had to draw on my spirit to guide me with its good energy, such as to be kind. Kindness would be the way within me if I were even to get things done.

Then I was over it. I asked for forgiveness after I felt sorry for all of those who hurt me in the past.

I realized that if they knew better, they would have treated me better. Then I felt sorry for myself. Everyone who hurt me moved on with life. I was still hurt and ruining my new drawn days because my mental mind was still hurting and broken. Then I cursed death for killing my daughter. Then I forgive death. I thanked it for easing her pain.

So instantly, I realized, life is full of junk. Life is full of good. But all I have is time to experience what I am born to fulfill. What the world lacks are more brilliant lights of compassionate minds and of non judgmental hearts that have learned to live by embracing all experiences with understanding and of love. That is what I have to focus on as I move forward.

Now is the courage to focus on the good, no matter what. Just as the Man of Peace said before in His past visits, just as he reveals now in His presence, the spirit of man is kind, the soul, the mind, the egos have to be transcended to its highest, through the power of love, which is the light and wisdom of the spirits of all men, women, children, and old; for these substances are the true spirit sustenance of the entire planet of humanity.

Forty-Two

The Hour Comes

Kindness is nonexistent unless you apply it to yourself. Be kind to your self's mind, and the world will be kind to you. For the self is the world. The mind's highest world is the world of the spirits before there is humankind in the flesh before his and her soul is birthed to blossom in his and her ultimate light; he/she is first breath of light and love. The spirit's consciousness is the kind substance that creates love from humanity's true body of peace out of the human's breath of tragedy.

—Evangeline

The hour I found the courage to face my sorrows, I felt I was on my own spiritual Armageddon. It was. It was a lot of crying. Cleansing the spirit of emotional gunk required a lot of tears.

Eventually, it happened. The tears that belonged to the past had dried away. The pain and darkness melted in the unknown wind. My brain held on to nothing by embracing the balance of calm that came after. I was emotionally emptied out. My vessel was light and clean. Then I heard and felt my spirit rise as I took a long deep breath of more calm. When I saw the bright beings coming and going, smiling and moving about, I knew the end of the old world, which was within my being had already happened; yet the love and the lessons it gave me is still and always there waiting to be seen, have taken part of my own evolution from a soul to spirit. All by honoring my spirit's source of light, the heart of the love, which is compassion, and through the gentle embrace of understanding, a subtle world opened up. It is its own secret. Its door is my own soul's surrender to the love of the spirits. The bodies of life and compassion are the breath of our eternal truth, the heart of consciousness, our throne of rest, our spirit home, the merciful, and graceful arms of our heavenly Father who loves all of His children on earth is how we open this secret door to peace.

Never Alone

Kindness is the way to peace. Peace is the breath of life that houses the eternal haven within the spirits of man.
—Evangeline

In this world, which is not just of the human mind, not just of the body, not just the purpose of the soul, as a mother, a true spirit dawns in validations that I am not alone. I never was. I am not lost. I never was. I am, no matter what the world around me says, never alone in spirit; for matter is a suit, a uniform for the spirits and energy. Who I am is the light of compassion, sourced in the heart and body of eternal love. I am love. I am as the bodies of pure consciousness, lighting the heavens around and above me, our spirit loved ones. I am a breath of pure love, as the light of the spirits dawn, embracing me through my entire breath in spirit, soul, mind, and body. I am the force of breath, which powers this body, which made up the soul that I am bestowed. I am now experiencing life as a woman in the flesh of Eve's suit the feminine body of the Holy Father's design. I am as every woman—is sacredly blessed, for it is my womb, and all mothers' wombs that earth's humanity will bear its children. Through such grace, I, as a woman, became a mother of beautiful Gaby. I am a loving force that is governing my own universe's mind's understanding and reason. I am a spirit of light. A driver of the soul, the mind, and the body, I am a child of the Father. I am the truth before I was even born into the flesh as a child of humanity.

Kindness is the way of the spirits, for all spirits are love before being vessels of matter prepared by the universe's earth's sacred dust.
—Evangeline

When Religion Alone Is Not a True Gift

While the mind of pain is busy creating fears toward hell, heaven comes to light up the minds of its hearts. When the heart of the mind is made open, the heaven of truth is revealed. All there is in heaven are spirits of love, the lights and the ways to the depthless ocean bodies of eternal peace, to all created beginnings, present, and ending of all human dreams.
—Evangeline

By writing the steps of my earthly journey, the dark world of my human mind—the creative basket filled with judgments of my ancestors' ideas that I was born a sinner—melted away. It had vanished and left me. How I shine, my light is in the absolute desire to magnify the love I have for our Father in heaven. He is the father of all love and glory of fantastic brilliance of peace on earth and in heaven.

Forty-Three

The Making of New Spaces

Surrender the human world and a new, light-filled, kind, and gentle world will open. It is the heaven of love. It is the world of peace. A new whole life is a light herein. This is the language of every heart.
—Evangeline

I was not angry that I was born poor. I did not know any other way. I was pleased that I was born to my mother and father, my sister and brother. I am so grateful for my family's ability to reach out to each other and calm all pain, sorrows, fears, and disappointments that have masked our lessons passed in the cycles of every season. Nature came and gave its best. It was good. The time came and gave its best. It was a blessing to see everyone grow. Our families grew with time. Despite the tragic nature of man-made laws, there was put in place kind justice, which the Father's love and His breath of peace shines onto the law of the land; a law which my own country of birth has not yet found—the pursuit of human equality; and not yet given the freedom to practice religion based on unity and compassion, mercy, and tolerance; for the law is governed by religion's guilt, and hunger; and the politics cravings to raise itself high in order to serve the cause of persistent greed in honor of the country's consistent oppression of its citizens, and its on going struggle to disengage from the torment of foreign wars have left many of its new generations of citizens unlearned, famished, and in constant brink of hunger just as our forefathers have been.

Yet now a mother here is a promised land, which through love for my husband, I am made equal as a human being, and because I am now its citizen, I am honored without being made to feel guilty if I was born Christian or not. In such a sense of freedom, I remain forever humble. Through the rights of citizenship, I am neither poor in the eyes of its government; nor am I made a sinner by the eyes of its countless religions. In this land, they call "the land of the free," my spirit is made free. What I regret most is having been raised with guilt and shame. Religion is neither good nor bad. It is unconscious of love. It is deadening to every heart's ears, blinding to the voices of fainthearted eyes, torturing to the mind of reason. It is condemning, to the light of the spirit's love. And to peace, it is a repulsive and disastrous wind. Guilt and shame, the judgments that breaks the mind paralyze the human soul and refuse the existence of the conscious spirit of love and breath of peace—the very reason the body of compassion must come to light the darkness with its love and peace.

After I surrendered guilt, I honored that I felt ashamed because I am living on earth, yet my daughter is dead. I realized death is nothing I created because I am bad. Death is part of the human season. Many people die. They die because their body is no longer healthy. It is the law of the consciousness that the spirits of love and peace are to be free. Death is not a punishment. It is a process nature must undertake, not to hurt me, but to free my daughter from her pain, free her from her heart disease, and free her from internal and emotional suffering.

"Children of light come to light the world of humanity with pure love. Children's births pave the world of mercy in the breath of peace. Children of love come to live in truth. That life should be living without a struggle. If living becomes suffering, the spirit is in the form of manifested diseases of mental tragedy. If loving becomes suffering and suffering becomes living, no spirit child of the God of peace may stay to serve the darkness of the mind and its gods, the mental universe is, the root cause of all diseases of human suffering," the Heavenly Father's family of angels explained.

This understanding made me realize my life is blessed because Gaby was birthed on earth. My family is blessed even in her death. She was born, so I may know her. She was born, so even when she died in the flesh, her spirit was to come and visit as often as she desires.

In accepting my life for what it was, I surrendered shame. I saw that there was only love. Even when we were struggling to keep her alive, everyone was there to serve and help our burden. Suddenly a whole new world appeared and opened its infinities before me.

I saw myself as a child—all smiles. I saw my father labored night and day to shelter me. Mother mended my bruised and injured wounds, kissed me, and cried with me when I was afraid. I knew I was loved. But when I went into the world, religion said I was a sinner. I've been mourning the truth since. Yet nothing changed despite hardships. My parents loved me. To my father, I am loved. To Mother, I am loved.

Now, all grown up and a mother, I found I am a spirit light in the vessel of newly awakened Eve. Now I am free of guilt. I am the cup that was poured out and made clean. I am stronger. I am new. Alive again. I can choose to allow myself to feel joy when it flows through my senses once again. In the love for myself, I am joyful. I am my breath.

> *No matter the age of the human vessel, each spirit is a child. It must remain a child of love.*
> —Evangeline

Eternal Space

> *A mother's love is an infinite ray of eternal space that lights the world of the human family in creations of conscious humanity time after time, life after life.*
> —Evangeline

As it stands in the current world, grief is told to be a *five-stage process*: *denial, anger, bargaining, depression*, and *acceptance*. For me, as a mother who was stung by the death of a beloved child, who has to face the world's cause of deep suffering, these five senses were just the beginning of the rest of my life. Our parenting responsibility is merely one of a title that we choose to partake in this one life. Our parenting is also a progressive evolution of our eternal spirit's wisdom, as we grow in knowledge as souls through our children's daily growth and experiences. The eyes of our children will differ in each of our children. Each will only be one-year-old one-time, and soon she or he will be two, three, four, and so on. We progress in knowledge, as they are in age, and will experience who they are as a human child, in each year's phases of time. Each child grows, so parents must grow in understanding and wisdom of being kind to themselves as a human mother and father. This kindness is the essence that will feed the souls, the minds, and the spirits of the children in each of us as our children themselves evolve in their magnificent light and wisdom.

It is every conscious mother's and father's dream to see their child achieve and manifest growth, kindness, healing of spirits, and humanity in service for good action and communication. Every child is an extensional body of our ancestors' dream, rooted in heaven's being of love and peace, meant to blossom further than our ancestors' hearts and lights, who themselves have lived and illuminated it on earth.

—Evangeline

Forty-Four

Extension of Life

Each child is an extension of love, light, wisdom, and body of its parents' existence in the universe of human creation.
—Evangeline

In losing a child, I lost all the phases of my own self-discovery, which my soul had expected to come to as Gaby experienced the stages of growing and discovering herself, had she stayed growing in her body. I learned that our growth comes in the projection of the essence of the presence of the people with whom we are surrounded. Learning as Gaby's mother, for me, halted when the time of her life as being a soul with me stopped. Yet though her body is no longer here, her spirit is now teaching me of her new life in the spirit world. She is teaching me what is true. We are spirit in love. We are light. We are eternal. And because we cannot die in spirit, we are only to keep learning and evolving in our purpose to shine love on the planet, because we are blessed to wear a divinely inspired suit, the sacred body of man and woman.

In this knowledge, I learned that everyone is governed by an eternal clock, a sacred gift of time. As long as we are in the flesh, our time ticks and keeps ongoing, and like all clocks, it will stop, yet new sets of learning transpire in spirit. Death of the flesh is not the end of our humanity. We keep learning in spirit. Now we are all blessed with a body to discover the grandest creation of spirit and matter within the sacred seen and hidden pockets of our universe. Of our birth and death, our creation of peaceful and kind and ever-loving humanity is of the highest dream. We are love. We are spirit. We are the eternal light that lights all wisdom with mercy and grace.

—Evangeline

PART EIGHT

Forty-Five

Heaven Is but One Thought Away

*The consciousness of love and truth is the
pure light space of infinite brilliance.*

—Evangeline

*Heaven has not a door; it is a presence of infinities of
white brilliance, of the pure light of eternity, cast from
earth onto the outside of all universes. It is a shining glory
of ultimate compassion, giving life to all that exists.*

—Evangeline

No money, no plane tickets, no luggage needed. When my heart speaks its kindness and seeks to love all, heaven opens. Loving spirits dawn upon me. Shining bodies, they smile. Children giggle in delight, eager to shine their presence on my wind. The heart of heaven is one brilliance, of loving bodies of our eternal families. I see my loved ones smile and peaceful light shining upon the earth as the Man on the Throne's body shines on all below. Before Him, all hearts are love, all beings are His peace.

—Evangeline

Without guilt. Having been pardoned and forgiven for the faults of my own upbringing, I seem to be okay with humanity's imperfections. I know now that we came to life's imperfections. We have all come to build *peace in mind, heart, body, and soul. We come to shine our eternal love and our light. We are the peace that has to end all wars; of minds, bodies, and souls, we are divine healers in the Holy Spirit's light, our Father's presence, through us and in us is forever and eternal.*

—Evangeline

Though my daughter's internal clock as a soul, as my human child, had stopped, her spirit body that is the love of her kind and innocent spirit remains present; she is as our ancestors' love, as our Spirit Father is eternal.

She comes without prior notice. She comes to give me love. She died in flesh; but rose in spirit. In spirit, she is lit up; now my guide, now my source of everlasting wisdom, she brings about the rest of the spirits to make amends and heal the ones left behind—families who are mourning the loss of their bright lights, which is their source of life, love, inspiration, joy, and wisdom. Family as they once knew existed remain one with our spirit, heart, and life.

The Spirit Is Not the Soul

The soul would go in circles as the world has done so in search of orders out of humanity's chaos. Patterns make up the world of suffering and the temporary joy of souls. But the spirit rises and tells its soul to walk the less-traveled path, to shine in full brilliance, for in love eternal, the soul is not alone; it is in the stillness of the soul that the spirit within self may become the illuminating light and love that may shine on to the planet world, of both known and the yet unknown realities of temporary creation.

—Evangeline

My heart, my dreams, my love still is here with time, wanting and yearning to fill the missing holes of Gaby's absence, both in the flesh and in the soul. It will not go away till I die. In spirit, contentedness is truth. Life is truth. Truth is light. Light and truth are the spirits' self-radiance. This is who she is as she appears now. Light and love in pure form. A brilliant light in my soul's time of darkness. She is love.

—Evangeline

I found my spirit's voice while my soul stumbled in words of what and who it is. I found that there are never acceptance stages in the order of the soul. Motherhood and fatherhood is a cycle. It is the built-in stages of programmed expectations, an automatically mirrored reality projected by our human order of progress. In the mind's projected reality, it is to be of what the world projects. The dream of the soul, though it may have been finished by our ancestors, we come and add to what they have left behind. The human expectation is carried on by others as their soul progresses. We are the souls; we dream of becoming. We are in the soul's dream manifested through our flesh. We are what we expected as seasons revealed them. The expectations of the soul, its cycle, keeps on with or without our spirit in it. It cannot stop because the body dies. Expectations of my soul for my daughter to come back the way she used to be in her body do not die just because the spirit of my daughter is no longer in its body. It is in my daughter's spirit's presence, light, and love that my soul is comforted and silenced.

—Evangeline

Forty-Six

Trade Suffering for True Love

When peace comes, it is because we have arrived in spirit; we acknowledge that we are the love we are seeking to experience within the soul of our one, colorful, kind, family of humanity.
—Evangeline

Healing of grief is difficult for the human mind to fathom. The human mind is not capable of a kind vision. It is overfilled with an endless kaleidoscope of human sufferings gallantly projected by outside visions of fears.

Kind vision is only weaved by the hearts of our consciousness, sourced from the love of our ancestors' brilliance of gentle and all-giving command as they embrace us by embracing our grace, mercy, and compassion. The mind is not the heart of our spirit. But we must understand its purpose to serve our spirits for shaping and creating what truth is. The truth is love. The truth is peace. The truth is light. The mind shall know who it must serve as it should be in the heart of our higher selves that it must obey. In grief, the heart is forsaken. The mind is injured. Like a broken recorder, it is at constant play and rewind. An injured mind does not have the ability to come into the focal point of the present experiences of kindness, light, and humanity's brilliant rays of love through actions and connections. Grief is surrendering of emotions and reality, which we have no control over. To grieve is understanding that we are powerless. To grieve is to honor the sacred acts of being human. It is letting go of that which is no longer serving our growth, that which taunts or halts our self-evolution, of our eternal self-discovery. It is shedding the old clothing and replacing it with a new room for our spiritual evolution.

Spiritual growth is the rising of one's spirit
above the expectations of the human mind.
—Evangeline

Though unseen, but lived and felt, our emotional body is a body itself. It is reality itself. Grief is its own body. This body is the emotional body of our minds. As a spirit divine, we must be okay to heal the body of our mind. The mind of mankind is also a house of suffering for all human souls. Grief is dying of all humanity's suffering, letting go of chaos, dying of fear and darkness. We must make way too for the Holy Spirit's descent, make room for the peace that is to come, for it has long yearned to rise through us in full glory. We are channels of peace. We must embrace the light, the dream, the love of our spirit's higher vibrational forces, to shine our spirit-light bodies, our higher self—by making a clean vessel, free of darkness, guilt, and fears. The gifts of new life, which have opened to us, have come in the passing of our ancestors. A loved ones death gives us a new road, which we must not and never walk alone. For the works of good are love and light. Light is infinite. It powers all spaces with such mercy. Compassion is love. Compassion is paved by our family's complete presence and union. Family's road is a boundless space of love and light, paved in one true and pure brilliance of the power of one good. The very power that we are fueled with will be our divine family's serenity of eternal love. The light and eternal love of their spirits are one with our being.

Forty-Seven

The Eternal Beauty

From heavens, the spirits dreamed. The dreamers are a father, mother, and children. The dream is to awaken the souls of humanity as one body of love, peace, and harmony; thus, we are birthed in time to come and to fulfill this divine dream. Humanity is the holy body of spirits of love, having granted our soul, to experience the bountiful fruits of this begotten, one and only sacred, divinely inherent, physical garden of love; where, the spirits' light of courage from the unborn, is welled out as compassion toward humanity; and the divinity of eternal wisdom of peace within each child's breath, is housed and nourished through the union of human family's hearts and minds, in fulfillment of time's promise, to usher in heaven on to the earth, upon each child's birth. For, in the union of the spirit and the flesh, heaven and earth are one.

—Evangeline

The beauty of letting go is allowing. Allow that you are important. Allow that you have the right to be free. In spirit, you are always free. Allow the truth to come through you. You are a free spirit at heart. Your love cannot be owned. Allow that you have the permission to love your spirit. No one can do that for your spirit but you, the soul, and the self, in the human that you are and in the child of the Father that you forever are always, even before time.

SHINE LOVE, JOY, AND PEACE!

The hands will labor as a man walks and sleeps under the sun but must rest in spirit when the heart has met the end of its humanity's season.

The eternal work is a decision to honor life by letting go of old sufferings. The traumas of death are powerful; traumas can be paralyzing as guilt suffocates the radiance out of the spirit's light. But shine in love, for you are the spirit that gives life and light to all of humanity.
—Evangeline

Know the truth. We don't have to leave the flesh to transcend our spirit minds. We don't have to be illuminated by dying in the flesh before we awaken to our true spirits' consciousness; we only need to surrender the guilt, trade the spirit's frustration of collective human suffering, just for one true breath—eternal and infallible peace, which our spirit is birthed as children, a breath that is in us for eternity; it is the spirit that lifts us above all the mountains of the entire earth.

We are eternal bodies of love; the breath and life of true light, that transcends the heavens above and descends below the bodies of multiple universes. Our lights are creation and matters' divinity.
—Evangeline

Decide to love and honor yourself. In so doing, that is what you will project in the world. For as divine eternal beings, as spirits, we breathe only one peace. It is in love that we breathe peace. We are to love unconditionally. We are the breath of eternal and external compassion. We must embrace without end. We are light. Yes, this is our spirit's true body. We must love all life with understanding and tolerance; for in so doing, we surrender suffering and bless it with a new life of love. Suffering will not end until it is given time, of surrender, of letting go. *Suffering waits for our blessings to disappear out of human creations.*
—Evangeline

EVANGELINE MENDEZ STEFAN

We need to honor the brief passage of grief before we can breathe love. It is in love and compassion to all humanity that we experience; we are indeed not just humans; we are its love. We are its compassion. We are its peace. We are its dreams; for we are in spirit transcendent beings, as our divine Father from whom we are in spirit are sourced. When suffering itself calls for its love and light, we answered the call. We send ourselves, to shine onto the heavens', in humanity's full brilliance.

—Evangeline

Forty-Eight

Human Life Is Earth. Earth As a Garden Is the Teacher of Life in Season. The Spirit Is Its Students. The Newborn Is Its New Life

Life—in all of its greatness and all of its ills—is teaching our spirits to come to terms with our eternal truth. We are the light and the breath of peace on earth. Just as Mother Earth is kind and ever-loving shall we tend and honor her love for our spirit's inner glory and brilliance. She is the womb of our humanity; her light and well-being are her children's spirits of love and peace.

—Evangeline

Acceptance of who we are eternally cannot happen until the stages of humanity have been acknowledged to exist. It is us here in this one life, contained within one season of our bodies' life that we now exist. Life is life. It is what it is. We are what we are. We are the humanity that has been manifested with time through our own evolutional experiences. We, as individual souls, must be one with our family to manifest our life's calling. For the calling of life is the good wisdom of the spirit, a gift from heaven.

So care, for we are in the womb of Mother Earth. She is our home. She is our refuge. She is our humanity. We are her birth. She is our lessons, we are her experiences, we are her humanity, and we come in time of her eternal gift, her seasons. Her womb is always peaceful. Humanity is her life's past, present, and future. We are her ultimate dream. We are her love. She craves to receive peace as our souls and spirits yearn to receive and give it as a blessing to all hearts of humanity; all of us who are here who hunger and thirst for the same food in order to experience the humble bounty of true life's harvest, to love and be loved as children, brothers, and sisters of one colorful and yet so brilliantly lit up in humility, we are to embrace our spirit virtue, her one whole and merciful, family of grace, as the Holy Father beacons for all of us children on earth. We are the earth's ultimate dream. We are her peace. We are her comfort. We are her gift of life. We are her one family of humanity. We are the Holy Father's breath and light, vesseled in earth's suit, a human body. Through her dust, our spirit and light are made conscious of human creations. We are this garden's marbles of creations. We are her spirit. We shall be conscious of this truth. She is our host. There is no one else like us in the universe. Mother Earth loves us no matter what. As the sun shines on all children and all creation, earth embraces all. No matter her seasons of creation, earth will make room for each vessel of the Heavenly Father's breath, the child of love to manifest as life's gift in all creation. Each child that is each of us is an innocent gift of love, from heaven. We only need to shape our soul to be kind before the spirit within us may shine good into the world. But we cannot guarantee who is to be our family. As children of man, we cannot guarantee that we will be loved by another human. We will not know if we are going to be taught kindness and compassion. We will not be certain if every day of our life, that our family will guide our soul with their wisdom of kindness, so we may in our soul be shaped by the light of their spirit's love. Even so, we come. Because when we are strong enough in spirit, we will become the love that we decide to be on earth. We can guarantee that Mother Earth will always cradle us in our magnificent journey. She was there for our ancestors yesterday. They crawled, they rose, ran till they fell. She was there for them when they decided to dream. She was with them when they stood, there when they were weakened, cradled to their end of human experience. Now she is here for all of us today. She cradles us now as we pave humanity's road for our tomorrow. No matter what, we must know her true being. She is our peaceful and kind host. We must acknowledge her true nature of grace. We must give back the kindness she's cradled the humanity from which we each are born. We must return her natural beauty. The sun shines for her. The moon supports her wisdom though the turning of her ocean tides. Humanity must honor her truth. Her nature is kind. She is our mother land. The bosom of our humanity. She is our kind mother of life. She is graceful. Without her ashes, without her fertile ground and sustaining waters, there is no life. There are no us. No family. No humanity. To the Holy spirit and its divine children of consciousness, the tree of love would not exist in the universe without her.

Mother Earth's Pain Is a Struggle Projected from Within Every Human Being's Inner Sufferings

Cultivate peace. Cultivate light. Cultivate love. Mother Earth is a fertile field in which a spirit must come and illuminate in light and wisdom. This divine grace of our Father in heaven is on earth because our spirit has come. From the light, we come to birth. Now human in the flesh, our purpose is to love, for it is our spirit that has come in the flesh to heal all pain of all hearts as we plant the seed of peace, light, and love into the grounds of Mother Earth's sacred consciousness.
—Evangeline

Mother Earth is fertile in peace. Though humans struggle to know and respect her, she is forever giving. She is a host to all glories of our Heavenly Father. Yet when she calls for her children, the spirit gods, we of consciousness, spirit divine come. However, for some of us, foreign to human ways, uncomfortable in the flesh, we become paralyzed by fear. In fear of getting hurt, we hide. When we hide, we hide not in our current fear alone; we are sheltered by our ancestors' traumas. In these inherited fears, which is not of our own making, we become lost and fade out of current hours of realities. Here, we do not grow in love. So we are lost from our divine purpose. Stunted from emotional love, we are not able to reply to Mother Earth's call to care for our home. She is our home. This island is our human home. She is our humanity's refuge. When our spirits are hurt and disrespected, it hides. When our spirit is nurtured, it grows and shines through our souls. Yet without the spirit's light, our souls are lost in the fear-based reality of mind-made darkness, which the earth and atmosphere do not create, but the collective minds impose on the masses. Do not be afraid. Love and shine peace, as this garden does. For Mother Earth's creation is a humble wind of peace, respect, and solitude.

Day and night, earth cradles us. When will we give back to it the peace and love it is continuously nourishing us in, despite man's collective terrors? When shall we embrace its everlasting respect, so our spirit may transcend peace in each of our souls?

Forty-Nine

The Purpose of Time Is to Heal and Build Again

Time carries us now and always. Time is an illusion to the spirit. But for humanity, it is a sacred season. It sustains, serves, and guides the power of love and peace of the spirit's soul to ignite and illuminate the eternal brilliance of heaven's hearts out into the human's world, family.
—Evangeline

Take the time to purge. Acknowledge that your pain exists. Your grief is to be given time, value, and importance. Do not believe that there is a god or other healers that will make things vanish for you. You, allowing your own breath to breathe out is allowing your light to come. It is your own light that is giving your soul the strength to embrace fear. You must acknowledge the source of your own light, love, and eternal body of wisdom by understanding. You will know who you are when you allow the power within you to shine, so you may in soul rise in the truth, that you are the lord of love who has come into flesh to shine a light on your own truth. Love is your light. Your light is true life. Darkness is fear. Fear is of mind-made beliefs, the creator of your own soul's sufferings.

In time you came. You came into humanity. Now, as the spirit of love, you must light the rays of your own eternal body of consciousness. Awareness is you in full light. You must rise to abolish the root cause of your own humanity's sufferings. In your child soul, you were first awakened to the darkness of systematic belief. You found yourself birthed in the dramas of families that you chose not. You come to be a brother and a sister of siblings you do not relate. Your soul will complain and defy the ways of your families at times. Be at ease. If you allow your spirit to shine through, it will speak the truth. It loves your family no matter what. No matter what, you care for them. The spirit shines. When love shines, the breath of peace comes. For the spirit that you are is of love, before you are given the mind, the body, and emotions of man. No matter what, you are told about who you are; you are in pure spirit, the light body of love. Your breath is your Spirit Father's breath in you, the same breath of your earthly father and mother. Your prism is life-giving essence, your breath of peace. Thus, when you forgive another soul's fears and turmoil, you light that space within you, which is brilliant love, the light of infinite space. When you decide to forgive, your compassion shines. Your breath in peace shines new dreams that allow the stillness in your mind, body, and heart to calm and solitude. For in spirit, you are always pure light of the infinite space.

Yet when you enter humanity, you find yourself in a soul. The soul without the spirit is total darkness. Humanity is a foreign language. Humanity's reality comes across as heavy emotional burdens. Such labors are weights on your soul. But love the spirit of those around you, and you will rise. Love and shine your spirit! Your spirit will be strengthened. Shine freely. Shine strong so that others will be reminded to shine their spirit. That in doing, such burdens, no matter how deep, will be no more for all those who suffer. Be reminded that humanity is a gentle and kind work for the whole heart of all humankind. We must be reminded that when each baby is born, it is into a cave of the mind of humanity. It is not yet born aware of its soul. It will rise as a human babe in fear. But when reminded who they are in the spirit of love, when children are nurtured through compassion and peace, comfort is their new souls' beginning. They can focus on being children without the burden of emotional guilt and spiritual pain. They, in turn, will not fear. They will shine on fear until fear forgets itself. They are at peace. They come to face the truth. Where adults get confused, children shine only love and are never confused. Children are aware that most mankind without knowledge of their own love and their own light have been raised to be the vessels of slavery and insecurities of others' fearful minds. If not careful, children will project what is before them. Children are the truth. They are the embodiment of love, light, peace, and joy of heavenly hearts; they are courage manifested as babes.

Why You Are Born

Humanity is in the cave of darkness, fears, and emotional burdens in the question of who it is and what it is about in the heart of its minds. Yet even when one spirit decides to shine love, by ways of compassion, forgiveness, and understanding, this gentle and eternal brilliance will make the suffering of the mind and heart vanish. You are spirit eternal. You are love eternal. Make way for your spirit to shine eternal love and peace, for such presence is your destiny. You are the light of the dark caves of your minds. You are the light and breath of your own humanity, wherever life and your feet take you.

—Evangeline

You are born to give light out on your current darkness, which was sourced from past darkness. You must not create any chaos for today. It will not be your time to clean it. Others will have to be called to make light out of that darkness that you have abandoned. Love is self-sustained. Peace is self-light from the source heart. In being human, forgive yourself. Make amends with others you hurt. Ask for forgiveness, where you lost the love of your mind. No matter how many years you may dwell in the flesh, be ready to forgive for eternity. Love had forgiven mankind before the idea of its creation was contemplated. You only are given one second to decide what it is that you will create. Chaos or peace. Breathe out your breath of peace. Bring the life of the heavens into your creation. Ask your spirit to shine its love and understanding. Be compassionate, at all cost. Reverse all darkness with compassion through understanding.

Thank yourself for being present on earth now. Be the light of all situations.

Today is filled with trillions of mistakes. Tomorrow, those who made mistakes today will be stronger, and compassionate teachers. They are enlightened human beings. Picture yourself having done the wrong that caused your pain. What will you do to yourself? Would you be kind and say to yourself, "Learn so next time you would not do it again"? Will you be compassionate to your brother, who is here to brave fears so he can be with you even if he knows he would wrong you? Will your heart shine toward that one brother or sister and guide him, love him or her no matter what? As a light being, even when your soul is afraid and hurt, you can light your own soul to freedom of compassionate love. Love your own soul. Serve breath to all spaces where darkness lurks. Darkness means that space of yourself, or the world, or in your mind that has not yet been illuminated with mercy and love. Breathe out; your heart will so shine to infinity. You are peace. You are the breath of heaven's life. Peace always comes with *forgiveness,* no matter who receives that forgiveness.

Peace will come to self when you release such eternal wealth to be bestowed on the earth's heart.

> *Give what you are born to give. The wealth of heaven is the eternal source of your spirit, love, and peace. Light the world. The world's darkness will know itself as love. Breathe out compassion; the world will thrive in the soft and gentle, pure light of brilliant grandeurs of mercy, calm, and peace.*
>
> —Evangeline

No matter how old you are. No matter how rich or poor you are. No matter how strong or weak you may think you are. No matter how smart or uneducated you find yourself. You only have one world to illuminate out of one breath, *darkness or light.* A lost and tired soul will create chaos by submitting to darkness, making darkness bigger. Chaos begets tantrums; anger begets frustrations. Frustrations build a house of hate within a soul who does not breathe love out into the world. Thus, suffering comes. Darkness is made.

Yet, even when the soul is lost, ask for its own spirit to come and give light to its world, the spirit will come and allow the soul to breathe love and peace. The awakened soul will illuminate a breath of peace, where eternal light is manifested, banishing all darkness no matter how big the emotional body has been.

Fifty

Holy Light. Holy Body of Eternal Love and Peace

Our Father in heaven is a loving and kind spirit. Our spirit flows from His eternal essence. He is love. He is peace. As our Father shines, so shall our soul, we must recognize the light of our spirit. We, in spirit must breathe peace in order to love. We must, as our father does, shine love to create a loving and kind world. A world of love. A world of peace.

We are a spirit family of wisdom and light, love and peace, compassion and mercy, while our vessel is in the season of the experiences of time, sustained by the secret code of intelligence of matter—the human suit—the body, which is powered by the unseen wind of the merciful host of the divine nature of universe's heavenly creation. From light, into the caves of the human mind's darkness, we come through as human children. We come to awaken the self-light of wisdom within. We have come to surrender humanity's grief of itself, to the past. So in to now, we rise to shine the sacred grace of love and peace of humanity's divinity and order every day of the rest of our lives.

—Evangeline

Love shines. Love is light. Light is a breath of peace. The soul must call for its spirit of light to come. For when love comes, the

Heavenly Father comes. His son comes. The mother of humanity of peace comes. All the angels come. All our ancestors will come. When we love, heaven comes on earth. All masks of darkness, of worries, burdens, and fear are of the past.

—Evangeline

Why Are You Born a Human Child?

You come to heal your life, your body, yourself. Thus, sufferings are a collection of modern superstitions, a pocketed belief that life has to be so difficult. This surrender is not of the spirit. It is the minds of the realities of the world you have been born. But even all created suffering calls for its gods. So, you are born. Suffering's existence is inevitable. But as a spirit of great wisdom and awareness, you do not shun sufferings. You embrace it, to understand its cause. Learn from it. You give it purpose as a teacher in your life. By honoring its presence, you are honoring its root, you know then the cause and the healing of your own suffering. It is in suffering that one yearns for answers. And when one receives, the light comes. Love rises from within. Empathy comes, fueling the heart with compassion. When the silent agony of pain is heard and honored, the presence of compassion summons the heart of love to come the father of that beloved spirit comes to comfort in light and breath of peace, His begotten child. Suffering vanishes. The journey to your higher self begins. Compassion is the highest and the purest light that shines the infinite and gentle space of pure luminosities of the heavens.

The law of the universe is cause and effect. Humanity is nature. Every soul is like a plant in the forest. Everything in nature must start from seed before it gives a stem and is called a seedling. Likewise, under this earth's sun, you, as a spirit, will become the buds that will evolve into flowers before you bear fruit. After humanity's experiences, your spirit of wisdom is your way back home; home is the wisdom that powers your brilliance. That brilliance is a home within your own light. The light is from the living brilliance of the throne of the kingdom of heaven. The King is the white luminosity of pure brilliant light, illuminating ever so gently His living heart with gentle essence powering the entire body of the universal brain with love—the breath of life. In His body of compassion, existence lives. The universe is a programmed cause and effect. What happened here will impact tomorrow, as it will have an impact somewhere else. Humanity and all other beings live in the brain of the universe. The brain is one body sharing one program to create, span, and multiply. Such creation is powered by the Holy Spirit's and His children's substance, love and peace. True creation is a manifestation of stillness and expansion. Heaven is not in the universal brain; heaven is the source of light, life force, and intelligence of the universe. The highest energy is the purest. It is pure white light. He is the source of all light. This light is the Maker's heart, the heart of the maker's love, His children. Humanity is fashioned by the Father's heart and mind of light and peace. Its door is compassion, embrace, tolerance, and unity. Heaven is a family. Family is one in spirit and in the body. Its law is to unite. The law is love and peace.

Fashioned by His presence, the light of the spirits is the Father's love. The breath of the spirit is peace in each man.

Sufferings do not exist in the heaven of *love* and *peace*. Even though you are in the world of man, know who you are. You are *love*. You are a breath of peace. Heaven is *you* in the flesh. For all spirits are of heaven's breath. You are a living flame of life. Peace, your breath of wisdom is the essence of life; living wisdom is already who you are in full consciousness. Be aware that love is your spirit.

Love is gentle. Love is kind. Love is compassion, understanding, and forgiving in full luminosity in action. Such wealth is the light of love. Shine your being wherever darkness sought you. Shine and set darkness free by giving it compassion and understanding by shining your light through service. You are the solution to darkness. Light is the wisdom and cure. Shine your heart so you yourself may be free. Give light to the world, for the world's darkness is caused by the lack of such spirit's love and peace, which is the presence of self's heavenly glory. Shine your body of love, for such substance gives life to the stunning brilliance of fantastic heaven's wholeness, in all man, and in all creation outside of man, which is nature and the universe. Blessed

SHINE LOVE, JOY, AND PEACE!

is the life that have you. You have come; for in glory and in grace, your Father in full brilliance has come in love and breath through you. *His love is you are in life, in love, in family, community, business, in services of humanity's creation of peace through every action. This eternal and external glory of self as conscious gods create light, peace, onto humanity's true, one narrow road to a lasting haven—you. A child arose that only a loving, unwavering, stillness, and ever-constant, merciful source, an ever-loving heart of infinite wisdom, a Father's brilliant heart of gentle love, light, breath, powering all creation with grace, mercy, and glory through you, in each child, of man and woman born on earth to walk and create a new, whole, and united family of humanity.*

—Evangeline

Fifty-One

Abandoned Souls No More

Your body is one sacred, glorified vessel of divinity's intelligent grace, natured in matter's substances of the earth's universe, yet powered by the infallible essence of your own spirit. Your spirit is light. You are the force of life. Your human name is your ticket to your mission on earth. Your consciousness is a vessel of truth, light, and everlasting wisdom of true light. Yet at any time you abandon your spirit's food of life, which is pure and gentle light of kindness, you disown the truth that you are loved; moreover, when you fail to shine the light of your own spirit, so your body may light up in spirit, many unconscious disembodied souls of unguided minds will nest in your soul and your body. Darkness and fears will then host your mind.

Honor your soul. Be conscious of the pure brilliance of your spirit light. You are its divine breath. You are the breath of kindness. You are pure love. You are the breath of peace. Peace is sourced in the heart of your Spirit Father. Your substance is mercy. For, you are the breath of His grace. He is a God of peace. You are a child of God, who is the father of peace. He is light. You are one body of His brilliant rays. Shine your love. Heal the darkness of the world. Shine your compassion. Give love to the universe. It is your physical heaven. The universe yearned for truth and light. It called for its god. You came. You are born to give it your understanding and love; as your Father in heaven breathes into the light of consciousness, the spirit, the child, you. You are the spirit of consciousness. Your spirit is His breath of peace, cast onto the body of human world-earth. Angels are human guides to all families on earth. You are the heaven of spirits' love and peace, while on earth. Listen at heart. In peace, you are guided, always. In love and mercy, you are protected at all times. Humankind, on earth when you choose to love, you bring forth the hidden light of the heavens into humanity's world. When you do good, you heal the pain of mankind. When you give understanding, you cure the source of earth's misfortune. You've come to humanity through your mother's womb, in order to temporarily walk on earth as you restore mankind's lost and dying light. You are humanity's living flames. For in love and peace, you are the breath of God's amazing grace. You are the light of love shining out of your human body. You are the breath of peace. Exhaling a kind and gentle, merciful, and graceful life into the world, you are heaven's presence on this planet island; you are never alone. For you are the living light of both heaven and earth.

—Evangeline

The soul will not have life, will not be given a purpose when the spirit, which must dwell in it, is not present. When the spirit is not present, love and awareness of truth will not be in the soul. Kindness and compassion are the heart's light. Without such light, the soul is lost.

The spirit of love from above that is pure light and love must nest in the body and express itself through the soul. For the soul is a created mission of the light and wisdom and breath of the spirit that inhabits it. A newborn is a new soul, a new name, and it is born with a new purpose. The newborn and the new name it is given must be driven by its divine spirit. For the spirit is the soul's awareness. The spirit is its consciousness. The spirit is its light. The soul is the sacred creation of love. The highest work of the spirit is compassion. It must go through the dark stages of life, bare the pain through sorrows until the spirit is called to rise within a soul. It is the spirit within each man that must shine out the light. It is when someone cares, understands, and accepts without judgment that the spirit projects the essence of the spirit's love through the world outside of self. Spirit is the soul's light. When the spirit comes, the pain and darkness of the mind leaves the soul. It is then that you are awakened stronger, shinier, sharpened, and brighter. You are, as we all are, the body of light, and peace within is our breath of existence. For what it is in heaven is spirit and what shall be on earth is the spirit of heaven's eternal love and peace.

In the Heavenly Father's love, each night is rest, calm, and solitude. His darkness is a cool, silent wind of peace and sweet lullaby. In His peace, each day is a sunrise of a new beginning. An infinite light in full glory shining on all creation. A new self. A new soul. A new being of wisdom in the space of new life is now in Him. A new mind of creation is all there is in full glory. In His love and peace is His arms, His presence in you, before you, through you; He shines in the simplistic grace of the world of His creation.

Today, you are new, whole, bright, and awakening into your own light, breathing your own eternal power of peace. Today, embrace your self's wisdom. Own your light. Let go of your mind. Let shine your heaven's light into this world of mankind. Let your brilliance illuminate. You are a living star. Light your being. In full light, mankind is good. Humanity is children's divinity of love and peace. Humankind in full glory is the ever-loving presence of mercy of the heart of compassion of your Father, your God of love and peace, from whom you have come out in full essence and breath always connected as one spirit in one home, one living star in the vast space of the universe; for He is the Father of all light, His entire being is your source of love. His breath weaves life in each breath you take. You, as the extension of Himself, have come on this planet as His child—the living light that weaves, shapes mankind out from His mind and heart of peace. Where your breath is, there is His presence of love within you.

Shine love. Shine peace. Be a child of love in full glory.
You were birthed a spirit of heaven on earth.
—Evangeline

SHINE LOVE, JOY, AND PEACE!

Love is not a religion that needs constant saving because it thinks life is an accidental anomaly. Love is peace itself, needing only to grow and be illuminated now wherever we, its spirit's body, find our footings. We are the immortal bodies of love. Amazing, eternal grace is our light; graceful, humble joy and peace are our eternal and external brilliance.
— Evangeline

Love is compassion in full illumination through kind thoughts of the mind and caring action of every human heart.
— Evangeline

Fifty-Two

The Secret Wealth of the Human Spirit

The languages of the conscious spirit of love:

The spirit is love. Love mends and guides the child within, when the soul fears, and when the mind hurts. Love shines its pure, white, and brilliant light when the world of humanity's minds seems hopeless and when times become dark. Love is the ever, gentle comfort, even when the heart is broken and in anguish. Love is the kind and soft voice within a human soul. Love is a light-filled and comforting vision of good dreams; it is the food of the mind when the mind is tired; moreover, when the mind is struggling to find its truth. Love is always humble, gentle, and soft in light, never rude. Love is self-respect. Love is honesty; even when the heart, mind, and soul are afraid of consequence, it breathes the truth and sets its own humanity free. Love is free to love, no matter what the mind thinks, no matter what the heart says, no matter what doubts and weaknesses give. Love is an expansive breath that powers all good domains. Yet, when the human domain is in darkness, it is the gentle voice of love within one's spirit that guides the soul to rise into the light of grace and joy. Love is humility. Love embraces all. Love creates. Love comes only to build a new dream. Love can never destroy. Love is eternal. Love heals. It restores all that is broken. Love is hopeful, joyful, and wishful. Love is perfect. Love is a newborn child. Love is innocent of the knowledge of sins. Love forgives all. Love accepts all. Love is wisdom. Love sees the truth and embraces the hidden truth in others. Love is friendly to self; it aims only for a lasting friendship that lasts for eternity; for eternal is its body. Love is eager to see the truth in all creation, for its own consciousness is truth. Love sees all the hidden possibilities, for it is the light that shines on the reason for the soul, heart, and mind to be happy. Love is conscious. Love is never prideful. Love validates the soul's heart and mind. Love is the perfect dream of its soul. Love flies beyond time. Love transcends time and space for a good cause. It is the highest order. Love is wisdom. Love is space. Love is self. Love is the spirit and soul's true body. Love nurtures the earth with peace, of grand yet humble wisdom. Love is never jealous, never frightful. Love is allowing. Love is a dream giver. Love weaves a good vision. Love lights the future. Love is the fulfillment of kind and conscious dreams. Love transcends the wind. Love powers the moon and sun. Love is the secret glue and life of all families on earth. Love powers the universe. Love powers the heavens' lights beyond the universe of matters and creations.

Love is a sanctuary of consciousness. Love is full illumination of its own being. Love is the light that shines on a child's giggles, play, courage, and carefree laughter. Love is spirits brilliance. Love is the man's spirit, powered by the heart of a conscious Father who is holy in spirit. Love is a child of mercy. For the Father's entire body is the pure light of mercy. Love is the breath of peace. Breath to breath, the Father and the child's breath is one substance—peace. The child is the extension of its father, and the Father is the sanctuary of the child. Love is the arms of compassion. Love is the breath of freedom, of the soul's mind, body, purpose, and being. Love is the spirit child in the self, that kind voice of its own soul. Love is truth. Love is humanity's light and life. Love is humanity's highest power. Love is a pure spirit. Love is never created. It is not a creation. It is a force that powers all consciousness to manifest the highest good for all creation. Love is divine. Love is the pure radiance of ultimate light. It illuminates itself through each man's soul, heart, and it ignites the mind. Love is self, yet in the same is above and beyond self. Love is the spiritual source that waters the universe of life, rest, and creation. While creation creates and renews, love powers and guides the system of its truth. Love is conscious only of its pure love. It knows not to judge. It is the brilliance of eternal and infallible beauty. Love's beauty rests in everyone, in all living spirits, and in everything that exists; for love is pure light, of awesome luminosities of morning glory that shines on all the heavens and the universe. Love is life itself, for it gives light to all. Love makes all live. Love is an eternal embrace. Love is a heavenly body of space of constant stillness. While judgments are made by the minds, the hearts, and the human tongues of human creations of fears and limitations, love floats freely as its sanctuary of pure glory, calling on all spirits to rise and to shine in glory. Love is the heavenly space of acceptance, an abode of pure embrace, and everlasting and eternal solitude of self's never-ending light of pure comfort. Love is the sprits true home when all human creation in times past, present, and future ends. Love is enthroned by our Father's whole being, of luminous brilliant body of pure light and peace, that transcends all lights above and below Him with the soft essence of His gentle heart, lighting all creation with ever-living wisdom of His eternal mind of calm, stillness, and solitude. His light-filled and life-giving breath comforts each child with ease, while He enfolds each babe onto His arms of eternal mercy and compassion. Love is the light of self in all creations. Love is the consciousness of heaven outside the universe. Love is the consciousness that powers the inner workings of all matters and systems within the universe. All creation has their beings through the breath, light, and body of this Holy Father's infinite love. Love is gentle. Love is kind. He is Holy, gentle and kind. Love is white light. The Father is radiant and pure. He exists as a Holy Spirit. He is a gentle being of grace. All human kindness is lit up in Him. He is the source of all great and kind intelligence. He is merciful. He is the breath of infinite wisdom. Love is all-knowing. Every child is all-knowing of His divine love. All children are His body of love in spirit. The Holy Spirit's infinite wisdom exists in every soul's consciousness. The Holy Spirit is the breath of every child's heart, mind, and body. Love is a brilliant grace. Love is not found on earth, it comes in each child's birth, and children are pure essences of the Holy Father's innocence. It is through every child's birth that the light and power of earth's humanity are sustained. Once the light and grace of love has been endowed on this planet's family, when all the love of a child is planted in the purpose it had been driven to serve, death releases the spirit to rest in the comfort of its Holy Father's arms and light. The child transfigures into full consciousness. The child is pure peace shining in all darkness. The child becomes *lit up. The spirit of the child is pure love. Love is kind. Love is gentle. Love is truth. Love is the spiritual service of conscious driven mercy, compassion, forgiveness, and fulfillment of the eternal dream. Love is the spirit that has come to earth to make conscious the evolution of the entire family of humanity. When humanity is lit up in consciousness, the spirit is guided to transcend beyond the darkness. In to the light, the spirit is to be united with its father, its home of consciousness, which is the arms of pure, gentle, soft, and living light of love. Home is a father of humanity's spirit—the Holy Spirit, humanity's God of peace, our Father in heaven. When creation ends, the spirit is born to its one single form—pure light. The spirit child transfigures itself to its natural body, a brilliant body of love and peace. Love is rest from the mind. Love is truth. Love is gentle and always kind*

—Evangeline

The Infinite and Ultimate Purity of the Human Spirit's Breath

Humanity's spirits are the brilliant rays of the Holy Spirit's breath and existence.
—Evangeline

Holy peace is; acceptance, forgiveness, tolerance, understanding, serenity, calm, service, non-violence, charity, truth, stillness, centering, compassion—self-knowing, honesty, love, eternal will, family, creativity, self-refuge, evolution, productive growth, fruitfulness, solitude, luminosities, purity, brilliance, internal space, wholeness, infinite space, infinite brilliance, eternal and external abundance, of ever-living breath sourced in the eternal to external creation, which powers all living wisdom.

Divine grace is pure white light of illuminating compassion, love, and peace. A living substance of consciousness that powers the space of life, the universe, the body, and the true and kind nature of each man, regardless of the color, sex, religion, and belief one is birthed into. Man

EVANGELINE MENDEZ STEFAN

is not a word. He is a living light, living breath of eternal glory of love and compassion, a vessel of living water of life's light, gloriously bestowed brilliance of infinite wisdom, flowing down in cyclic order from a fountain of love and peace, its source, wherever his feet walked, the past, the present, and the future with his family on earth. Each human is born to fulfill the heaven's grace during his short journey in the time of human creation.

—Evangeline

Fifty-Three

Living Vision

I see Him, sitting humbly on His throne. Love is light. He is white light. Light and wisdom are pure luminosity of His body. Light is the power of the universe's creation. Peace is the entire brilliance that gives life to the space that surrounds Him. Peace is His living breath. Peace is the space of brilliance of calm solitude. Below His feet floats an eternal basketball-size universe. The universe is busy. It's a living holographic brain of subtle vibrations of infinite degrees of lights. He shines the gentle, brilliant light of peace originating from His entire being, nourishing every space and fiber of the universe's life, which is living below His throne. In body and light, He sat watchful over the light within the universe. I saw that the light of the universe is from His radiance. His body radiates in all spaces within the sacred ball of creations, which encompasses all spaces with His breath of divine consciousness. I understood. The universe has its being because of His love; His mercy and compassion are the living force of all creations. Heaven and the universe have life because of His light and presence. He is where He is because the universe is itself before Him. The universe cannot exist without Him; neither would He be a Father of Peace, without the peace and love that shines out of the universe's creations. Because the universe exists, He has His throne. Without Him and without the universe, peace would not be in existence. The water of life, which gives essence to peace, would not be without His light. Creation without His gentle presence would be no more. Without peace, without love, without light, the spirit of humanity would cease to exist. Without a

Father of love and peace, without the joy of life's wisdom and consciousness of humanity's holy love and spirit, humankind will remain unconscious of its divine origin, where life has come from and will continue to exist in the darkness of humanity's limitation as it is only governed by the fears of human mind.

—Evangeline

The world—seen and unseen—is powered by one, and only light. The source of light is spirit. His body is love. His breath is the breath of every human being on earth. All creation within the universe is His presence.

He is the luminosity of mercy and kindness, a divine and ever-living glory that powers the life of true human creation. All creation that is good is in Him. The gentle and loving world is good, for it is His Fatherly heart. The good is Himself in all creation. True creation is in Him. The world is good. His heart illuminates all darkness. All darkness lights up in His presence. In all the darkness, He casts Himself, for all that is hidden finds itself as a radiant light. There is nothing in creation that does not contain His light, for all things rose from His light. All darkness calls for Him; He sends His beloved children. His children come to be lost in darkness, but every child is the living seed of kind manifestations. After all journeys, home is His Majesty's divine arms. His love for His children shines beyond the universe of all creation. All creation's wisdom rises and celebrates His soft, kind, and merciful presence. Everything is space. All spaces live in His ever-loving grace.

—Evangeline

Tell every heart of man.
Mankind is the vessel of nature's kindness and grace. However, the Holy Spirit breathes into this vessel, the breath of life called spirit, the bearer of intelligent wisdom of love who becomes conscious of its humanity's daily experiences of itself in the world of evolution. This spirit creation is divine wisdom. Wisdom is the breath of spirits that are born into a

human family in a quest for the peaceful, loving, all-inclusive, all-giving humanity—the conscious spirits of creation.

—Evangeline

Spirit is light. Light is love. Spirit is peace. The human family is patterned from the spirit of the Holy Father, the Holy Mother, and our brothers' and sisters' eternal wisdom of light. Humanity's children are spirit consciousness. Peace is the breath of creation; every human are God's children, for all living breath in each man is only peace. The Father's spirit is light. Light is the vital energy of life that embodies the forces of creation. His breath is the breath of our being. The Spirit Father is Holy in His light and love. Mercy and compassion His being, within His spirit, shines and guides brightly upon His children of love, and peace. Children are spirits—the spirits of all human souls in creation, are all mankind—being attached to His body in the space of distant breath of gentle flames; humanity is fashioned in His light and being. One spirit, mind, and body, in full light, one family of humanity is His breath, united as a whole body of pure white illuminating and life-giving radiance, a holy creation. Family of mankind.

—Evangeline

Fifty-Four

Tree of Life

Humanity is a gift from our ancestors' sacrifices and courage. They are the roots of who we are now. We are the branches, the leaves, and the flowers of the tree of human life. We are born simply to have the privilege to come as burning flames of life's torches. To keep the game of life filled with blossoms of compassion, is our service to this humanity. We build our perfected dreams. We rise each day in the creation of conscious human families, with which we learn from things that are not yet so good. Our ancestors pave the road of life. Everyone before us made the road bigger and stronger. Thus, though humanity is built on the foundation of trials and sacrifices, compassion, and tolerance, we have come to give them rest. We have come to give our family the light, which is our love. Pass it on. You are humanity's spirit presence here to partake in the creation of a good family. We come. We rise. We evolve as the builders of conscious humanity.

We are merely here shortly to make way for humanity's kind and bright future. Humanity's spirit is the light and love of heaven who walk on planet earth. We are pure spirits sent to come in order to create in grace and truth, no matter how short or long the unexpected wind or darkness stays. We are that stay, after all darkness passes. We build to survive, no matter what. We have come to light the way for the unborn. Shine love. Shine peace. Give humanity its love—your body and breath; it is you, the spirit of love in the flesh. Where there is no road, build one according to your needs. Build love. Make way for the good in you to shine. Peace is you. Build in the space of peace. Peace is heaven's breath. Peace is the spirit's food and sanctuary. Where there is darkness, shine on that space, for you, have come as its light. You are love. You are peace. You are the heaven on earth shining at all human darkness.

—Evangeline

Don't just believe in love. You are its brilliance. You are its breath. Shine your being. The universe's life is within you in love and peace.

—Evangeline

You Are Light

"Child, I have them." The Holy Father said as He sits compassionately, lighting earth with His presence. A baby girl and boy just died out of the earth. Now one by one they are cradled in spirit on His lap, carefully with absolute love. His radiance rests in the return of His divine children. Sleeping soundly, comforted brightly and softly, they return to rest upon Him, unto the beat and light of His heart and being. In pure radiance and comfort, the child is at ease, at home in peace. In His arms, every child of humanity, no matter how far the distance traveled in the womb of the universe, is a holy union of coalescing lights. The soft brilliance of joy is the purity of bodies and breaths of the Father and His child's wholeness. The child and the Father are one. Holy is the Father whose arms of love are gracefully radiating to comfort Himself in glory, as the child who's divine in spirit returns back to His arms. The child is holy. For, the Father of the spirit in every child is holy; breath to breath, light to light, the Father is the Holy child's home.

—Evangeline

You are the radiance of eternal love. You are the breath of peace. Life is you!

Where there is darkness, compassion is your breath of life.

Where there are pain and tears, you light up your kindness, wisdom, and ever-loving mercy.

Where there is poverty, you light up with compassion. Shine the glory of your infinite wisdom and mercy, for peace is you at ease.

Where there is grief, light up your brilliant glory of understanding; for, the ever-living embrace of your Heavenly Father's hands is you in eternal wisdom. Your conscious presence on earth is the extended force of divinity's glory, sent through spaces of creation to make conscious the purpose of this begotten planet earth's life. You are the flame of living mercy that has come to light your families' love—the breath of your entire being.

Love is you. Love is compassion in action.

—Evangeline

There are times in life when the pain in our being is too painful to contain. But, in this pain, only eternal mercy and grace of our loving guardian angels, our family, and the Holy Spirit and our Lord of peace await to help ignite the force that empowers our hearts to shine the light within. We are our hearts, mind, and body's conscious forces. We come in order to heal not only ourselves but be humanity's grace and gentle comfort.

—Evangeline

For Guidance

In your need for self-validation, divine guidance, and closure from death and loss, in your quest to obtain love and peace; in your hunger to experience your divine glory, you must experience your own spiritual transformation. In spirit, you must light in glory. The glory is your divine love and peace. Connect with the living Jesus and the ever-living and loving Heavenly Father of Peace, the Heavenly Mother of Peace, Mother Mary, your guardian angels, and your beloved ones in heaven. If you are ready to accept how loved you are in spirit, please e-mail BEYONDHEARTBEATS.COM to schedule a reading service—spiritually, emotionally, physically—we are here to help. Angels are always with you, guiding you.

SHINE LOVE, JOY, AND PEACE!

If you want to discover your spiritual light or you are in dire need of emotional transformation from grief, pain, and loss, and you want to receive an awe-inspiring healing of your own spirit from PTSD (post-traumatic stress disorder), addiction, or obtain guidance on jobs and home issues, or in need of closure from grief, with the aid of your guardian angel's gift of peace and love, in the comfort of your own home, most importantly, while in Hawaii to schedule an appointment for your spiritual reading, please contact (808) 341-1772. Clinic hours: Monday–Friday 9:00 a.m.–5:00 p.m. (Hawaii Standard Time). Weekend hours are available upon request. Please see the website: Beyondheartbeats.com

New in spirit. Shine Love, Joy, and Peace!

Every broken heart wants to be heard and be made whole. The mind wants to feel at ease in the ocean of safety through understanding. The body wants to shine love through kindness. The breath yearns to in-hale and ex-hale the calm rays of the brilliant light of joy and peace; as the Heavenly Father bestows His entire being mercifully and gracefully, through His divine and transcendent presence in nature's calm and solitude. Illuminating His heart through the creation of time's everlasting; within, the constant cycles of eternal and external manifested dreams— to shine Himself in each of His child's awesome love; and, to be the never-ending breath of forgiveness in each mankind's soul—peace.
—Evangeline

Humankind: Shine Yourself. For you are not bound by your mind's ills, not jailed by the your bodies' circumstantial limitations, not bound by limiting trauma of your emotional bodies. You are a spirit. You are free. You are light. You are love. You are the peace you are seeking to breathe out into the world. You are a spirit that makes conscious of the universe's ongoing and ever expansive creation of love and peace within earth's humanity.
—Evangeline

To shine in spirit, you must cleanse emotionally. Love yourself. Heal your grief. Write your story!

TEN STEPS TO GRIEF RECOVERY

1. **The Shock, Numbness, Bargaining, and Denial**

    Write how your feel to overcome the zombie-state of grief.

2. **Anger**

    Write how you feel to overcome the anger of grief.

3. **Power of Guilt and Shame**

    Write how you feel to release and overcome the emotional trauma of guilt and shame of grief.

4. **A Necessary Road to Self-Redemption**

    Write what grief has taught you about finding your own voice.

5. **Surrendering to Life's Course**

    Write what you accept about your grief and why you value the lesson it gave you.

6. **The Demeaning Power of Depression**

    Write how you are processing the emotional feeling of depression to overcome your grief to feel your inner balance. The mixture of emotions are feelings of sadness, anger, tears, afraid, and bouts of wanting to be alone or want to move, exercise with music, comfort eat, or not eat, these are are all okay examples during this time of your sacred journey.

7. **Learning to Understand: Life goes on, Love keeps on growing, Love will Keep on Shining.**

   Write how you see life now as it gives Love to you today. Take a moment to feel your inner self. What language of Love do you see in yourself today? List your progress of feeling. How are you taking care of yourself to feel light and happy?

8. **The Physical Manifestation of Fear**

   Write how you are self-checking your health. Do you feel hungry? Do you eat fruits and vegetables with every meal? How is your taste? Do you have pain? What part of the body? When will you make time to see your general and mental health Doctors to address the issue? Remember you are there to educate your doctors about what is happening with you. You have the right to feel heard. You are forming the team for your well-being and self care to live a balanced and healthy life. Remind yourself you are going to be okay. You've decided to take action.

9. **Let go of Control over this Earthly life. Let the God of Love and Peace Come. Nature and Love Will Take Care of the Rest in Time.**

   Write to the Creator of your peaceful and loving life. What are you going to surrender? Why must you let go, in order to trust life and live free again?

10. **Acceptance**

Write what you are thankful for about your loved one who has risen in spirit—back home to Heaven where he or she came from before birth to join you down here in life, to gift you with a sacred and blessed experience of divine humanity on earth.
Would you change anything?
Would you live life over again with this spirit if you were given a second chance to do so?
List the blessings of your life now.
Thank yourself for being here on earth.
Thank life for its gift of family and Love.

Shine! Thank God—The Father of a Kind and Loving Grace—for your breath of peace, your body of love and light, and your soul of conscious breath of joy—Amen.

About the Author

Evangeline resides in Hawaii. She is the spouse of a US Navy (thirty-year veteran), an AFAA-certified physical fitness and wellness teacher, a trainer and coach for Navy, Army, Marines and their families since 1992. She is a certified regression therapist for PTSD recovery and a spiritual life coach. She has traveled the world in support of her community's heart—military families physical, mental and spiritual wellness, wherever the Navy had taken them.

After the loss of her one and only daughter at the time in 2011, with the Heavenly Father's orders, she founded BEYONDHEARTBEATS.COM, a practice committed to healing the Heavenly Fathers children through His divine presence. A visionary and a spiritual healer, a universal messenger of Jesus, The Heavenly Father, Mother Mary, the Buddha, our guardian angels, children, and our beloved ones in spirit, she travels the world as a link between heaven and earth in service of peace and love to all families who are in need of spiritual light in their time of darkness.

She gives love in times of chaos and pain. Peace in times of fear. The spirit of Jesus, the Living Man of Peace, and the Living Holy Father come in full illumination through her to comfort and heal those who are in dire need to receive love, light, compassion, mercy, kindness and peace through loving and gentle guidance. Jesus and Buddha make way for families to have peace on earth through the aid of our ancestors' spirits' loving and intercessional prayers. Our Father, Mother Mary and the multitude of loving angels often cross over to ask for Evangeline's help to voice out their presence during families' ordeals with sickness, death, dying, grief, healing, births, jobs, family interventions and marriage restoration.

With the Holy Spirit's divine presence, the physical journey to wellness and recovery is often achieved with ease and gentle grace. Evangeline helps the brokenhearted obtain spiritual, emotional, physical and mental freedom through divine knowledge of their own truth, love and peace. In a time of the Holy Spirit's presence, eternal love is the only healing light that our family's hearts need for ultimate calm, wholeness and peace while we journey through the rest of our life on earth. In spirits of truth, our family is life. She began Amazing Grace in September 2017 as a community outreach project to gather in the spirit of love, peace and comfort, which meets every first Saturday of each month in Hawaii to unite those who walk alone in need of support and guidance during their hour of emotional, spiritual and physical trials.

Printed in the USA
CPSIA information can be obtained
at www.ICGtesting.com
CBHW010834051024
15376CB00007B/60